A Course in English Grammar

R. N. Bakshi

Orient BlackSwan

ORIENT BLACKSWAN PRIVATE LIMITED

Registered Office
3-6-752 Himayatnagar, Hyderabad 500 029, Telangana, India
e-mail : centraloffice@orientblackswan.com

Other Offices
Bengaluru, Bhopal, Chennai, Guwahati, Hyderabad,
Jaipur, Kolkata, Lucknow, Mumbai, New Delhi,
Noida, Patna, Vijayawada

First Published 2000
Reprinted 2004, 2005, 2008, 2009, 2010, 2015, 2017

ISBN : 978 81 250 1846 9

Typeset by
Anita Rao
Hyderabad

Printed by
Seth Informatics
Kolkata 700 035

Published by
Orient Blackswan Private Limited
3-6-752 Himayatnagar, Hyderabad 500 029, Telangana, India
e-mail : info@orientblackswan.com

Contents

Preface v

Chapter 1 Simple Sentence Patterns

1.1 Subject and predicate 1
1.2 Form and function 2
1.3 Basic patterns 9
1.4 Intransitive and transitive verbs 26
1.5 Semantic roles 27

Chapter 2 Nouns and Articles

2.1 Countable, uncountable and proper nouns 40
2.2 Genitive 45
2.3 Articles 49
2.4 Use of articles 53

Chapter 3 Noun Phrase

3.1 Introduction 64
3.2 Parts of a noun phrase 65
3.3 Modifiers of the noun head 66

Chapter 4 Verb Phrase

4.1 Introduction 89
4.2 Structure of the verb phrase 90
4.3 Finite and non-finite verb phrases 96
4.4 Modifiers of the verb 98

Chapter 5 Adjectives and Adverbs

5.1 Adjectives 111
5.2 Adverbs 118
5.3 Adverbials 127

Chapter 6 Tenses and Modal Auxiliaries

6.1 Tenses 135
6.2 Modal verbs 163

Chapter 7 Complex Sentences - I

7.1 Introduction 177
7.2 Subordinate and superordinate clauses 180

7.3 Subordinate clause and matrix clause 184
7.4 Structure of a subordinate clause 187
7.5 Functions of a subordinate clause 199

Chapter 8 Complex Sentences - II
8.1 Adjectival clauses 254
8.2 Appositive clauses 267
8.3 Adverbial clauses 269
8.4 Analysis of complex sentences 281

Chapter 9 Coordination
9.1 Introduction 292
9.2 Compound sentences and coordinate clauses 292
9.3 Ellipsis in coordinated clauses 296
9.4 Meaning related to coordinating conjunctions 299
9.5 Coordination of the constituents of a sentence 300

Chapter 10 Focus
10.1 Simple sentences and focus 303
10.2 Cleft sentences 305
10.3 Pseudo-cleft sentences 306
10.4 Extraposition 307
10.5 Existential sentences with introductory 'there' 307

Chapter 11 Prepositions and Phrasal Verbs
11.1 Prepositions 309
11.2 Phrasal verbs 326

Chapter 12 Word Formation
12.1 Root, base and affix 340
12.2 Simple, complex and compound words 346
12.3 Other processes of word formation 352

Key to Exercises 356

Bibliography 423

Index 424

Preface

The main aim of this book is to make advanced students of English understand grammatical categories and their inter-relationships. Since this is an introductory book on English grammar, I have not followed any one particular model to present grammatical structures and categories.

In the last thirty years two models of grammar, transformational, generative and systemic, have emerged as very popular models of grammatical analysis in the USA, Britain, and India. However, the most useful description of English grammar from the point of view of an advanced second language user, a native speaker and a teacher of English language is to be found in *A Comprehensive Grammar of English* by R. Quirk, S. Greenbaum, G. Leech and J. Svartvik. It is this approach that has been central to the preparation of this book. However, I have also derived from the basic principles of transformational grammar in chapter 4 on the Verb Phrase and chapters 8 and 9 on Complex Sentences. This eclectic approach to English grammar will, I feel, help the reader in understanding the workings of the English language. In the preparation of this book, I have relied greatly on grammarians such as R. Quirk, S. Greenbaum, G. Leech, P. Corder, L. G. Alexander, J. Thomson and A.V. Martinet as sources of reference. I have also found Collins Cobuild English Grammar very helpful in the explanation of certain grammatical categories.

Each section in a chapter is based on the discussion of a grammatical category along with illustrative sentences. This is followed by exercises. In some chapters, particularly the ones on complex sentences and on tenses and modal auxiliaries, these are of two kinds. The first set helps the learner in sentence construction based on the category explained, while the second set is more analytical in nature. This set requires the student to apply the rules that have been learnt. Another important feature is that the form is related to meaningful use. Many of the exercises focus on the semantic aspects of language.

This book can be used as a coursebook for B.A. (Hons) English, B.Ed (English Methods), M.A. English, M.Phil. English and the Postgraduate Diploma in the Teaching of English. The book can also be used independently by students. College and university lecturers in English will find the book useful for a better understanding of English grammar. It will also be of immense help to English teachers in schools. School teachers can use this book to gain an in-depth understanding of English grammar. The book can also be of help in the training of college and university lecturers at Academic Staff colleges of various universities.

There are four academicians, who have influenced my professional career and my understanding of the workings of the English language. Dr. Paul. L. Love was my teacher and colleague at Baring Union Christian College, Batala, Punjab, where I took my M.A. degree. It was due to his encouragement and persuasion that I went to the Central Institute of English and Foreign Languages, Hyderabad to do my PGDTE and M.Litt. At CIEFL I came under the influence of Professor S. K. Verma, then Professor and Head of the Department of Linguistics and Contemporary English. Professor Verma's lectures on grammar helped me in understanding the principles underlying grammatical structures. Many sections of this book are a result of this understanding. Later, I went to University College of North Wales, Bangor and my understanding of English grammar was further widened through the courses on English grammar by the late Dr Michael Anthony and Professor A. Thomas. Dr Anthony made me realise the importance of meaning in English grammar and Professor Thomas extended the scope of English grammar in analysing texts. Needless to say Professor Thomas's influence in preparing the exercises is very obvious. I am greatly indebted to these teachers.

I am grateful to my students at CIEFL, Regional Centre, Lucknow, the Faculty of Arts and the Faculty of Education, University of Taiz, Yemen, where I class-tested several parts of the book. I own special thanks to Mr. A. K. Ojha, of CIEFL, Regional Centre, Lucknow, who helped me in many ways to give final shape to this book. I am also grateful to my wife, Shefali, my son, Varoon and my daughter, Shailaja, who inspired me to write this book and bore the evenings they had to spend without me while this book was being written.

Lucknow Raj. N. Bakshi

November 5, 1997

1

Simple Sentence Patterns

The number of simple sentence patterns in English is small and limited. Once the concept of simple sentence patterns is understood, it becomes easier to understand complex and compound sentence structures. Several examples of simple sentences given in this chapter may appear simpler than the sentences we usually come across or use in speech and writing. However, it is important to first understand the concept of simple sentence patterns. We will later discuss how these simple sentence patterns may be expanded.

1.1 Subject and predicate

A simple sentence in English consists of two parts: **subject** and **predicate.** Notice the division of these sentences into subject and predicate:

Subject *(Noun Phrase)*	**Predicate** *(Verb Phrase)*	
Birds	fly.	[1]
Birds	fly in the sky.	[2]
Gowri	is a doctor.	[3]
John	is tall.	[4]
Asha	is in the library.	[5]
The dog	chased/a rat.	[6]
The old man	told us a story.	[7]
The committee	elected him/Mayor.	[8]
He	dyed his shorts red.	[9]

The above sentences illustrate that the subject of a sentence can be a **noun** (*birds, Gowri, John, Asha*), **a noun phrase** (*the dog, the old man, the committee*) or a **pronoun** (*he*). A noun, a noun phrase or a pronoun may be treated as part of a noun phrase (NP). The NP functions as the subject of a simple sentence.

The predicate is more complex than the subject. In sentence 1 the predicate is just the main verb *fly*. In sentence 2, however, the predicate consists of the main verb *fly* and the prepositional phrase *in the sky*, which functions as the **adverbial.** Similarly, sentence 6 has the predicate *chased a rat* with *chased* as the main verb and *a rat* as the noun phrase. Notice that *a rat* functions as the object in sentence 6. Thus we find that a predicate can have only the verb or it can have the verb followed by several constituents.

Exercise 1

Identify the subject and the predicate in these sentences:

1. Her younger brother is a famous doctor.
2. The finance minister has given us tax concessions.
3. Meera runs very fast.
4. The food smells good.
5. All the old employees are unhappy.
6. Her teachers consider her intelligent.
7. Varun is sitting in the corner.
8. The Board's decision has made us happy.
9. The university has framed a new rule.
10. The old students have gone out for dinner.

1.2 Form and function

We can analyse a simple sentence either on the basis of formal categories like noun, noun phrase, verb, adjective, adverb or prepositional phrase or in terms of functional labels like **subject, verbal, object, complement** or **adverbial.** We need to distinguish between these two categories.

While discussing sentences 2 and 6 in section 1.1, we assigned two different labels to the constituents after the verb. For example, in 2 *in the sky* is treated as a prepositional phrase and an adverbial. Similarly, *a rat*, in 6, is treated as an NP and an object.

NP_1	V	NP_2	Prep Phrase	
Asha	met	Rakesh	in the office.	[10]
S	V	O	(Adv)	

If we analyse sentence 10 according to formal labels, we say it has the structure:

a. NP_1 - V - NP_2 - Prep Phr

If we analyse the sentence according to functional labels, we say that it has the structure:

b. S - V - O - Adv

Analysis **a** does not indicate the relationship between NP_1 and NP_2.

Analysis **b** gives us a better understanding of the relationship between NP_1 and NP_2. Similarly, we may analyse sentence 11 as follows:

NP_1	V	NP_2	
John	is	a doctor.	[11]
S	V	C	

Thus the formal analysis will be:

a. NP_1 - V - NP_2

and the functional analysis will be:

b. S - V - C

Again analysis **a** fails to indicate the relationship between NP_1 and NP_2.

Analysis **b** clearly indicates that a *doctor* in 11 is the complement of the subject, *John*.

There are basically five main functional constituents or elements of sentence structure. They are subject, verb, complement, object and adverbial. An adverbial is an optional constituent of a sentence. An important thing to remember is that a sentence is made up of a minimum of two constituents, subject + verb and a maximum of five constituents, subject + verb + object + complement + adverbial.

Examples:

The army advanced. [12]
S V

The shirt looks nice. [13]
S V C

Kapil Dev hits the ball. [14]
S V O

Mukesh bought a briefcase yesterday. [15]
S V O (Adv)

The Board nominated Farooq the captain on Tuesday. [16]
S V O C (Adv)

We will discuss each one of these constituents briefly.

Subject: Every statement in English begins with a subject. The subject of a verb is usually a noun, pronoun or a noun phrase. The subject noun, pronoun or noun phrase is tied to or is in agreement with the verb. This means a singular third person subject noun in a sentence which is in the present tense must have a singular verb and all other subject nouns (first and second person singular and plural and third person plural) must have a plural verb.

Examples:

Lions **roar.** Dogs **bark.**

We add **-s** or **-es** after the first form of the verb to form singular verbs.

The lion **roars.** The dog **barks.**

To sum up, some of the characteristics of the subject are:

- It is a noun, pronoun or a noun phrase. (In 7.5.1, you will notice that a complex sentence may, sometimes, have a clause as the subject.)
- It is the first constituent of a statement.

  The sun rises in the east [17]

- It has number and person agreement with the verb.

  The lion **roars.** [18]

  Roshan **was** absent yesterday. [19]

- When a sentence in the active voice is turned into the passive voice, the subject voice of the active voice sentence becomes the object of the passive voice sentence.

  Kamal painted that **glass.** [20]

  That glass was painted by **Kamal.** [21]

Verb: The verb is the second constituent of a statement. Basically there are three types of verbs:

a. linking verbs

b. intransitive and

c. transitive verbs

What comes after the verb is greatly determined by the type of verb used.

a. A linking verb requires a complement or more precisely a subject complement to complete it. The linking verb, in a way, links the subject and its complement.

In the sentence,

His mother	is	a doctor.	[22]
S	LV	Cs	

is serves as the linking verb and *a doctor* is the complement of the subject, *his mother*.

Similarly in the sentence,

Razia	looks	tired.	[23]
S	LV	Cs	

Razia is the subject and *tired* is the complement of the subject.

b. An intransitive verb is complete by itself. This means that an intransitive verb does not require an object or complement to complete it. It is possible to use an adverbial after an intransitive verb but it is an optional constituent. Whether we want to use an adverbial after an intransitive verb or not depends on how much information we want to convey to the listener/reader.

Mukesh	argues.		[24]
S	InTrV		
Mukesh	argues	forcefully.	[25]
S	InTrV	(Adv)	

Sentence 24 is grammatically complete by itself but one may like to add the adverbial *forcefully* to convey more information.

c. A transitive verb requires an obligatory object after it. Most of the transitive verbs can be passivised. In other words, we cannot change a sentence into its passive form, if its main verb is a linking verb or an intransitive verb. Only sentences with transitive verbs can be changed into their passive forms.

Arundhati Roy	has written	this novel.	[26]
S	Tr V	O	

I	watched	this film	yesterday.	[27]
S	Tr V	O	(Adv)	

Notice that *yesterday* (Adv) in 27 is an optional constituent.

Complement: As noticed earlier, a complement follows a linking verb and completes the sense of the verb. The complement tells us something more about the subject. In a way, the subject and the complement have the same referent, that is, they refer to the same person or thing.

This suit	is	**expensive.**	[28]
S	LV	Cs	

In the above sentence the subject, *the suit* and the complement, *expensive* refer to the same thing. We will later discuss how an object can also have a complement.

Object: Objects are of two types, **direct object** and **indirect object.** If a verb requires only one object, it has to be a direct object and it comes right after the main verb, which is a transitive verb. A direct object usually refers to a person or thing, which is affected by the action of the verb.

Mukesh	hit	the ball	with force.	[29]
S	TrV	Od	(Adv)	
She	wrote	a letter	in the morning.	[30]

An indirect object also comes immediately after the main verb, but is usually followed by a direct object. An indirect object usually 'receives' the action of the verb.

Rita	told	us	a story.	[31]
S	TrV	Oi	Od	
Rajesh	asked	him	a question.	[32]

Adverbial:

1. An adverbial can be a one-word adverb, a noun phrase, a prepositional phrase, or a clause.

Vina sleeps **here.** (*adverb*) [33]

We watched *Jurassic Park* **last night.** (*noun phrase*) [34]

Salma sleeps **on the mat.** (*prepositional phrase*) [35]

Rohit sleeps **after he has his dinner.** (*clause*) [36]

2. Adverbials, as compared to the other constituents of a sentence, are mobile and do not have a fixed position. Adverbials can occur in the beginning, in the middle and at the end of a sentence.

Quickly,	I	jumped	over the wall.	[37]
(Adv)	S	InTr	(Adv)	

I	**quickly**	jumped	over the wall.	[38]
S	(Adv)	InTr	(Adv)	

I	jumped	over the wall	**quickly.**	[39]
S	InTr	(Adv)	(Adv)	

3. There is no restriction on the number of adverbials in a sentence. The other constituents of a sentence are limited in number. There can only be one subject, one main verb, one complement and one or two objects but in theory there can be any number of adverbials in a sentence. In practice, however, there may not be more than three or four adverbials in a simple sentence.

As a child	I would	**quickly**	jump	**over the wall.**	[40]
(Adv)		(Adv)		(Adv)	

Exercise 2

Underline the adverbials in these sentences and mention whether each is an adverb, a prepositional phrase or a clause:

1. They play while their parents are away. ( )
2. Gita writes with a pen. ( )
3. Rasool and Suresh run whenever they see a dog. ( )
4. I sleep there. ( )
5. Soldiers rest when they are on leave. ( )
6. She ran fast. ( )
7. The boy studied in the room. ( )
8. Babies cry loudly. ( )
9. Asha goes to her office in the afternoon. ( )
10. The bombs exploded continuously. ( )

1.3 The Basic patterns

We noticed in section 1.2 that normally a sentence has the subject in the first position and the verb in the second position. What is used after the verb depends on what type of verb is used. Therefore, we will discuss the basic patterns from the point of view of the verb. We will also study the various constituents of a sentence pattern from the point of view of form and function.

1.3.1 Linking verbs

There are basically two types of linking verbs: **be** and others. We will first discuss **be.**

Be has the following forms:

Present	Past
is/am/are	was/were

Any one of these forms can be used as a main verb.

In addition to **is/am/are, was,** and **were,** we can have **will be, shall be, can be, has been, have been** as linking verbs.

A linking verb requires a complement to complete it.

S	LV	Cs	
They	were	happy.	[41]
Meera	is	very tall.	[42]
That dog	is	dangerous.	[43]
The book	was	interesting.	[44]
NP	V	Adj	

S	LV	Cs	
Rakesh and Mohan	are	lawyers.	[45]
His father	has been	an officer.	[46]
Sakina	is	a nurse.	[47]
John and Lily	are	teachers.	[48]
NP_1	V	NP_2	

A linking verb is a verb that functions as a linking device between the subject and the complement. In sentences 41 to 48 above, the linking verbs have the sense of *may be described.* A complement is usually an adjective, *happy, tall, dangerous, interesting* in sentences 41 to 44 or a noun phrase *lawyers, an officer, a nurse, teachers* in 45 to 48. A complement gives us a 'characteristic' of the subject NP and is thus related to the subject.

Exercise 3

Underline the linking verbs and the complements in these sentences. Mention whether the complement is a noun phrase or an adjective. There are a few sentences which do not have a linking verb.

1. The boys were busy.
2. The Indians were the winners.
3. She slept inside.
4. Her brother is a fool.
5. The policeman may be right.
6. The lunch is tasty.
7. She gave me a pen.
8. My mother is industrious.
9. His father is a doctor.
10. Lal Bahadur Shastri was a great leader.

It is also possible to have an adverbial of time or place after the linking verb **be.** Such an adverbial functions as an **adverbial complement.** (*Adv. Comp*)

S	LV	(Adv Comp)	
Prakash	is	in the library.	[49]
NP	V	Prep Phr	
Ravi	was	downstairs.	[50]
NP	V	A	
The examination	will be	on Tuesday.	[51]
NP	V	Prep Phr	

Notice that in 49, *in the library* is a prepositional phrase, in 50 *downstairs* is an adverb and in 51, *on Tuesday* is a prepositional phrase. All three function as adverbial complements. We do not call them complements as we do in the case of adjectives and nouns because an adverbial complement, strictly speaking, does not 'describe' the subject as in the case of a noun or an adjective. However, an adverbial complement does tell us about the place/time in relation to the subject. In fact, it may be more appropriate to call them **subject-related adverbials.**

Exercise 4

Complete each of these sentences in two ways, one with an 'adjective' or an 'NP' and then with an 'adverbial':

1. His book was ....
2. Delhi is ....
3. Mukesh was ....
4. The meeting will be ....
5. The cricket team has been ....
6. The car is ....
7. The players were ....
8. Her grandfather is ....
9. Professor Kapoor is ....
10. The policeman was ....

There is a second category of linking verbs. These are verbs like:

appear	*feel*	*look*	*seem*	*smell*
sound	*taste*	*become*	*get*	*grow*

S	LV	Cs	
John	feels	happy.	[52]
This dog	seems	restless.	[53]
The music	sounded	strange.	[54]
NP	V	Adj	

S	LV	Cs	
His aunt	became	a judge.	[55]
This	will remain	a secret.	[56]
NP_1	V	NP_2	

Notice that verbs like *appear, feel, look, seem, sound, taste, get* and *grow* may be followed by an adjective functioning as the subject complement. A few verbs like *become, remain, seem,* and *appear* may be followed by an NP functioning as the subject complement.

Exercise 5

Analyse the constituents of each one of the sentences below, mentioning the form and function of each constituent. Use labels like NP (Noun Phrase), V (Verb), Adj (Adjective), A (Adverb), Prep Phr (Prepositional Phrase) for the form and S (Subject) IntrV (Intransitive Verb), LV (Linking Verb), Adv (Adverbial) and C (Complement) for the function.

1. Rajesh is a doctor.
2. The students played in the ground.
3. My brother has become a professor.
4. The comedian laughed.
5. His sister is tall.
6. The cat slept under the table.
7. I feel fine.
8. Mary seemed sad.
9. Vinod talks softly.
10. Kalpana must have been the thief.

Exercise 6

Complete these sentences with the constituent (element) mentioned under each blank:

Example:

John .... continuously.
InTrV

You can use **speaks/spoke** **laughs/laughed** **sleeps/slept**

1. His mother .... a teacher.
LV

2. They seemed ....
C

3. .... appears happy.
S

4. Mita amd Kunal wrote ....
Adv

5. My cousin is ....
C

6. Mira ....
InTrV

7. The food tastes ....
C

8. Feroz and Sanjay .... policemen.
LV

9. Philip shoots ....
Adv

10. They were ....
C

Adverbial position

As mentioned in 1.2, an adverbial is usually (though not always) an optional element of a sentence and may be used with any one of the sentence patterns, depending upon how much information we want to convey. Therefore it is possible to use an adverbial with a linking, intransitive, or transitive verb.

Examples:

Hema	runs	fast.	[57]
S	InTrV	(Adv)	

Shom	looked	happy	at the party.	[58]
S	LV	Cs	(Adv)	

Her father	has been	a doctor	for many years.	[59]
S	LV	O	(Adv)	

All the three sentences above have an adverbial at the end. Whereas *runs* is an intransitive verb, *looked* and *has been* are linking verbs. However, *fast, at the party* and *for many years* are optional elements. It is likewise possible to use an adverbial with a transitive verb.

1.3.2 Intransitive verbs

Subject + Intransitive Verb

An intransitive verb denotes an action or event which does not refer to anything other than the subject. In other words there is nobody or nothing to receive the action of the verb. In this sense, an intransitive verb is complete by itself. However, we may use an adverbial with an intransitive verb to convey more information to the listener or reader. As mentioned earlier, a noun, pronoun or noun phrase, (NP) is used at the subject position. We will use NP as a term for a noun, pronoun or noun phrase.

S	InTr	
Mukesh	fainted.	[60]
NP	V	

S	InTrV	(Adv)	
She	laughed	loudly.	[61]
NP	V	A	

Examples of intransitive verbs are given below:

ache	*advance*	*apologise*	*apply*	*argue*	*awake*
bargain	*bark*	*blaze*	*blow*	*breathe*	*come*
cough	*cry*	*crush*	*fall*	*go*	*laugh*
pause	*rise*	*run*	*stand*	*sit*	*weep*

1.3.3 Transitive verbs

A transitive verb requires an object to complete it. Transitive verbs are of three types:

a. Monotransitive

b. Ditransitive

c. Complex transitive

Monotransitive verbs:

1. A monotransitive verb requires a direct object to complete it. A direct object is a pronoun or a noun phrase.

2. A direct object can be an answer to **what or whom.**

S	Tr V	Od	
He	addressed (*whom*)	**the audience.**	[62]
He	has read (*what*)	**this novel.**	[63]
NP_1	V	NP_2	

3. It is possible to use an adverbial with a monotransitive verb.

He	addressed	the audience	**in the hall.** (Adv)	[64]
I	read	this novel	**recently.**	[65]

4. Although a direct object is an NP, it does not have the same referent as the subject. Thus the subject and the direct object refer to two different persons or things. Notice the use of NP_1 and NP_2 for the subject and the direct object in sentences.

5. A monotransitive verb can be passivised. The **subject** of the active sentence becomes the **object** and the **object** of the active sentence becomes the **subject** of the passive sentence.

India won the match.	(*active*)	[66]
The match was won by India.	(*passive*)	[67]
Monica has built a house.	(*active*)	[68]
A house has been built by Monica.	(*passive*)	[69]

Here is a list of monotransitive verbs:

abolish	*describe*	*love*	*visit*	*abuse*	*enjoy*
make	*wash*	*watch*	*accept*	*find*	*many*
achieve	*follow*	*meet*	*lose*	*use*	*get*
need	*admit*	*hear*	*receive*	*afford*	*help*
remember	*believe*	*hold*	*say*	*bring*	*keep*
see	*call*	*know*	*start*	*carry*	*lead*
study	*close*	*like*	*take*	*cut*	*acknowledge*

Exercise 7

Label the verbs in these sentences as 'transitive', 'intransitive' or 'linking':

1. Naresh has taken my car. (   )
2. His mother has been ill. (   )
3. I need a coat. (   )
4. My coat is warm. (   )

5. Your wife is standing outside. ( )
6. She met the director yesterday. ( )
7. My friend visits me every Sunday. ( )
8. She slept in the morning. ( )
9. Your skirt looks very pretty. ( )
10. They have started the game. ( )

Exercise 8

Identify the different constituents of these sentences. Label both the form and function of each. Label them as NP, V, Adj, A, Prep Phr for the form and Sub, InTrV, TrV mono, LV, Adv for the function:

1. John has been a university professor for five years.
2. She boarded the train with her baggage.
3. The servant polished the car on Friday.
4. The driver turned sharply.
5. The vice-chancellor delivered the speech in the hall.
6. The leader of the opposition criticised the government at the press conference.
7. Rita looked unhappy at the party.
8. The policeman carried his rifle on his shoulder.
9. I bought this book in Delhi.
10. She followed him everywhere.

Exercise 9

Complete these sentences with the constituents mentioned below the blanks:

1. My brother .... this building.
   TrV mono
2. Sunita .... talented.
   LV

3. Arnaz constructed .... last year.
   Od Adv

4. Our dog ....
   TrV mono Od

5. My father has been .... for years.
   Cs

6. We .... the party immensely.
   TrV mono

7. His father has planted .... in the garden.
   Od

8. The girls ....
   InTrV Adv

9. Samson .... yesterday.
   InTrV Adv

10. The car turned ....
    Adv

Ditransitive verbs:

There are a group of verbs (TrVdi) in English which require two objects, an indirect object, and a direct object.

S	TrV di	Oi	Od	
He	gave	his daughter	a present.	[70]
Our aunt	told	us	a story.	[71]
She	offered	me	her car.	[72]
Arun	brought	John	a book.	[73]
NP_1	V	NP_2	NP_3	

1. The indirect object can be defined as the recipient of the action. The indirect object indicates **to whom** or **for whom** the action of the verb is carried out.

2. The indirect object can be a noun or a pronoun or a noun phrase.

3. When there is a sentence with a ditransitive verb, the direct object is usually a noun, or an NP. We cannot normally use a pronoun as direct object with a ditransitive verb. However, it is possible to use a pronoun as direct object with a monotransitive verb.

S	TrV mono	Od		
I	know	him.		[74]
NP_1	V	NP_2		

S	TrVdi	O	Od	
Our aunt	told	us	a story.	[75]
NP_1	V	NP_2	NP_3	
* Our aunt	told	us	it.	[75a]

Notice that whereas *him* (pronoun) is possible as the Od in 74 *it* (pronoun) as the Od in 75a is not possible.

4. Three different subscript numbers on the three NPs in sentences 73 -75 indicate that the three noun phrases in these sentences have different referents.

5. The direct object may often be replaced by a prepositional phrase beginning with **to** and **for.** In such a case

   a. the prepositional phrase is used after the direct object and

   b. it is possible to use the pronoun as the object.

Sheila	bought	me	a book.	[76a]
Sheila	bought	a book	for me.	[76b]
Sheila	bought	it	for me.	[76c]

She	gave	the boy	a book.	[77a]
She	gave	a book	to the boy.	[77b]
She	gave	it	to the boy.	[77c]

Notice that in 76c and 77c the pronoun **it** has been used as a direct object.

6. Some sentences with ditransitive verbs have two passive forms. These two passive forms are possible because there are two objects after the ditransitive verbs and therefore, it is possible to use either the indirect object or the direct object as the subject of the passive sentence.

    She gave the boy a book. [78a]

    The boy was given a book (by her). [78b]

    A book was given the boy (by her). [78c]

    A book was given to the boy (by her). [78d]

    It is possible to omit the agent (*by her*) in the passives.

    The passive with the indirect object as the subject is more common than the passive with the direct object as the subject.

    When the direct object is used as the subject, it is more usual to use the prepositional phrase rather than the indirect object after the verb. Therefore, between 78c and 78d the latter is more usual.

Some of the common ditransitive verbs in English are:

ask	*bring*	*give*	*grant*	*pay*
leave	*lend*	*make*	*offer*	*tell*
promise	*send*	*serve*	*teach*	

Exercise 10

Complete these sentences using suitable indirect and direct objects:

	S	TrVdi	Oi	Od
1.	Our teacher	told		
2.	Sudhakar	wrote		
3.	They	paid		
4.	She	asked		
5.	I	granted		

Exercise 11

Replace the indirect object by a prepositional phrase in these sentences. Place the prepositional phrase at the most natural position:

1. Radha sent her brother a box of biscuits.
2. My mother bought me a bicycle.
3. Mr Kapoor wrote us a letter.
4. He found her a house.
5. Sham paid me the money.

As in the case of the earlier sentence patterns, it is possible to use an adverbial after the direct object.

They gave Mary a bicycle. [79a]

They gave Mary a bicycle **yesterday.** [79b]

Rakesh sent Meera a birthday card. [80a]

Rakesh sent Meera a birthday card **on Wednesday.** [80b]

Exercise 12

Rewrite each of the sentences in Exercise 11 using an adverbial after the direct object.

Exercise 13

Complete these sentences adding a 'ditransitive verb', an 'indirect object' and a 'direct object' to form a sentence:

1. The teacher ....
2. The shopkeeper ....
3. Leander ....
4. My father ....
5. Our gardener ....
6. The lawyer ....
7. The director ....
8. The commanding officer ....
9. Mohini ....
10. The minister ....

Complex transitive verbs:

The complex transitive verb requires a direct object but a direct object is followed by an object complement.

S	TrV comp	Od	Co	
The school	elected	Rakesh	secretary.	[81]
She	called	him	an idiot.	[82]
His remark	made	her	angry.	[83]
The judge	found	the complaint	false.	[84]

The object complement can be an NP or an adjective. For example, in 81 and 82 *secretary* and *an idiot* are NPs and in 83 and 84 *angry* and *false* are adjectives.

S	TrV comp	Od	Co	
All of us	consider	him	a genius.	[85]
NP_1	V	NP_2	NP_3	

S	TrV comp	Od	Co	
They	chose	Alka	their leader.	[86]
NP_1	V	NP_2	NP_3	

S	TrV comp	Od	Co	
Samir	called	Meena	foolish.	[87]
His teachers	consider	Varun	intelligent.	[88]
NP_1	V	NP_2	Adj	

2. Notice that the object complement (NP or Adj) and the object (Od) have a common referent. Whereas in the case of the linking verb, the complement refers to the subject, in the case of the complex transitive verb, the complement refers to the object.

3. Though the object complement can be an NP, it cannot become the subject of a passive sentence.

   If we wish to passivise the complex transitive verb, there will be only one passive and only the direct object becomes the subject of the passive sentence.

   They chose Alka their leader. [86a] (*their leader* is Co)

   Alka was chosen their leader by them. [86b] (*their leader* is Cs)

   Thus whereas in 86a *their leader* is the Co, in 86b *their leader* is the Cs. However, the relationship between *Alka* and *their leader* has not changed in 86b because even in 86b *their leader* is related to *Alka*.

4. As in the case of the earlier sentence patterns, it is possible to add an adverbial to these sentences also.

   They chose Alka their leader **at the meeting.** [89]

   He dyed his shirt red **after the party.** [90]

Exercise 14

Identify the form and functionof each constituent in these sentences:

1. His mother gave Peter an apple in the morning.
2. The sun rises in the east.
3. Uma will become a pilot next year.
4. We watch television every evening.
5. The company offered her a high salary.
6. The minister considers his secretary very patient.
7. Neeta called Roshan a fool.
8. She sleeps till eight in the morning.
9. Our gardener has planted cauliflower recently.
10. The General Manager asked him difficult questions during the interview.
11. Meena looked cheerful at the party.
12. The child was crying.
13. Our finance minister is far-sighted.
14. Doordarshan has started five satellite channels.
15. The Principal declared Monday a holiday.

Exercise 15

The functional labels for sentence patterns have been given below. Write three sentences for each of the sentence patterns. Identify the form for each of the constituents of the sentences:

1. Sub + InTrV
2. Sub + LV + Cs
3. Sub + TrV mono + Od
4. Sub + TrV di + Oi + Od

5. Sub + TrV + Od + Co
6. Sub + InTrV + (Adv)
7. Sub + LV + Cs + (Adv)
8. Sub + TrV mono + Od + (Adv)
9. Sub + TrVdi + Oi + Od + (Adv)
10. Sub + TrV Comp + Od + Co + (Adv)

1.4. Intransitive and transitive verbs

There are a few verbs in English which are usually intransitive but may be used as transitive verbs in certain contexts.

S	InTrV		(Adv)	
The car	stopped		near the bridge.	[91a]
S	TrV	Od	(Adv)	
Mohan	stopped	the car	near the bridge.	[91b]

Notice that *stopped* in 91a is an intransitive verb and in 91b it is a transitive verb. Similarly, we have

He	ran	fast.	[92a]
He	ran	a race.	[92b]

Some other intransitive verbs which can be used as transitive verbs are:

drive	*sing*	*close*	*turn*	*study*	*dance*
open	*read*	*cook*	*court*	*call*	*escape*
shoot	*sink*	*stand*	*write*	*play*	

Middle verbs

There is another small number of verbs in English which always occur in the active form and do not have any passive form.

We **had** a party last night. [93]

This cannot be changed into a passive sentence.

* A party was had last night.

Some of the middle verbs are:

It **costs** rupees ten. [94]

This box **weighs** five kilograms. [95]

As these middle verbs are followed by NPs, they may be treated as transitive verbs. However, the NP used after such verbs does not function as an object and hence these verbs are called **middle verbs.**

Exercise 16

Distinguish between the patterns of each pair:

1a. She ran on the track.	b. She ran a race.
2a. The soup tasted delicious.	b. She tasted the delicious soup.
3a. Rakesh called for her a taxi.	b. Rakesh called her a spoilsport.
4a. He cooks fish in the evening.	b. He cooks in the evening.
5a. This bag weighs fifty kg.	b. Mohan weighed this bag.
6a. Rita found the girl intelligent.	b. Rita found the girl a room.
7a. I will study tonight.	b. I will study the file tonight.
8a. She bought a book yesterday.	b. She bought me a book yesterday.
9a. They elected him secretary.	b. They elected him tonight.
10a. The judge found him guilty.	b. He felt guilty.

1.5 Semantic roles: In 1.2, we discussed the form and function of the different elements of a clause. However, there can be a number of participants performing different semantic roles in a clause.

Khazi opened the door with a key. [96]

The key opened the door. [97]

The door opened. [98]

If we analyse the above sentences in terms of functional analysis, we find that *Khazi*, *the key* and *the door* are subjects in 96, 97 and 98 respectively.

However, the semantic roles played by *Khazi, the key* and *the door* remain constant whether they occur as the subject, the object or any other position in the clause or sentence.

The semantic roles played by these nouns are:

Khazi: agent *the door:* affected *the key:* instrument

Therefore, whereas *Khazi* is the agent, *the door*, the affected and *the key*, the instrument in 97, there is no agent in 98. Sentence 97 has *the key* as the instrument and *the door* as the affected.

Agentive and affected roles

The usual semantic role of a subject of a clause which is followed by a monotransitive verb is of the **agentive participant.** This simply means that the agent (human or animate) initiates an action denoted by a verb.

Shefali hit the ball with force. [99]

The carpenter is cutting the wooden sheet. [100]

The most typical role of the direct object is that of the **affected.** In a simple sense, it receives the action of the verb.

Mohini slapped her son in the park. [101]

Edward sold his house last week. [102]

Notice that in a passive voice sentence the subject may be the **affected.**

The ball was hit with force. [103]

The wooden sheet is being cut by the carpenter. [104]

In 103, *the ball* is the **affected** and similarly in 104, the *wooden sheet* is the **affected** and the carpenter is the **agentive.**

Exercise 17

Identify and label the 'agentive' and the 'affected' in these sentences:

1. Rita is writing a letter.
2. The book was torn by my younger sister.
3. This play will be staged by Standard 4 students.
4. The dog chased the cat.
5. My mother is reading a book.

Beneficiary and attribute

Another important semantic role performed by an element of a clause is the **beneficiary.** The beneficiary is the person for whom or for whose benefit a particular action is carried out. The semantic role of a beneficiary is usually carried out by the indirect object in an active sentence and by the subject in a passive sentence, if the subject has been derived from the indirect object in an active sentence.

Kevin gave her a pen. [105]

My brother was paid a handsome amount by his employer. [106]

Certain middle verbs like *have, own, weigh* and *possess* may have the subject with a beneficiary role.

My brother owns two houses. [107]

This bag weighs twenty kilos. [108]

Certain verbs of perception like *taste, smell* and *feel* may also have subjects in the beneficiary role.

He tasted the tomato soup. [109]

I felt a pain in the leg. [110]

Quirk *et al* (1985: 741) mention that the typical semantic role of a subject complement and an object complement is that of an **attribute.** They distinguish between two subtypes of the attribute: **identification** and **characterisation.**

Identification

Priya is my sister. [111]

She became a pilot. [112]

Her parents called her Susie. [113]

Characterisation

She has been very successful. [114]

The soup tastes good. [115]

Our director made us comfortable. [116]

The Prime Minister considered the experiment a success. [117]

Instrument

The instrument role is performed by a thing (usually inanimate) by means of which an action is carried out:

She opened the door with a key. [118]

The key opened the door. [119]

They bound him with a thick rope. [120]

A thick rope bound him. [121]

The bus knocked him down. [122]

I used a knife to open this box. [123]

Notice that the element performing the semantic role can be used at the subject (sentences, 119, 121 and 122) or object (sentence 123) or adverbial (sentences 118 and 120) positions.

Exercise 18

Identify and label the semantic roles of different participants - 'agentive', 'affected', 'beneficiary',' attributive' and 'instrument' in these sentences:

1. My father's car was stolen by a thief.
2. My mother hit the ball with a stick.
3. Seema sliced the potatoes with a knife.
4. That girl is my friend.
5. They elected him president.
6. That building is very impressive.
7. Rajesh bought his son a bicycle.
8. The milk has turned sour.
9. They made her the captain of the hockey team.
10. They built her a house.

Subject as affected

We discussed earlier that the subject of the passive of a monotransitive verb can be in the affected role. In addition, the subject of an intransitive verb has usually the affected role.

The chair was lying in the corner. [124]

The car turned left on the bridge. [125]

Similarly, the subject of linking verbs followed by the subject complement (in the attributive role) may be treated as in the affected role.

Varinder is a doctor. [126]

Notice that in some cases the object of the transitive verb in an affected role may be used as the subject of an intransitive verb in the affected role.

She is preparing **tea.** (*Od affected*) [127]

The tea is being prepared. (*S affected*) [127a]

Keshav opened **the door.** (*Od affected*) [128]

The door opened. (*S affected*) [128a]

Locative and temporal

Some subjects and NPs in adverbials may perform locative or temporal roles.

It is hot in **Lucknow in June.** [129]
(locative) (temporal)

Tomorrow is a holiday. [130]
(temporal)

Delhi is cold in winter. [131]
(locative)

I met her **at the station.** [132]
(locative)

Exercise 19

Analyse these sentences identifying the functions of each element and the semantic roles, wherever possible, as in the first two examples:

	S	V	Oi	Od	(Adv)
i.	I	shall give	her	my car	tomorrow.
	agentive		beneficiary	affected	temporal

	S	V	(Adv)
ii.	The tiger	was killed	in the field.
	affected		locative

1. Her sister has been a dancer for several years.
2. It is humid in Mumbai during the rains.
3. She is boiling milk in the kitchen.
4. The milk is boiling.
5. Monish is my cousin.
6. The Principal made him the monitor of the class.
7. My uncle remained silent.
8. The opposition supported the new bill.
9. The dog was hit by a train.
10. She was presented a watch on the occasion.

1.6 Sentence types and illocutionary acts

In this chapter, all the sentences discussed or presented for illustrations have been examples of declarative sentences. On the basis of the structure of a sentence, or what is called formal classification, simple sentences fall under four major categories.

a. **Declaratives:** These are sentences which have the subject as the first element followed by verbal and other elements, if any.

   Geeta bought him a pen on Tuesday. [133]

   New Delhi is the capital of India. [134]

b. **Interrogatives:** These are of two kinds:

   i. **Yes-No interrogatives** have the auxiliary placed in front of the subject.

   Are you attending the meeting today? [135]

   Do you like fish? [136]

ii. **Wh- interrogatives** have a **wh-** word placed in the initial position of a sentence.

What did he pay you for the work? [137]

When are you going to Gwalior? [138]

c. **Imperatives:** These are sentences which do not have a grammatical subject. Therefore, they begin with the main verb as the first element of the sentence.

Open the door. [139]

Give me a glass of water. [140]

d. **Exclamatives:** These are sentences which are introduced by **what** or **how** but have the subject-verb order of a declarative sentence and end with the subject and the verb and an exclamation mark.

What a fine day it is! [141]

Usually four discourse functions are associated with the four sentence types mentioned above:

a. Statements usually convey information.

b. Questions usually seek information.

c. Directives usualy instruct/order someone to do something.

d. Exclamations usually express a fact that the speaker is impressed by something.

Thus 133 and 134 are statements, 135 - 138 are questions, 139 and 140 are orders and 141 is an exclamation.

However, we notice that several sentences may not have an association between the sentence type and its normal discourse function.

Don't go near the tiger.
(*imperative but an act of warning*) [142]

Could you pass the salt please?
(*interrogative but a request*) [143]

You are going to Varanasi tonight?
(*declarative but a question*) [144]

You can play outside for an hour.
(*declarative but giving permission*) [145]

Sentences 142 - 145 indicate that in actual use a sentence may perform an act which may not be associated with its discourse function. The above sentences are, in fact, utterances. An utterance performs a particular speech act in a given situation and context keeping in view the listener.

Quirk *et al* (1985: 804) mention,'Utterances of sentences are *SPEECH ACTS*... to refer to a speech act identified with reference to the communication intention of the hearer.'

An illocutionary act is an utterance, the significance of which is understood in a social interaction. Illocutionary acts can be explained as interactional functions such as greeting, congratulating, asserting, accusing, questioning, thanking, warning,ordering, promising, requesting, apologising, congratulating, giving permission, leave-taking, praising, etc.

What a fine boy he is! [146]

Sentence type: *exclamative*
Illocutionary act: *praising*

Would you like a cup of tea? [147]

Sentence type: *interrogative*
Illocutionary act: *offering*

Father to child: 'You have got zero in maths.' [148]

Sentence type: *declarative*
Illocutionary act: *criticising*

Exercise 20

Mention the sentence type and illocutionary act for each of these sentences:

1. A member of parliament in Lok Sabha: 'Is it right to increase taxes on essential commodities?'
2. Teacher to students: 'The earth revolves round the sun.'
3. I'm awfully sorry I couldn't attend the meeting.
4. What a talented girl she is!
5. Will you open the door please?
6. Senior to junior: 'You have not been working on this project.'
7. Senior to junior: 'You may go on leave from Monday.'
8. London is foggy during winter.
9. The food is ready.
10. I think you'd better return this car.

1.7 Concord

This refers to the agreement or relationship between two grammatical units in such a way that a certain feature of A requires a certain feature of B.

As discussed in 1.2, the most common type of concord in English is between the third person singular subject in the simple present tense and the verb.

a. A singular subject in the simple present tense requires a singular verb.

   My father goes to office by bus. [149]

b. A plural subject in the simple present tense requires a plural verb.

   Her brothers go to office by car. [150]

c. A subject in the first person singular or plural requires a plural verb.

I go to office by van. [151]

d. If the verb **be** is used as a linking verb/auxiliary with *I* it requires the form *am*.

I am watching television. [152]

e. If the subject is a noun phrase, the form of the noun head would be used for concord with the verb.

The boy standing near the corner **is** a hockey player. [153]

The boys standing near the corner **are** hockey players. [154]

f. Finite and non-finite clauses at the subject position are treated as singular.

What he needs is a change of place. [155]

Playing cricket is compulsory in our school. [156]

g. The verb, **be** in the past tense also has concord between the subject and theverb.

She was singing in the classroom. [157]

They were singing in the classroom. [158]

h. Anything indicating measurement of weight, distance, etc. takes a singular verb.

Twenty miles is a long distance. [159]

Hundred kilograms is a lot of weight. [160]

i. Certain nouns coming together but treated as singular also take a singular verb.

Bread and butter was served at breakfast. [161]

j. Using the principle of proximity, when two nouns or noun phrases are linked by **or,** the verb agrees with the noun which is nearest to it.

Either **she or her mother is** attending the function. [162]

Either **she or her brothers are** attending the function. [163]

k. A noun at the subject position with *as well as* or *with* is treated as a singular noun.

Karan, **as well as his friend is** responsible for this act. [164]

l. The subject preceded by one of is followed by a singular verb.

One of my friends wants to meet you. [165]

m. When a subject has a plural noun after phrases like *a number of, a majority of* we usually use a plural verb.

A large number of teachers were invited to the seminar. [166]

The majority of the residents are attending the meeting. [167]

n. Certain collective nouns like government, board, faculty are used both as singular or plural nouns.

The government has not imposed any new taxes. [168]

The government have not imposed any new taxes. [169]

The faculty is discussing the new pay scales. [170]

The faculty are discussing the new pay scales. [171]

Several grammarians distinguish between **grammatical concord** and **notional concord.** If the singular noun takes a singular verb and the plural noun takes a plural verb as in a, b, c and as illustrated above, it is treated as grammatical concord. However, if the form of the noun is singular but is notionally treated as plural and is followed by the plural verb, it is treated as notional concord as in 169 and 171.

o. A singular verb is also used after a subject with *every* and *each* and compounds like *everyone, everybody, anyone, anybody, noone, nobody.*

Every teacher keeps two registers in this school. [172]

Noone listens to me. [173]

Exercise 21

Rewrite these sentences with the right form of the auxiliary verb given within brackets:

1. Either your father or his colleagues (have) spoken about it.
2. The board (have) decided to give two increments to everybody.
3. Nobody (be) listening to him.
4. The army (have) established a new command.
5. Everyone (have) to draw this map.
6. The majority of the officers (work) during vacation.
7. A lot of people (have) complained.
8. Two thousand rupees (seem) a reasonable price for this.
9. A large number of doctors (be) attending the conference.
10. Either your father or your sister (be) responsible for this mess.

2

Nouns and Articles

2.1 Countable, uncountable and proper nouns

Nouns may be generally divided into two categories: **countable** and **uncountable.** Countable nouns are those nouns which have singular and plural forms:

book - books	man - men
dog - dogs	woman - women
pen - pens	child - children

We can, for example, make a count of *books, dogs,* etc. We can say *a book, two books, three books, a hundred books, a thousand books,* etc. The singular form is used to refer to one person or thing and the plural form is used to refer to more than one person or thing.

There are certain nouns which refer to general things like material, mass, a quality or an abstract idea. Such nouns are called uncountable nouns. Uncountable nouns have only one form i.e. the singular form. These nouns cannot be counted: *rubber, food, anger, sugar, water,* etc.

Noun-verb agreement

a. **Countable nouns:** We use a singular verb with a singular noun and a plural verb with the plural noun in the simple present tense:

   A **student wants** to see you. [1]

   Some **students want** to see you. [2]

b. **Uncountable nouns:** As an uncountable noun usually has a singular form, we use a singular verb with an uncountable noun in the simple present tense.

   Water freezes at 0° C. [3]

Some countable nouns have the same form for singular and plural.

I saw **an aircraft** at the airport. [4]

I saw **several aircraft** at the airport. [5]

Some other nouns with the same singular and plural forms are:

deer, fish, sheep, fruit, etc.

Quantifying uncountable nouns: Uncountable nouns usually denote gaseous, liquid or solid states or abstract ideas, which cannot be counted. However, there are certain expressions of quantity like *piece, item, slice,* etc. which can be used before such uncountable nouns. Such expressions are called **partitives**.

a drop of water	a block of ice	a piece of cake
a cup of tea	a bottle of milk	a pinch of salt
a slice of bread	a kilo of flour	a piece of paper
a loaf of bread	a blade of grass	a litre of oil
an acre of land	a gallon of water	a jet of water

Partitives used with countable nouns: It is possible to use partitives with some singular and plural countable nouns:

a branch of a tree	a page of a book
a block of houses	a herd of cattle
a pack of cards	a pack of cigarettes

Mass nouns: There are a few mass nouns which are usually used as uncountable nouns but can occasionally be used as countable nouns. When they are used as countable nouns, they have a special meaning.

Can I have **a cup of tea,** please? [6]

Can I **have a tea,** please? [7]

Can I have **a lemon juice,** please? [8]

There is hardly any difference in meaning between 6 and 7. In sentence 7, *a tea* means *a cup of tea.*

Collective nouns: There are certain nouns like *government, board, faculty* which can be treated both as singular or plural nouns:

The government wants to impose new taxes. [9a]

The government want to impose new taxes. [9b]

The board has decided to grant leave to all the officers. [10a]

The board have decided to grant leave to all the officers. [10b]

Some other collective nouns are:

army	*family*	*committee*	*group*	*community*
press	*herd*	*staff*	*club*	*team*

Some collective nouns only have the singular form and are hence only used with a singular verb.

The aristocracy does not have the same status today as it had in earlier times. [11]

Some collective nouns are only followed by the plural verb.

The people are waiting for the President. [12]

The police are looking into the matter. [13]

Nouns with plural forms only: Some nouns like *trousers, scissors, spectacles,* etc., have only plural forms and are followed only by the plural verb.

His **trousers were** torn. [14]

She left her **spectacles** on the table. [15]

Some such nouns are:

belongings	*braces*	*briefs*	*jeans*	*leggings*	*parts*
pyjamas	*trunks*	*underpants*	*shorts*	*laces*	*forceps*

Some nouns have the plural form but are followed by a singular verb.

Billiards is not a very popular game these days. [16]

The 7.30 news gives the details of national happenings. [17]

Nouns ending in **-ics** are usually treated as singular.

Linguistics is the science of language. [18]

Other examples are:

mathematics	*physics*	*economics*
acoustics	*phonetics*	*politics*

Proper nouns: When we use the actual names of people we use proper nouns. Proper nouns are always written in capital letters:

Varun Akram Elizabeth Radha

There is no determiner used before a proper noun.

We may use the title of a person before his/her name.

In such a case, we usually use the surname or the full name of a person after the title.

Professor Kapoor Dr Lahiri President Narayanan

Professor Mahesh Kapoor General Sharma

A few titles such as King, Queen, Prince, Princess, may be followed by the person's first name:

King Mahendra Princess Anne Queen Elizabeth

Masculine and feminine nouns: Some nouns in English have distinct masculine and feminine forms and thus they may be referred to by the pronouns **he** or **she.**

> I met **a boy** yesterday on the road. **He** asked me if I could help him cross the road. [19]

> There is **a girl** outside the classroom. **She** wants to talk to you. [20]

Such nouns may be called **contrasting nouns** as these nouns have contrasting masculine and feminine forms.

son - daughter   father - mother   uncle - aunt
husband - wife   man - woman   nephew - niece

There is a group of nouns which has contrasting masculine and feminine forms but the feminine form can be formed by adding **-ess** to the masculine form.

host - hostess   prince - princess   emperor - empress
waiter - waitress   god - goddess

There is a set of nouns which ends in **-man** or **-woman** and can either be masculine or feminine:

salesman - saleswoman   postman - postwoman
policeman - policewoman

Some nouns, which were traditionally treated as masculine nouns, because they have **-man** ending are nowadays used by many native speakers with **-person** ending so as to avoid gender bias.

chairman - chairperson   spokesman - spokesperson

Some other nouns, which were traditionally either masculine or feminine, are used in their neuter forms:

air hostess - flight attendant   foreman - superior
mailman - mailcarrier

Nouns with dual gender: There is a large class of nouns in the neuter gender which can be referred to by **he/she** depending upon the sex of the person:

foreigner	doctor	clerk	writer	professor
shopkeeper	secretary	reader	officer	assistant
lecturer	teacher	typist		

I met **my doctor** yesterday. **He** asked me to see **him** on Monday. [21a]

I met **my doctor** yesterday. **She** asked me to see **her** on Monday. [21b]

Some animals have masculine and feminine distinction:

bull - cow	cock - hen	tiger - tigress
dog - bitch	lion - lioness	stallion - mare

Usually the pronoun used to refer to these animals is **it**. But occasionally one may use **he/she** to refer to these animals, particularly if they are our pets.

In the case of other animals like *cat, monkey, snake, sparrow, crow*, etc., there is no masculine and feminine distinction and they are referred to by **it.**

2.2 Genitive

The genitive case of nouns in English is formed by apostrophe **s** ('s) in English. Apostrophe **s** ('s) is usually added to a noun referring to a person or an animal.

John's book is lying on the table. [22]

I have poured milk into the **cat's** plate. [23]

Apostrophe s ('s) can also be used with things associated with a group of people and public institutions.

The **government's policy** on tax reforms will definitely attract more foreign investment. [24]

India's freedom movement was non-violent. [25]

I attended the **bank's annual meeting.** [26]

In written English **'s** is used after a singular form but with the plural form, we may use only the apostrophe. Similarly singular nouns ending in **s** may either have the apostrophe or the apostrophe **s**.

boy's college	boys' college
Ross's book	Ross' book

However, we may add the apostrophe **'s** after the plural form of a noun which does not end in **s**. For example:

children's clothes

The genitive can be used with:

a. names of people and other nouns indicating possession.

I saw **Ramesh's house** on my way to office. [27]

Meena's book is lying in the corner. [28]

The boy's parents want to see you. [29]

Your neighbour's father is very old. [30]

b. animal names, particularly higher animal names.

I have kept **the cat's plate** on the table. [31]

He twisted **the dog's tail.** [32]

c. names of cities, states, countries, continents.

India's future depends on its foreign policy. [33]

Everything is all right with **Lucknow's electric supply system.** [34]

d. nouns expressing time.

Yesterday's newspapers carried the story about the earthquake in Maharashtra. [35]

We like **Monday's TV programme.** [36]

My son enjoyed **his three weeks' vacation.** [37]

e. nouns expressing a place, home, shop, place of work, etc.

You might meet her at the **baker's** (at the baker's shop). [38]

She should be at **Rakesh's** (at Rakesh's house). [39]

Exercise 1

Rewrite these sentences using the plural forms of the nouns:

Example: A dog is a faithful animal.
Dogs are faithful animals.

1. This fan needs repair.
2. That chain is made of stainless steel.
3. A cat dislikes a dog.
4. I bought a book yesterday.
5. A TV set is sold at a lower price these days.
6. A child below five is not allowed inside the planetarium.
7. The Bajaj company has manufactured a good scooter.

8. A computer has become essential for most organisations.
9. I own a cow.
10. A monkey can be dangerous.

Exercise 2

Fill in the blanks with either the singular or the plural form of the nouns in brackets:

1. My .... studies in class V. (son)
2. My .... play their radio loudly. (neighbour)
3. The .... that you bought for me are lying on the table. (book)
4. The .... is good for health. (sunflower)
5. The .... are lying on the lawn. (chair)
6. The .... whom you met at the station wants to see you. (man)
7. The .... whose mother gave you a gift is waiting for you in the common room. (girl)
8. The .... were kept in the fridge. (potato)
9. The .... in the attic are a nuisance. (mouse)
10. The .... were waiting for us. (child)

Exercise 3

Use the noun given in brackets with 'a/an + singular noun' if it is a countable noun, or an expression of quantity if it is an uncountable noun:

Examples: I met a .... yesterday. (brilliant boy)

I met a brilliant boy yesterday.

I requested her to give me .... (water).

I requested her to give me a glass of water.

1. I bought .... from the corner shop. (bread)
2. She gave me .... yesterday. (pot)
3. Radha wants .... (milk).
4. There is .... lying on the floor. (paper)
5. There is .... lying on the floor. (pen)
6. My mother gave my sister .... at breakfast. (cake)
7. My mother gave my sister .... at breakfast. (apple)
8. My father planted .... in our house. (tree)
9. Tom brought home .... last night. (dog)
10. Rasheeda wanted .... (tea).

2.3 Articles

2.3.1 Generic reference

An article along with the noun head may refer to the given noun in a generic sense:

Dogs are faithful animals. [40]

A dog is a faithful animal. [41]

The dog is a faithful animal. [42]

Sentences 40, 41 and 42 refer to the class **dog** without referring to an individual dog and therefore, *dogs, a dog, the dog* in the above sentences are said to have **generic reference.**

Gold is a precious metal. [43]

Milk is good for health. [44]

Air is essential for health. [45]

However, nouns also have **non-generic reference.**

There is **a dog** barking outside. [46]

I need **a pen.** [47]

In the above sentences the reference is to the individual and not to the class.

If a noun is non-generic, it can either have a **specific** or a **non-specific reference.** A noun has specific reference if the speaker has a specific individual in mind. If the speaker does not have a specific individual in mind but any individual belonging to the class referred to, then the noun is non-specific. Notice that in sentence 46 *a dog* is non-generic and specific, because the speaker can identify the *dog*. The speaker is talking of a particular *dog*. However, in 47, *a pen* is non-generic and non-specific, because the speaker is not talking of a particular *pen* but any *pen*.

Balu wants to plant **a mango sapling** in his garden. [48a]
(He has bought **one** from the nursery.)

Balu wants to plant **a mango sapling** in his garden. [48b]
(He will buy **one** from the nursery.)

In sentence 48a, *a mango sapling* is specific because *Balu* has already bought it and thus the sapling is a specific sapling, whereas in 48b, *a mango sapling* is non-specific because *Balu* has yet to buy *a mango sapling* and hence it can be any mango sapling.

Farha has been in love with **a doctor.**
She wants to get married to him. [49a]
(***specific***)

Farha wants to get married to **a doctor.**
(***non-specific***) [49b]

2.3.2 Definite and indefinite reference

If a noun has a specific reference, then it may have either a **definite** or an **indefinite reference.** In the case of specific and non-specific distinction, one looks at the speaker's point of view, that is, whether the speaker knows the individual or he does not. If the listener can identify the individual, then it is a definite noun. If the listener cannot identify the individual, then it has an indefinite reference.

> I bought **a car** yesterday. (***specific, indefinite*** *because the listener cannot identify the car*) [50]

> I met **the doctor who treated you** yesterday. (***specific, definite*** *because the listener can identify him*) [51]

The definite reference to a noun depends on the shared knowledge between the speaker and the listener or the writer and the reader. The shared knowledge between the speaker and the listener can be related to situational or linguistic reference.

Situational reference: is related to the extralinguistic situation. The extralinguistic situation may arise either from the immediate situation or from the general understanding of the universe.

> When will the train arrive? (*at the railway station*) [52]

> Have you taken your dog for a walk? (*at home*) [53]

> The vice-chancellor is visiting our college next week. [54]
> (*knowledge about who the vice-chancellor is*)

> The President will address the nation. [55]
> (*knowledge about who the President is*)

Anaphoric reference: is linguistic reference and refers to the information given earlier in the discourse.

> There was **a man** and **a woman** living in a forest. **The man** was fifty years old and **the woman** was fifty-five years old. [56]

The definiteness of *the man* and *the woman* in the second is with reference to *a man* and *a woman* in the first sentence.

> Monisha brought **a cat** and **a dog** here yesterday but her father asked her to return **the dog.** [57]

Cataphoric reference: is also linguistic reference but it refers to information that is given later in the discourse.

> **The man** that Kumar met at the press was a minister. [58]

The definiteness of *the man* is with reference to the relative clause *that Kumar met at the press* later in the sentence.

> **The girl** writing on the wall is a painter. [59]

Exercise 4

Identify the article features of the nouns in bold letters in these sentences. (Mention whether they are generic/non-generic, specific/ non-specific, definite/indefinite. In the case of definite, mention the type of reference.)

1. **Wood** is used for building houses and making household furniture.
2. **The girl** eating ice cream is Vani's sister.
3. Kalam needs **a house.**
4. Mukta wants to appoint **a manager**. She has already issued an appointment letter to him.
5. Subeda wants to get **a book** issued from the library. She has left the book on your table.
6. **An apple** a day keeps the doctor away.
7. I saw **the film** that you suggested yesterday.
8. Vinod wants to appoint **a manager.** He is holding interviews on Wednesday to select a person for the post of manager.
9. **Iron** is important for the growth and development of children.
10. I saw **a film** on television last night.

2.4 Uses of articles

There are two kinds of articles in English. **A/an,** is the indefinite article and **the** is the definite article. In addition we also need to learn when not to use an article. This is referred to as **zero** article. The use of articles in English depends on whether a noun is countable or uncountable.

2.4.1 The indefinite article: a/an

Whenever a countable singular noun begins with any one of the vowels, a, e, i, o, u, we use the article **an** before the noun:

an apple, an engagement, an officer

The indefinite article **a** is used before singular, countable nouns beginning with consonants:

a church, a man, a shoe, a book, a girl

We need to modify the above statements regarding the use of **a** and **an** before a singular countable noun. The use of **a** or **an** depends on the following vowel or consonant sound rather than the following vowel or consonant sound at the beginning of a noun:

an apple	an officer	a man

but

a large apple	a young officer	an old man

The general rule is that we use the article **an** before a vowel sound in a noun phrase with a countable singular noun as the noun head and we use the article **a** before a consonant sound in a noun phrase with a singular noun as the noun head. So we say *a university, a union,* though all these nouns begin with the letter **u,** because the sound is a consonant sound, **yu.** We also say *an hour, an honest man, an heir,* because the initial consonant sound is not pronounced in these words.

Exercise 5

Use* a *or* an *before each of these noun phrases:

1. .... long train	2. .... airy room
3. .... table	4. .... ass
5. .... beautiful flower	6. .... ideal house
7. .... factory	8. .... old factory
9. .... very old factory	10. .... well decorated hall
11. .... extremely cold winter	12. .... very old man
13. .... man	14. .... bicycle
15. .... inkpot	16. .... iron gate
17. .... brass gate	18. .... expensive coat

We use **a/an** with a singular countable noun when we use one individual person or thing to make a general statement about all people or things of that type. In other words, **a/an** can be used before a singular countable noun when the singular countable noun is used in the generic sense. *A dog is a faithful animal* implies that *all dogs are faithful animals.*

An airconditioner can be of great help in summer. [60]

Here are some more uses of **a/an:**

a. before a noun functioning as a subject complement after a linking verb. This is done to give more information about someone or something.

Monica is a **painter.** [61]

His father was a **judge.** [62]

Radha is a **bank officer.** [63]

b. when someone or something is mentioned for the first time.

We bought **a car** last month. [64]

I met **an old friend** at the market yesterday. [65]

My sister brought home **a parrot** and **a rabbit** yesterday. My father asked my sister to let **the parrot** loose. [66]

c. to talk about a thing or a person in an indefinite way.

I met **a man** on the way. [67]

This means that you met one man on the way but either you don't know who he was or you do not wish to specify who he was.

He was eating **a mango.** [68]

A man wants to meet you. [69]

We've killed **a tiger.** [70]

d. with mass and uncountable nouns. However, it is possible to use **a/an** with an uncountable noun when it has prenominal or postnominal modifiers.

He has **a good knowledge of computer science.** [71]

A clear understanding can solve this problem. [72]

2.4.2 Zero article

We do not use an indefinite article:

a. when a plural countable noun is used in a generic or general sense.

Tigers can run very fast. [73]

Mangoes are in great demand in the west. [74]

Trees are our friends. [75]

b. when uncountable nouns are used in a generic sense.

Water is necessary for our survival. [76]
(*water in general not a specific water*)

Oil is used for frying. [77]

Wood is used for building houses and making furniture. [78]

English is an international language. [79]

c. before proper nouns.

I met **Hussein** yesterday. [80]

Narlikar is going to Delhi tomorrow. [81]

d. before the names of countries.

India has liberalised its economy. [82]

She comes from **South Africa.** [83]

e. before the names of cities, towns and villages.

Ujjain is an ancient city. [84]

She lives in **Malihabad.** [85]

f. before the names of streets and parks.

They live in **Park Street**. [86]

Lady Hydari Park is very beautiful. [87]

g. before meals.

We had **lunch** at 2 p.m. [88]

Breakfast is served between 8 and 9 a.m. [89]

h. before nouns like *school, hospital, bed, church, class, college, university, work.*

She goes to **college** in the morning. [90]

I went to **bed** at 10 p.m. last night. [91]

Indu goes to **church** every Sunday. [92]

i. before means of transport, like *by air, by bus, by car, by land, by sea, by ship, by train.*

We went to Goa **by bus.** [93]

I always travel **by train.** [94]

Exercise 6

Fill in the blanks with a/an, if necessary. Leave the blanks unfilled if no article is necessary:

1. Suresh's father is .... teacher. He goes to .... school at 8 a.m. by ...... bus.
2. I saw ...... cat yesterday. It was carrying .... rat in its mouth.
3. He met with ...... accident last week. He is still in .... hospital.
4. We bought ..... house last year. It is made of ..... wood, ... cement and ...... plaster.
5. ...... smoking is injurious to health. Therefore, our country should not allow .... production of .... cigarettes.
6. Vasanta has planned to open ..... school. She has applied for .... no-objection certificate from the state government to start her school.
7. .... mangoes grow in abundance in India and .... apples grow in abundance in Australia.
8. We will go by ...... train and my sister will go by .... bus to Delhi.
9. .... Air is an essential element for .... life on .... earth.
10. .... rain is good for .... agriculture but .... excessive rain can cause floods.

Exercise 7

Explain the use or non-use of articles in the nouns in bold letters in the following sentences:

Examples:

A camel is **a beast of burden.** (The indefinite article **a** is used before *camel* because *camel* has generic reference here.)

Liza has been **a dancer** for five years. (The indefinite article **a** is used before *dancer* as *a dancer* is the subject complement of the subject, *Liza.*)

1. **Horses** are faithful to their masters.
2. **Electricity** is important for industrial development.
3. I met **Vidya** yesterday.
4. I saw **an elephant** on my way to your house.
5. **A scooter** can be very useful for your daily visits to the various hospitals.
6. We went for **dinner** to my grandmother's house last night.
7. I have **a clear conscience.**
8. He goes to **hospital** at 8.30 a.m.
9. My mother bought **a television set** for us.
10. She is going to **Patna** by train.

2.4.3 The definite article 'the':

The main use of the definite article, **the,** is for definite reference. In this sense it can be used before singular and plural countable nouns and with uncountable nouns. The definite article, **the,** is used when the noun is specified:

> There is an apple and an orange in the bowl.
> **The apple** is overripe but **the orange** seems fresh. [95]

However, **the** can also be used before singular countable nouns in the generic sense.

The definite article **the** is used:

a. before nouns which refer only to one person, group, thing or group. This can be due to situational reference as mentioned in section 2.3.2. The situational reference may be due to the immediate situation or due to a general knowledge of the situation that the speaker and hearer share.

Can I see **the manager?** (*at a bank*) [96]

The Principal wants to see you. (*at a college*) [97]

The President is visiting Wardha on Tuesday. (*of India*) [98]

The moon revolves around the earth. (unique reference, the only one of its kind) [99]

b. before a noun which has become definite because it has been mentioned a second time. In other words, the noun has an anaphoric reference.

She bought a bus and a taxi last month. She has got the licence to run **the bus** on the Delhi-Kanpur route and she has given **the taxi** to her son to run it as a local taxi. [100]

c. before a noun which has been identified or made unique because it has cataphoric reference, that is, the noun has been modified by a relative clause or a phrase following it.

The dog barking over there is very ferocious. [101]

The President of France will visit India next month. [102]

The man in the red shirt is a preacher. [103]

d. with superlatives and ordinals used as modifiers of the noun.

Shikha is **the best student** in our class. [104]

Charles was **the first person to** board the plane. [105]

Cricket is **the most popular game** in India. [106]

e. before different parts of the body.

He hurt himself on **the chin.** [107]

The insect bit her on **the forehead.** [108]

f. before nouns which refer to only one place or organisation in a particular place. If there is only one hospital in the city, then one can use **the** before hospital.

I am going to **the museum.** [109]

We swam in **the river.** [110]

g. with nationality adjectives and other adjectives used as noun heads.

The English have signed an economic treaty with **the French.** [111]

The rich can be helpful to **the poor.** [112]
(the + adjective has generic reference)

h. with time sequence and parts of the day.

Our University has planned to start vocational courses **in the near future.** [113]

In the beginning, the Mughal Empire did not have a well-organised administration. [114]

You can meet me **in the evening.** [115]

She was not well **in the morning.** [116]

i. with buildings and objects, when they refer to the structures.

Notice the differences between the following pairs of sentences:

The church was designed by Jim Hopkins. [117a]

He has gone to **church.** [117b]

He has gone **the office** to assess the damage. [118a]

He has just left for **office.** [118b]

j. before proper nouns in some cases.

i. with the surnames of couples or families.

The Sharmas have invited us for dinner tonight. [119]

I met the **Tyagis** on the way home. [120]

ii. before the names of newspapers.

The Times of India	The Hindu
The New York Times	The Guardian

iii. before geographical proper nouns which have an invariably plural form.

the Himalayas	the Netherlands
the West Indies	the Midlands

iv. before certain other geographical proper nouns. There are no grammatical reasons for the of use **the** before the names of such countries, states or cities.

the Punjab   the Hague   the Sahara

v. before names of hotels, restaurants, theatres, cinema halls etc.

the Oberoi Sheraton	the Globe
the Clarks Avadh	the National Library

k. to make general statements. In this sense it is not used as a definite article but functions more as an indefinite or a zero article. Thus we have three ways of making general statements.

The dog is a faithful animal.
(*all dogs are faithful animals*) [121]

A dog is a faithful animal. [122]

Dogs are faithful animals. [123]

Exercise 8

Use **the** ***wherever necessary:***

1. She's going to .... hospital to consult Dr Mathew.
2. .... girl sitting in the corner seems to be Kaushal's cousin.
3. .... youngest girl was given the prize.
4. .... earth revolves around .... sun.
5. I read .... Hindustan Times every morning before going to ...... office.
6. I entered .... hospital through the side gate.
7. I went to Valsad .... last month and stayed in .... house where I was born.
8. .... next meeting of the Board of Directors will be held in ..... Hague.
9. Columbus was one of .... greatest seamen in history.
10. We visited .... British Museum during my stay in London.

Exercise 9

Insert **a, an** ***or*** **the** ***wherever necessary:***

1. I took children to zoo on Sunday. We saw tiger and panther in zoo. Tiger seemed to be very young and ferocious but panther was old and looked harmless.

2. Nita's father was engineer. He worked for construction company. Company was owned by Russian.
3. We couldn't see road in front of us. Therefore, we parked car on side of road and waited for clear weather to set in.
4. Tea can be very refreshing in evening. I often have friends come over for cup of tea and pleasant chat.
5. You must buy refrigerator because it is necessity these days.
6. She hired taxi to visit Amritsar.
7. Mac bought scooter and car last year. But as he is in need of money, he wants to sell car.
8. She hit him on head.
9. Prime Minister is visiting Jammu next Monday and therefore, Chief Minister wants to have meeting of all Secretaries.
10. Oil is essential for the industrial development of country.

Exercise 10

Explain the use of articles before the nouns in bold letters in the following sentences: (Examples as in exercise)

1. She goes to **bed** at 10a.m.
2. **The Times of India** is one of the leading newspapers in India.
3. **Oil** can float on water.
4. We shall meet in **the evening** and discuss this problem.
5. Please take **the dog** outside.
6. **The best player** will get this medal.
7. **The shirts lying on that shelf** are rather expensive.
8. We need **a dog** to guard our house. When you get one please inform us.
9. **The Chopras** will meet the Governor tomorrow.
10. We saw a film at **the Mayfair theatre** yestraday. **The film** was a real classic.

3

The Noun Phrase

3.1 Introduction

We noticed in chapter 1, that a noun phrase occupies different positions in a sentence. Thus a noun phrase may function as subject, direct object, indirect object, subject complement, object complement or even the object of the preposition in a prepositional phrase.

S	LV	Cs	
Our Principal	is	efficient.	[1]

S	TrVmono	Od	
I	saw	**the Principal.**	[2]

S	TrVdi	Oi	Od	
Mary	gave	**the Principal**	a book.	[3]

S	LV	Cs	
Her mother	is	**a Principal.**	[4]

S	TrVcomp	Od	Co	
The Board	appointed	Rakesh	**the Principal.**	[5]

S	TrV	Od	(Adv)	
Mr Kapoor	left	the building	**with the Principal.**	[6]

3.2 Parts of a noun phrase

The sentences that we speak, write or read in real life may have noun phrases more complex than the ones we have seen above. We find that often the noun phrase consists of a number of words so that one is able to identify the noun easily. Therefore, it is possible to modify a noun with a number of modifiers.

The noun phrase consists of a noun head (NH) which is the most important word in a noun phrase and all the modifiers that accompany it:

> **The tall girl wearing a blue frock** is my cousin. [7]

Notice that in the above sentence *the tall girl wearing a blue frock* is a noun phrase functioning as the subject. The most important word in this noun phrase is *girl* and therefore, *girl* is the noun head. Other words/ phrases like *the, tall* and *wearing a blue frock* only modify the noun head *girl*. The noun head is the minimal grammatical part of the noun phrase which can form a noun phrase. For example, grammatically, instead of using the above sentence, we can use the one below:

> **Usha** is my cousin. [8]

where *Usha* is the noun phrase and the subject.

> **The car** is parked outside. [9]

In this sentence, *the car*, is a simple noun phrase. In order to make this noun phrase more specific, we can say:

> **The car that John gave his daughter** is parked outside. [10]

Notice that it is not grammatically necessary to modify the noun head with one or more modifiers. It is quite appropriate to use sentence 9 if we know which *car* the speaker is talking about. We may use 10 either if there are two or more *cars*, or to give more information to the listener.

Exercise 1

Circle the noun head in the noun phrases underlined:

1. The boy standing in the corner is our college captain.
2. John has bought an old car.
3. She owns a big house in Delhi.
4. I met your younger brother yesterday.
5. Their eldest son has been selected for the foreign services.
6. The huge dog that we saw in the morning looked ferocious.
7. The tall girl eating ice cream is very angry.
8. The book that you gave me yesterday is lying on the table.
9. Her latest novel is a historical romance.
10. I saw your new English teacher.

3.3 Modifiers of the noun head

A noun head can be modified by a number of modifiers. Basically, the modifiers of the noun head are of two types: **prenominal modifiers** and **postnominal modifiers.** Prenominal modifiers are used before the noun head.

Prenominal modifiers <NH> Postnominal modifiers

the tall <man> [11]

<Vikram>, who is waiting for you outside [12]

the tall <man> whom we met yesterday [13]

Thus we have three possibilities:

a. prenominal modifier + <NH> as in [11]

b. <NH> + postnominal modifier as in [12]

c. prenominal modifier (s) + <NH>
+ postnominal modifier(s) as in [13]

3.3.1 Prenominal modifiers

3.3.1.1 Determiners: Determiners are a very important subclass of prenominal modifiers. Many of the nouns are usually preceded by a determiner. A determiner signals a noun. Determiners are words like these:

Articles	Possessives of Pronouns	Possessives of Proper Nouns	Demonstratives
	my	Edward's	this
the	our	Jane's	that
	your		
	their		
a/an	his	Varun's	these
	her	Shailaja's	those
	its		

Examples:

the table	Edward's pen
a book	Varun's cat
our house	this cat
your house	those dogs

A characteristic of determiners is that they are mutually exclusive. This means two or more determiners cannot occur before an NP.

* the my table	the clerk's table
* the that cat	the cook's pan

However, the possessives of nouns like *clerk's, cook's* etc., are not determiners. They can be used after a determiner and are called genitives: the *clerk's table, the cook's cat*. For further explanation of the genitive, see section 3.3.1.7

3.3.1.2 Postdeterminers: Postdeterminers follow determiners (in case there is a determiner present). They precede an adjective or any other prenominal modifier used before the noun head. Postdeterminers can be:

cardinal numerals: *one, two, three ....*

ordinal numerals: *first, second, third ....*

others: *next, last, (a) few, fewer, fewest, little, much, many, more, most, less, least, ...*

Examples:

the two < books >	the next < shop >
the second < boy >	many < people >

It is possible to use more than one postdeterminer with a noun head:

the first three < months >	the next four < days >

3.3.1.3 Predeterminers: Predeterminers are a small subclass of prenominal modifiers, which can be placed before determiners. They are words like:

a. *all, both, half*

b. *double, twice, thrice*

c. *one-third, one-fourth*

d. *such, what*

Predeterminers, like determiners are mutually exclusive.

Examples:

Pre-D	**D**	**NH**
all	his	< books >
both	her	< brothers >
three times	his	< salary >

Exercise 2

Underline and label the noun head and the prenominal modifiers in these noun phrases:

1. both his friends
2. three times her salary
3. her first three books
4. twice a day
5. little water
6. a few men
7. half the amount
8. the last six months
9. Arun's twentieth birthday
10. Ayesha's last wish

3.3.1.4 Adjectives: An adjective is one of the most frequent prenominal modifiers used between the determiner and the noun head.

Examples:

D	Adj	NH
the	tall	< girl >
the	old	< house >
the	long	< rod >

It is possible to use more than one adjective before a noun head.

Examples:

D	Adj	Adj	NH
his	new	red	< shirt >

When there is more than one adjective before the NH, the usual order is: first, the qualitative adjective, followed by the colour adjective, followed by the classifying adjective.

a	small	blue	oval	< ring >
the	beautiful	green	<house>	

Exercise 3

Fill in the blanks with appropriate adjectives in the following sentences:

1. Mukesh has bought a .... car.
2. The .... man wants to talk to you.
3. She gave me a .... book.
4. Sophia has written me a .... letter.
5. The .... dog barked at every one.
6. Her father built a .... house.
7. Anil's .... film is very successful.
8. It was a .... party.
9. Your .... photographs are with Ravi.
10. The .... table is lying in the corner.

Adverb as modifier of an adjective: It is possible to modify or intensify the adjective by modifying the NH. This means a premodifying adjective may itself be modified by some of the adverbs.

Examples:

D	Adv	Adj	NH
an	extremely	good	< idea >
a	very	handsome	< man >
that	rather	old	< house >

Exercise 4

Fill in the blanks with one of the adverbs and one of the adjectives given below:

extremely rather fairly very absolutely (*adverbs*)

heavy impossible high old long
tall long sensible faithful fierce (*adjectives*)

1. It was a (n) .... work.
2. A(n) .... girl wants to meet you.
3. She has written a(n) .... novel.
4. *Gone with the Wind* is a(n) .... film.
5. It is a(n) .... table.
6. They have constructed a(n) .... wall.
7. A(n) .... fridge is lying in your shop.
8. Nita is a(n) .... girl.
9. A dog is a(n) .... animal.
10. We saw a(n) .... lion in the zoo.

3.3.1.5 Present and past participles used as prenominal modifiers:

The ***-ing*** and ***-ed*** participles when performing the function of adjectives can also function as prenominal modifiers.

This is a very interesting < novel >. [14]

The rising < prices > will affect the budget. [15]

Frozen < peas > have become very popular. [16]

She had a frightened < look >. [17]

Mohan is a very sophisticated < man >. [18]

Like other adjectives, it is possible to modify the ***-ing*** and ***-ed*** participles with adverbs. However, there is a restriction on the use of adverbs with some participles.

For example, in 14 and 18 *very* has been used before *interesting* and *sophisticated.* However, it may not be possible to use an adverb before the ***-ing*** participle in these sentences:

He is going to contest the forthcoming election. [19]

* He is going to contest the very forthcoming election. [20]

We've just moved into a finished house. [21]

* We've just moved into a very finished house. [22]

3.3.1.6 Nouns: Sometimes, a noun can also function as a prenominal modifier, i.e., a noun may modify the noun head.

Examples:

D	**N**	**NH**
the	cotton	< shirt >
a	cricket	< player >
the	film	< industry >

Exercise 5

Fill in the blanks with one of the nouns given below:

tennis	steel	chemistry	village	entertainment
morning	iron	copper	insurance	finance

1. She left Mumbai by the .... train.
2. The .... jug is lying in the kitchen.
3. The electricity company has used .... wires.
4. The .... *sarpanch* wants to see you.
5. Vibha has submitted her claim to the .... company.
6. With the coming of new singers, the .... industry is making a lot of money.
7. Our neighbour's daughter has taken admission in the .... department.
8. Karan hit the dog with an .... rod.
9. Steffi Graf is one of the top .... players.
10. We signed a .... deal last night.

It is possible to use an adjective before a noun functioning as the modifier of the noun head. This kind of modification is possible if we want to give more information about the noun or noun head:

I like **that fast swimmer.** [23]

I like **that girl swimmer.** [24]

Notice that in 23 *fast* is an adjective and in 24 *girl* is a noun modifying the noun head *swimmer.*

I like **that fast girl swimmer.** [25]

In 25 we have used both *fast* and *girl* as prenominal modifiers. The sequence of these two modifiers is fixed. The noun is used immediately before the NH and the adjective is used before the noun.

the new gas company   that low garden fence

When we have both the noun and the adjective as prenominal modifiers, the context determines whether the adjective modifies the noun or the noun head. But sometimes such premodification may lead to ambiguous noun phrases.

D	**Adj**	**N**	**NP**
that	small	baby	product

The above NP is ambiguous because *small* may either modify *baby* or *product*. If *small* modifies *baby*, then it would mean *a product for small babies*. On the other hand if *small* modifies *product*, then it would mean *a small product for babies*.

Exercise 6

Use the words in each list given below to form a noun phrase with the pattern: D (Adv) - Adj - N - NH. Then use each noun phrase to form a complete sentence:

1. village, her, old, house, extremely
2. new, college, my, friend
3. rather, player, that, football, tall
4. the, Doordarshan, latest, channel
5. captain, fairly, that, young, army
6. formal, notebook, his, grammar
7. box, red, metal, that
8. compact, dictionary, his, English
9. very, a, man, young, bright
10. absolutely, water, this, mineral, pure

3.3.1.7 Genitive: The genitive is a noun used with the apostrophe **s** ('s) and indicates possession. We noticed while discussing determiners in section 3.3.1.1, that *Edward's*, *Varun's* etc., are determiners and are mutually exclusive of the other determiners. Thus we have,

Edward's book *the book* *that book*

However, it is possible to say

her father's book

Now we find that, though *father's* is a genitive or a possessive form, it is not mutually exclusive of the other determiners. We may, therefore, conclude that the possessive forms of pronouns and names are determiners as they are mutually exclusive of the other determiners. However, when there is a noun which refers to a person, an animal or a public institution but is not a name, the possessive form of such a noun may be preceded by a determiner:

his mother's coat *my daughter's wedding*

the fisherman's net *the dog's ear*

It is possible to use an adjective as a prenominal adjective before or after the genitive:

his mother's old coat *the old fisherman's net*

my youngest daughter's wedding

However, whether we use an adjective before or after the genitive will depend on how much information we want to convey. If an adjective is used before the genitive, then it modifies the NP (genitive). On the other hand, if the adjective is used before the NH, it modifies the NH itself.

Group genitive: Quirk *et al* (1985: 328) mention that in the case of the group genitive, the genitive is attached to a postmodifier.

For example:

the Queen of England's estate

Notice that the *estate* belongs to *the queen* and not to *England.* Therefore, the possessor in the above example is *the queen* and not *England.* The apostrophe **'s**, therefore, is not added to *the queen* but is delayed and added to *England Estate*, therefore, is the NH and the *queen of England's* is determinative. According to Quirk *et al* (1985: 1276) 'Determinative function means that the genitive noun phrase functions like a definite determiner.' Following Quirk *et al* (1985: 1345), one can analyse the above NP as follows:

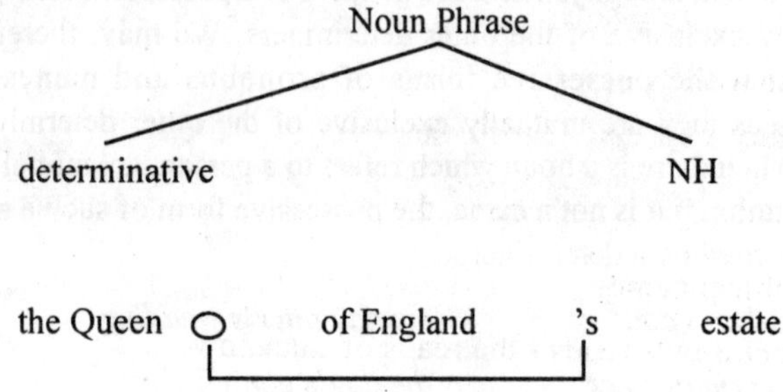

The above figure indicates that whereas **'s** belongs to *the queen,* it has been delayed and added to the noun head of the prepositional phrase. A few other examples are:

the University of Delhi's Vice-Chancellor

my father-in-law's business

Exercise 7

Analyse the following noun phrases:

1. my mother-in-law's car
2. the President of India's visit
3. The Profpssor of Linguistics' room
4. The Finance Minister of India's budget speech
5. Edward VIII's reign

The genitive is generally used with:

a. personal names.

Rakesh's book　　　**Kiran's** car

b. people and higher animals.

my daughter's house　　　**the dog's** bark
the doctor's clinic　　　**the horse's** leg

c. genitive denoting time.

last week's news　　　**a month's** salary
today's special TV programme

The genitive/the of + NP can be used with several inanimate nouns:

a. geographical names.

Lucknow's roads - the roads of Lucknow
Europe's economy - the economy of Europe

b. heavenly bodies.

the earth's atmosphere - the atmosphere of the earth

c. nouns referring to organisations etc.

the company's annual budget - the annual budget of the company.

the university's executive council - the executive council of the university.

However, with certain things the of + NP rather than the genitive is used:

the side of the car	* the car's side
the end of the match	* the match's end
the corner of the street	* the street's corner

In the above cases, we have discussed the genitive which is followed by the noun head. However, the genitive can also occur without the following noun head . Such a noun phrase may be treated as a reduced noun phrase.

Elliptic genitive: The head of the noun phrase may be omitted as it can be understood or retrieved from the context.

My house is smaller than *Sharma's.* (Sharma's house) [26]

This year's Holi festival was better than *last year's.* (last year's Holi festival) [27]

Sheetal's was the oldest car. (Sheetal's car) [28]

Local genitive: The local genitive is less elliptic in the sense that there is only a general or vague retrievability of the noun head.

We'll have a party at **Rakesh's.** [29]

It generally means *the place where Rakesh* lives, but the hearer may not know whether it is a *house, hostel, building* etc.

Generally speaking local genitive can be used:

a. for a place of residence

We met at **my sister's.** [30]

She stayed **at Kapoor's.** [31]

b. for professional establishments and commercial firms

I'm going to **the grocer's.** [32]

Indica is the best car from **the Tata's.** [33]

Post-genitive: An **of** construction is combined with a genitive to produce a post-genitive. For example,

a friend **of my brother's** a pupil **of his**

Nouns functioning as post-genitive are either proper nouns or count nouns. The use of post-genitive is to indicate the indefiniteness. Notice the difference between the following two phrases:

my brother's friend (presupposes definiteness)	a friend of my brother's (presupposes indefiniteness)

3.3.2 Postnominal modifiers

As in the case of prenominal modifiers, there are several modifiers of a noun phrase that can be used as postnominal modifiers.

3.3.2.1 Prepositional phrases: A prepositional phrase is the most frequent postnominal modifier in English.

I met a < girl > **with red hair** yesterday at the bus stop. [34]

The < man > **in the blue shirt** seems to be a CBI officer. [35]

The < shops > **along this road** have already been sold. [36]

Some more examples:

the < road > at the back	the < house > in the front
the < book > on Nehru	the < garden > beside the river

Exercise 8

Underline the prepositionai phrases modifying the noun head in these sentences:

1. The big car with four headlights is very expensive.
2. I saw a man in a black suit.
3. The main road from London to York is quite wide.
4. Edward is a student of English.
5. He has plastered the roof of his house.

3.3.2.2 Relative clauses: Relative clauses can be introduced by the relative pronouns, **who, whom, whose, which** and **that.** A relative clause is a finite clause. (*For details on relative clauses see chapter 7 and for the details on finite clauses see chapter 8*).

A relative clause can function as a postnominal modifier.

The < man > **who is standing at the door** wants to meet you. [37]

I want to see the < girl > **who attended our party with you.** [38]

The < story > **that he told us** was very interesting. [39]

This is the < dog > **which won the first prize at the dog show.** [40]

3.3.2.3 Non-finite clauses: There are three non-finite clauses which can function as postnominal modifiers. *(For a detailed discussion of non-finite clauses, see chapter 7*).

Present participle or -ing clause:

The < girl > **eating ice cream** is my cousin. [41]

The < man > **writing a letter** is my teacher. [42]

Some grammarians consider the present participle clause used as the postnominal modifier as the reduced form of the relative clause. Compare 41 and 42 with 43 and 44.

The < girl > **who is eating ice cream** is my cousin. [43]

The < man > **who is writing a letter** is my teacher. [44]

Notice that although the ***-ing*** clauses (as in 41 and 42) are without any tense, the tense is interpreted on the basis of the tense in the main clause.

The boy weeping next door sounded sick.
(*the boy was weeping next door*) [45]

The man carrying a bag turned out to be our manager.
(*the man was carrying a bag*) [46]

Exercise 9

Change each one of these sentences into noun phrases with a non-finite participial clause. Then use each of the noun phrases in a sentence:

Example: The girl is sitting at the table.
The girl sitting at the table is my neighbour.

Example: A cat is sitting near the window.
I saw a cat sitting near the window.

1. A dog is barking at the cat.
2. The boat was sailing slowly.
3. The plane was flying in the air.
4. The teacher is writing on the blackboard.
5. A crow is eating bread.

Past participle or *-ed* clause:

A noun may be modified by an ***-ed*** clause.

The < child > **neglected by her parents** found life difficult. [47a]

The < car > **repaired by the mechanic** could sell at a good price. [48a]

We may treat the clauses in bold as i) reduced forms of a relative clause and ii) as passive in nature.

The < child > **who was neglected by her parents** found life difficult. [47b]

The < car > **that was repaired by the mechanic** could sell at a good price. [48b]

Thus, we can conclude that the ***-ing*** participle clause is related to the active form and the ***-ed*** participle clause is related to the passive form.

Exercise 10

Change these active voice sentences into the passive voice, then use the passive sentence as a noun phrase with an -ed participle phrase and finally use each of the noun phrases in a sentence:

Example: The wind drove the snow.

The snow was driven by the wind. (*passive*)

The snow driven by the wind. (*noun phrase*)

The snow **driven by the wind** came down the mountain at a tremendous speed. (*sentence*)

1. Our engineers have recently made a machine.
2. They showed a film on TV this week.
3. Manoj wrote a letter.
4. They have mentioned a problem above.
5. Pandit Jawahar Lal Nehru wrote the *Discovery of India.*

Infinitive clauses: Like the ***-ing*** and ***-ed*** participle clause, the infinitive clause may also be treated as the reduced relative clause. In the case of ***-ing*** and ***-ed*** participle clauses the subject and **be** of the relative clause is omitted. However, in the case of the infinitive clause, the subject, object or an adverbial and sometimes even the complement may be omitted.

An < instrument > **to test blood infection** has been installed at the district hospital. [49]
(*which can test blood infection*) (subject + modal omitted)

He has got a < room > **to stay.** [50]
(*where he can stay*) (adverbial + subject + modal omitted)

The < man > to approach is Professor Rai. [51]
(*whom you should approach*) (object + subject + modal omitted)

In sentences 49, 50 and 51, the infinitive clause or its underlying relative clause is in the active form. It is possible to have an infinitive clause in the passive form.

He was the youngest < person > to be elected. [52]
(*who was elected by the people*)

This is the < method > to be followed for investigation. [53]
(*which will be followed for investigation*)

Exercise 11

Change the relative clauses in these sentences into infinitive clauses:

Example: This is the method **that will solve this sum.**
This is the method to solve this sum.

Example: The man **whom you should see** is Dr Das.
The man to see is Dr Das.

1. The place **where you can stay** is the Institute hostel.
2. We need students **who can study this problem.**
3. He is the right man **who can take a decision.**
4. I need something **that I can eat.**
5. That is most suitable time **when you can practise.**

There are some **to- infinitive clauses,** functioning as postnominal modifiers which do not have any corresponding finite relative clause.

Rakesh lacks the ability to pass this examination. [54]

The agreement to set up a petroleum plant has been finalised. [55]

They signed a proposal to start a school. [56]

Exercise 12

***Combine these pairs of sentences in such a way that sentence* b *of each pair becomes a non-finite clause modifying a noun phrase of sentence* a.**

Examples:

i a. The dog is very docile.

b. It is sleeping under the table. (*transform it into* ***-ing*** *clause*)

The dog < it is sleeping under the table > is very docile.

The dog which is sleeping under the table is very docile.

The dog sleeping under the table is very docile.

ii a. The fridge is working well now.

b. It was repaired by my father. (*transform it into* ***-ed*** *clause*)

The fridge < it was repaired by my father > is working well now.

The fridge that was repaired by my father is working well now.

The fridge repaired by my father is working well now.

iii a. The first woman has been selected.

b. She will work on this project. (*transform it into* ***to-*** *infinitive clause*).

The first woman < she will work on this project > has been selected.

The first woman who will work on this project has been selected.

The first woman to work on this project has been selected.

1. a. I saw a girl.

   b. She was swimming in the pool. (*transform it into* ***-ing*** *clause*)

2. a. That man wants to meet you.

   b. He is standing under the tree. (*transform it into* ***-ing*** *clause*)

3. a. The problem is quite difficult.

   b. It has been mentioned above. (*transform it into* ***-ed*** *clause*)

4. a. Your willingness has been appreciated.

   b. You will attend the meeting. (*transform it into* ***to-*** *infinitive clause*)

5. a. She asked me to bring the book.

   b. It was lying on the table. (*transform it into* ***-ing*** *clause*)

6. a. The scooter is for sale.

   b. It is parked near the gate. (*transform it into* ***-ed*** *clause*)

7. a. You have no reason.

   b. You refuse it. (*transform it into* ***to-*** *infinitive clause*)

8. a. The boy is my cousin.

   b. He is running in the field. (*transform it into* ***-ing*** *clause*)

9. a. The candidates have arrived.

   b. They will be interviewed by us. (*transform it into* ***-ed*** *clause*)

10. a. Everyone liked the dress.

    b. It had been designed by your mother. (*transform it into* ***-ed*** *clause*)

3.3.2.4 Appositive phrase: It is possible to use a noun phrase as a postnominal modifier of a noun head. A noun phrase, thus used, gives information about the noun head.

> Dr Mehta, **our Principal,** has been awarded a UGC fellowship. [57a]
>
> Our college magazine, ***Deep Shikha*,** is published three times a year. [58a]
>
> Your neighbour, **Mrs Gopal,** wants to talk to you. [59a]

a. Commas are used before and after the appositive phrase because it is separate from the noun head.

b. The noun head and appositive phrase have a common referent. Notice that in 57a *Dr Mehta* and *our principal*, refer to the same person and in 58a *our college magazine* and *Deep Shikha* refer to the same thing.

c. The relationship between the noun head and the appositive phrase is similar to the relationship between the subject and the complement of a subject.

> Dr Mehta is our principal. [57b]
>
> Our college magazine is Deep Shikha. [58b]
>
> Your neighbour is Mrs Gopal. [59b]

3.3.2.5 Minor postmodifications:

Adjectives: Adjectives usually function as prenominal modifiers. However, when an adjective is used as a postnominal modifier, there are two possibilites:

1. The postposed adjective is modified by an adverb.

> I find my < wife >, **usually cheerful**. [60]

2. There are two adjectives used at the postnominal position.

A < man > **old and tired,** approached me. [61]

Our < friend >, **happy and jovial,** teased everyone at the party. [62]

Adverbs: Some adverbs may also function as postnominal modifiers.

The < people > **upstairs** are very friendly. [63]

The < conditions > **there** are pretty bad. [64]

Nouns:

The < party > **last night** was fantastic. [65]

3.3.3 Multiple postmodification

A simple case of multiple modification can be of a noun that has got more than one postnominal modifier.

The < girl > **in the corner eating ice cream** [66]

Thus in 66, we have two postnominal modifiers, i. a prepositional phrase, *in the corner* and ii. an ***-ing*** participle, *-eating ice cream.*

Simple and complex noun phrases: A simple noun phrase is a noun head without any modification, or a noun head with only a determiner. Thus, *Mary, he, the girl* etc. are simple noun phrases. Noun phrases with one or more than one prenominal or/and postnominal modifier are complex noun phrases. These noun phrases are thus **complex noun phrases.**

the beautiful flower

the beautiful flower in the hand of the statue

the tall man standing in the corner

Exercise 13

Analyse these noun phrases in detail. Identify the noun head and then identify each type of prenominal and/or postnominal modifier:

1. that tall boy standing near the door
2. both his younger brothers, who studied with me
3. her most expensive pen that she bought at an auction
4. a few back issues of our college magazine
5. the seventh UGC Refresher Course for teachers of English
6. all those tall hockey players running with their sticks
7. his small white dog which he bought last year
8. both his elder sisters sitting near the door
9. the long garden fence of my house that was built two years ago
10. the blue paper box covered with silk paper

4

The Verb Phrase

4.1 Introduction

In chapter 1, we mentioned that the second constituent of a sentence is the verb. In sentence 1 *sleeps* is the verb.

Seema **sleeps** in the afternoon. [1]

Similarly, in sentence 2 *is sleeping* is the verb.

Seema **is sleeping** in the room. [2]

and in sentence 3 *has been sleeping* is the verb.

Seema **has been sleeping** for two hours. [3]

Thus we notice that whereas *sleeps* is the main verb (MV) in sentence 1, *is* is the helping verb or auxiliary verb and *sleeping* is the MV in sentence 2, and *has* and *been* are *auxiliaries* and *sleeping* is the MV in sentence 3. However, there seems to be some grammatical relationship between **is** and ***-ing*** of *sleeping* in sentence 2 and again there seems to be some relationship between **has** and ***-en*** and **be** and ***-ing*** in sentence 3. Therefore, we find that the second constituent of a sentence (what we call **verb** in chapter 1) can be more than the MV. Thus, it would be appropriate to call it the **verb phrase.** In this chapter we will discuss the structure of the verb phrase in detail.

Another grammatical relationship that we notice in sentences 1, 2 and 3 above is that *in the afternoon* modifies *sleeps* in sentence 1, *in the room* modifies *is sleeping* in sentence 2 and *for two hours* modifies *has been sleeping* in sentence 3. These modifiers of the verb phrase, as discussed in chapter 1, are adverbials. In this chapter, we will also discuss the modifiers of the verb phrase in detail.

4.2 Structure of the verb phrase

The verb phrase (VP) has two constituents: the **auxiliary** (aux) and the **main verb** (MV).

VP → aux + MV

Thus 4, 5 and 6 can be analysed as follows:

She **has been reading** the newspaper since morning. [4]

Ali **has finished** his work. [5]

I **shall meet** you tomorrow. [6]

		aux		MV
has been reading	=	has been	+	reading
has finished	=	has	+	finished
shall meet	=	shall	+	meet

This analysis is very general. However, we notice that the auxiliary can have more than one subconstituent. As the analysis of *has been reading* indicates in 4, the auxiliary comprises **has + been**. Another thing to notice here is that the tense is always part of the auxiliary. In a very simple analysis, which will be modified in this section later, we notice that tense is carried by **has been, has** and **shall** in 4, 5 and 6 respectively. However, if there is no word like **has, is, shall**, etc. in a sentence, as in 7 below, we still maintain that the tense is carried by the auxiliary.

She **finished** her work soon. [7]

Thus the analysis of the VP, *finished* in this sentence will be as follows:

VP → aux + MV

aux → tense (T)

T → past

MV → *finish*

Another point to remember is that in English we have only two tenses - present and past. We do not have any future tense as such in English. Many books on English grammar mention that **shall** and **will** indicate future tense, but when we learn the verb forms of **shall** and **will,** we say **shall** and **will** are the present forms and **should** and **would** are the past forms. Nevertheless, it is possible to express future time in English. We will discuss this in detail in chapter 6.

Let us analyse some more sentences to understand the structure of the VP in detail.

Umesh **is reading** the newspaper. [8]

Umesh **has read** the newspaper. [9]

Umesh **has been reading** the newspaper. [10]

The VP *is reading* in sentence 8 can be analysed as:

VP → aux + MV

aux → T + (*be* + *-ing*)

T → present

MV → *read*

We can indicate it as follows:

T + (*be* + *-ing*) + MV

pres + *be* + *-ing* + *read* = *is reading*

Notice that what we finally get is the tense (present) and **be** clubbed together as *is* and ***-ing*** and *read* clubbed together as *reading*. Thus we can say that the progressive aspect in English is expressed by (**be**+***-ing***).

Similarly, the VP *has read* in sentence can be analysed as follows:

VP → aux + MV

aux → T + (*have* + *-en*)

tense → present

MV → *read*

We can indicate it as follows:

T + (*have* + *-en*) + MV

pres + *have* + -en + *read* = *has/have* + *read*

(*the past participle form of the verb read*)

Again **pres + have** have been clubbed to get **has** and ***-en*** + *read* have been clubbed to get *read* here. Thus we can say that the perfective aspect in English is expressed as *-en* + *read.* Now we can analyse the VP *-has been reading* - in 10 as follows:

VP → aux + MV

aux → T + (*have* + *-en*) + (*be* + *-ing*)

T → present

MV → *read*

We can represent it as follows:

T + (*have* + *-en*) + (*be* + *-ing*) + MV

pres + *have* + *-en* + *be* + *-ing* + *read* = *has/have been reading*

The perfective aspect (**have** + ***-en***) and progressive aspect (**be** + ***-ing***) are always shown in parentheses. This means that the perfective and progressive aspects are always optional constituents of the verb phrase and the tense and the MV are always obligatory constituents.

However, the above rules cannot generate the VP in 11, which can be analysed as follows:

I shall meet you tomorrow. [11]

VP → Aux + MV

Aux → T + (M)

T → present

M → shall

MV → *meet*

Thus the VP which can generate any active sentence in English can be represented as:

T + (M) + (*have* + *-en*) + (*be* + *-ing*) + MV

Notice that as in the case of the perfective aspect (**have** + ***-en***) and the progressive aspect (**be** + ***-ing***), the modal (M) is also an optional element of the verb phrase. There is a fixed order of the various elements of the verb phrase. The tense or T is always the first element, followed by modal or (M), perfective (**have** + ***-en***), progressive (**be** + ***-ing***) and the main verb or MV.

The tense is always carried by the first element of the verb phrase:

Monisha **is playing** in the ground. [12]

Vivek **has been living** in this house for the last four years. [13]

Basu **talked** to Mohini in the morning. [14]

Notice that in 12 and 13 the tense is carried by **is** and **has been,** and in 14 the tense is carried by *talked*.

Exercise 1

Analyse the elements of the verb phrase in each of these sentences. First, give the general analysis and then the specific analysis as shown in these examples:

Examples:

i. She has been sleeping since morning.

General Analysis: T + (*have* + *-en*) + (*be* + *-ing*) + MV

Specific Analysis: pres + *have* + *en* + *be* + *-ing* + sleep

ii. Ravi might have met her.

General Analysis: T + (M) + (*have* + *-en*) + MV

Specific Analysis: past + *may* + *have* + *-en* + meet

1. Robert was singing in his room.
2. Sunita has finished the work.
3. Meena goes to office at 9 in the morning.
4. Javed is playing in the field.
5. Rajiv must have reached college today.
6. Vijay might have done it.
7. Rafiq has been sleeping since morning.
8. Kunal was talking to Manisha in the class.

Exercise 2

Write full sentences on the basis of the following strings of the verb phrase. You may use any subject, object, complement or adverbial of your choice to write full sentences.

Examples:

i. past + (be + -ing) + watch

Sentence: Ravi was watching a film in his room.

ii. pres + (*have* + *-en*) + (*be* + *-ing*) + read

Sentence: She has been reading a novel since morning.

1. past + can + have + -en + examine
2. pres + work
3. past + be + -ing + run
4. past + may + have + -en + meet
5. pres + have + -en + be + -ing + practise
6. past + can + have + -en + be + -ing + play
7. past + sing
8. pres + will + telecast
9. past + be + -ing + drive
10. pres + shall + go

The following formula:

VP → T + (M) + (*have* + *-en*) + (*be* + *-ing*) + MV

can generate the verb phrase in active voice sentences. However, it cannot generate passive voice sentences. Thus, whereas the VP in 15 below can be generated using the above formula,

Mr Rao saw a bear yesterday. [15]

A bear was seen by Mr Rao yesterday. [16]

the VP in 16 cannot be. Thus we need to expand the above formula for the VP to be able to generate passive voice sentences. The expanded formula will be as follows:

VP → T + (M) + (*have* + *-en*) + (*be* + *-ing*) + (*be* + *-en*) + MV

This means that the fixed order for the various elements of the VP is as above. The tense (T) is always the first element, followed by the modal (M), perfective (**have** + ***-en***), progressive (**be** + ***-ing***), passive (**be** + ***-en***) and the MV. Only the T and the MV are obligatory elements. The modal, perfective, progressive and passive are optional elements.

Thus the general and specific analysis for 16 will be as follows:

General Analysis: T + (*be* + *-en*) + MV

Specific Analysis: past + (*be* + *-en*) + *kill*

This book could have been published without much delay. [17]

The matter was being discussed by the members at the meeting. [18]

Sentence 17:

General Analysis: T + M + (*have* + *-en*) + (*be* + *-en*) + MV

Specific Analysis: past + *can* + *have* + *-en* + *be* + *-en* + *publish*

Sentence 18:

General Analysis: T + (*be* + *-ing*) + (*be* + *-en*) + MV

Specific Analysis: past + *be* + *-ing* + *be* + *-en* + discuss

Exercise 3

Give the general and the specific analyses for the verb phrases in the following sentences:

1. He was examined by the police.
2. Your proposal is being considered at the meeting.
3. Lucknow has been visited by several Prime Ministers.
4. Your parcel will be delivered to you tomorrow.
5. This might have been done by Rakesh.

4.3 Finite and non-finite verb phrases

In the previous section, we discussed the structure of the verb phrase in terms of the auxiliary and the verb phrase. We noticed that the auxiliary comprises an obligatory element, the **tense** and the optional elements - the **modal,** the **perfective,** the **progressive** and the **passive.** A verb phrase can also be distinguished according to whether it is **finite** or **non-finite**. A verb is finite if it carries tense and non-finite if it does not carry tense.

I **told** Mohini that her father **had arrived.** [19]

I **asked** Mohini **to receive** her father. [20]

Notice that in 19 there are two verb phrases *told* and *had arrived.* Both *told* and *had arrived* carry the past tense. Thus *told* and *had arrived* are finite verb phrases.

In 20, there are two verb phrases *asked* and *to receive.* Whereas *asked* carries the past tense, *to receive* does not carry any tense. Thus *asked* is a finite verb phrase and *to receive* is a non-finite verb phrase. As we shall see in chapter 7, the main clause must have a finite verb phrase. It is only the dependent or subordinate clause that can either have the finite or non-finite verb phrase.

Entering the room, I found the book on the shelf. [21]

Bill hates **sending** her memos. [22]

In 21 *entering* is the non-finite verb phrase as it does not carry any tense and *found* is the finite verb phrase as it carries the past tense. Notice that *entering* has been used in the subordinate clause. Similarly in 22 *hates* is the finite verb phrase as it carries the present tense but *sending* is the non-finite verb phrase as it does not carry tense. Again *sending* is used in the subordinate clause.

Thus a clause with a finite verb phrase is called a **finite verb clause** or **finite clause** and a clause with a non-finite verb phrase is called a **non-finite verb clause.** It may be pointed out here that although a non-finite verb does not carry tense, its tense can be interpreted from the tense of the main clause.

Exercise 4

Underline the verb phrases in these sentences and then identify whether a given verb phrase is 'finite' or 'non-finite':

1. She has been sleeping.
2. I know where he has left the keys.
3. While coming out of my room, I saw Rita in her car.
4. Mary wants to see you.
5. To work like that can be tiring.
6. Chandran has finished his work.
7. He got up early to catch the train.
8. Having completed her work, she went out for a walk.
9. Asif asked her if she could attend the dinner.
10. I noticed that she was tired.

4.4 Modifiers of the verb

As we saw in chapter 3, the head noun can be modified by a large number of modifiers. Similarly, the verb can be modified by a number of modifiers. The modifiers of the verb are known as **adverbials.** The term **adverbial** is used for all the modifiers of a verb. There can, therefore, be different types of adverbials modifying the verb. For example, there can be a one-word adverb, a noun phrase, a prepositional phrase or an adverbial clause (finite or non-finite) used as an adverbial:

I met him **there.** [23]

I met him **every hour.** [24]

I met him **at the airport.** [25]

I met him **while he was leaving for Delhi.** [26]

In 23 - 26, *there* (adverb), *every hour* (noun phrase), *at the airport* (prepositional phrase) and *while he was leaving for Delhi* (finite clause) are all adverbials. Similarly, there can be a non-finite adverbial clause.

He works **to earn money.** [27]

He works **standing at the table.** [28]

He works **seated at the table.** [29]

Sentences 27 - 29 have non-finite adverbial clauses as modifiers of the verb. Finite and non-finite adverbial clauses will be discussed in detail in chapter 7.

As discussed in chapter 1, adverbials are mobile as compared to the other elements of the sentence. The position of adverbials is flexible in order to have a different focus on the adverbial. The normal position of adverbials is the end of the sentence/clause. Sentences 23 - 29 have adverbials at the **sentence-end** position.

The second position of adverbials is the **sentence-initial** position.

In the beginning, his lecture was very interesting. [30]

Suddenly, he turned towards the left. [31]

As he was very poor, I helped him. [32]

When an adverbial is used at the beginning of a sentence, it carries the **focus.** (*see chapter 10*)

The third position where an adverbial can occur is the **sentence-medial** position. The adverbial can occur between the subject and the main verb, or the auxiliary and the main verb.

She **immediately** took away her purse. [33]

Mani, **in the meantime,** repaired the television. [34]

He has **almost** finished painting. [35]

4.4.1 One-word adverbs

One-word adverbs can be classified into four basic kinds of adverbials expressing **time, place, manner** and **degree.**

Adverbs of **time** can be subdivided into adverbs of frequency and duration. Definite time is usually expressed by noun phrases, adverbs and prepositional phrases.

Some of the adverbs functioning as adverbials of frequency are:

always	*continually*	*continuously*	*frequently*	*generally*
usually	*normally*	*occasionally*	*often*	*rarely*

We **always** go on vacation in June. [36]

Maria is **usually** late for class. [37]

She **rarely** misses her class. [38]

He was **regularly** attending the evening session. [39]

Adverbs of **duration** indicate how long something happens or lasts. Some of the adverbs of duration are:

always briefly indefinitely long permanently temporarily

He is **temporarily** working in our office. [40]

They have **permanently** shifted to the civil lines. [41]

Adverbs of **manner** indicate the manner in which an action is/was/will be carried out. Some of the adverbs of manner are:

angrily	*awkwardly*	*badly*	*beautifully*	*carefully*
clearly	*closely*	*coldly*	*comfortably*	*correctly*
quietly	*easily*	*efficiently*	*firmly*	*fluently*
freely	*gently*	*honestly*	*peacefully*	*properly*

She shouted at me **angrily.** [42]

Mahesh touched the ball **gently.** [43]

The inspector searched his pockets **thoroughly.** [44]

I need it **urgently.** [45]

Adverbs of **degree** give us information about the degree to which an action expressed by a verb is performed. Some of the adverbs of degree are:

absolutely	*almost*	*awfully*	*completely*	*considerably*
deeply	*enormously*	*entirely*	*extremely*	*fully*
greatly	*immensely*	*nearly*	*partly*	*purely*
strongly	*surprisingly*	*wonderfully*		

I **absolutely** agree with you. [46]

The enemy **strongly** defended their position. [47]

I **almost** forgot to inform her. [48]

We **deeply** regret this error. [49]

Adverbs of **place** indicate the place or position of the action. Some of the adverbs of place are:

ahead	*away*	*downstairs*	*upstairs*
here	*there*	*nearly*	

He was running **ahead.** [50]

Bina always sleeps **there.** [51]

Exercise 5

Identify and underline the one-word adverbials in these sentences. After each sentence classify the adverbials as frequency (F), duration (D), place (P), manner (M) and degree (D):

1. Indira normally reaches office at 10 a.m ....
2. She always has lunch with us. ....
3. The minister spoke to her softly. ....
4. I fully agree with you. ....
5. Sharada rarely misses lectures. ....

6. The district magistrate dealt with the problem firmly. ....
7. She generally draws pictures beautifully. ....
8. The board deeply mourned his death. ....
9. He plays there regularly. ....
10. She was sewing inside. ....
11. He always prepared his lectures carefully. ....
12. She rarely drove her car carelessly. ....
13. He seldom loses his temper. ....
14. She often spoke to him coldly. ....
15. The opposition strongly opposed the motion. ....
16. Aruna is sleeping upstairs. ....
17. We have always lived here. ....
18. Our college has been closed indefinitely. ....
19. The demonstration was held peacefully. ....
20. They were looking sideways awkwardly. ....

4.4.2 Noun phrase adverbials

Some noun phrases may also function as adverbials but they are not very frequent in English. For example:

> Liz went **home.** (***home** is an adverbial of place*) [52]
>
> He studies for **two hours every day.**
> (***two hours** and **every day** are adverbials of time*) [53]
>
> No classes will be held **this Friday.**
> (***this Friday** is adverbial of time*) [54]
>
> We played **the whole day.**
> (***the whole day** is an adverbial of the period of time*) [55]

As these noun phrases functioning as adverbials are used immediately after the verb, one may tend to consider them as objects. However, whether such a noun phrase is an object or not can be tested.

i. All the four noun phrases in 52 - 55 cannot answer the question **what** or **when.**

ii. None of the sentences 52, 53, or 55 can be passivised.

* Home went by Liz. [56]

* The whole day was played by us. [57]

Secondly, the noun phrase in 52 - 55 can answer the question **where** or **when.**

Exercise 6

Identify and underline the adverbials in these sentences. After each sentence classify the adverbial as one-word adverb (A) or noun phrase (NP).

1. The test will be held this evening. ....
2. I could not sleep the whole night. ....
3. She has painted the picture carefully. ....
4. I like this food a great deal. ....
5. Iqbal rarely attended parties. ....
6. We shall work for a little while. ....
7. You should not do it next time. ....
8. Divya has gone upstairs. ....
9. Naresh rested a little while. ....
10. I vividly remember it. ....
11. I will do it this way. ....
12. Bikram died the next day. ....
13. Anita would occasionally visit us. ....
14. It can be easily done. ....
15. The plane will leave soon. ....

4.4.3 Prepositional phrases

Prepositional phrases are the most frequent adverbials used to modify a verb.

Examples:

Birds fly **in the sky.** [58]

Vinita sat **near me.** [59]

A prepositional phrase may be used before the main verb, before the auxiliary and the main verb, or between the auxiliary and the main verb.

She, **in the meantime,** wrote an essay.
(*before the MV*) [60]

She, **in the meantime,** was writing an essay.
(*before the auxiliary and MV*) [61]

She was, **in the meantime,** writing an essay.
(*between the auxiliary and the MV*) [62]

It is possible to use a prepositional phrase functioning as an adverbial after the direct object.

I met Hira **at the party.** [63]

Rahul ate sandwiches **during the break.** [64]

There can be two or more prepositional phrases used as adverbials in a sequence after the verb.

We shall study **in school during the lunch break on Monday.** [65]

I met Hira **at the party on Sunday.** [66]

It may be possible, sometimes, to change the sequence of two or more prepositional phrases. For example, sentence 66 may be rewritten as:

I met Hira **on Sunday at the party.** [67]

Prepositional phrases, like one-word adverbs, can express different meanings.

a. **Place**

The dog is sitting **in the kennel.** [68]

She sat **under the tree.** [69]

Mohini went **to Delhi.** [70]

I met Vikram **at the bus stop.** [71]

He wrote something **on the blackboard.** [72]

b. **Direction and movement**

The bird flew **over the lawn.** [73]

The panther ran **across the grass.** [74]

We went **up the hill.** [75]

Rita moved **towards the pond.** [76]

We walked **along the river.** [77]

c. **Time position**

Veena reached office **in the evening.** [78]

Our examination will be held **on Tuesday.** [79]

I have dinner **at 7 p.m.** [80]

Sunit was born **in 1979.** [81]

The meeting will be held **in May.** [82]

d. **Duration**

We stayed there **for two months.** [83]

You can speak **during the meeting.** [84]

Arti slept **throughout the journey.** [85]

e. **Means and instrument**

Rita opened the door **with an iron rod.** [86]

I go to office **by car.** [87]

I sent him the message **by telex.** [88]

f. **Manner**

The shop assistant talked to us **with courtesy.** [89]

She behaved **like her mother.** [90]

He made the sofa **with great skill.** [91]

g. **Cause, reason or motive**

We could not reach home **because of the heavy rain.** [92]

The bus met with an accident **due to the driver's carelessness.** [93]

I went to Mussorie **for the conference.** [94]

Exercise 7

Underline the adverbial prepositional phrases in these sentences and classify each prepositional phrase according to its meaning:

1. Mohini is studying in the library. ....
2. For four days, we couldn't eat anything. ....
3. We went to Delhi by train. ....
4. The plane will leave in the morning. ....
5. In the meantime, I rushed to the doctor. ....
6. The examination could not be held because of the holiday. ....
7. He threw the ball towards me. ....

8. The meeting will be held in the conference room during the lunch break on 28 July. ....
9. Satish kept on talking during the film. ....
10. The Prime Minister was taken to the Rashtrapati Bhavan in the horse-carriage. ....

In chapter 3, section 3.3.2.1, we discussed that a prepositional phrase can also be used as a postnominal modifier, that is, it can modify a noun head in the noun phrase and thus function as an adjectival. In this chapter, we have discussed that a prepositional phrase can function as an adverbial. Thus a prepositional phrase can function either as the modifier of a noun or a verb. Sometimes because of this dual function, a prepositional phrase may appear to be ambiguous.

I waved at the girl **with a smile.** [95]

Notice that in this sentence *with a smile* may either modify the verb *waved* at or it may modify the noun *the girl.*

He saw a girl **on the porch.** [96]

Notice that this ambiguity arises only when the prepositional phrase occurs after a noun used as the direct object in a sentence.

Exercise 8

Underline the prepositional phrases in these sentences. After each sentence write (Adj) if the prepositional phrase modifies the noun, (Adv) if the prepositional phrase modifies the verb and (Amb) if it is ambiguous.

1. The children laughed at the soldiers behind the fences. ....
2. I met Seema in college. ....
3. My neighbour opened the door with a hammer in two minutes. ...
4. She hit the girl with the stick. ....
5. The dog behind that fence is very ferocious. ....

6. He pressed the dried leaves between the pages. ....
7. The girl in the red shirt jumped into the pool. ....
8. We waited in the auditorium for two hours ....
9. The horse killed the donkey with three legs. ....
10. The boy in the blue suit is a test player. ....

4.4.4 Adverbial clauses

Clauses can also function as adverbials in complex sentences. Adverbial clauses are discussed in detail in chapter 8, section 8.3. However, we will discuss adverbial clauses briefly in this section so that their relationship to the other adverbials can be understood. As we shall discuss in chapter 7, section 7.1, a complex sentence has two or more clauses. One of the clauses is the main or principal clause and the other(s) is/are the subordinate clause(s).

I met him **then.** [97]

I met him **on Tuesday.** [98]

I met him **while he was coming out of his room.** [99]

I helped him **because he was in need.** [100]

Notice that the highlighted constituents in 97 - 100 are adverbials. In 97 *then* is a one-word adverb, in 98 *on Tuesday* is a prepositional phrase and in 99 and 100 *while he was coming out of his room* and *because he was very poor* are clauses. Adverbial clauses are introduced by conjunctions/subordinators like *when, as soon as, until, while, where, after, if, as if, though, although, because, since, as, in order that,* etc.

A few more examples of adverbial clauses are:

Ring me up **when you reach Mumbai.** [101]

She went to office **because she had to type a letter.** [102]

I'll buy a pen for you **if I go to Delhi.** [103]

Mukesh gave me the money **as soon as he got his salary.** [104]

4.4.5 Non-finite present participial (*-ing*) and past participial (*-ed*) adverbial clauses

Present participial (***-ing***) and past participial (***-ed***) clauses can also function as adverbials.

Lila sat there **eating ice cream.** [105]

She left the room **laughing at my suggestion.** [106]

Lila sat there **neglected by her parents.** [107]

Persuaded by his wife, he went to attend the meeting. [108]

As discussed in chapter 3, section 3.3.2.3, the present participial and past participial clauses can also modify a noun head at the postnominal position in a noun phrase.

The girl **wearing a blue T-shirt** is a hockey player. [109]

The girl **neglected by her parents** couldn't pay her fees. [110]

Notice that the participial phrases in the above sentences function as postnominal modifiers.

Exercise 9

Underline the participial phrases in these sentences. After each sentence write MN if the phrase is a postnominal modifier and MV if the phrase is an adverbial.

1. She took her breakfast walking around the room. ....
2. The novels written by my father are selling like hot cakes. ....

3. The glass lying on the ground was in pieces. ....
4. Meena entered the room frowning at Ravi. ....
5. The girl laughing at Jivan is a nurse. ....
6. The song played at the party has been written by Monisha. ....
7. Sudha spoke to me smiling gently. ....
8. The man sitting at the table is from the intelligence department. ....
9. He sat there shaken by the event. ....
10. The lady standing near the school is a champion rider. ....

Exercise 10

Underline the adverbials in these sentences. Classify the adverbials as follows:

*one-word adverb **(A)***	*adverbial clause **(adv. cl.)***
*noun phrase **(NP)***	*present participial **(-ing cl.)***
*prepositional phrase **(prep phr.)***	*past participial clause **(-ed cl.)***

1. My mother cooked food last night sitting on the chair. ....
2. India dealt firmly with the other country's propaganda. ....
3. Please inform me if you need help. ....
4. We shall attend the party at Clark Avadh this evening. ....
5. I rested a little while. ....
6. I last saw him when he lived in Lucknow. ....
7. My father always ate with gusto. ....
8. He fell, wounded by the bullet. ....
9. Raja sold his house because he had migrated to the U.S.A.
10. Naresh never misses my lecture. ....
11. She touched the flowers gently. ....
12. She has not met me since she came back from England. ....
13. Rajni boarded the plane waving at all of us. ....

5

Adjectives and Adverbs

5.1 Adjective

An adjective may occur as a single word before a noun as a prenominal modifier or as a subject complement or an object complement.

Devi met an **intelligent** girl at the museum. [1]

Rita is **tall.** [2]

The plan made him **happy.** [3]

An adjective itself may be modified by an adverb or by a phrase or a clause. In such a case, it is treated as an adjective phrase.

Devi met a **very intelligent** girl at the museum. [4]

Rita is **fairly tall.** [5]

The plan made him **extremely happy.** [6]

In examples 4 - 6 the adjectives have been modified by the adverbs, *very, fairly* and *extremely*. Adjectives can also be modified by adjective complements at the post-adjectival positions. Thus the structure of an adjective phrase can be presented as follows:

(Pre-adjectival) Modifier	Adjectival Head	(Post-adjectival) Modifier

Pre-adjectival modifiers are also known as **intensifiers** and post-adjectival modifiers are also called **adjectival complements.**

She is hopeful that **she'll pass with grade 'A'.** [7]
(*that- clause as adjectival complement*)

She is glad **to meet you.** [8]
(*to- infinitive as adjectival complement*)

My sister is afraid **of loud noise.** [9]
(*prep phr as adjectival complement*)

Exercise 1

Identify the adjective phrases in these sentences. Also identify the adjective head and pre-adjectival and post-adjectival modifiers, if any. In the case of post-adjectival modifiers, specify the type of complement.

1. She will be extremely happy to hear this.
2. My brother was a little hesitant to say this.
3. He is very eager to meet you.
4. My sister is devoted to her son.
5. Meera is doubtful of passing the examination.
6. Madan was afraid that his sister might not return.
7. I am certain that he'll attend the meeting.
8. Rita was surprised that I knew the story.
9. She is willing to accompany you.
10. This plan is fraught with danger.

5.1.1 Syntactic functions of adjectives

5.1.1.1 Attributive and predicative: The most frequent use of an adjective or an adjective phrase is either as prenominal modifier before the noun head or as subject complement or object complement.

When adjectives occur as prenominal modifiers, they are called **attributive adjectives:**

a small boat **a tall** girl

Adjectives functioning as subject complement or object complement are called **predicative adjectives.**

Vanita is **intelligent.** [10]

I find Vanita **intelligent.** [11]

Most adjectives can be used either in the attributive or predicative position. However, there are a few adjectives which are restricted to either the attributive or predicative position.

Attributive only

the **main** story	* *the story is **main***
an **utter** nonsense	* *the nonsense is **utter***

my **old** friend (*notice that in **my friend is old, 'old'** has a different meaning*)

a **little** cottage	my **monthly** salary
a **pure** thriller	her **former** husband
the **simple** truth	the **only** occasion
a **true** scholar	a **criminal** lawyer
an **absolute** crook	an **atomic** scientist

Predicative only

All of us were **asleep.**	* *the asleep man*	[12]
The maid is **unwell.**	* *the unwell maid*	[13]

1. Some adjectives can only be used as complements of the subject after a linking verb. These adjectives are, therefore, predicative.

The girl felt **glad.**	* *a glad girl*	[14]
The dog is **alive.**	* *the alive dog*	[15]
The pupils felt **uneasy.**	* *the uneasy pupils*	[16]

2. Many adjectives which have complements after them can only be used at the predicative position.

I am **aware of the danger.**	[17]
She is **prone to ill health.**	[18]

He is **fond of her.** [19]

I am **willing to do it.** [20]

They are **unable to help you.** [21]

Some of the adjectives that are followed by a complement are:

glad	*happy*	*reasonable*	*annoyed*	*pleased*
delighted	*angry*	*good*	*hopeless*	*amused*
pleased	*delighted*	*afraid*	*proud*	*fond*
convinced	*tired*	*answerable*	*liable*	*sure*
sorry	*surprised*	*convinced*	*ashamed*	*furious*

Exercise 2

Make sentences with the adjectives given below. Then state whether each has been used at the attributive or predicative position:

weekly, afraid, tall, wonderful, answerable, unwilling, eastern, occasional, glad, delighted, fond, incapable, thin, daily, liable, tired, elder, anxious, pleased, wide

5.1.1.2 Participle adjectives: There are a large number of adjectives in English which have ***-ing*** or ***-ed*** forms and are called **participle adjectives:**

this **amazing** picture - this picture is **amazing**

the **shocking** news - the news was **shocking**

the **bored** student - this student is **bored**

Some of the **-ing** adjectives are:

amusing	*annoying*	*astonishing*	*boring*	*charming*
confusing	*depressing*	*disgusting*	*disturbing*	*dying*
interesting	*pleasing*	*refreshing*	*shocking*	*sickening*

Some of the **-ed** adjectives are:

alarmed	*amazed*	*amused*	*annoyed*	*armed*
bored	*confused*	*convinced*	*concerned*	*depressed*
disappointed	*disgusted*	*dried*	*embarrassed*	*established*
frightened	*furnished*	*interested*	*infected*	*irritated*
pleased	*paid*	*shocked*	*surprised*	*trained*

5.1.1.3 Compound adjectives: Compound adjectives comprise two or more elements:

an **absent-minded** professor   a **second-class** ticket

a **handmade** basket   an **airtight** container

Compound adjectives can be of the following types:

a. *Adjective + participle*

good-looking, good-tempered, kind-hearted, easy-going, long-lasting, nice-looking, fresh-baked, widespread

b. *Noun + participle*

fact-finding, record-breaking, mouth-watering, air-borne, air-conditioned, custom-built, home-trade, mass-produced

c. *Noun + adjective*

airsick, duty-free, ice-cold, airtight, dustproof, fireproof, homesick, tax-free, age-old, brick-red, bottle-green, blood-red, dove-grey

d. *Adjective + adjective*

reddish-brown, Anglo-Indian, tragi-comic, socio-economic, deaf-mute

5.1.2 Types of adjectives

We can divide adjectives into four types:

a. **Qualitative adjectives:** These adjectives identify a quality that a person, animal or thing has:

happy, tall, beautiful, small, big, tiny

a **happy** girl	a **small** table
a **tall** boy	a **big** dog
a **beautiful** lady	a **tiny** bird

Qualitative adjectives are usually gradable. This means they have the comparative and superlative degrees.

tall	taller	tallest
beautiful	more beautiful	most beautiful

Gradable adjectives can be modified by intensifiers:

a **very beautiful** girl
a **rather big** dog
an **extremely** high fence

b. **Classifying adjectives:** These adjectives place a noun in a particular class that it belongs to. Classifying adjectives are words like *central, direct, medieval, golden, international, regional.*

the **central** government	a **golden** casket
the **direct** flight	an **international** conference
a **medieval** king	a **regional** issue

Classifying adjectives are nongradable and, therefore, do not have comparative and superlative degrees. They are usually not modified by intensifiers.

Some other classifying adjectives are:

agricultural	*American*	*annual*	*basic*	*civil*
commercial	*daily*	*western*	*economic*	*educational*
electric	*general*	*historical*	*industrial*	*Indian*
legal	*national*	*modern*	*political*	*public*
loyal	*scientific*	*social*	*solid*	*urban*

c. **Colour adjectives:** Adjectives referring to colour are called colour adjectives.

brown shoes **dark brown** hair

his **black** eyes a **light blue** shirt

These colour adjectives can be mixed to express different shades.

her **greenish blue** eyes his **reddish brown** shirt

Colour adjectives are gradable.

d. **Emphasising adjectives:** These adjectives emphasise the feelings of the speaker. Words like *real, absolute, utter* are emphasising adjectives.

a **real** bliss an **absolute** fool **utter** rubbish

When two or more adjectives of different types are used as prenominal modifiers, the usual order is:

qualitative adjective colour adj. classifying adj. noun head

a **large brown wooden** table the **new central** government

her **small blue** eyes his **small black digital** watch

Exercise 3

Make noun phrases by putting these words in the right order. Then identify the types of adjectives used before it:

1. box, a, metallic, white, little
2. calm, the, wind, Western
3. the, political, party, new
4. heavy, a, vehicle, commercial
5. a, dress, blue, beautiful
6. the, equipment, agricultural, new
7. Kashmiri, red, a, delicious, apple
8. famous, building, the, Victorian
9. the, regime, weak, military
10. successful, the, national, party

5.2 Adverbs

5.2.1 Adverb forms

-ly Adverbs: -ly is a derivational suffix with the help of which many adverbs are derived from adjectives including participial adjectives:

quick - quickly	beautiful - beautifully
honest - honestly	fortunate - fortunately
bad - badly	quiet - quietly

They were studying **quietly.** [22]

She completed the work **quickly.** [23]

Most adverbs ending in **-ly** have their meanings similar to the adjectives they are derived from.

She is **beautiful.** [24]

She danced **beautifully.** [25]

However, there are a few adverbs ending in **-ly** which do not have the same meaning as their related adjectives. For example, *hard* (adj) and *hardly* (adv) do not have a corresponding meaning. *Hardly* means 'not very much' and does not have the corresponding meaning of *hard*. In fact, *hard* and *hardly* can both be used as adverbs.

This butter is very **hard.** [26]

She **hardly** worked during the vacation. [27]

She worked very **hard.** [28]

Some other adverbs of this kind are:

lately, scarcely, shortly

Other derivational adverbs:

-wise/ways: clockwise, lengthwise/sideways

-wards: northwards(s), backwards(s), leftward(s)

He cut the sheet **lengthwise.** [29]

She drove **northwards.** [30]

-fashion: schoolboy-fashion

-style: cowboy-style, Indian style

Identical adjective and adverb forms:

There are some adjectives which have common adverb forms:

early, fast, long, straight

She ran **fast.** [31]

Uninflected adverbs:

There are a number of commonly used adverbs which are not derived from adjectives or any other part of speech and are, therefore, uninflected:

here	*there*	*up*	*down*	*upstairs*	*downstairs*	*in*
out	*inside*	*outside*	*on*	*off*	*now*	*then*
just	*only*	*well*	*back*	*under*		

They went **up.** [32]

She is sleeping **outside.** [33]

Exercise 4

Make sentences with these adverbs:

downstairs, long, nicely, southward, happily, then, clockwise, shortly, suspiciously, early

5.2.2 Grammatical functions

There can be three grammatical functions performed by adverbials. Accordingly these are called **adjuncts, conjuncts** and **disjuncts.** In this section, we shall distinguish these three categories from one another. However, in the following sections, we shall study only adjuncts.

5.2.2.1 Adjuncts: An adjunct can usually be placed in the position of an adverbial (*see chapter 1, section 1.2*).

Our grandmother **always** treated us **gently.** [34]

She was standing **under the tree.** [35]

They came **by car.** [36]

I met him **last night.** [37]

I helped him **because he needed money.** [38]

She **quickly** came to meet me. [39]

He **always** drives the car **slowly.** [40]

a. Adjuncts like S, O and C, can be elicited by the **wh-** word in a **wh-** interrogative sentence.

Who came to meet you? {*Shefali (S)*} [41]

What is her father? {*a doctor (C)*} [42]

Who(m) did you meet at the party? {*Ronaldo (O)*} [43]

Why did you help him? {*because he needed money (A)*} [44]

How did she treat you? {*gently (A)*} [45]

b. An adjunct can also be the focus of a cleft-sentence.

It was **last night** that I met her. [46]

It was **intentionally** that she didn't return the book. [47]

It was **by car** that they took him to hospital. [48]

5.2.2.2 Disjuncts: Adverbials which function as disjuncts convey the speaker's comment or attitude towards what is said.

Frankly, I don't agree with you on this point. [49]

In all frankness, she will not pass the examination. [50]

Notice the two tests applied to adjuncts above cannot be applied to disjuncts.

How does he agree with you on this point? [51]

* It is **frankly** that I don't agree with you on this point. [52]

* It is **in all frankness** that she will not pass the examination. [53]

Quirk *et al* (1985: 613) state:

> Adjuncts are similar in the weight and balance of their sentence role to other sentence elements such as subject and object. ...
>
> Disjuncts by the same analogy, have a superior role as compared with the sentence elements; they are syntactically more detached and in some respects 'superordinate', in that they seem to have a scope that extends over the sentence as a whole.

To be frank, her writing is awful. [54]

In short, your essay requires improvement. [55]

Actually, she didn't want to say so. [56]

If I can speak frankly, you cannot be admitted to our course. [57]

Personally, I find this film full of terror. [58]

Briefly, he is a good and honest worker. [59]

Rightly, she did not accept his offer. [60]

Putting it broadly, your proposal with modifications is acceptable. [61]

Some other disjuncts are:

apparently	*bluntly*	*broadly*	*consciously*
frankly	*foolishly*	*generally*	*honestly*
unfortunately	*hopefully*	*certainly*	*actually*
officially	*theoretically*	*possibly*	*surprisingly*
in broad terms	*in all fairness*	*in short*	
much to our regret	*if I may say so*		

5.2.2.3 Conjuncts: Conjuncts, like disjuncts, are grammatically different from adjuncts.

I couldn't attend the meeting; **therefore,** I don't know the minutes. [62]

She couldn't attend the meeting; **however,** she sent her secretary to attend it. [63]

* It is therefore that I don't know the minutes. [64]

* It is however that she sent her secretary to attend it. [65]

Conjuncts like disjuncts perform a superordinate role. Whereas a disjunct is a comment on the whole sentence or expresses the speaker's attitude towards what is said, a conjunct performs the function of conjoining two independent sentences or two coordinate clauses in a sentence. Thus they function as cohesive devices.

Lata has passed the MBA examination and is preparing for the civil services examination. **Besides,** she is also preparing for the NET examination. [66]

We visited south India last year. **First,** we went to Bangalore and **then** we went to Ooty. [67]

Some other examples of conjuncts are:

accordingly	*again*	*consequently*	*else*
further	*hence*	*incidentally*	*in other words*
instead	*in conclusion*	*moreover*	*as a result*
to conclude	*briefly*	*nevertheless*	*next*

Exercise 5

Identify the adverbials in these sentences. Mention whether each adverbial is an 'adjunct', 'disjunct' or 'conjunct'.

1. She wants to become a pilot. However, her father wants her to be a doctor.
2. Luckily, I had played this role earlier.
3. She has given her application for the publication grant. Personally speaking, I'm not in favour of such a grant.

4. I met her at the party on Tuesday. She asked me to meet her in college on Wednesday. However, she couldn't come to college as she fell ill after the party.
5. My uncle had a heart attack while he was travelling by the Rajdhani to Mumbai. Fortunately, there was a doctor travelling in the same coach. Therefore, my uncle got medical aid immediately and could reach Mumbai safely.
6. When I reached her place, she had already left for office.
7. Surprisingly, mangoes have arrived rather late in the market.
8. My brother greatly admires Sujata. Incidentally, Sujata also admires him.
9. She didn't like the food. Therefore, we had to cook again.
10. Kavita and Shanu happily agreed to our proposal. Actually, they were looking forward to such a proposal.

5.2.3 Syntactic functions of adverbs

Adverbs can function as modifiers of different parts of speech and phrases.

5.2.3.1 Modifier of adjectives: An adverb can be used before an adjective as a pre-adjectival modifier. It is called an intensifier when it occurs as the modifier of an adjective.

I am **awfully** sorry. [68]

It is **extremely** cold here. [69]

That **extremely** tall girl is my cousin. [70]

Some other examples are:

very rare	**strikingly** tall
relatively big	**rather** late
absolutely right	**highly** proficient
fairly small	**too** sharp

5.2.3.2 Modifier of verbs: An adverb modifies a verb.

She **immediately** wrote a letter to him. [71]

He **always** plays **fast.** [72]

The table was so heavy that he could **hardly** lift it. [73]

I have **recently** bought a set. [74]

5.2.3.3 Modifier of adverbs: An adverb of degree may premodify another adverb.

She came back **pretty** fast. [75]

I visit her **quite** often. [76]

She speaks **extremely** quickly. [77]

He played football **extremely** well. [78]

I met her **fairly** recently. [79]

5.2.3.4 Modifier of noun phrases: The intensifiers **quite** and **rather** can modify a noun head in a noun phrase.

It was **quite** a match. [80]

It is **rather** a shame. [81]

There are a few adverbs which can be used as postnominal modifiers:

the paragraph **below**	the day **before**
the people **upstairs**	the girl **there**

In some cases the adverb can function either as a prenominal or a postnominal modifier.

the **above** sentence	the sentence **above**
the **upstairs** room	the room **upstairs**
the **downstairs** people	the people **downstairs**

5.2.3.5 Modifiers of prepositional phrases: Prepositions of time and place may be premodified by adverbs functioning as intensifiers.

She drove **close** behind our car. [82]

We left her home **soon** after 9 o' clock. [83]

The plane flew **directly** above our house. [84]

The vegetables were lying **all** over the place. [85]

She finished her project **well** within time. [86]

5.2.3.6 Complement of prepositions: A few adverbs expressing time and place may be used as complements of prepositions.

She was sitting over **there.** [87]

I had not met him till **then.** [88]

He spoke to me from **inside.** [89]

They live over **there.** [90]

How do we get out of **here?** [91]

She has received an invitation from **abroad.** [92]

5.2.3.7 Modifiers of predeterminers:

About half his salary was given to him. [93]

She received **roughly** double the amount. [94]

Nearly one-third of the members attended the meeting. [95]

Exercise 6

Identify the adverbs in these sentences and mention the syntactic function each one of them performs:

1. Rita has always lived there.
2. It is a rather expensive dress.

3. The sentence below is a quotation.
4. I've just finished lunch.
5. She read the story aloud.
6. It is lying right in front of you.
7. It was quite a party.
8. It was a simply marvellous trip.
9. An economically backward nation must invest in education.
10. They came to the meeting pretty late.
11. She was sleeping up there.
12. She rarely drove her car carelessly.
13. I met a highly talented girl during the train journey last week.
14. They came close behind us.
15. She met almost all the students at the inaugural session.
16. She always speaks very softly.
17. The people upstairs are making a noise.
18. The house that we purchased is fairly small.
19. I know her pretty well.
20. Nearly two-thirds of the party members could not arrive in time.

5.3 Adverbials

As discussed in 4.4, an adverbial can be a one-word adverb or an adjunct, a noun phrase, a prepositional phrase, a finite adverbial clause, a non-finite **-ing** clause or a non-finite **-ed** clause.

She walks **fast.** (*adjunct*) [96]

She fasts **every Tuesday.** (*NP*) [97]

I met him **at the airport.** (*prep phrase*) [98]

My brother saw her **while she was crossing the road.** (*finite adverbial clause*) [99]

My mother cooks food **sitting on a chair.** (*non-finite* ***-ing*** *adverbial clause*) [100]

She ate dinner **seated near the TV set.**
(*non-finite -ed adverbial clause*) [101]

5.3.1 Position of adverbials

End of the clause: The normal unmarked position for adverbials is the end of the clause. In sentences 96-101, the adverbials have been used at the end of the clause.

Beginning of the clause: This position is used for emphasis or can be considered the marked position for adverbials.

In the end, the hero and heroine get married. [102]

Suddenly, she left the room. [103]

After all the guests left, the hostess rang up the cook to thank him. [104]

In the middle of the clause: This position is usually described as the position between the subject and the verb. This position is more common for one-word adverbs or adjuncts than for other adverbials.

She **suddenly** left the room. [105]

He **regularly** exercises in the morning. [106]

I **really** liked the movie. [107]

Multiple adverbials at the end position:

a. If there is more than one adverbial at the end position, the shorter adverbial is placed before a larger one.

He waited **cheerfully** in the classroom. [108]

They were sitting **quietly because the teacher had asked them to do so.** [109]

b. Adverbials of time and place can be used in either order though some people feel comfortable with an adverbial of place first and then an adverbial of time.

I met her **at the party last night.** [110]

I met her **last night after eight o' clock.** [111]

They studied **in the library after eight o' clock.** [112]

They studied **after eight o' clock in the library.** [113]

5.3.2 Semantic functions of adverbials

We have separately discussed the semantic functions of adverbials under sections 4.4 and 7.3. In this section, we shall consolidate the semantic functions of adverbials.

5.3.2.1 Adverbials of time: (*Also see sections 4.4.1, 4.4.2, 4.4.3, and 8.3.1*) Adverbials of time can be of three types:

a. adverbials of definite/indefinite time

b. adverbials of frequency

c. adverbials of duration

Adverbials of definite/indefinite time: Definite time is usually expressed by noun phrases, adverbs, and prepositional phrases.

I shall meet you **tomorrow.** [114]

This building was constructed **in 1946.** [115]

The meeting will be held on **20 April.** [116]

I have **just** finished the meal. [117]

You can take the lecture **afterwards.** [118]

Adverbials of frequency: Some of the adverbs of frequency are:

always	*continually*	*continuously*
frequency	*generally*	*usually*
normally	*occasionally*	*often*
rarely	*regularly*	*seldom*
never	*daily*	*monthly*

Occasionally a noun phrase like *every Saturday*, and a prepositional phrase like, *from time to time,* may also be used as adverbials of frequency.

She **occasionally** visited the library. [119]

They are **daily** paid their wages. [120]

We have extra lectures **every Saturday.** [121]

Adverbials of duration: (*also see sections 4.4.1 and 4.4.3*). Adverbials of duration indicate how long something happens or lasts.

Adverbs and prepositional phrases are generally used as adverbials of duration. Some of the adverbs of duration are: *always, briefly, indefinitely, long, permanently,* and *temporarily.* Some of the prepositional phrases expressing duration are: *for three months, during the meeting, throughout the journey,* etc. Noun phrases like *a short while, all day* and *adverbial clauses* with conjunction **till** can be occasionally used as adverbials of duration.

We **briefly** discussed your project. [122]

She is **temporarily** being transferred to Hyderabad. [123]

Mary was sleeping **during the meeting.** [124]

The director visited the centre **for a short while.** [125]

They played football **the whole day.** [126]

They waited for us **till we returned from Aminabad.** [127]

5.3.2.2 Adverbials of place: (*also see sections 4.4.1, 4.4.2, 4.4.3 and 7.3.2*) Adverbs, noun phrases, prepositional phrases and adverbial clauses can function as adverbials of place.

Adverbials of place can denote either a) position or b) direction and movement.

Position

They were sitting **there.** [128]

They play **under the tree.** [129]

She is sleeping **upstairs.** [130]

They went **where the plane had landed.** [131]

Direction and movement

They went **home.** [132]

She walked **along the river.** [133]

5.3.2.3 Adverbials of manner: (*also see sections 4.4.1, 4.4.3 and 7.3.6*) Adverbs of manner indicate the manner in which an action **is/ was/will** be carried out. Some of the adverbs of manner are:

angrily	*beautifully*	*carefully*	*correctly*
dangerously	*firmly*	*freely*	*gently*

She **beautifully** bowed to the audience. [134]

He spoke **softly.** [135]

A few prepositional phrases are used as adverbials of manner:

He always treated his nephews **with great affection.** [136]

She behaves **like her grandmother.** [137]

My brother always argues **with fervour.** [138]

She behaves as **if she were a minister.** [139]

5.3.2.4 Adverbials of means and instrument: The most frequent adverbials of means and instrument are prepositional phrases.

My son goes to school **by bus.** [140]

She opened the bottle **with a tin opener.** [141]

I sent him a letter **by fax.** [142]

5.3.2.5 Adverbials of viewpoint: Viewpoint adverbials can be paraphrased from a point of view or from the point of view.

Economically, India is far better than many other developing countries. [143]

Technically, it is a sound proposal. [144]

Theoretically, you can build a beautiful house with this money. [145]

From the government's point of view, this film needs to be banned. [146]

5.3.2.6 Courtesy adverbials: There are a limited number of adverbs which can express courtesy or civility. The most common adverbs are *kindly, cordially, graciously, please.*

Would you **kindly** permit us to hold the party? [147]

He **graciously** consented to be the Chief Guest. [148]

Could you **please** open the door? [149]

5.3.2.7 Intensity adverbials: Intensity adverbials either intensify/ amplify or tone down the meaning of a lexical verb. Therefore, intensity adverbials are of two types, a) amplifiers and b) downtoners.

Amplifiers: Amplifiers intensify the meaning of a lexical verb. Amplifiers are adverbs like:

absolutely	*badly*	*completely*	*entirely*
enormously	*extremely*	*fully*	*greatly*
highly	*intensely*	*thoroughly*	*strongly*
terribly	*utterly*	*immensely*	*totally*

I **absolutely** agree with you. [150]

She **very badly** needed rest. [151]

The Principal **strongly** objected to the new rules. [152]

I **completely** forgot to congratulate her. [153]

Downtoners: Downtoners lower the effect of the lexical verb. Downtoners are adverbs like:

almost	*barely*	*hardly*	*more or less*
nearly	*partially*	*partly*	*slightly*

I **almost** forgot to congratulate her. [154]

She has **more or less** finished the novel. [155]

He **hardly** knows us. [156]

5.3.2.8 Focussing adverbials: Focussing adverbials can focus attention on a part of a clause. The focus of attention can be the whole predicate or a single constituent of a clause.

a. **Restrictive adverbials** restrict the meaning of the lexical verb to the part focussed. These are words like *alone, just, merely, only, purely, simply,* etc.

We teach semantics and grammar **only.** [157]

We grade them **purely** on the basis of the final examination. [158]

They were **merely** discussing the important points for discussion. [159]

She was **simply** requesting you to allow her to take the examination. [160]

b. **Additive adverbials:** These adverbials indicate that the given utterance is focussed for its truth with reference to an utterance made earlier. Additive adverbials are usually adjuncts like: *also, either, even, further, neither, nor, similarly,* etc.

I played the piano and Rajinder **also** did the same in the evening. [161]

Neither she nor he attended the meeting. [162]

Exercise 7

Identify the adverbials in these sentences. Also mention the semantic functions of each adverbial:

1. She was sleeping there under the tree, while we were chatting here.
2. The Vice-Chancellor has temporarily appointed him the Dean.
3. He acts as if he were the boss.
4. From our point of view, this is an excellent proposal.
5. Could you kindly inform us of your decision?
6. We shall discuss this matter on Monday.
7. She has recently seen this movie.
8. She completely forgot to attend the lecture.
9. I generally reach office at 9.30 a.m.
10. Rekha hardly studies at night.

6

Tenses and Modal Auxiliaries

6.1 Tenses

As discussed in chapter 4, the verb phrase carries tense and the main verb as obligatory elements and the modal, progressive, perfective and passive as optional elements.

We discussed the structure of the verb phrase in chapter 4 and in this chapter we will discuss the uses of the various tenses in English. At the beginning of the discussion of each tense we will also briefly discuss its form.

6.1.1. Simple present

Form

In order to write a sentence in the simple present tense, we use the first form of the verb. However, if the subject is in the third person singular like *he, she, it, Nilima, Sohrab* etc., we use the first form of the verb followed by the suffix **-s** or **-es.**

If the subject is in the first person singular or plural, the second person singular or plural or the third person plural, we use only the first or the root form of the verb.

She **sleeps** till eight o'clock in the morning. [1]

He **goes** to office by bus. [2]

They **work** in a bank. [3]

I **write** to my wife every week. [4]

This bus **stops** after every ten kilometres or so. [5]

Use

i. **Habitual actions:** This use of the simple present tense is achieved through the use of adverbials like *always, often, generally, usually, everyday, every week, every month.*

My father goes to work by car. [6]

It rains here practically everyday in summer. [7]

We visit Simla every year. [8]

ii. **General or permanent truths:**

The earth revolves around the sun. [9]

Honesty is the best policy. [10]

Water turns into steam when heated. [11]

iii. **Thoughts and feelings at the present moment:**

She is tired. [12]

Maria looks weak. [13]

I feel sad. [14]

iv. **Commentary and demonstrations:**

Kapil Dev bowls to Imran Khan. Imran Khan hits the ball and Sidhu stops the ball at mid-on. There's no run. [15]

Rakesh passes the ball to Balbir and Balbir sends it across to Vijay. [16]

Take four eggs and a pinch of salt. Beat the eggs in a bowl and then add salt. [17]

Colonel Naik walks towards the President. He salutes the President. [18]

v. **Future:** The simple present tense is used for fixed events related to timetables and programmes, or something which is the result of 'natural law'.

The train leaves at 6.30 p.m. [19]

The sun rises at 5.30 tomorrow. [20]

vi. **Past or historic simple present:** There can be various interpretations of this use of the simple present tense. It can be used

a. for extended commentary, that is, to interpret past events as if they were actually happening in the present.

A man comes to my office yesterday and asks for rupees ten thousand. Before I say anything to him, he points a pistol at me. [21]

b. with verbs of communication to indicate the present effect of the information received in the past.

She tells me that you have been away to Colombo. [22]

I hear you have bought a new house. [23]

c. with reference to the work of a writer.

In *The Merchant of Venice*, Shakespeare describes the main plot in Act IV. [24]

Exercise 1

Interpret the use of the simple present tense in each of the following sentences:

1. The matinee show begins at 3.30 p.m and ends at 6.00 p.m.
2. We leave for Udaipur tomorrow.
3. The sun rises in the east.
4. He looks handsome.

5. Dickens describes the social life in the nineteenth century in his novels.
6. This peak remains snow-clad throughout the year.
7. The college reopens on 6 January.
8. I go to university by bus.
9. The Prime Minister walks towards the raised platform to unfurl the flag.
10. Pour milk and cream into the bowl and whisk them.

6.1.2 Present progressive tense

Form

The present progressive is formed with the present form of the auxiliary **be**, (**is**/**am**/**are**) + the present participle (**v** + **ing**) form of the main verb:

Reema **is reading** a book. [25]

I **am writing** a letter. [26]

They **are watching** television. [27]

Before we discuss the use of the present progressive tense, we need to discuss the distinction between **stative** and **dynamic** verbs.

Stative verbs: refer to a state, quality or condition. Stative verbs are normally not used in the progressive **-ing** form. The verbs **be** and **have** used as main verbs are stative verbs because they are followed by the complement of the subject, which has a permanent quality:

Manda is a bank officer. [28]

Arun is very industrious. [29]

Shaila has brown eyes. [30]

Afzal has curly hair. [31]

We cannot say:

* Manda is being a bank officer. [32]

* Shaila is having brown eyes. [33]

Sentences 32 and 33 are ungrammatical because **be** and **have** as main verbs cannot be used in their progressive form. In short, a linking verb is not normally used in its continuous form.

Similarly verbs like *contain, belong, matter, consist* and *own* are stative verbs and thus cannot be used in the progressive (**-ing**) form.

This box **contains** salt. [34]

Our house **belongs** to my grandfather. [35]

I **own** this house. [36]

Thus stative verbs can be divided into the following categories:

i. **Relational verbs:** Verbs like *be, have, contain, belong, matter, consist, own* are relational verbs.

ii. **Perception verbs:** These verbs are related to one of the senses of perception like *see, hear, feel, smell, taste* etc.

I see a man outside. [37]

I hear you. [38]

I smell something burning. [39]

I feel better. [40]

These verbs refer to involuntary perception. If a verb refers to a voluntary perception we can use it in the progressive form. Thus, we have verbs of voluntary perception like *look, listen to, watch* etc., which can be used in the progressive form.

She is looking at the picture. [41]

I'm listening to music. [42]

The modal auxiliary **can** may be used before the involuntary perception verbs mentioned above:

I can see a man outside. [37a]

I can hear you. [38a]

Here **can** does not have any meaning.

iii. **Attitudinal verbs:** These verbs refer to mental or emotional states, and feeling or opinion. Verbs like *assume, believe, dislike, expect, feel, forget, hate, hope, know, like, love, mind, notice, remember, see, think, understand, want, wish,* etc. are attitudinal verbs:

I dislike her. [43]

I forget his name. [44]

She knows you. [45]

Dynamic verbs: Dynamic verbs can be used either in their simple forms or in their progressive forms. Dynamic verbs can be classified as follows:

i. **Action verbs:** Action verbs refer to actions which require an agent to perform the actions. These verbs refer to activities related to duration. Verbs like *write, read, ask, work, play, walk, run, call, laugh* etc., are action verbs:

She is playing in the field. [46]

Roger is running after the dogs. [47]

Prateek is writing a letter. [48]

Aziz is reading a book. [49]

Notice that action verbs can be either intransitive or transitive.

ii. **Intransitive verbs:** Intransitive verbs refer to a change of state or position. They can be of two types:

a. They can be verbs like *arrive, change, die, draw, improve, stop* etc.

All the patients are improving. [50]

The train is stopping over the bridge. [51]

b. They can be linking verbs like *get, become, grow,* and *turn* which refer to a change of state:

She is growing tall. [52]

The jelly is becoming red. [53]

iii. **Sensation verbs:** These verbs refer to physical sensation. Verbs like *burn, feel, glow, hurt* etc., are sensation verbs. However, there is hardly any difference in meaning between the simple present and the progressive forms of sensation verbs.

She is feeling better. [54a]

She feels better. [54b]

Her face is glowing. [55a]

Her face glows. [55b]

iv. **Momentary verbs:** These verbs refer to the repetition of the event taking place. Momentary verbs are verbs like *shake, knock, nod, jump, open, close, bank, hit, shoot, tap,* etc.

She is knocking at the door. [56]

The peon is opening the door. [57]

He is shaking his head. [58]

Exercise 2

Use the simple present or the present progressive form of the verbs in brackets according to the context of the sentence:

1. Mona (seem) very ill today. She (wear) a sweater.
2. I (listen) to whatever you are saying. I (hope) you (hear) me too.
3. Shweta (own) that car.
4. He (have) two dogs in his village house.
5. Subha (wait) for me outside. I (want) to go with her.
6. This toy (belong) to me.
7. Dilip (need) a new house. He (work) very hard this year to earn money.
8. I (think) I should leave now. My wife (wait) for me in her office.
9. The food (taste) good. That is why Minal (eat) well today.
10. I (remember) I met her last year.

Use

i. We use the present progressive tense to describe things that are happening or are in progress at the present moment. We may use adverbials like *now, in the morning, just* etc.

Ted is sleeping in the room. [59]

The Principal is dictating a letter at the moment. [60]

She is just having her lunch. [61]

ii. We may use the present progressive tense to describe temporary situations. It may be used to describe happenings which are not habitual actions but are thought to be happening for a limited period.

I am working in a bank these days. [62a]

Sentence 62a means that **I don't usually work in a bank.**

I work in a bank. (*habitual situation*) [62b]

iii. We use the present progressive to express repeated action referring to habitual actions. In this sense, the use of the present progressive is similar to the simple present (habitual actions) in a way but it refers to a repeated habitual action which is continually repeated. Adverbials like *always, continually, constantly, repeatedly* etc. are used with the present progressive to describe repeated actions.

She is always talking about her achievements. [63]

He is repeatedly asking for money. [64]

iv. The present progressive can be used to express future with reference to definite *plan, arrangement* or *programme*. Usually, an adverbial of future time like *tomorrow, tonight, next week, on Monday* etc. is used to distinguish this use of the present progressive from the other uses of this tense.

We are leaving for Ahmedabad tomorrow. [65]

They are spending their vacation in their village this year. [66]

The train is leaving at 8 o'clock tonight. [67]

Exercise 3

Interpret the use of the present progressive tense in each of the following sentences:

1. She is playing tennis there.
2. The DD Metro is showing *Gandhi* tomorrow.
3. Vijay is studying in the library.
4. Sudha is working as an accountant in our firm for a month.
5. He is closing the door.
6. Shalini is waiting for you in her office.
7. She generally plays badminton but she is playing cricket today.

8. I'm visiting my doctor tonight.
9. She is always humming to herself.
10. The children are constantly making a noise.

6.1.3 Present perfect

Form

The present perfect tense is formed by using the helping verb (auxiliary) have + the past participle form of the main verb.

I **have written** this letter. [68]

We **have already issued** instructions regarding this matter. [69]

He **has just finished** his breakfast. [70]

Use

The interpretation of the present perfect is based on:

- the occurrence of the time-duration adverbials like *so far, for the last two months, all my life* etc.
- the 'character' of the verb, i.e. whether a verb implies that the action tends towards and reaches a certain goal and conclusion, e.g., *buy, sell, achieve, contrive, persuade,* etc., or whether a verb which obviously does not imply such a goal or conclusion, e.g. *walk, sing, sit, love, admire,* etc. Jesperson (1954) calls them **conclusive** and **non-conclusive** verbs. The present perfect can only be used with conclusive verbs.
- the general context

i. **Resultative:** The present perfect is used to refer to past events/ actions to imply that the result of that event has observable results. In this sense, the present perfect occurs with conclusive verbs.

Arvind **has bought** a new car. [71]
(*he bought a car in the past and the car is still with him*)

His toy car **has been broken.** [72]
(*it's still not been mended*)

He **has cut** his finger with a knife. [73]

If we replace the present perfect by the simple past tense in sentences 72, 73, we get the following sentences, which are acceptable but have different interpretations:

His toy car was broken. [74]
(*but now it is mended*)

He cut his finger. [75]
(*it has probably healed*)

Sentences 74 and 75 do not show any results in the present.

ii. **Continuative:** This use of the present perfect is used to express an action which began in the past and which has continued in the present. We usually use **since** or **for** after the verb with this use of the present perfect tense.

I **have lived** in Mumbai since 1990. [76]
(*I began living in Mumbai in 1990 and have continued until now.*)

The house has been empty for ages. [77]

The use of an adverbial of duration is compulsory if one has to use the present perfect in the continuative sense. Without an adverbial, a sentence may have the sense of the indefinite past.

We have lived in Shillong.
(*some time in the past*) [78]

iii. **Indefinite past:** The present perfect is also used with reference to an indefinite past related to the present moment. In this case the time is unspecified.

Have you been to Nigeria? [79]

I have been a taxi driver. [80]

I have not read Dickens. [81]

The adverbials *ever, never,* or *before,* can reinforce the indefinite meaning in such sentences.

iv. **Recent past:** The present perfect may also be used to express something that happened only a short time ago. The adverbials like *just, recently* and *already* are used to express this meaning of the present perfect tense.

She has recently joined our office. [82]

Sunit has already finished typing. [83]

v. **Completion:** In this sense the idea is that some previously assigned goal has been reached:

I have removed the stones. [84]

He has pressed the button. [85]

Notice that any verb will be conclusive under this interpretation because the goal is achieved. The completion will have the interpretation of 'an act as completed at the present moment.' (Curme 1935: 358)

If we use the simple past tense in sentences 84 and 85, we get:

I removed the stones. [86]

He pressed the button. [87]

Notice sentences 86 and 87 represent an action indicated in the past but they may sound odd without an adverbial of time or adverbial of place. It would be more natural to say:

I removed the stones yesterday. [88]

Otherwise, these sentences have to be understood in a particular context.

vi. **Hot news:** McCawley (1971) feels that one of the interpretations of the present perfect is 'hot news' as in:

Malcolm X has just been assasssinated. [89]

McCawley (1971) mentions that the hot news sense is 'to report hot news'. Similarly sentence 90 will have the meaning of 'hot news'.

He has met with an accident. [90]

In sentences 89 and 90 the happenings of the past are related to the present because they are new to the addressee. Notice the following two sentences in the past tense:

Malcolm X was assassinated. [91]

He met with an accident. [92]

Both sentences 91 and 92 cannot be interpreted in the sense of hot news. They only refer to happenings in the past. In fact in sentence 91 the information may not be new to the addressee at all. Sentence 92 would be more natural with an adverbial of past time.

He met with an accident last week. [93]

6.1.4 The present perfect progressive tense

Form

This tense is formed by **has been/have been** + the present participle (v + **ing**) form of the main verb.

Rita has been working with us since 1997. [94]

I have been painting this room since morning. [95]

She has been knitting the sweater for the last two weeks. [96]

Use

i. **Action in progress from the past to the present:** The present perfect progressive may be used to refer to an action that started in the past and is still happening.

We have been living in this house since our childhood. [97]

She has been watching television for two hours. [98]

or it may refer to an action that ended in the recent past.

I have been trying to solve the problem. [99]
(but now I have stopped)

It has been raining. [100]

ii. **Result of the recent past events seen now.**

Your eyes are red. You've been crying. [101]

Your house is leaking. Has the overhead tank been overflowing? [102]

iii. **The present perfect and the present perfect progressive.** One may use the present perfect for an activity where the action is complete and the present perfect progressive for an activity where the action is in progress:

I've cleaned the car. [103a]

I've been cleaning the car. [103b]

I have read this novel. [104a]

I've been reading this novel. [104b]

In some cases, there is no difference between these two tenses.

I've worked in this office since 1992. [105a]

I've been working in this office since 1992. [105b]

Use of ***for*** and ***since:*** **For** and **since** are generally used with the present perfect or the present perfect progressive tense.

i. **For** is used to express a period of time:
for ten minutes, for eight years, for a long time

We have lived in this house for twenty years. [106]

They have been living in Saigon for twenty years. [107]

He has been using your telephone for the last two years. [108]

ii. **Since** is used to express a point in time:
since morning, since Friday, since 1991, since last week, since last year, since 10'0clock

I have been teaching in this school since 1995. [109]

Madona has taught in this school since 1994. [110]

He has been working in this garage since 6 o'clock. [111]

Exercise 4

Interpret the use of the present perfect/present perfect progressive tense in each of the following sentences:

1. She has gone to sleep.
2. Sharmila has written on the blackboard.
3. She has been crying for the last two hours.
4. Have you ever met Mr Quirk?
5. They have not spoken to each other for long.
6. The Prime Minister has resigned.
7. That house has been vacant since December.
8. They've built a new house.

9. She has stayed with us for eight months.
10. I've read this novel.

Exercise 5

Explain the difference in meaning, if any, between the following pairs of sentences:

1. a. We have visited Srinagar every year since we moved to Delhi.
   b. We have been visiting Srinagar every year since we moved to Delhi.
2. a. She has cleaned the windows.
   b. She has been cleaning the windows.
3. a. We have lived here for two years.
   b. We have been living here for two years.
4. a. I have waited for her for two hours.
   b. I have been waiting for her for two hours.
5. a. He has written a novel.
   b. He has been writing a novel.

6.1.5 Simple past

Form

The simple past tense is formed with the past form of the verb by adding **-d** or **-ed** to the base form of the verb. In the case of irregular verbs, **-d** or **-ed** is not used.

We **translated** ten pages yesterday. [112]

I **met** Rita at the airport. [113]

Use

i. The simple past tense is used to indicate activities or states in the past, without any connection with the present. There is usually, though not always an adverbial of past time in the sentence.

I got Indira's letter **yesterday.** [114]

I saw him **at the Bhusaval station last month.** [115]

Sometimes, in place of an adverbial of time, an adverbial of place may be used to indicate past time.

What did you do **in Bhubaneshwar?** [116]
(*that is, when you were there*)

Did you meet Fatima **at the station?** [117]
(*that is, when you were there*)

Sometimes the past tense can be used for a context outside language but having a presumed common knowledge between the speaker and the listener. (Leech and Svartvik,1975)

Did the postman bring any letters? [118]
(*It is understood that the postman comes at a given time in the day*)

If we use the present perfect in place of the simple past in sentences 114 and 115, we get unacccptable sentences.

* I have got Indira's letter yesterday. [119]

* I have seen him at the Bhusaval station last month. [120]

However, if we use the present perfect in place of the simple past in sentences, 116, 117 we get acceptable sentences:

What have you done in Bhubaneshwar? [121]

Have you met Fatima at the station? [122]

This shows that the present perfect cannot be used with the adverbials of definite time: *yesterday, last month,* but it can be used with the adverbials of place, *in Calcutta, at the station.*

Notice the difference in the meaning between sentences 116, 117 on the one hand and sentences 121, 122 on the other. Whereas sentence 116 implies that the listener is no longer *in Bhubaneshwar,* sentence 121 implies that he is still there. In sentence 117, the listener is no longer *at the station* whereas in sentence 122 he is very much there.

ii. The simple past tense may be used in the -if clauses used to indicate unreal conditions.

If he worked hard, he'd pass. [123]

The 'real' condition is,

If he works hard, he'll pass. [124]

Some other examples are:

If I went to the moon, I would bring a lunar rock for you. [125]

If I were in your place, I would not resign. [126]

The 'unreal' or hypothetical past is also used in some other adverbial clauses:

She behaves as if she were a queen. [127]

He dances as if he were a professional. [128]

Supposing we asked him, would he agree? [129]

Anyone who said that would be crazy. [130]

iii. The simple past is also used to express a tentative or polite attitude in questions or requests.

Did you want to try anything on, sir? [131]

Did you ask for something? [132]

I thought I might call on you this evening. [133]

I wondered if you could help us. [134]

iv. The simple past is used for reported speech. If the reporting verb is in the simple present tense, the verbs in the reported speech are also changed into the past. Therefore, if the reporting clause is in the past, the reported clause is also changed into the past:

'I am happy', he said to me. [135]

He told me that he was happy.

However, if the speaker feels that what the reported clause expresses is still true, he may use the present tense:

She told the class that the show is open the whole week. [136]

Exercise 6

Explain the meaning of the simple past tense in each of the following sentences:

1. She sang a song at the gathering.
2. Did you want to speak to me?
3. If he visited her, she'd help him.
4. She directed two plays in 1998.
5. If I were you, I wouldn't do it.
6. He told you that you would visit us the next day.
7. I wondered if you could come with us.
8. She said that the sums were difficult.
9. He lost his father last month.
10. He behaves as if he owned the company.

Exercise 7

Explain the difference in meaning between the sentences in each of the following pairs:

1. a. I was ill all night.
   b. I have been ill all night.
2. a. Did the postwoman come?
   b. Has the postwoman come?
3. a. The noted film actor, Kiran Kumar, got the Filmfare Award.
   b. The noted film actor, Kiran Kumar, has got the Filmfare Award.
4. a. The late Mayor visited our school.
   b. Our school has been visited by the late Mayor.
5. a. I cleaned the store yesterday.
   b. I have recently cleaned the store.
6. a. Newton believed in an omnipotent God.
   b. Newton has explained the movement of the moon.
7. a. His sister was an asthmatic all through her life.
   b. His sister has been an asthmatic all through her life.
8. a. Dr Kapoor came to town.
   b. Dr Kapoor has come to town.
9. a. Who broke this doll?
   b. Who has broken this doll?
10. a. Did you see *The Poseidon Adventure*?
    b. Have you seen *The Poseidon Adventure*?

6.1.6 The past progressive

Form

The past progressive tense is formed by using **was/were** + the present participle (**-ing**) form of the main verb.

They were sleeping when I visited them. [137]

Sunita was reading a novel when she received this message. [138]

Use

i. The past progressive tense is used for actions which were in progress or continued in the past. It does not indicate the beginning or the end of the action. It may be used with a specific point of time. When we use the past progressive tense with a point of time, the assumption is that the action expressed by the verb started before that time and most probably continued after it.

They were playing football at 5 p.m yesterday. [139]
(*they were playing before 5 p.m. also*)

She was waiting for her car at 11a.m. yesterday. [140]

ii. The past progressive is more often used in a complex sentence. The main clause of the complex sentence may be in the past progressive tense and the adverbial clause of time with the conjunction **when** may be in the simple past tense.

When the bell rang, she was studying in the library. [141]

Rakesh was sharpening a pencil, when the lights went out. [142]

It is possible to use the adverbial clause beginning with **while, just as,** or **when** in the past progressive, describing an action or event.

While I was entering the lift, the door closed. [143]

Just as we were leaving the office, it began to rain. [144]

iii. The past progressive tense is also used with adverbials beginning with **all**: *all night, all evening, all yesterday*. Notice that these adverbials express continuity.

Mallaya was talking all evening yesterday. [145]

It was raining all last week. [146]

6.1.7 Past perfect

Form

The past perfect tense is formed using **had** + the past participle (**-ed**) form of the main verb.

My mother had left before I reached home. [147]

They had called the doctor before the ambulance arrived. [148]

Use

i. **Past in the past:** The past perfect tense is used to express an action which happened or took place before another action in the past. We use the past perfect tense for the event that happened later.

The train had left before we reached ths station. [149]

I loved the dish. I'd never eaten it before. [150]

I hired this house last month. I had been told that it was a good house. [151]

In some cases the past perfect and simple past tense may be interchangeable because the time sequence may indicate what happened first.

After he attended the meeting, he went home. [152]

I hired this house last month. I was told that it was a good house. [153]

However, in some cases the use of the past perfect instead of the simple past can bring about a change in meaning.

When I reached home, they rang up the police. (*at that moment*) [154]

When I reached home, they had already rung up the police. (*before I reached there*) [155]

ii. **Reported speech:** If the reporting verb is in the simple past tense and the reported verb is in the present perfect tense, the reported verb is changed into the past perfect tense in the reported speech.

He said to me, 'I have finished the work.' [156]

He told me that he had finished the work. [157]

If the reporting verb is in the simple past tense and the reported verb is also in the simple past tense, the reported verb is changed into the past perfect tense in the reported speech.

She said to me, ' I finished the work yesterday.' [158]

She told me that she had finished the work the previous day. [159]

iii. **Unfulfilled condition:** The past perfect tense is also used in the adverbial clauses of condition, where the condition remained unfulfilled in the past. The subordinate clause usually consists of **could/might/should.** The main clause has **would** + **have** + the past participle.

If he had worked hard, he would have passed. [160]

If she had bought it last month, we would have given her a 25% rebate. [161]

If Mina had paid the money, we could have extended her stay in the guest house. [162]

6.1.8. Past perfect progressive

Form

This tense is formed by using **had been** + the present participle **(-ing)** form of the main verb.

Our director had been working till late evening before this incident. [163]

She was tired. She had been mowing the lawn the whole afternoon. [164]

Use

The main use of the past progressive is to indicate the duration of an action over a period of time upto a past time.

The child has been playing outside till her parents arrived. [165]

Our mechanic fell down all of a sudden. He had been working in the sun since morning. [166]

Exercise 8

Identify the tense in the sentences/clauses in bold letters and then explain the use of the tense in each of the following sentences:

1. When I reached her table, **she had already ordered two cups of tea.**
2. When I reached her table, **she ordered two cups of tea.**

3. She told me that **she had already bought a house.**
4. **If Mary had arrived in time,** we would have allowed her to take the examination.
5. **They were playing cricket** in the morning yesterday.
6. **The driver had been washing the car** until the time we left.
7. She reached the cinema hall late. **She had been reading the latest issue of India Today.**
8. **She was having her lunch,** when I went to meet her.
9. When I went to meet her, **she had already had her lunch.**
10. We reached the station **before the train had arrived.**

6.1.9 Expressing future time

There are several ways of expressing time in English; however, the two most common ways of expressing future time are: i) with the modals **will/shall** and ii) with **be + going to**

i. Use of **will/shall: Will/shall** + the base form of the verb is used to make a prediction or express an opinion about something over which one does not have any control.

I'll meet you tomorrow. [167]

It will rain in the evening. [168]

Monika will take your class on Monday. [169]

Some native speakers will use shall with **I/we** as the subject.

I shall take your class on Monday. [170]

We shall hold elections for class representatives on Monday. [171]

It may be pointed out that some native speakers do not maintain the distinction between **will/shall.**

ii. Use of **be + going to** + the base form of the main verb.

We are going to introduce computer courses very soon. [172]

You are on the edge of the staircase; you are going to fall down. [173]

be + going to is used for future actions which are going to happen soon. By using **be + going** to one foresees something which will possibly happen.

iii. **Simple present tense:** As mentioned earlier in section 6.1.1, the use of the simple present tense for the future time has the interpretation of fixed events related to timetables and programmes or something which is the result of the 'natural law':

The moon rises at 7p.m. tomorrow. [174]

The plane leaves at 4.30p.m. [175]

The examination begins on Monday. [176]

iv. **Present progressive tense:** As mentioned in section 6.1.2, the present progressive can be used to express future with reference to a definite plan, arrangement or programme. Usually an adverbial of future time like *tomorrow, tonight, next week* or *Monday* is used to distinguish this use of the present progressive from the other uses of this tense.

We are starting the French course in November. [177]

I am taking leave from next Monday. [178]

The company is holding elections on Sunday. [179]

v. **Will/shall + be + the present participle:** This structure is used to express an action in the future time, which will be the result of a preplanned arrangement or will happen as a matter of course.

I shall be meeting you on Friday afternoon. [180]
(*already arranged/planned*)

The train will be running at the speed of 150 kms/hr. [181]

We shall be nearing Hyderabad by this
time tomorrow. [182]

vi. **be to** + the base form of the verb

This structure is used to express an official arrangement or plan.

The President is to visit Shimla next month. [183]

The CBI is to hold an enquiry soon. [184]

vii. **be about to + the base form of the verb:** This structure is used to express an action which is going to happen in the near future.

The plane is about to leave. [185]

The film is about to start. [186]

Exercise 9

Explain what sense of future time is expressed in each of the following sentences:

1. The sun sets in the west.
2. We shall be meeting the vice-chancellor on Wednesday.
3. He will chair the session in the afternoon.
4. He will be paying you the money tomorrow.
5. The Chief Minister is to visit Belgaum next month.
6. The train is about to arrive at the platform.
7. It will be very hot in April this year.
8. I am going to see her tomorrow.
9. This block is going to fall down.
10. The train is leaving at 7 in the evening.

Exercise 10

Read each of the following passages/dialogues carefully. Identify the tense and aspect (if any) of the verb phrase of the finite clause and then explain the meaning expressed by the verb phrase:

1. I met Mohini at the airport in June last year. I had gone to receive my brother. I saw her standing in the corner. She was wearing a brown suit . I realised that she had been my classmate in school. I went to her and she immediately recognised me. She told me that she had come to the airport to receive her father.

2. Rina: Have you seen, *Mother India* recently?

   Tim: No, I haven't.

   Rina: It has been running at Dreamland for the last three weeks.

   Tim: Yes, I know it. I am going to see it on Monday. I have already bought the tickets for my family.

3. Take 250 gms of flour, four eggs, 100 gms sugar and 75 mls groundnut oil and make a dough. Then beat the eggs and whisk them and add sugar.

4. Hamid: John, the train is leaving four hours late. What shall we do now? Poor Lily will be waiting for us at Kurnool station on Tuesday morning.

   John: There's another train which leaves at 5 in the evening. We'll go by this train and reach Kurnool on Tuesday morning.

   Hamid: That'll be good. After you've got the reservation, I'll go and ring up Rina.

5. I was going to my office on Tuesday morning. It was a bright day and the sun was shining. I was driving my car at a slow speed, when I saw Minu. She was holding a book in her hand. I stopped my car and called her, but by then she had walked into a lane.

6. Mr Sethi: Has the postman come?

   Ajay: No, he hasn't. You look very anxious for letters these days.

   Mr Sethi: Yes I do. I've been waiting for my son's letter for more than two weeks now.

   Ajay: I think I should ring him.

   Mr Sethi: I think I should. I'll ring him up this evening.

7. Asif bowls to Sachin. Sachin hits the ball and it goes to the square leg boundary for a four. Iqbal picks up the ball and returns it to Asif. India are two hundred for three.

8. The Prime Minister is to visit Chandigarh next Monday. The Prime Minister's secretary announced it at the hurriedly called press conference yesterday. The Prime Minister will inaugurate the International Seminar on Linguistics. Later during the day, he will return to Delhi.

9. Manu: Have you been to Nepal?

   Teja: Yes, I've been to Nepal twice.

10. I saw her as we were coming out of my office. She told me that she'd been waiting outside my office since 5 p.m. I asked her to come in and ordered tea. While having tea with me, she told me that she had been looking for a job for two years.

6.2 Modal verbs

6.2.1 General characteristics of modal verbs

Modal verbs are also called **modal auxiliaries.** They are different in use from other auxiliaries or helping verbs and are therefore treated separately. The following are the modal verbs used in English:

can, should, may, might, will, would, shall, should and must

In addition to these modal verbs also called **central modals** there are other modals called **marginal modals.** (Quirk *et al* 1985). Marginal modals are *dare, need, ought to* and *used to.*

Both central and marginal modals are used primarily to express our relationship with other people. These are used to indicate our attitude towards what we are saying. Modal verbs may be used to grant permission to someone, to indicate someone's ability to do an action, to express a situation that is possible or to indicate an action that is necessary.

6.2.2 Special characteristics of modal verbs

i. A modal is always followed by the base form of the verb.

   Prema can sleep on the floor. [187]

   She might visit you in the evening. [188]

ii. For the sake of simplicity, one may say that *will, can, may* and *shall* have the past tense forms *would, could, might* and *should.* The other modal verbs have only one form. This means that a modal verb cannot have **-s** after it with the the third person singular subject in the present tense. It cannot have the present participle and past participle forms.

   Rita will reach Delhi tomorrow. [189]

   You must visit her next week. [190]

iii. Although the four pairs of modals, like *will-would* mentioned above have been treated as the present and past forms, their functions are different from the functions of the present and past forms of the main verbs. The use of the past form with modal verbs has the interpretation of tentativeness.

   Can I borrow your pen? [191a]

   Could I borrow your pen? [191b]

   I may see you tomorrow. [192a]

   I might see you tomorrow. [192b]

iv. In some sentences, the use of the past form with the modal verb has the interpretation of pastness.

He can lift 100 kgs [193]

He could lift 100 kgs when he was young. [194]

Similarly, the past forms of these modal verbs are also used in the reported speech.

Rakesh said to me, ' I will see you tomorrow.' [195]

Rakesh told me that he would see me the next day. [196]

v. Negatives can be formed by adding **not** after the modal. In the case of **ought to,** the negative particle **not** is used after **ought.**

I may not come tomorrow. [197]

She could not attend classes regularly. [198]

Sagar ought not to have done this. [199]

vi. Questions are formed by placing the modal in front of the subject. In the case of **ought to, ought** is placed before the subject and *to* is placed after it.

Could you give me a call in the evening? [200]

Ought we to go now? [201]

Exercise 11

Change the following sentences into their negative forms:

1. We will play football this evening.
2. John can carry heavy loads.
3. They may visit us tomorrow.
4. She could finish her work in time.
5. You should write to him.

6. You must sit there.
7. They should visit the hostel.
8. Renu will attend the class on Monday.
9. Vijay may take your car.
10. She can attend my lecture today.

Exercise 12

Change the following sentences into yes/no questions:

1. Professor Kumar will take our class tomorrow.
2. I could meet you at the bus stand.
3. He will go now.
4. I can eat this piece of bread.
5. We may leave this room now.
6. You can see me in the evening.
7. I may borrow your car.
8. You will open the window.
9. We shall watch the film.
10. We ought to wait for some more time.

6.2.3. Interpretations of modal verbs

6.2.3.1 Ability: We use **can** to talk about someone's ability in the present.

Sarita can work for twenty hours a day. [202]

Farida can drive a truck. [203]

Notice that sentence 202 can be paraphrased as:

Sarita **is able/has the ability to work** for twenty hours a day.

Similarly sentence 203 can be paraphrased as:

Farida **is able/has the ability** to drive a truck.

We can use **could** to express past ability, that is, the ability that one possessed in the past.

Sonali could work for twenty hours when
she was a girl. [204]

Ajay could play the guitar when he was in college. [205]

Notice that sentence 204 can be paraphrased as:

Sonali was able to play for twenty hours when she was a girl.

6.2.3.2 Permission/asking for permission: There are four modal verbs, **can, could, may** and **might,** which can be used either to grant permission or to ask for permission. In a general sense we can use **can, may** or **could** to talk about permission or to grant permission.

You can use the library from tomorrow. [206]

You may use the library from tomorrow. [207]

We could use the library ten years ago. [208]

Notice that both sentences 206 and 207 can be paraphrased as:

You are permitted to use the library from tomorrow.

or

You are allowed to use the library from tomorrow.

Sentence 208 can be paraphrased as:

We were permitted to use the library ten years ago.

May is more formal than **can,** when either of them is used to express permission and **could** is used to express permission in the past. **Can, may, could** and **might** can also be used for permission, though the use of **might** is rather rare and highly formal.

Can I use your telephone, please? [209]

Could I use your telephone, please? [210]

May I use your telephone, please? [211]

All the three senetences can be paraphrased as:
'*Am I allowed to use your telephone*?'

May is more formal than **can** in this sense. **Could** and **might** being past forms are more polite.

Could I meet you in the evening? [212]

Might I leave you now? [213]

However, **might** as mentioned earlier, is rare these days.

Exercise 13

Rewrite the following sentences using* can, could *or* may *in place of the italicised words:

Examples:

i. He *is able* to drive a car. (*He can drive a car*)

ii. *Am* I *allowed* to borrow your car? (tentative)
(*Could I borrow your car*?)

iii. *Am* I *allowed* to borrow your car? (formal)
(*May I borrow your car?*)

1. Jane *is able* to fly a plane.
2. *Am* I *allowed* to drive this car? (informal)
3. Rehman *was able* to attend the meeting yesterday as he took the morning train to Jabalpur.
4. She *is able* to walk ten kilometres everyday.
5. *Am* I *allowed* to borrow some books from the library? (tentative)
6. They *were able* to operate this machine, when they were young.
7. *Are* we *allowed* to take part in the discussion? (tentative)
8. *Are* we *allowed* to attend the conference? (formal)
9. He *is permitted* to participate in the national games. (formal)
10. You *are allowed* to borrow my car tomorrow. (informal)

6.2.3.3 Possibility: The four modal verbs **can, could, may** and **might** can be used to express possibility. Let us first discuss **can** and **may.**

She can be at home now. [214]

She may be at home now. [215]

Can expresses theoretical possibility and **may** expresses factual possibility. Therefore, **can** has a weaker possibility.

Could and **might** express tentative possibility as compared to **may.**

Ms Bhalla may take our class tomorrow. [216]

Ms Bhalla might take our class tomorrow. [217]

The difference between 216 and 217 is that the speaker in 217 is less sure of the possibility; otherwise there is no difference between the two sentences. Some people feel that **may** expresses the meaning of possibility and if one is less sure, one can use either **might** or **could**. Thus, we may say that **can** expresses factual possibility. **Could** and **might** also express factual possibility but one is less sure when one uses **could** and **might.**

Exercise 14

***Rewrite the following sentences using* can, may, could *or* might:**

Examples:

i. It is possible that this engine will work. (theoretical possibility)
(*This engine can work.*)

ii. It is possible that it will rain tomorrow. (factual possibility)
(*It may rain tomorrow.*)

iii. It is possible that he is attending the meeting. (less sure)
(*He could/might be attending the meeting.*)

1. It is possible that I will win the prize. (less sure)
2. It is possible that the best of pilots make judgement errors. (theoretical possibility)
3. It is possible that Mira is in her office. (factual possibility)
4. It is possible that the state will be placed under the Governor's rule. (theoretical possibility)
5. It is possible that Debashish will visit Ahmednagar next week. (factual possibility)
6. It is possible that Kailash is on his way to the bank. (factual possibility)
7. It is possible that the team is preparing for the final match. (factual possibility)
8. It is possible that our team will win the match. (less sure)
9. It is possible that the house is still vacant. (factual possibility)
10. It is possible that Rita will pass the examination. (factual possibility)

6.2.3.4 Requests: We can use **can, could, may, might, will** and **would** to make requests.

i. **Can** is used to make a simple request in an informal manner.

Can I sit with you? [218]

Can you lend me your book? [219]

ii. **Could** is also used to make a request. The use of **could** to make a request is considered tentative and therefore more polite than **can.**

iii. **May** and **might** are more formal than **can** and **could** to make requests. Requests made with **might** are rather rare and unusual.

May I know your name, please? (formal) [220]

Might I know if the results have been declared? [221]

iv. **Will** and **would** can also be used to make polite requests for actions in the immediate or distant future.

Will you open the door, please? (now) [222]

Will you lend me your book? (now or later) [223]

Would you open the door, please? (now) [224]

Would you lend me your book? (now or later) [225]

6.2.3.5 Suggestions:

i. The most common way to make a suggestion is by using an interrogative sentence beginning with **shall** and **we**.

Shall we see this film today? [226]

Shall we leave now? [227]

Shall we continue with this problem? [228]

ii. Another way of making a suggestion is by using **could/might** in a declarative sentence.

We could see this film today. [229]

You might build your house there. [230]

iii. **Should** and **must** can be used in a declarative sentence if the speaker strongly suggests or persuades the listener to do a particular thing.

You should speak to your lawyer. [231]

You must ring him up. [232]

Exercise 15

Change each of the following sentences into a request or a suggestion with the help of the modal verb suggested in brackets:

Examples:

i. I want to read that book. (request with *can*)
Can I read that book?

ii. I want to attend the French class. (request with *may*)
May I attend the French class?

iii. We may attend the prayer. (suggestion with *shall*)
Shall we attend the prayer?

iv. We may meet the Principal. (suggestion with *could*)
We could meet the Principal.

1. You may have lunch with us tomorrow. (request with **would**)
2. You may switch on the television please. (request with **will**)
3. We may have dinner now. (suggestion with **shall**)
4. I want to drink a glass of fresh lime juice. (request with **can**)
5. You lend me your car, please. (request with **could**)
6. I want to meet the Principal. (request with **could**)
7. I want to borrow this book from the library. (request with **may**)
8. You may visit your grandfather. (suggestion with **should**)
9. You may drop me at my hostel. (request with **would**)
10. We walk down to the market. (suggestion with **could**)

6.2.3.6 Necessity: The most common modal verb to express necessity is **must.**

You must attend the meeting tomorrow. [233]

I must go home now. [234]

Notice that sentence 233 can be paraphrased as:

It is necessary for you to attend the meeting tomorrow.

and sentence 234 can be paraphrased as

It is necessary for me to go home now.

6.2.3.7 Obligation: When we want to introduce the meaning of obligation, that is when we wish to say that something needs to be done or is the right thing to do, we use **ought to** or **should.**

You ought to exercise during the camp. [235]

He should report to work at 9 a.m. everyday. [236]

The past tense of these two modal verbs are **ought to have** and **should have.**

She ought to have met me at the airport yesterday. [237]

Exercise 16

***Write the following sentences using* ought to , should, ought to have *or* should have:**

Examples:

i. It is necessary for you to submit the application today.
   You should submit your application today.

ii. He was obliged to inform you that he would not meet you today.

He ought to have informed you that he would not meet you today.

1. It is necesary for you to see the doctor next week.
2. Enakshi is obliged to support her aged parents.
3. It is necessary for her to use these glasses.
4. We are obliged to respect our teachers.
5. They were obliged to see the Principal in the morning.
6. It is necessary to finish our work on time.
7. He was obliged to take your permission before he took a week's leave.
8. Visitors are obliged to park their cars outside the colony gates.
9. You are obliged to report to work within ten days.
10. It is necessary for students to wear their games uniform on Saturdays.

6.2.3.8 Needn't and mustn't: Needn't expresses the sense of not having the necessity to do something.

You needn't take the test. [238]
(*you have already passed it*)

Karim needn't pay the money. [239]
(*somebody has already paid for him*)

Mustn't is used when something should not be done.

You mustn't miss this rare opportunity. [240]
(*you are not likely to get it again*)

Since John has a cold he mustn't come out
in the rain. [241]
(*if he does the cold will worsen*)

Exercise 17

***Fill in the blanks with* needn't *or* mustn't:**

1. You .... go to the market. I have already bought vegetables for two days.
2. You .... go out to the market. Curfew has been clamped over the city.
3. Rekha .... neglect her studies. She didn't do well in the last test.
4. Vicky .... attend extra classes. He did very well in the last term.
5. I .... build a house. My father has transferred our ancestral house to me.
6. He suffers from high blood pressure. He .... eat a lot of salt.
7. You .... go to work today. It has been declared a public holiday.
8. You.................. take leave today. There is a lot of work that needs to be finished.
9. The children .... disturb the neighbours.
10. You .... visit her in the hospital everyday. Her sister is constantly by her side.

6.2.3.9 Some other uses of modal verbs:

Future prediction: **Will** and **shall** are used to express future prediction.

We shall visit Ooty next year. [242]

Probability: **Should** and **ought to** express probability either in the present or the future.

Rita should have/ought to have reached Bilaspur by now. [243]

Venissa should/ought to be there soon. [244]

Hypothetical: **Would** is used in sentences expressing unreal conditions.

If I were you, I wouldn't do it. [245]

Exercise 18

Interpret the meaning of each modal verb in the following sentences:

1. The director could be in his office.
2. If she worked hard, she would pass.
3. They ought to have sent you the letter.
4. John can run ten miles at a stretch.
5. She may meet you tomorrow.
6. Could you pass on the salt, please?
7. Shall we discuss the agenda now?
8. May I see you in the morning?
9. I could drive a car when I was just fifteen years old.
10. They should have reached Surat by now.
11. You must apologise to her.
12. She might see the governor tomorrow.
13. Mira may be in the library.
14. May I sit with you?
15. Could I use your typewriter please?
16. They should have seen this film.
17. You mustn't miss my lecture tomorrow.
18. She should have informed you that she will not attend the meeting.
19. She might see him tomorrow.
20. Children should take care of their parents.

7

Complex Sentences - I

7.1 Introduction

In chapter 1, we stated that a simple sentence is made up of only one clause.

That girl is very talented. [1]

A sentence that consists of two or more clauses is a **complex sentence.**

S	TrV	Od	(Adv)	
I	saw	him	then.	[2]
He	was coming		out of his office.	[3]

Both 2 and 3 are simple sentences. We can combine 2 and 3 in such a way that sentence 3 is used as an adverbial in the position of **then** in sentence 2. We can form a complex sentence by combining sentences 2 and 3 as follows:

S	TrV	Od	(Adv)	
I	saw	him	**while he was coming out of his office.**	[4]

Notice that, *while he was coming out of his office* is an adverbial clause. Thus a complex sentence may have two or more subject-predicate structures, whereas a simple sentence has only one subject-predicate structure. A few more examples of complex sentences are:

I know that Mohan is a bank manager. [5]

What you told me is true. [6]

I helped him because he was very weak. [7]

The man whom you met at the party is a doctor. [8]

All the sentences from 5 - 8 are complex sentences. Whereas 5 - 7 are one type of complex sentence, 8 is of a different kind. Notice the brief analysis of sentences 5 - 7:

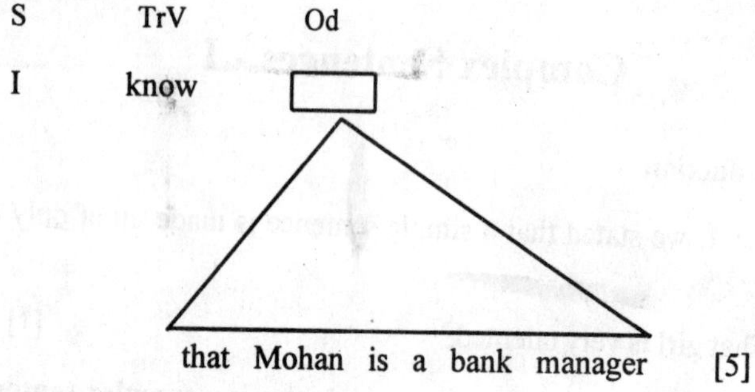

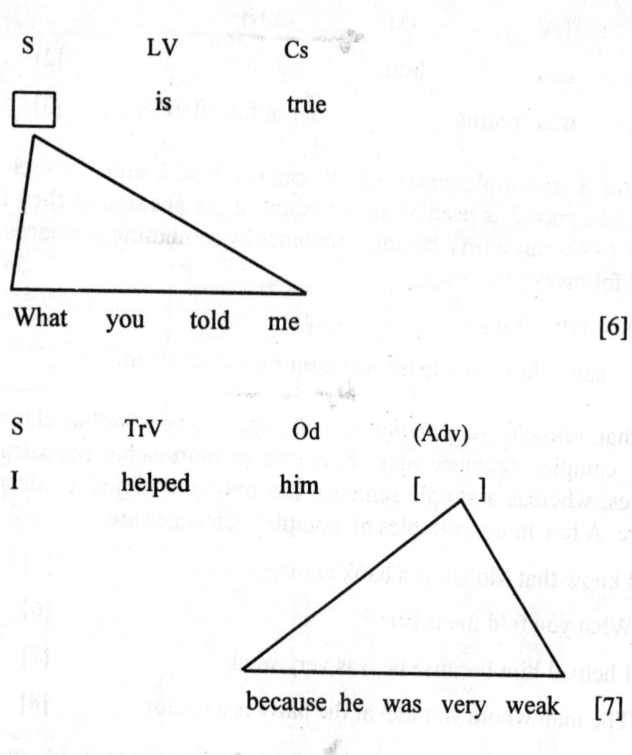

Notice that the subordinate clauses in 5 - 7 are inserted in the slots of one of the elements of the sentences. The subordinate clause in 5 is placed at the object position, in 6 at the subject position and in 7 at the adverbial position.

However, the analysis of 8 will be as follows:

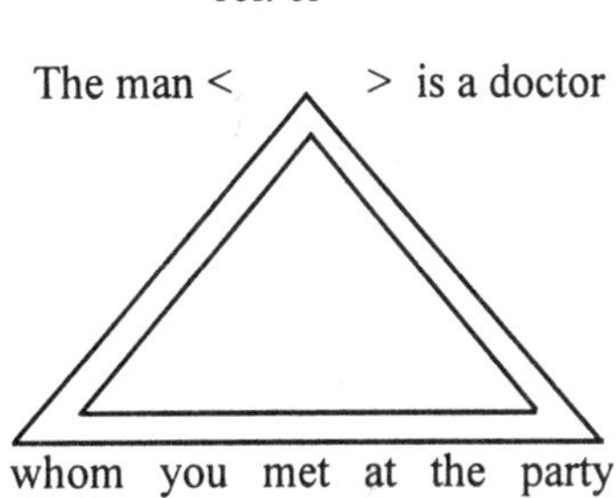

Whom you met at the party has not been placed in the position of any one of the five sentence elements, S, V, C, O, Adv. It is inserted into the sentence in such a way that it modifies the noun phrase *the man.*

There is an easy test to identify the number of clauses in a sentence. One may count the number of main verbs in a sentence and the rule is that the number of main verbs in a sentence is equal to the number of clauses in a sentence. (*see chapter 4 for the definition of a main verb*)

Meenakshi is **reading** a book. [9]

Notice that 9 has only one main verb i.e. *reading*. Therefore, it has only one clause and thus is a simple sentence.

I **went** to his house because he **needed** my help. [10]

Sentence 10 has two main verbs, *went* and *needed* and therefore, it is a complex sentence with two clauses. *Because he needed my help* is the subordinate clause.

I **feel** that he will **come** here if we **send** him the money. [11]

Notice that 11 has three clauses because it has three main verbs: *feel, come* and *send.* The subordinate clauses are: i. *that he will come here* ii. *if we send him the money.* The conjunctions used with the subordinate clauses are **that** and **if.** Sentence 11 can be analysed as:

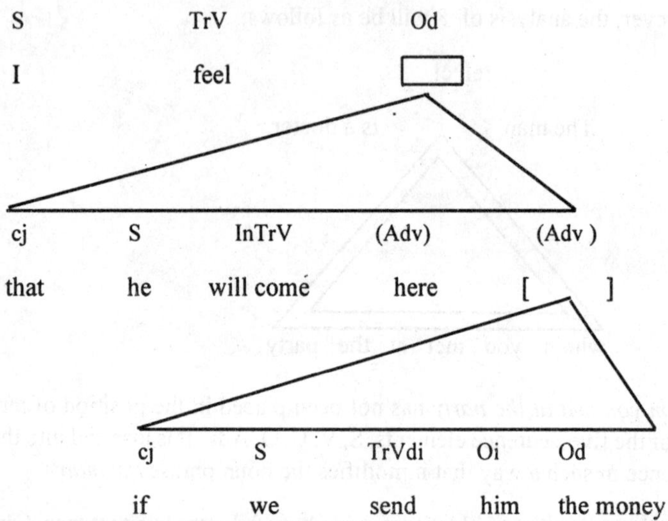

Notice that a subordinate clause may also be used at the beginning of a sentence:

When I last met him, he was writing a novel. [12]

That the earth is round is a fact. [13]

When I last met him and *that the earth is round* are subordinate clauses. *When* and *that* are conjunctions in sentences 12 and 13 respectively.

7.2 Subordinate and superordinate clauses

Vikas told me that he had bought a house. [14]

Although he has bought a car, he always rides his scooter. [15]

We may analyse sentence 14 as follows:

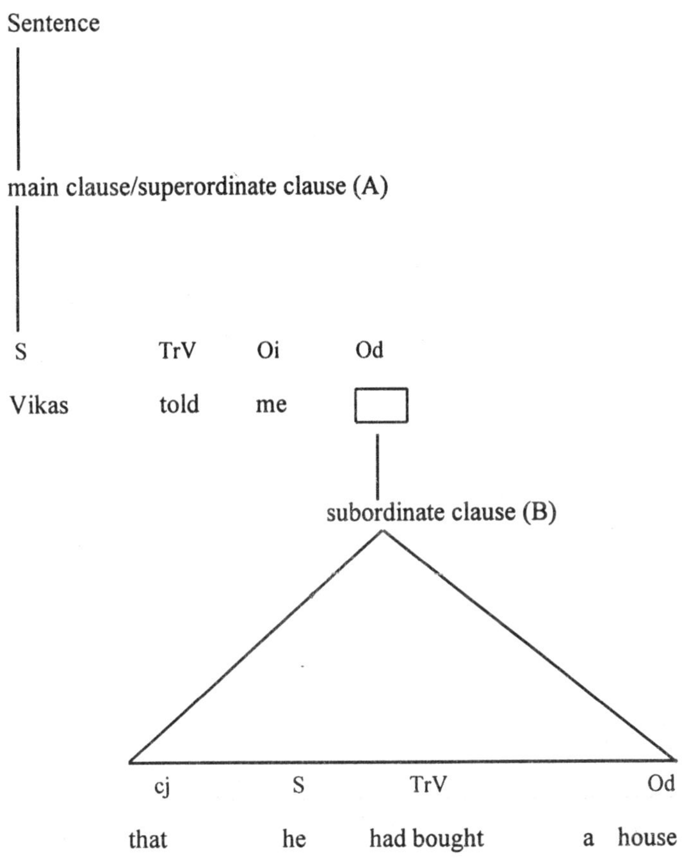

Thus 14 has two clauses. There is clause A, which is the main clause and also the superordinate clause and there is clause B, which is a subordinate clause.

Sentence 15 can be analysed as:

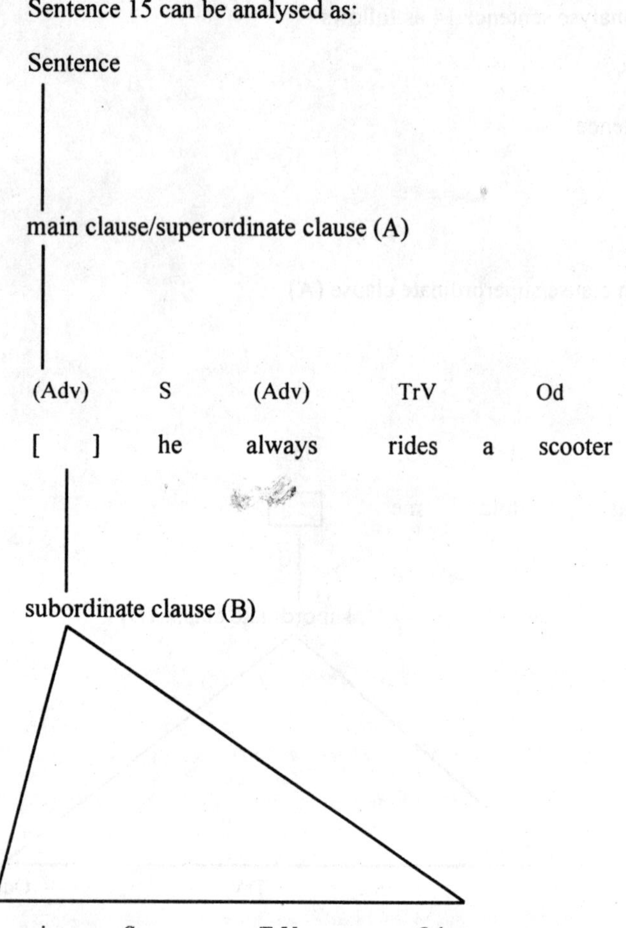

Now let us look at sentence 16, which has three clauses:

> He told me that his father joined the company
> when he was young. [16]

We may analyse sentence 16 as:

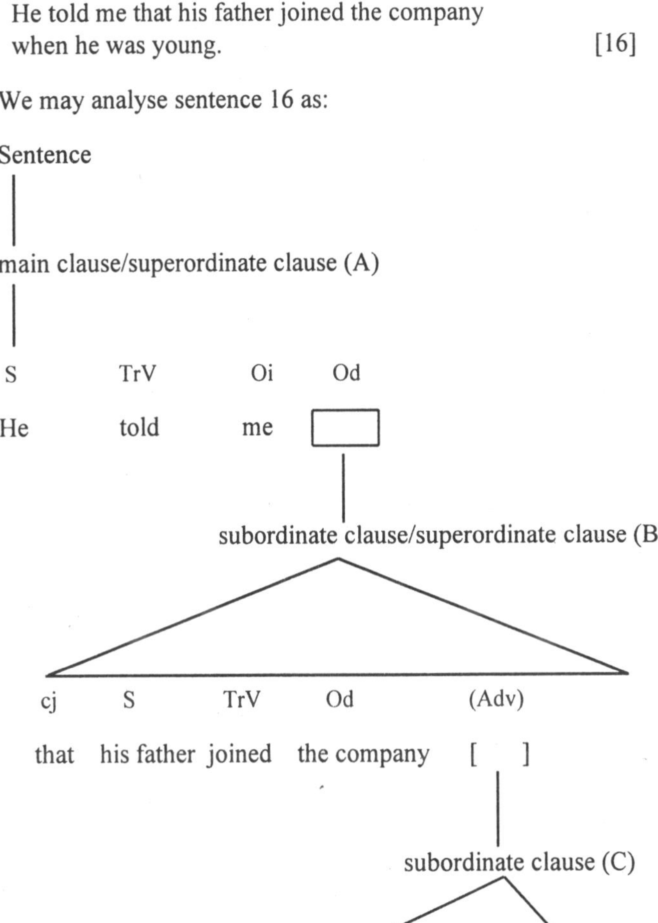

Notice that clause A is superordinate to clause B. Clause B, which is a subordinate clause to clause A, is in turn superordinate to clause C. Thus clause B is superordinate to clause C but subordinate to clause A. Therefore, a superordinate clause can be the main clause or a subordinate clause as long as it has a clause subordinate to it.

7.3 Subordinate clause and matrix clause

While discussing the previous sections in this chapter, we mentioned that the subordinate clause functions as part of the superordinate/main clause. Let us look at sentence 14:

Vikas told me that he had bought a house. [14]

As explained earlier,

S	Tr	Oi	Od
Vikas	**told**	**me**	☐

is the main clause/superordinate clause

	cj	S	TrV	Od
and	**that**	**he**	**had bought**	**a house**

is the subordinate clause

Similarly sentence [17] can be analysed as:

I saw him while he was crossing the road. [17]

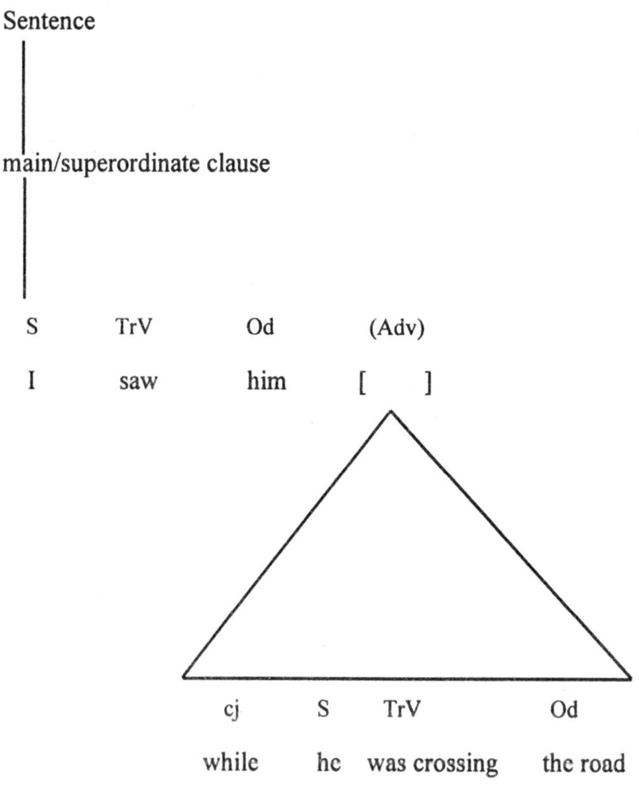

Thus when we analyse a complex sentence in terms of the main clause/ superordinate clause and the subordinate clause, we need to include the subordinate clause in the main/superordinate clause. For example, if we analyse sentence 14 we cannot say that *Vikas told me* is the main clause. The main clause in sentence 14 is *Vikas told me* Od [ ], and then in the slot for Od we use the subordinate clause. Similarly, in sentence 17 we cannot say that the main clause is *I saw him* but the main clause is *I saw him Adv* [ ] where the slot for the adverbial is completed by a clause. Thus the main/superordinate clause and the subordinate clause in a complex sentence are not separate entities but are interrelated to each other. However, on some occasions, we may not go into the detailed analysis of a complex sentence. In such instances we may like to distinguish the subordinate clause from the rest of the sentence. In such cases whatever is left before or after the subordinate clause is the **matrix clause**. Thus in 14 *Vikas told me* is the matrix clause and *that he had bought a house* is the subordinate clause. Similarly in 17 *I saw him* is the matrix clause and *while he was crossing the road* is the subordinate clause.

Exercise 1

Identify the matrix clauses and subordinate clauses in these complex sentences. Write down the matrix clause, the subordinate clause, and the conjunction for each sentence:

1. The fact is that he has never attended the meeting. ....
   ....
2. I shall help you if you pass this examination. ....
   ....
3. He noticed that she was wearing his daughter's dress. ....
   ....
4. I shall see you after I have finished my lecture. ....
   ....
5. He told me that the Prime Minister would visit Lucknow. ....
   ....
6. Although I reached the college at 9 a.m., I couldn't see the Principal. ....
7. The rumour was that she had been dismissed. ....
   ....
8. As Shakti had returned early, we went out for a week. ....
   ....
9. You may leave the class as soon as you have finished your paper.
   ....
10. I last met him when he lived in London. ....
    ....

7.4 Structure of subordinate clauses

Subordinate clauses can be broadly divided into three categories:

a. finite subordinate clauses

b. non-finite subordinate clauses

c. verbless clauses

7.4.1 Finite subordinate clauses

A clause with a finite verb phrase is a **finite clause.** We discussed in detail the distinction between finite and non-finite verb phrases in chapter 4, section 4.3. Briefly, a verb is finite if it carries **tense** and it is non-finite if it does not carry **tense.** Another important thing to remember is that the main clause or the matrix clause is always a finite clause. The main clause or the matrix clause can never be a non-finite or a verbless clause.

He told me that Sheela had stood first. [18]

Sentence 18 can be analysed as:

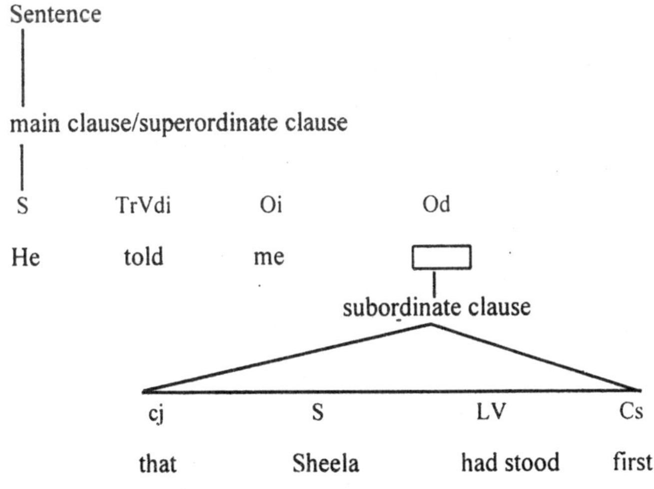

Notice that in 18 both the main clause, *he told me* Od and the subordinate clause, *that Sheela had stood first* have finite verbs, *told* and *had stood* because both the verbs carry tense. Thus the subordinate clause is a finite clause in 18. Similarly, 19 and 20 have finite subordinate clauses:

We had lunch **as soon as we reached Gulmarg.** [19]

I'll see Mr Mehta, **if I visit Valsad.** [20]

7.4.2 Non-finite subordinate clauses

As mentioned earlier in section 4.3, a non-finite subordinate clause has a non-finite verb phrase, which does not carry tense:

He fell on the floor **while entering the room.** [21]

I hate **his sending her reminders.** [22]

Notice that in 21 and 22 the non-finite subordinate clauses, *while entering the room* and *his sending her reminders* do not carry tense. However, we should remember these points about subordinate clauses:

a. Although the non-finite/verbless subordinate clause does not carry tense, it usually has the same time reference as the main clause.

b. We can treat non-finite and verbless subordinate clauses as clauses because they have the same functional elements as finite clauses.

c. For the sake of understanding, we may even treat non-finite and verbless clauses as reduced forms of finite clauses.

Sentence 21 may be analysed as:

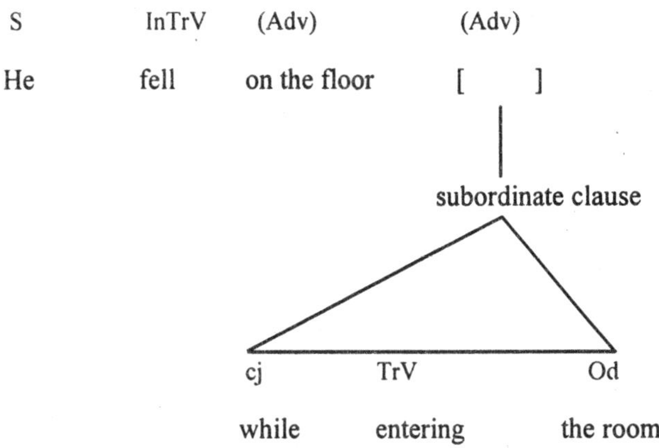

It is also possible to treat 21 as the reduced form of 21a.

He fell on the floor **while he was entering the room.** [21a]

Similarly, 22 can be analysed as:

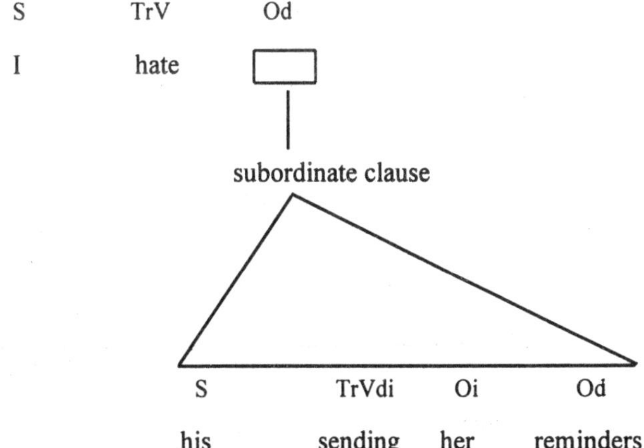

We may treat 22 as a form of 22a.

* I hate that he sends her reminders. [22a]

The verb *hate* cannot be followed by a **that** clause. But we can easily understand that the complex sentence 22 seems to have been derived from two simple sentences:

I hate it. [23a]

He sends her reminders. [23b]

A few more examples of non-finite subordinate clauses are:

I want him to study hard. [24]

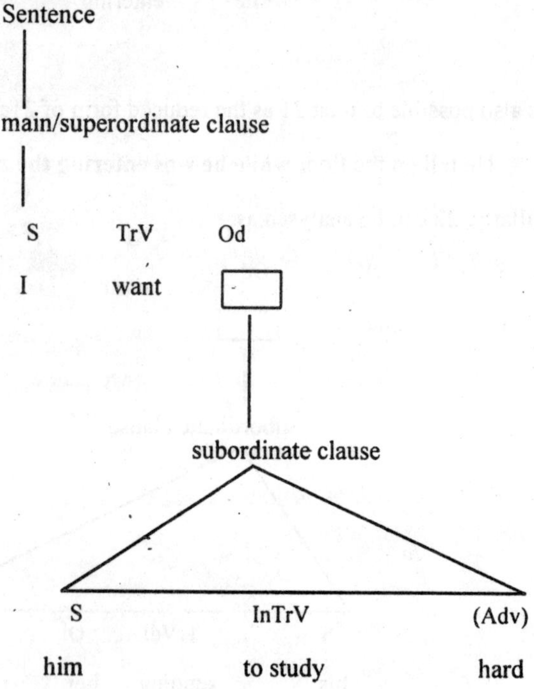

Mukesh reached the station at 5 a.m. in order to catch the first train. [25]

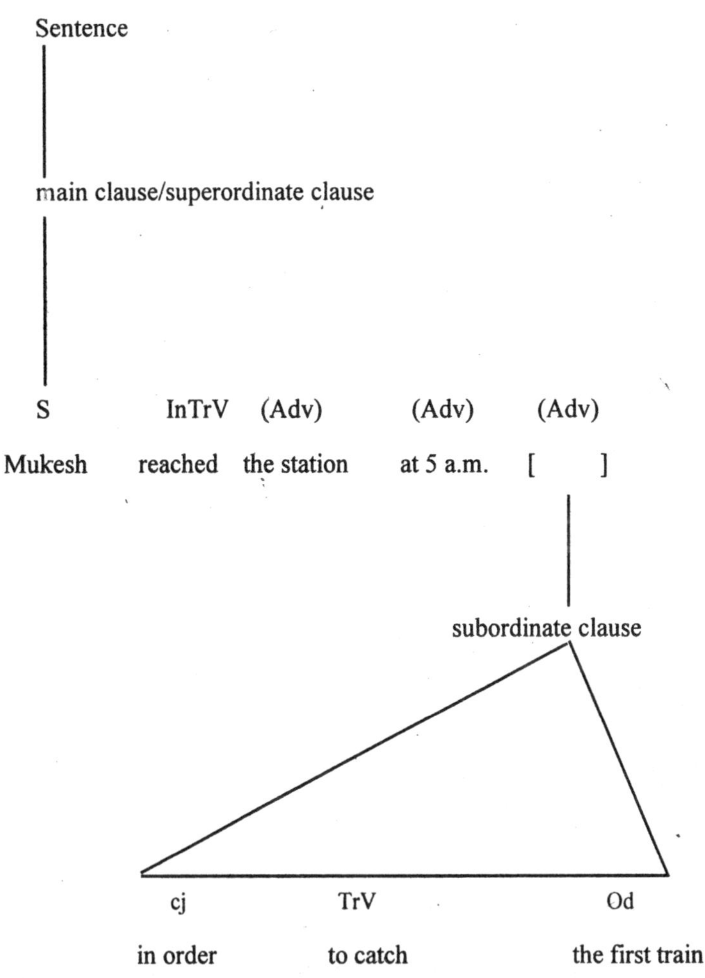

Having finished his work, he came to my room. [26]

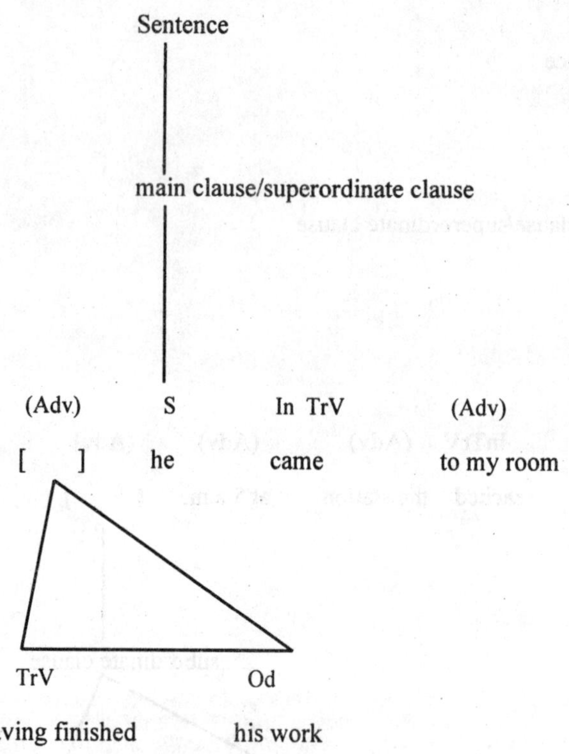

7.4.2.1 Types of non-finite subordinate clauses: Non-finite subordinate clauses are of four types:

a. **to-infinitive**

She wants **to be a pilot.** [27]

The right thing would be **for him to work hard.** [28]

b. **bare infinitive**

All I wanted to do was **drink a glass of water.** [29]

Bare infinitive is very rare as a subordinate clause.

c. **-ing participle**

Singing in the classroom can be disturbing. [30]

I like **his singing in the classroom.** [31]

d. **-ed participle**

Covered with snow, he suddenly entered the room. [32]

Completed in 1993, the project brought worldwide acclaim for India. [33]

7.4.3 Verbless clauses

For the sake of convenience, a verbless subordinate clause may be treated as the reduced form of a finite clause. The elements of the verbless clause which have been dropped can be recovered with reference to the main clause:

Although always happy, he did not love anyone. [34]

This sentence may be treated as the reduced form of 34a.

Although he was always happy, he did not love anyone. [34a]

Sentence 34 can be analysed as:

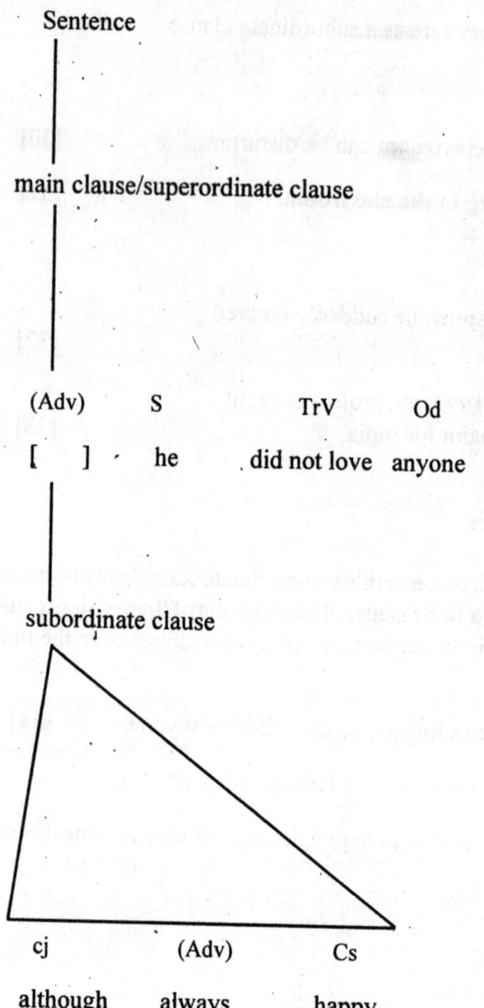

Similarly, sentence 34a can be analysed as:

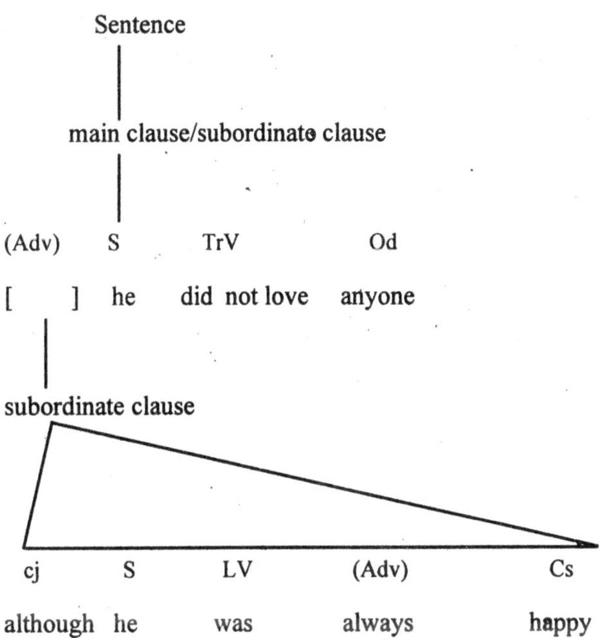

Red with rage, she caught hold of his collar. [35]
(*as she was red with rage...*)

Illustrate your answer, **wherever possible.** [36]
(..., *wherever it is possible*)

The meeting can be held next week, **if necessary.** [37]
(..., *if it is necessary*)

While at the NDA, he was an underofficer. [38]
(*while he was at the NDA...* ,)

Exercise 2

Analyse these sentences into the main clause and subordinate clause (finite, non-finite or verbless) as shown in the examples:

i. She presumed that you had left early.

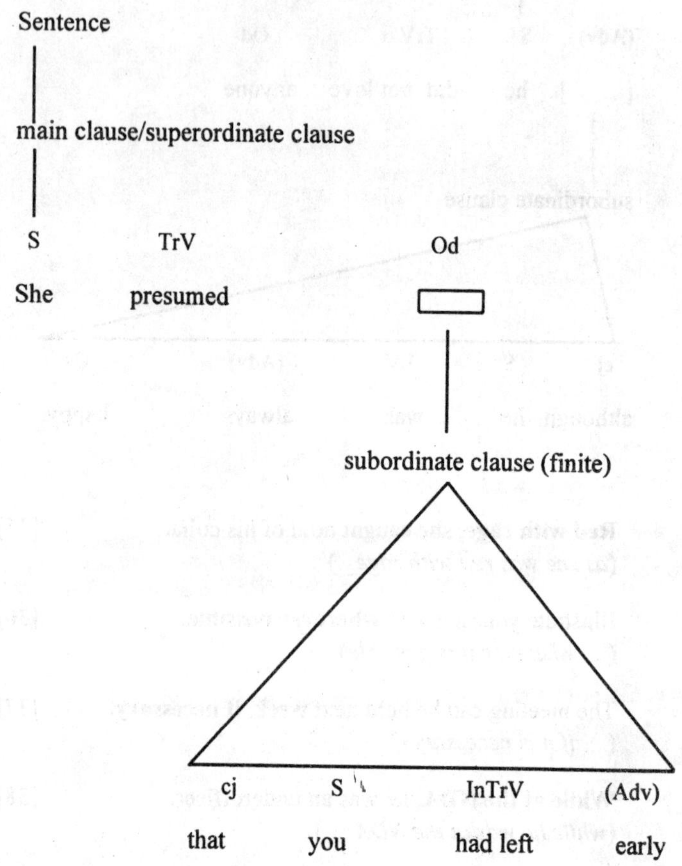

ii. I love watching films on the DD Metro.

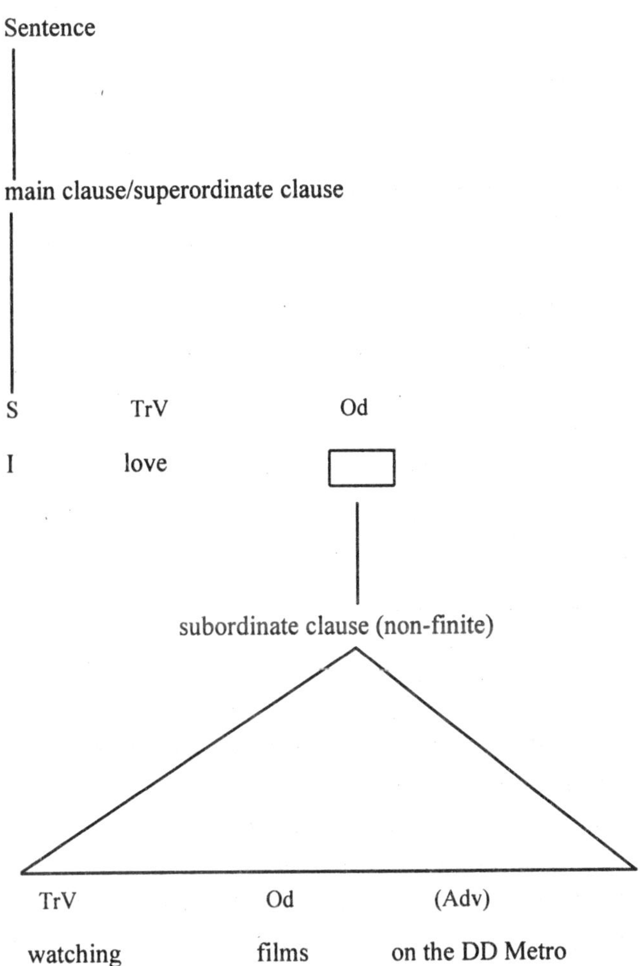

iii. While at Delhi University, he wrote five articles.

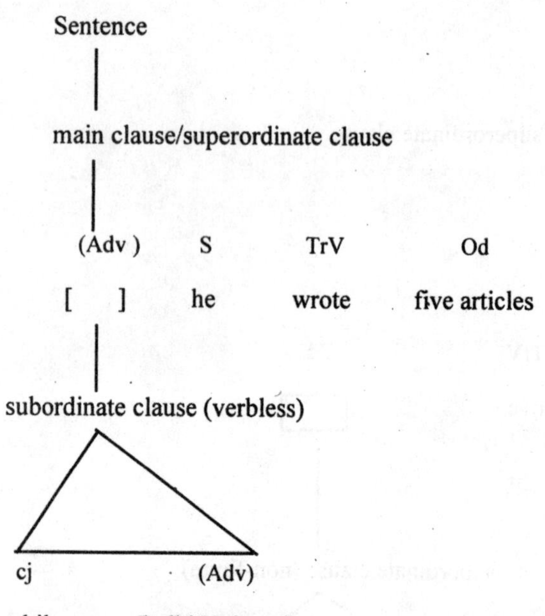

1. I reached college before her examination had begun.
2. She wants to study in the library.
3. If I go to Connaught Place, I'll buy a shirt.
4. He proved that his results were correct.
5. For John to drive his car is a very difficult task.
6. She enjoys swimming in the evening.
7. She found that her locker had been opened.
8. My assumption is that fertilizer prices will be reduced.
9. When in difficulty, press that button.
10. I feel better after taking this medicine.

7.5 Functions of subordinate clauses

Subordinate clauses can perform the functions of the various elements of a sentence. Thus a subordinate clause may function, among others, as the subject, object, complement and adverbial in a sentence.

7.5.1 Nominal clauses

Nominal subordinate clauses perform the functions of the noun phrase in a sentence.There are six types of nominal clauses:

a. **that-** clauses

b. **wh-** interrogative clauses

c. **yes-no** interrogative clauses

d. nominal relative clauses

e. **to-** infinitive clauses

f. **-ing** clauses

The first four types are finite nominal clauses and the last two, i.e., **to-** infinitive and **-ing** clauses are non-finite nominal clauses.

7.5.1.1 That- nominal clauses: These can function as:

a. **Subject:**

That he will be elected the Prime Minister is expected by everyone. [39]

That she has seen this film proves her interest in art films. [40]

Sentence 39 can be analysed as follows:

Sentence 39 is derived from two simple sentences:

This is expected by everyone. [a]

He will be elected the Prime Minister. [b]

Sentence b is inserted in the subject position of sentence a:

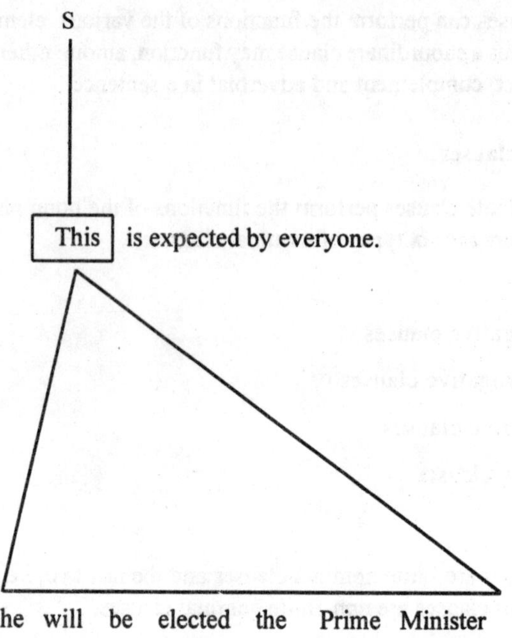

As a general rule, whenever two or more simple sentences are combined to form a complex sentence, a conjunction or a subordinating conjunction is required. In this case the subordinator **that** is required, so that we get:

> **That he will be elected the Prime Minister** is expected by everyone. [39]

Thus *that he will be elected Prime Minister* has been used at the subject position. Finally, we can indicate the relationship between the main clause and the subordinate clause in 39 as follows:

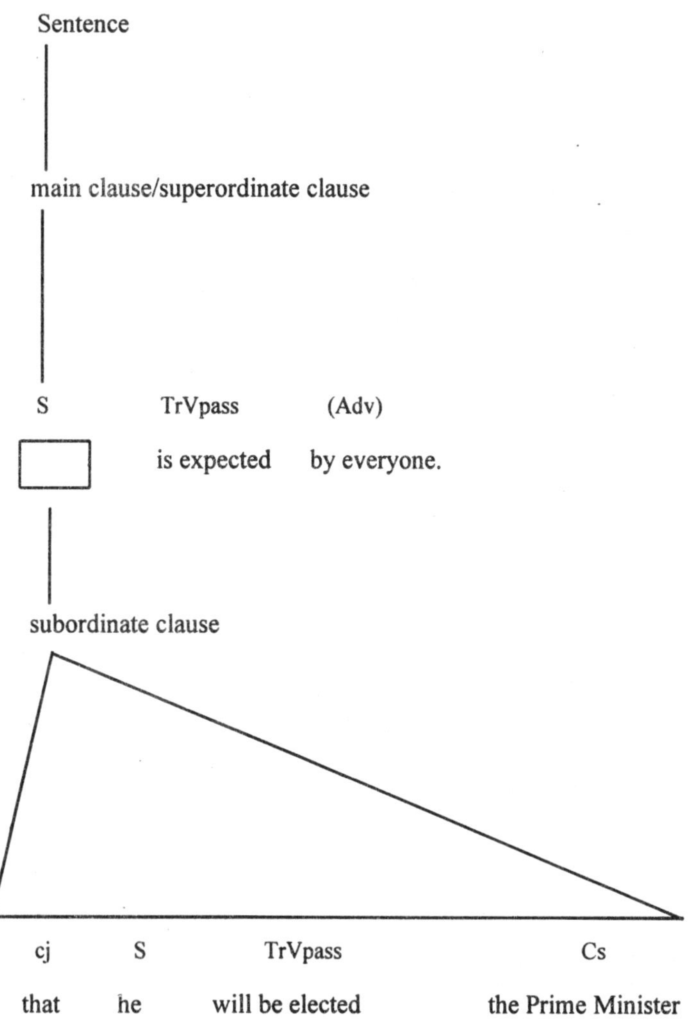

cj S TrVpass Cs

that he will be elected the Prime Minister

Sentence 40 can be analysed as follows:

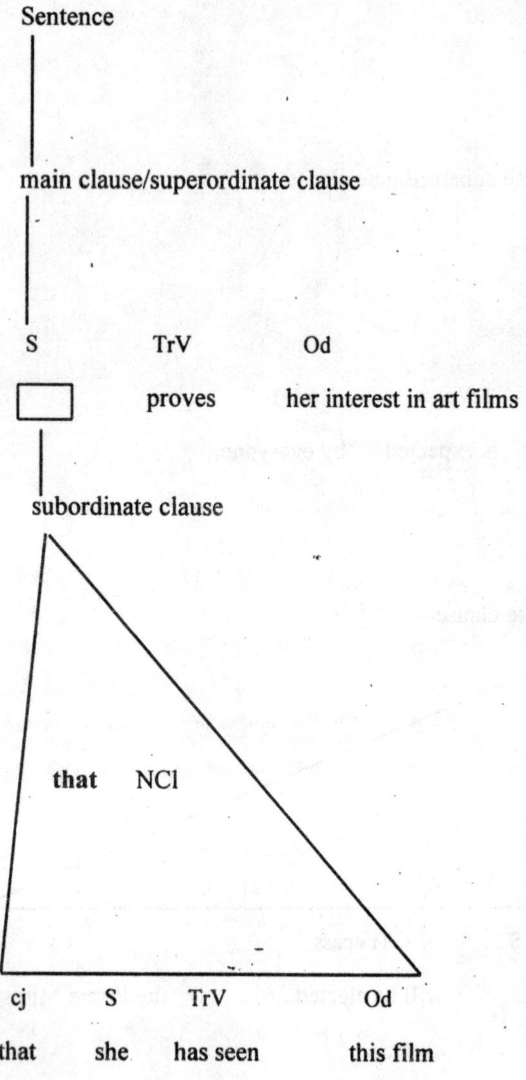

Exercise 3

Use sentence* b *as the 'that'-noun clause at the subject position of sentence* a *in each one of these pairs of sentences:

1. a. It did not come as a surprise to anyone.
   b. India won the one-day series.
2. a It has brought credit to the school.
   b. Kunal has stood first in the ISC examination.
3. a It indicates her popularity in the international community.
   b. She will meet the President of the USA.
4. a. It has not changed our government's policy.
   b. The troops have been withdrawn.
5. a. It raised the morale of the battalion.
   b. Rajinder was promoted as Lieutenant Colonel.

Exercise 4

Analyse these sentences into the main clause/superordinate clause and the subordinate clause indicating the elements of each clause. You may follow the analysis of sentence 40 above as illustration.

1. That she had become a pilot has thrilled everyone.
2. That India is the largest democracy is very creditable.
3. That his father is alive is no less than a miracle.
4. That she does not know him demonstrates her lack of social skills.
5. That America is a super power is a known fact.

b. **Direct Object:** A **that-** nominal clause can function as the direct object of a monotransitive or ditransitive verb:

I know that Mohinder has passed the examination. [41]

She assumed that you would attend the meeting. [42]

He told me that she was not right. [43]

Sentence 41 can be analysed as:

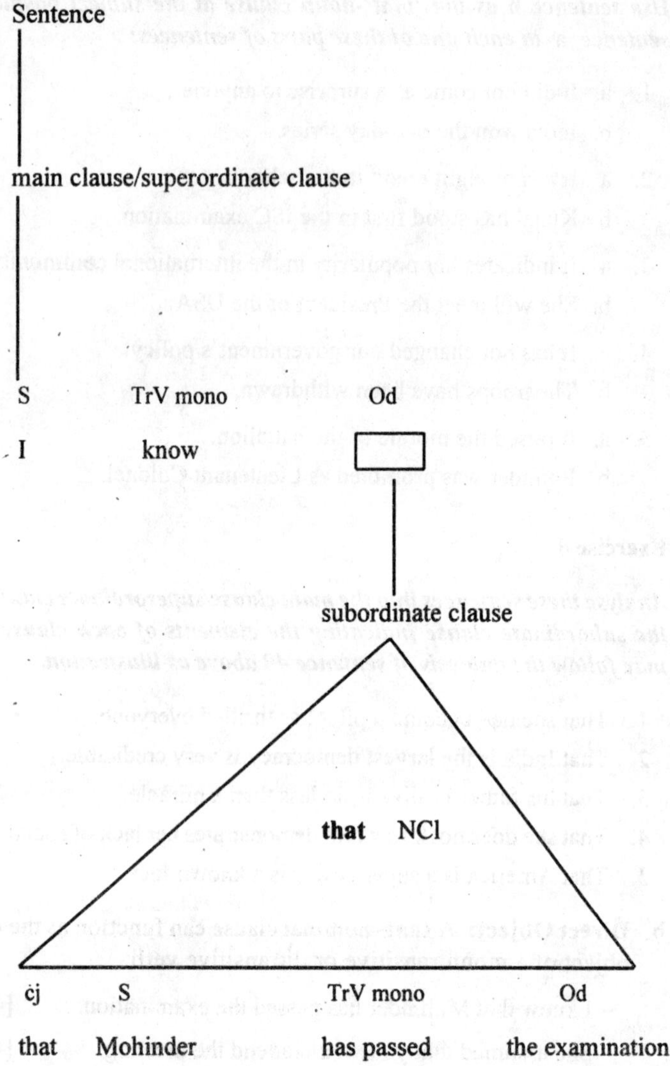

Similarly, sentence 43 can be analysed as :

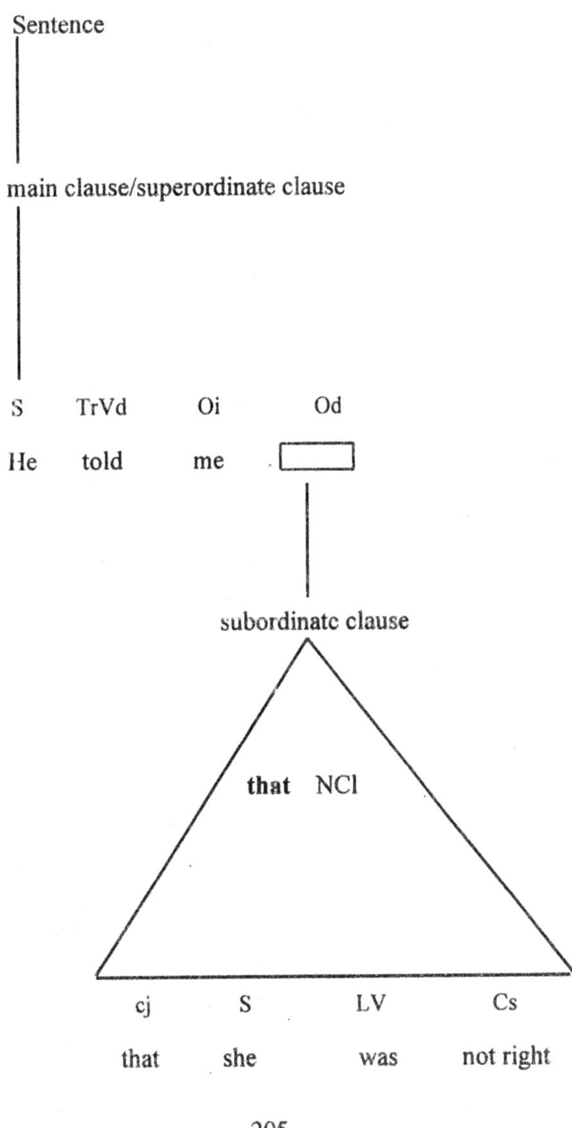

It is possible to drop the conjunction **that** in the **that-** nominal clause when it occurs at the direct object position. **That** as conjunction can only be dropped in an informal situation. So instead of 41, 42 and 43 one could say:

I know Mohinder has passed the examination. [41a]

She assumed you would attend the meeting. [42a]

He told me she was not right. [43a]

In 41a, 42a and 43a, the conjunction **that** has been dropped. This means that there is a slot for the conjunction **that** and the conjunction has been dropped from this slot. In other words, what we can say is that there is a use of the **zero** ø conjunction. Therefore, 42a can be analysed as:

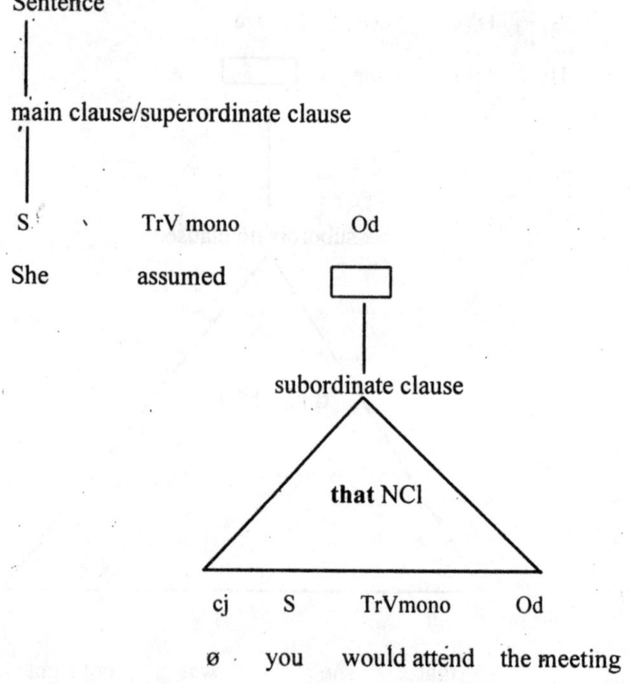

Some of the verbs that can have **that**-noun clause at the direct object position are:

accept	*admit*	*agree*	*announce*	*assume*
believe	*conclude*	*confess*	*confirm*	*complain*
declare	*decide*	*demand*	*discover*	*dream*
feel	*found*	*hear*	*hope*	*infer*

Exercise 5

***Combine sentences* a *and* b *in these pairs of sentences in such a way that sentence* b *becomes the* that-*nominal clause used as the object of sentence* a:**

1. a. Kamlesh accepted it. b. Her sister had taken the money.
2. a. She told me something. b. You were coming here on Tuesday.
3. a. I regret it. b. She did not give me the discount.
4. a. Vikram dreamt it. b. He had become a general.
5. a. We heard it. b. You are going to the USA.

Exercise 6

Analyse these sentences into the main clause/superordinate clause and the subordinate clause indicating the elements of each clause. You may follow the analysis of sentences 41and 43 above as examples:

1. She feels that we should buy a car.
2. The minister announced that the bridge would be constructed within a week.
3. She is insisting that we should pay an advance on the rent.
4. Mohini suggested that we should go on vacation.
5. The general has ordered that the troops should move immediately.

c. **Subject complement:** The **that**-nominal clause can also function as the complement of the subject:

The fact is that he never attended the meeting. [44]

The recommendation was that all the employees should be promoted. [45]

There is a limited number of nouns like *fact, suggestion, reply, remain, answer, story, message* - that can have a **that**- nominal clause as their complement. The analysis of sentence 44 is:

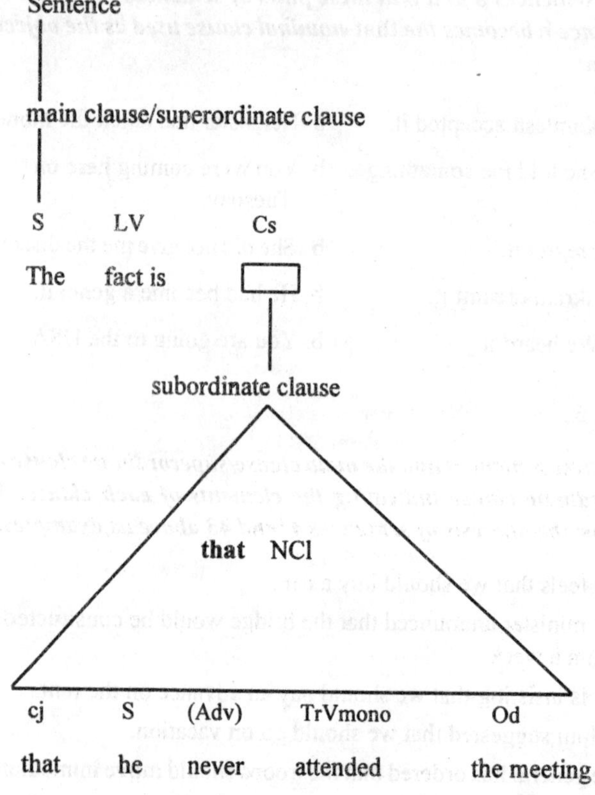

As in the case of the object position, the conjunction **that** can be dropped at the subject complement position in the informal style.

The fact is he never attended the meeting. [44a]

The recommendation was all the employees should be promoted. [45a]

Sentence 45a can be analysed as:

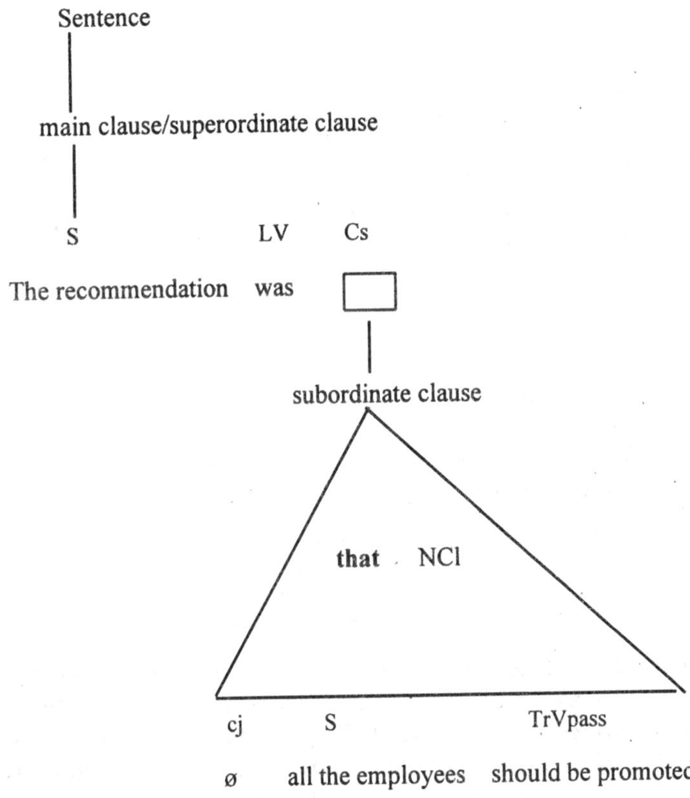

Exercise 7

***Combine sentences* a *and* b *in these pairs of sentences in such a way that sentence* b *becomes the* that- *nominal clause used as the complement of the subject of sentence* a:**

1. a. The chances are these.
   b. We will win the match.
2. a. The suggestion was this.
   b. The meeting should be held after two months.
3. a. The assumption is this.
   b. Democracy will survive.
4. a. The decision was this.
   b. Varun would be given a scholarship.
5. a. My advice is this.
   b. You should attend the interview tomorrow.

Exercise 8

Analyse these sentences into the main clause/superordinate clause and subordinate clause indicating the elements of each clause:

1. The feeling is there should be no examination.
2. The hope is we shall get help.
3. The reply is that we should start the project.
4. The report is that the interest rate has decreased.
5. The news is that India has won the cricket match.

Appositive clause: The **that-** nominal clause can also function in apposition to a noun phrase. There is a difference between the **that-nominal clause** functioning as the subject, object or subject complement and the **that-** nominal clause functioning as appositive. While the **that-** clause replaces one of the elements of the main clause in the case of the subject, object and subject complement positions, the appositive clause is inserted into the main clause. Thus the appositive clause is loosely attached to the main clause. We shall indicate the appositive clause through a double-lined triangle to distinguish it from the other elements of the sentence.

> The news story that the Prime Minister is resigning has been refuted by the Prime Minister's office. [46]

> The recommendation that all the employees should be promoted has been implemented. [47]

We notice that sentence 46 is made of two simple sentences.

> The news story has been refuted by the Prime Minister's office. [a]

> The Prime Minister is resigning. [b]

Sentence **b** is inserted into sentence **a** at the position of the postnominal modifier of the *news story* so that we get sentence 46. Therefore, 46 can be analysed as:

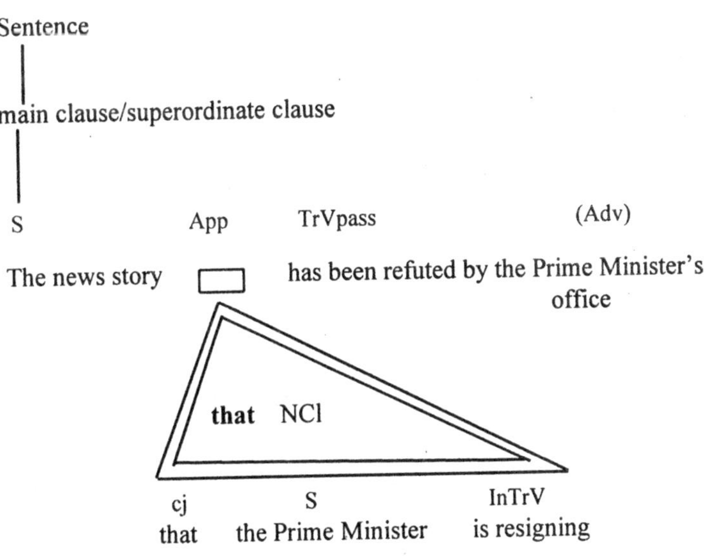

The head of the noun phrase with which an appositive clause can be used is a general abstract noun like *fact, idea, reply, remark, answer, recommendation, message, suggestion.* We shall discuss the appositive clause in comparison to the relative clause in chapter 8, section 8.2.

Adjectival complementation: The **that-** nominal clause can sometimes be used as the postmodifier of an adjective.

I am glad that she has passed. [48]

We are sorry that we could not attend the party. [49]

We were annoyed that you had not informed us. [50]

Sentence 48, again, is made of two simple sentences:

I am glad about something. [a]

She has passed. [b]

When we combine **a** and **b,** we get 48 so that sentence **b,** *she has passed,* replaces *about something*, which functions as the postmodifier of the adjective, in sentence **a.** We can, therefore, analyse 48 as:

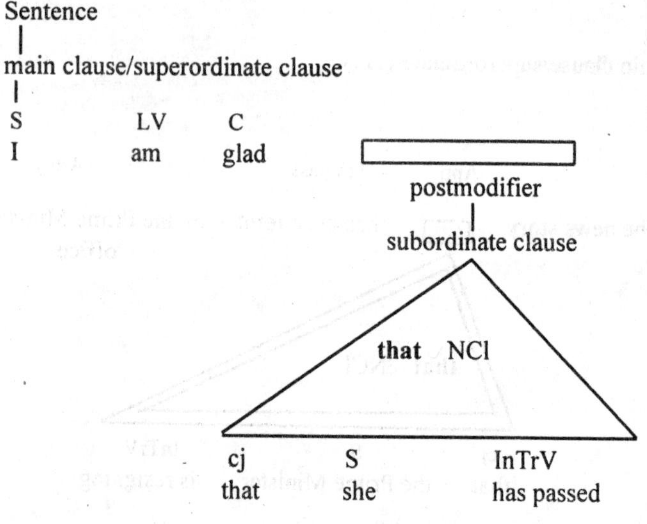

Some of the adjectives and past participles that can be followed by a **that-** clause are:

afraid	*aware*	*alarmed*	*amazed*	*annoyed*	*astonished*
certain	*confident*	*disturbed*	*glad*	*grateful*	*happy*
hopeful	*pleased*	*proud*	*sad*	*shocked*	*sorry*

It is possible to drop the conjunction **that** in an informal style:

I am glad she has passed. [48a]

Exercise 9

Analyse these sentences into the main clause and subordinate clause:

1. Kiran is certain that she will get this job.
2. I am afraid you cannot join this course.
3. She is astonished that Rahul could do it.
4. I am convinced that he is a great writer.
5. We were hopeful that she would survive.

Extraposed: In this case the **that-** nominal is postponed, i.e., it is placed at the end of the clause. This happens when the **that-** nominal clause is used at the subject position followed by **be** as the linking verb and the subject complement:

S LV Cs

That he is not going to help you is clear. [51a]

Sentence 51a can be transformed into 51b by shifting the **that-** nominal clause to the end of the sentence:

Anticipatory Subject LV Cs Postponed (extraposed) subject

It is clear that he is not going to help you. [51b]

Notice that when the **that-** nominal clause, *that he is not going to help you*, is postponed, the position of the subject at the beginning of the sentence is replaced by the anticipatory subject *it*. Sentence 51a may sound little odd, whereas 51b is more acceptable. In 51a the subject is rather long and heavy. The single-word complement *clear* in 51a is no match for the heavy subject, *that he is not going to help you*. Thus, in order to balance the long and heavy subject in the beginning, it is replaced by the anticipatory *it* and the real subject is delayed or postponed to the end of the sentence. However, if the predicate is also long, then the subject may not be postponed.

> That the summer vacation has been shortened
> will not affect our admission policy. [52]

7.5.1.2 Wh- interrogative clauses: Wh- interrogative clauses can function as:

Subject:

> **What he has done** does not concern me. [53]
>
> **How you complete this job** depends on your skill. [54]

Sentence 53 is derived from two simple sentences:

> It does not concern me. [53a]
>
> What has he done? [53b]

Sentence **b** is inserted in the subject position of sentence **a:**

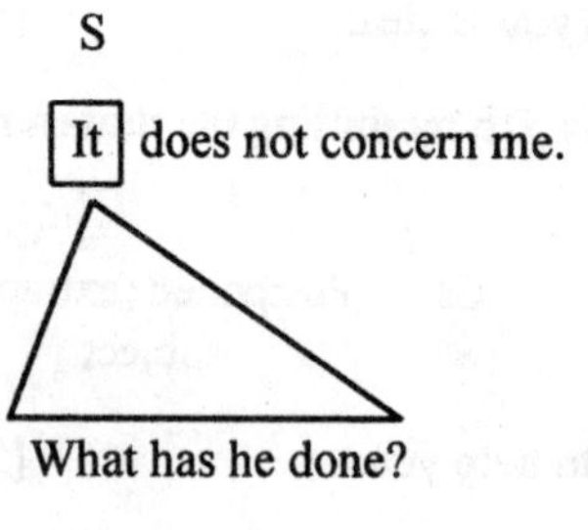

S

It does not concern me.

What has he done?

In the case of **wh-** interrogative clauses, the **wh-** word itself functions as a subordinating conjunction. In 52 **what** functions as the subordinating conjunction. In addition, the **wh-** word functions as the S, O, C or Adv element of the subordinate clause. As a general rule, the subordinate clause has the structure of a declarative clause. Therefore, the inversion of *has* and the subject *he* does not function in the subordinate clause. Thus we get sentence 53:

What he has done does not concern me. [53]

In this sentence, *what he has done*, is the subordinate clause functioning as the subject. We can indicate the relationship between the main clause and the subordinate clause in sentence 52 as follows:

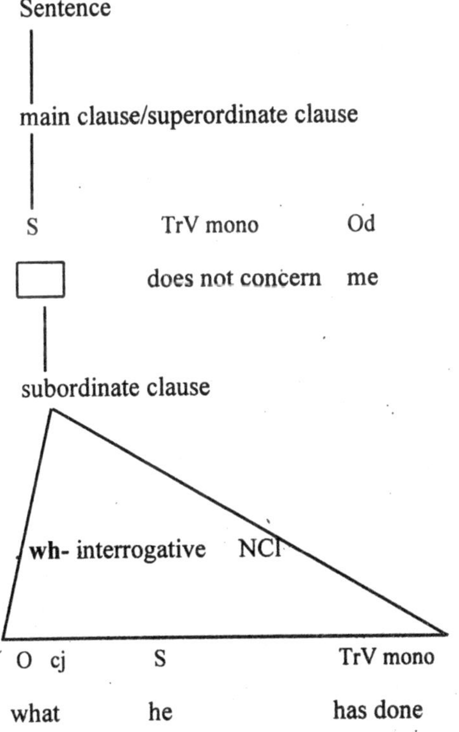

Direct object:

I don't know **where he has left the keys.** [55]

She asked me **why they were not coming.** [56]

Sentence 55 can be analysed as:

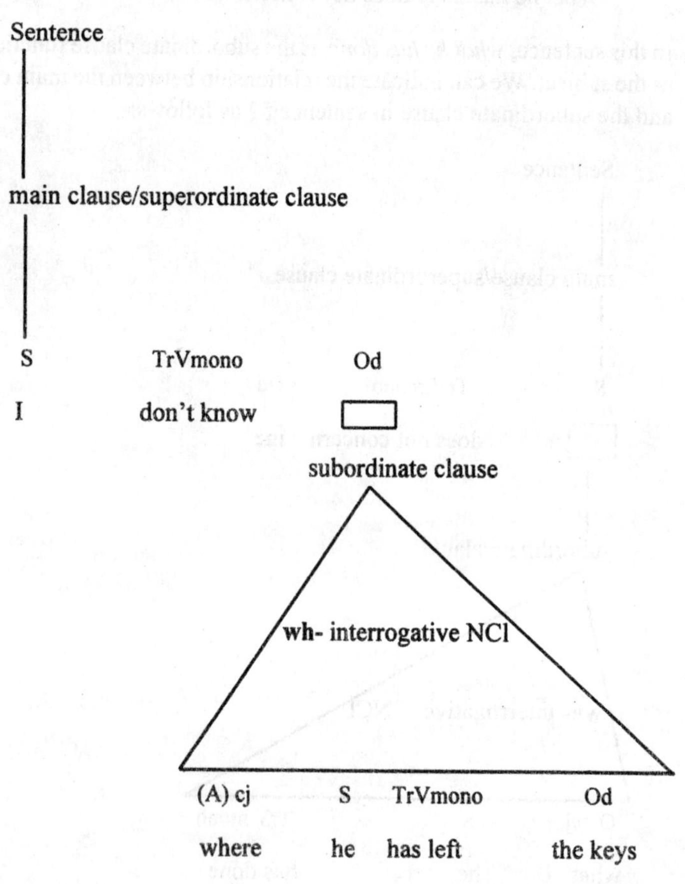

Similarly sentence 56 can be analysed as:

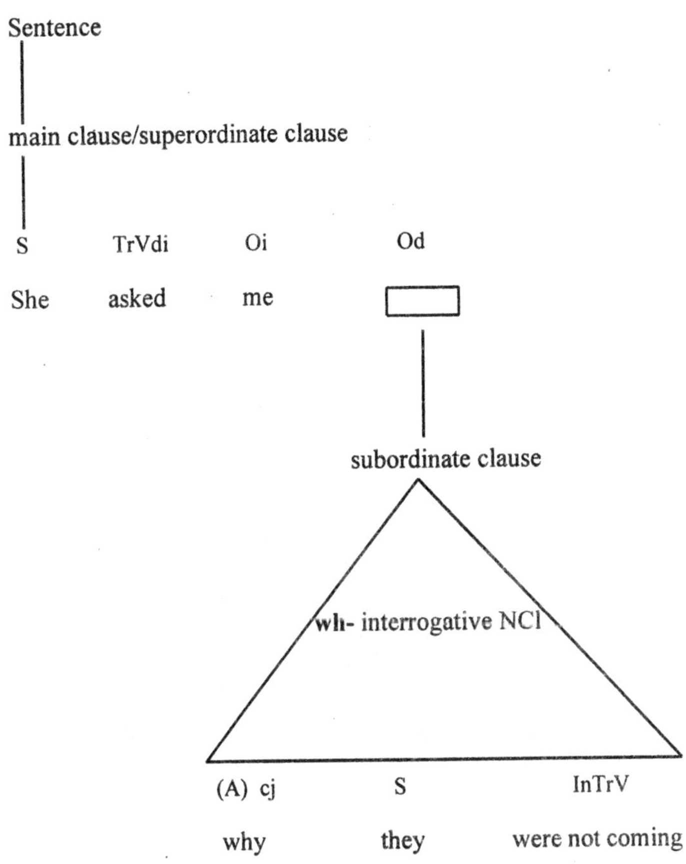

Subject complement:

The question is how we can solve this problem. [57]

The problem is why he can't attend classes. [58]

Sentence 58 can be analysed as follows:

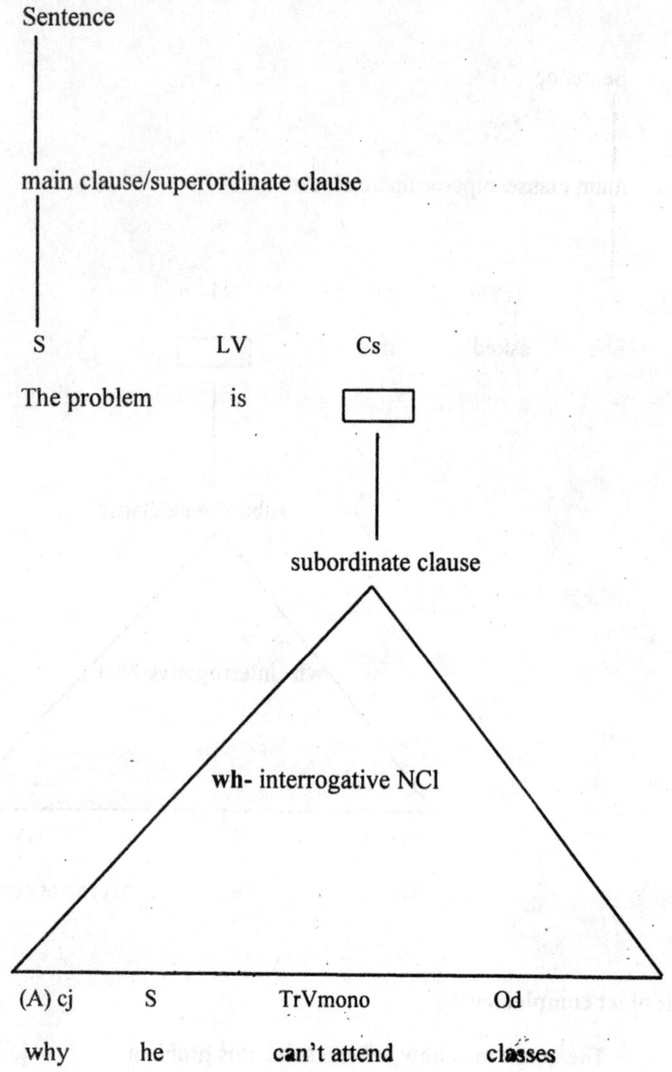

Appositive:

His question, why she did not attend the meeting, is important for this inquiry. [59]

Sentence 59 can be analysed as follows:

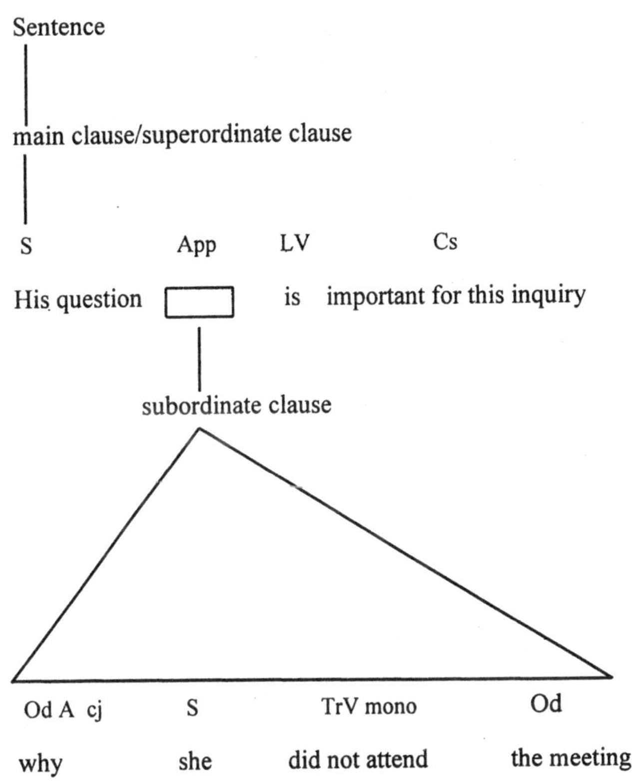

Adjectival complementation:

I was not sure **what she would say.** [60]

Meera was careful **how she spent the money.** [61]

We can insert a preposition between the adjective and the **wh-** interrogative clause in the case of some adjectives:

I was not sure of what she would say. [60a]

Meera was careful about how she spent the money. [61a]

Sentence 60 can be analysed as:

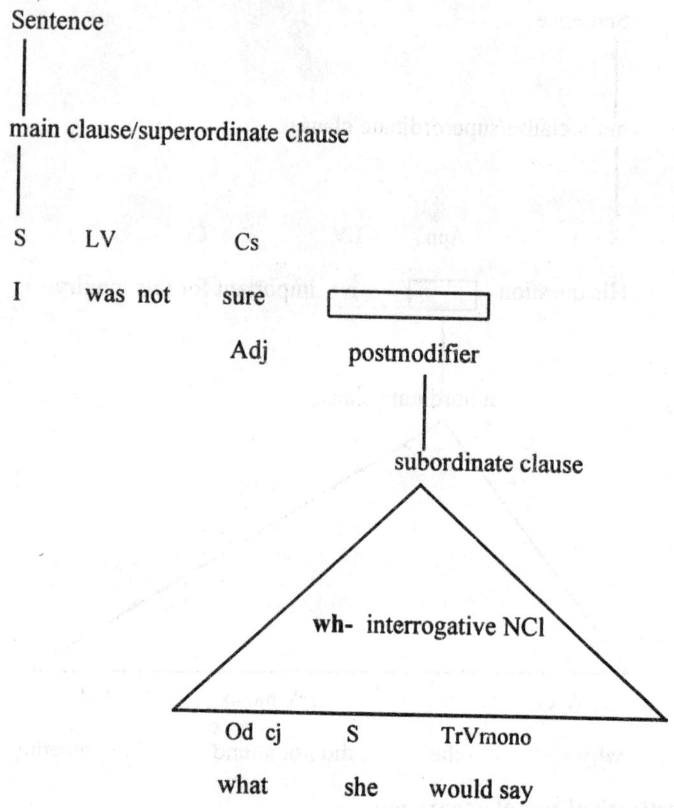

It was obvious why she behaved like that. [62]

It is unknown who constructed this pillar. [63]

Notice that in 62 and 63 the **wh-** interrogative clauses are extraposed subjects with the following structure:

anticipatory subject						extraposed subject
It	+	be	+	Cs	+	wh- clause

Exercise 10

***Combine these pairs of sentences in such a way that the* wh-*interrogative sentence is used as a* wh-*interrogative clause in place of* it:**

1. a. It is a secret.
   b. When will the Prime Minister arrive?
2. a. I know it.
   b. Why didn't he take the examination?
3. a. The best solution is this.
   b. What have you suggested?
4. a. It will depend on the Principal.
   b. How is the college run?
5. a. I can't tell it.
   b. Why did she arrive late?

Exercise 11

Analyse these sentences into the main clause/superordinate clause and the subordinate clause:

1. Why he could not win will be discussed at the next meeting.
2. Elizabeth asked me when the meeting would end.
3. The problem is who will teach this course.
4. I never believed what you told me.
5. His success depends on how he runs his business.

6. **I** was not sure of what she would say.
7. His question, why the matter was not reported to the police, should be answered immediately.
8. She was not certain when the examination would begin.
9. What you want is justified.
10. She didn't know how Nasreen would respond to her question.

7.5.1.3 Yes-no interrogative clauses: Subordinate **yes-no** interrogative clauses can be used for all those functions for which **wh-** interrogative clauses are used. However, we will mainly consider four major functions: subject, object, complement, and extraposed subject in detail.

Subject:

Whether he buys a house or a flat is his decision. [64]

Whether you attend the class or not does not matter now. [65]

Sentence 64 is derived from two simple sentences:

It is his decision. [a]

Does he buy a house or a flat? [b]

Sentence **b** is inserted in the subject position of sentence **a.**

S

It is his decision.

Does he buy a house or a flat?

As we stated in the previous section on **wh-** interrogative clauses, the subordinate clause has the structure of a declarative sentence. In addition, in the case of **yes-no** interrogative clauses we use the conjunction **whether/if. If** has a restricted use. In the case of the **yes-no** interrogative clause used at the subject position only **whether** is used. The relationship between the main clause and the subordinate clause for 64 can be shown as:

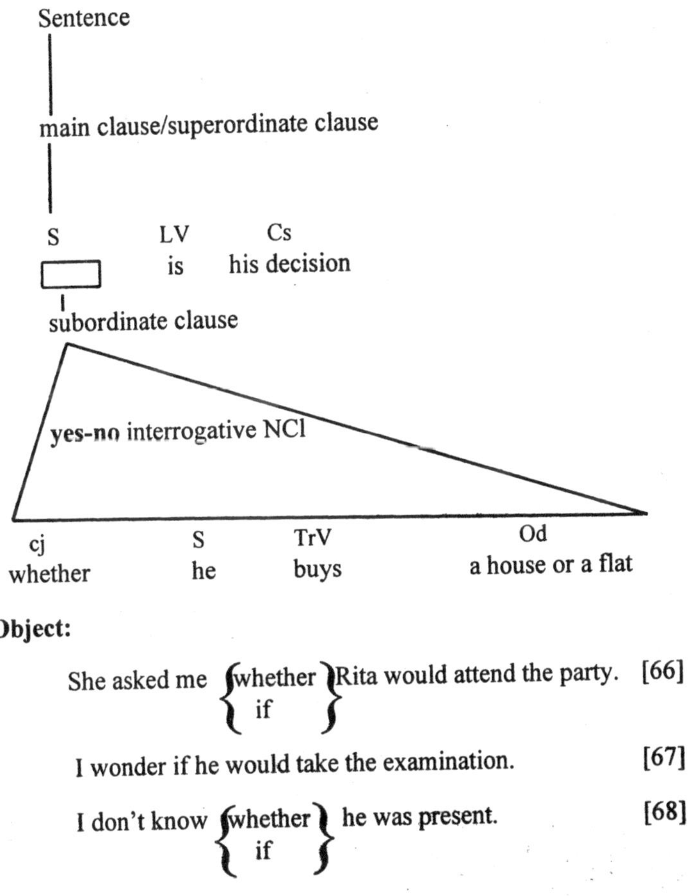

Object:

She asked me {whether / if} Rita would attend the party. [66]

I wonder if he would take the examination. [67]

I don't know {whether / if} he was present. [68]

Sentence 66 can be analysed as follows:

This sentence is derived from two simple sentences:

Od

She asked me [something.] [a]

Would Rita attend the party? [b]

Sentence **b** is inserted in the direct object position of sentence **a.**

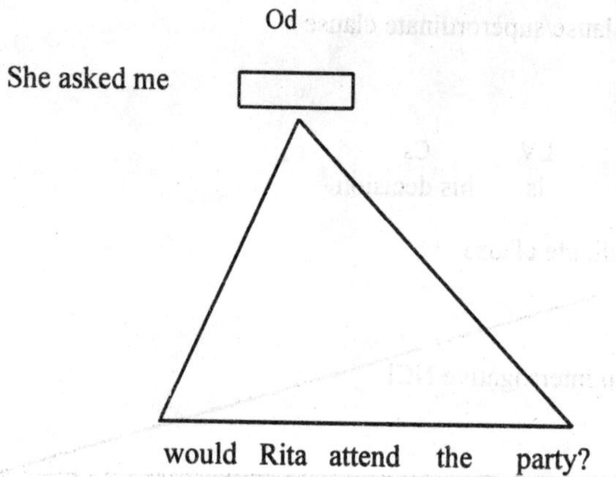

Whether or *if* is used as subordinating conjunction and the subordinate clause has the structure of the declarative sentence so that *would Rita attend the party*? is changed to {*whether* / *if*} *Rita would attend the party.*

Sentence 67 can be presented as follows:

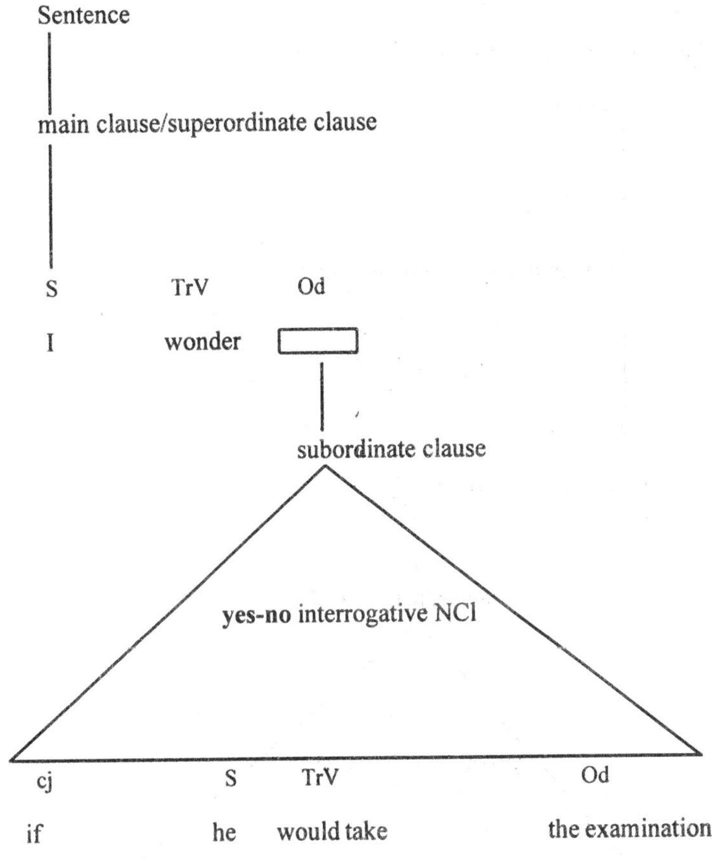

Notice that the use of **if** as conjunction is more frequent when the **yes-no** interrogative clause is used at the object position than at the other positions in a sentence.

Subject complement:

The question is whether she can contest the election. [69]

My problem is whether I can complete the project during the vacation. [70]

Sentence 69 can be presented as follows:

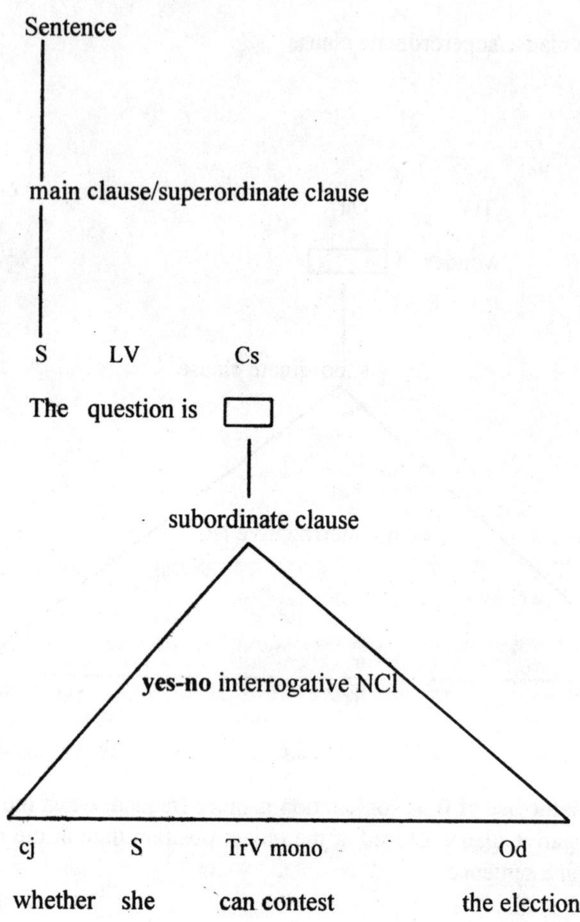

Notice that **if** cannot be used as conjunction when the **yes-no** interrogative clause is a subject complement.

Extraposed subject: The **yes-no** interrogative clause may also be used as the postponed subject:

It does not concern me {whether / if} he likes my lectures or not. [71]

It is immaterial whether he takes the examination or not. [72]

Sentence 71 can be analysed as follows:

As *whether/if he likes my lectures or not,* is an extraposed or delayed subject, 71 has been derived from sentence 71a.

Whether he likes my lectures or not does not concern me. [71a]

Sentence 71a can be transformed into sentence 71 by shifting the **yes-no** interrogative clause to the end position.

Anticipatory Subject	TrV	Od	postponed (extraposed) subject
It	does not concern	me	{whether / if} he likes my lectures or not.

The **if** clause cannot be used at the subject position but it can be used as the delayed subject.

Appositive:

His question, **whether she would vote for us,** has not been answered. [73]

Adjectival complement:

I am not sure {whether / if} I should attend the meeting. [74]

The use of **yes-no** interrogative clauses as appositive and adjectival complement is not very frequent.

Exercise 12

***Combine these pairs of sentences in such a way that the* yes-no *interrogative sentence is used as a subordinate clause in place of* it/ this/something *in sentence* a:**

1. a. It depended a great deal on her recovery.
   b. Could she take part in the game?
2. a. Our main concern is this.
   b. Will she join us before lunch time?
3 a. Jivan asked her something.
   b. Had she worked earlier?
4. a. It is your decision.
   b. Do you study or play?
5. a. She asked me something.
   b. Could Meena stay with them?

Exercise 13

Analyse these sentences into the main clause/superordinate clause and the subordinate clause, and label the elements of each clause:

1. I wonder if he could lift that stone.
2. The question is whether he ever borrowed a book from the library.
3. Whether he goes to Delhi or to Calcutta depends on his result.
4. I don't know if he wants me to join the company.
5. It is immaterial whether she takes part in the dance or not.
6. I am not certain if he can do this job successfully.
7. Whether Rajiv has written this letter or not is not clear to me.

8. I am not sure whether she would pass the examination.
9. Mohini enquired whether the postman had come.
10. It is irrelevant whether you help us or not.

7.5.1.4 Nominal relative clauses: Nominal relative clauses function like nominal clauses and resemble **wh-** interrogative clauses, because they are introduced by a **wh-** element. However, nominal relative clauses in some ways resemble noun phrases or modifiers of the noun phrase. Like relative clauses, nominal relative clauses can refer to concrete and abstract things including human beings.

Whoever did this is a genius. [75a]

I ate **whatever was left on the table.** [76a]

In 75a *whoever did this* is the nominal relative clause used at the subject position. *Whoever did this*, may be paraphrased as:

The person who did this is a genius. [75b]

In 75b, *the person who did this*, is the subject and *who did this*, is the relative clause modifying the noun *the person*, and *the person who did this*, is the noun phrase. What has happened in 75a is that the head noun, person and the relative pronoun, *who* have been merged together and what we get is *whoever*. Thus in a nominal relative clause, the head noun and the relative pronoun merge into a **wh-** element.

Similarly, we can paraphrase sentence 76a and get 76b.

I ate **the food which was left on the table.** [76b]

The head noun, *food*, is merged with the relative pronoun *which* into a single word *whatever*. Thus, we may assume that the nominal relative clause is derived via the relative clause. Therefore, we may say that 75a is derived from these simple sentences:

The person is a genius. [a]

He did it. [b]

Sentence **b** is inserted in sentence **a** in such a way that sentence **b** is transformed into a relative clause. (*For details on relative clauses, refer to chapter 8, section 8.1*).

The person < he did it > is a genius.

We get sentence c:

The person who did it is a genius. [c]

When, *the person*, and *who*, are merged, we get, *whoever*. We may analyse sentence 75a and 76a into the main clause and subordinate clause as follows:

Sentence 75a

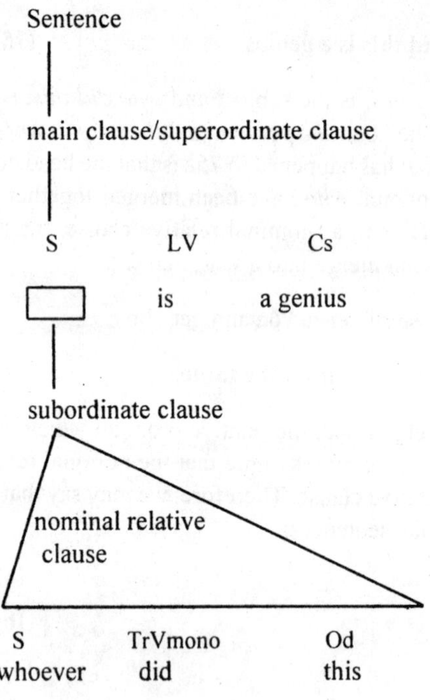

Sentence 76a:

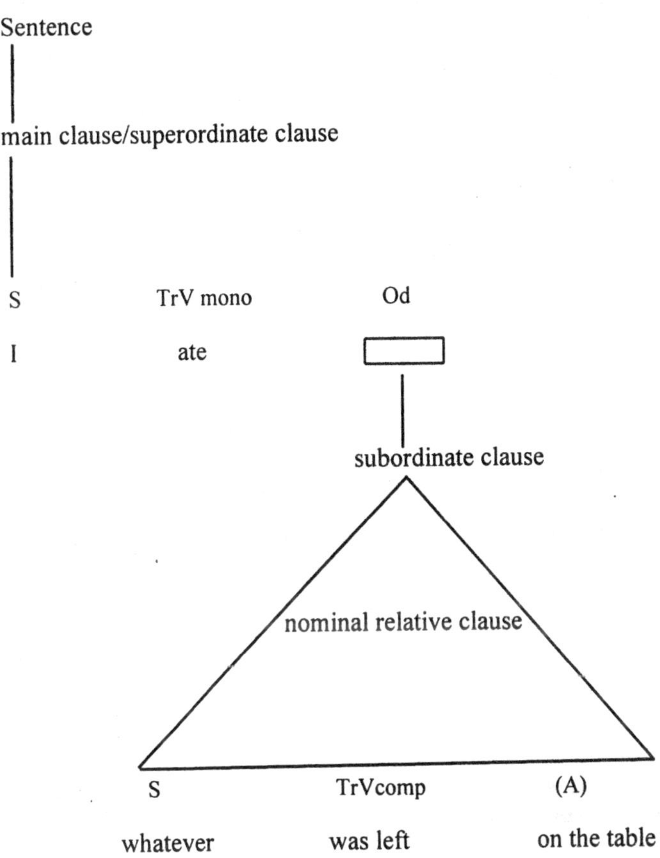

The **wh-** elements in a nominal relative clause can function as subject, direct object, subject complement, etc.

Subject:

Whoever did this is a genius. [75a]

I ate **whatever** was left on the table. [76a]

Direct object:

What he said was true. [77]

Subject complement:

He is not happy with **what** his son has become. [78]

Object complement:

I didn't like **what** he called his office. [79]

Nominal relative clauses can also function as subject, direct object, subject complement, and object complement:

Subject: **What he told you** was true. [80]

Direct object: He told you **whatever he knew.** [81]

Subject complement: She is **who you want to see.** [82]

Object complement: She called him **whatever came to her mind.** [83]

Prepositional complement: You can go to **whoever you like.** [84]

Exercise 14

Analyse these sentences into the main clause/superordinate clause and the subordinate clause:

1. You may take whatever you need.
2. She called him whatever she liked.
3. What he saw was a flash gun.
4. That is where I was born.
5. You can give me whatever you have.
6. You can clean it with whatever you have at home.
7. Whoever knocked at the door must have been in a hurry.

8. I liked what you gave her.
9. I'm who you want to interview.
10. He believed what you told him.

7.5.1.5 To- infinitive nominal clauses: To- infinitive clauses can function as subject, direct object, subject complement, appositive and adjectival complement. **To-** infinitive clauses are non-finite clauses and do not carry tense.

Subject:

For me to act on stage is not possible. [85]

To watch *Jurassic Park* in the theatre is my keen desire. [86]

We may analyse 85 as follows:

It is derived from two simple sentences:

S

It is not possible. [a]

I act on stage. [b]

Sentence b is inserted in sentence a at the subject position, so that we get:

S

[ ] is not possible [c]

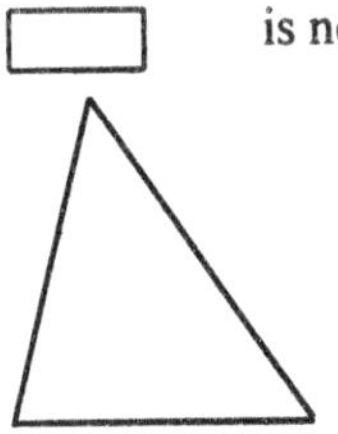

I act on stage

As **that** is used as the subordinating conjunction in a **that-** nominal clause, **for-to** is used as the subordinating conjunction in the case of **to-** infinitive clauses. **For,** if used in a **to-** infinitive clause, should not be treated as a preposition. If we treat it as a preposition, it will not be directly linked to the subordinate clause. As shown in the analysis of sentence 85, there is no grammatical rule by which **for** can be inserted as a preposition. Therefore, **for** is a part of the subordinating conjunction, the other part being **to. For** is placed before the subject and **to** before the verb of the subordinate clause. In the case of pronouns, the object case is used after **for,** even though the pronoun is the subject of the subordinate clause. Thus from **c** above, we get sentence 85:

For me to act on stage is not possible. [85]

Although **for-to** is a part of the subordinating conjunction, for the sake of clarity and convenience, we may treat **for me** as the subject and **to act** as the verb of the subordinate clause. Therefore, sentence 85 may be represented as:

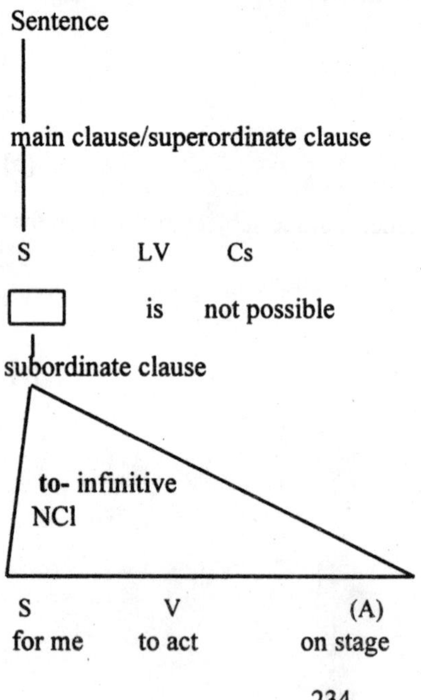

There are **to-** infinitive clauses, such as 86, which do not have the subject but the subject can be understood from the structure of the main clause. Sentence 86, therefore, is derived from the two simple sentences:

S

It is my keen desire. [a]

I watch *Jurassic Park* in the theatre. [b]

Sentence **b** is inserted in sentence **a** at the subject position.

S

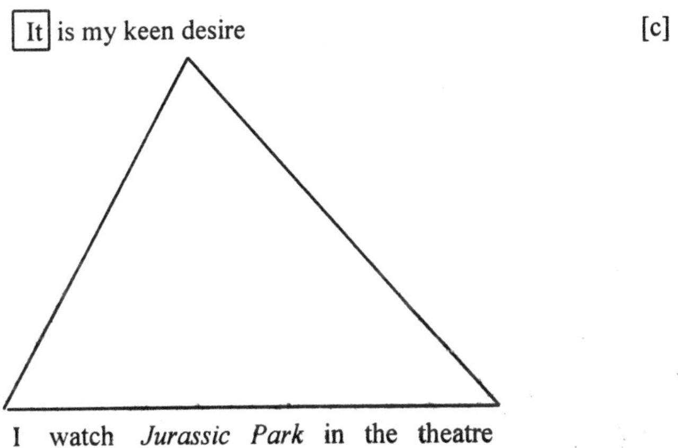

Using **for-to** as conjunction, sentence d is derived.

For me to watch *Jurassic Park* in the theatre
is my keen desire. [d]

As the subject of the subordinate clause *I* (*for me* in d) has a common referent in the possessive pronoun *my* (part of the subject complement of the main clause) *it* is dropped and sentence 86 is derived.

To watch *Jurassic Park* in the theatre is my keen desire. [86]

Sentence 86 can be represented as:

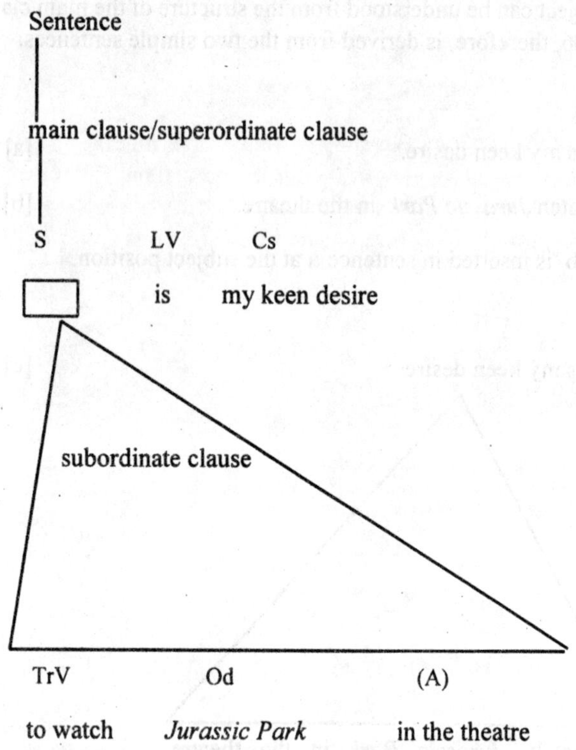

to watch *Jurassic Park* in the theatre

The subject is also dropped in those infinitive clauses, used at the subject position, where the subject refers to a generic human noun.

To err is human. [87]

is derived from

For anyone to err is human.

Direct object:

She likes **to watch the DD Metro show.** [88]

I want her **to watch the DD Metro show.** [89]

There are two important observations on the use of the **to-** infinitive clause at the position of the direct object.

i. If the subject of the **to-** infinitive clause has a common referent in the main clause, **it** is dropped, e.g. sentence **88**.

ii. If the subject of the **to-** infinitive clause does not have a common referent in the main clause, then **it** is retained but **for** is dropped. **For** is not used, when the **to-** infinitive clause is used at the direct object position. Sentences **88** and **89** can be presented as follows:

Sentence 88:

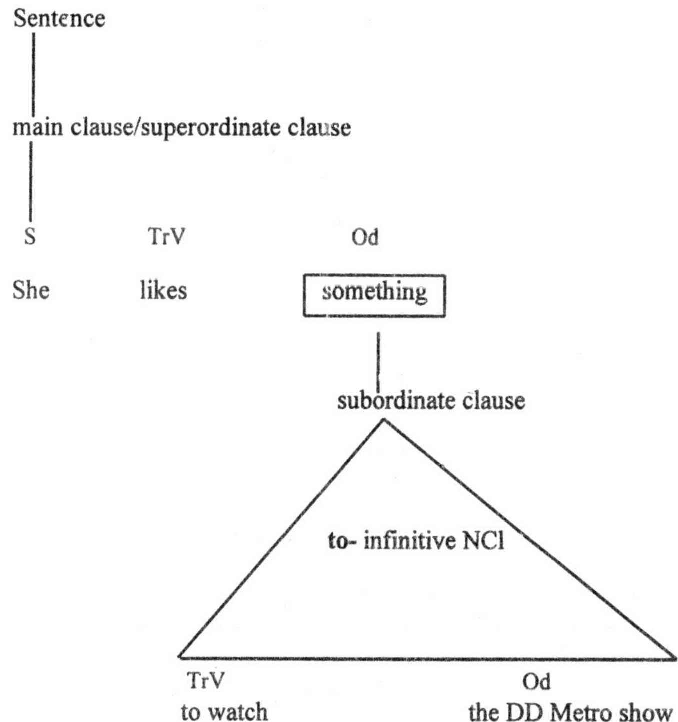

Sentence 89:

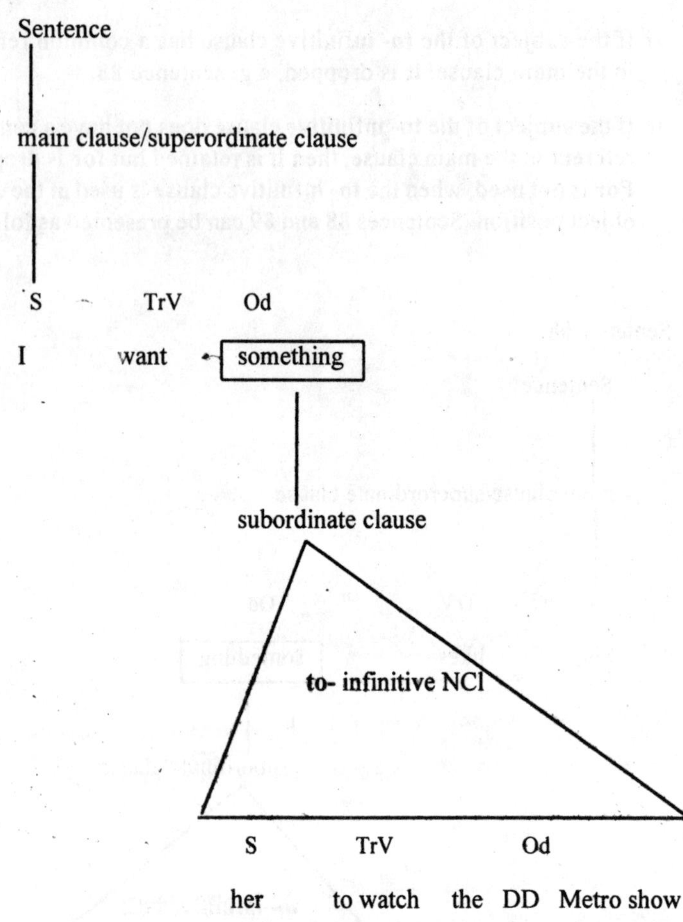

In the case of ditransitive verbs, a slightly different analysis is required. Ditransitive verbs like, *advise, teach, tell,* require an indirect object before the **to-** infinitive clause as the direct object position is used. The direct object after such verbs should not be confused with the subject of the **to-** infinitive clause.

Compare sentences 90 and 91.

I want **him to take rest.** [90]

I advised him **to take rest.** [91]

Notice that *want* in 90 is a monotransitive verb.

Him to take rest is the direct object. Sentence 90 can be represented as:

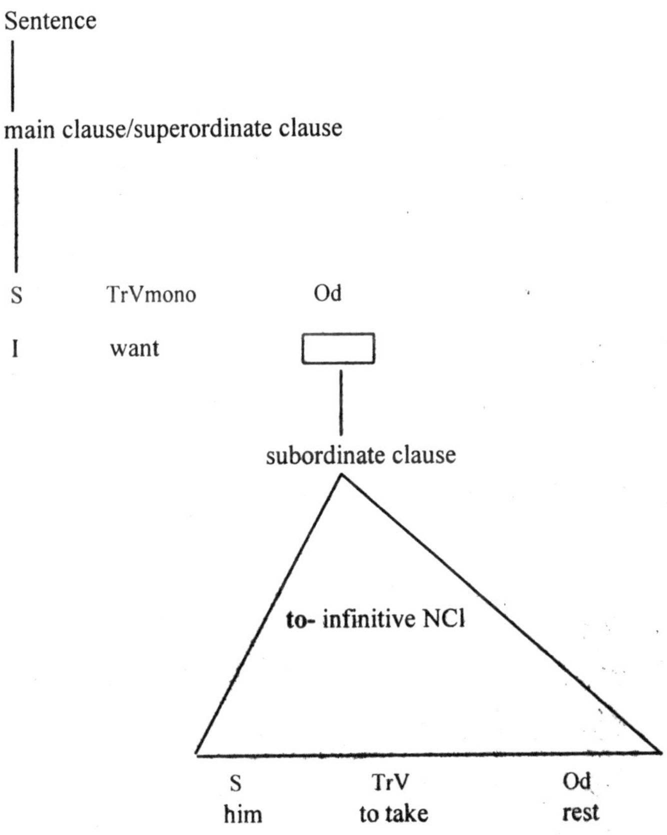

Advised in 91 is a distransitive verb and thus requires two objects. Sentence 91 can be represented as:

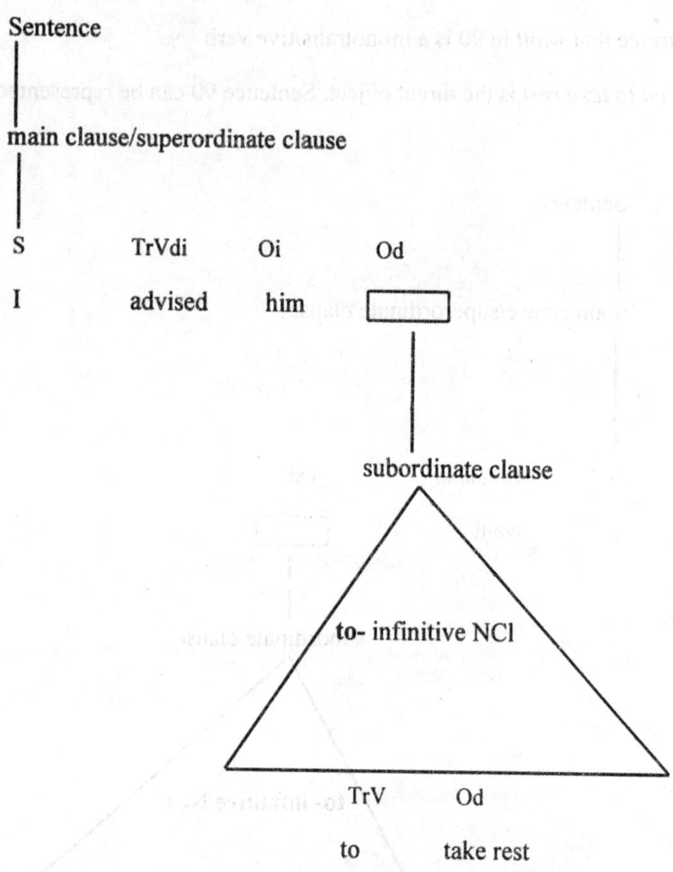

Sentence 91 can be derived from two simple sentences **a** and **b**:

I advised him something. [a]

He took rest. [b]

Sentence **b** is inserted in sentence **a** at the direct object position so that we get **c.**

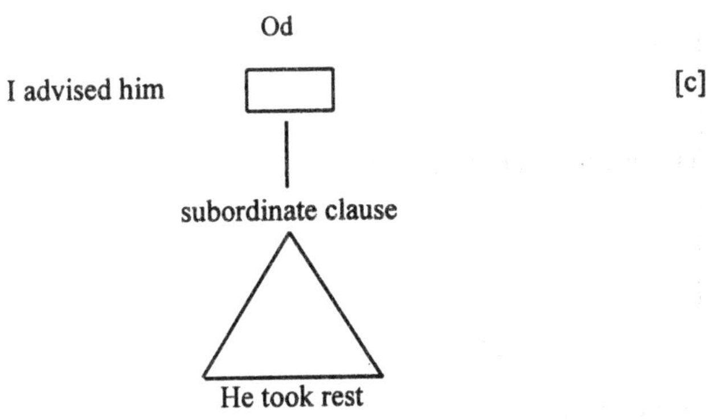

[c]

Using the conjunction **for-to,** we get **d.**

I advised him for him to take rest. [d]

As the subject of the subordinate clause *for him* in **d** and the indirect object of the main clause have common referents, the subject of the subordinate clause *for him* is dropped and we get 91.

I advised him to take rest. [91]

Some more examples of ditransitive verbs with **to**- infinitive clauses are:

I asked her **to be regular.** [92]

She requested me **to help her.** [93]

Subject complement:

The best thing is **to relax.** [94]

His ambition is **to become a lawyer.** [95]

Sentence 94 can be represented as:

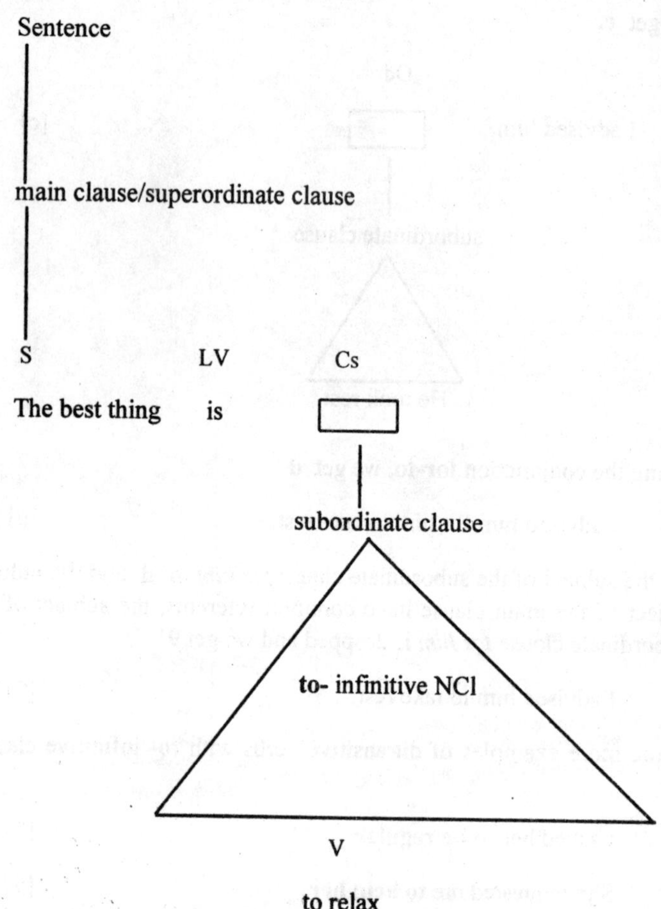

Appositive:

My plan, to attack the enemy from the left wing, has been accepted by the commanding officer. [96]

Your desire, to visit Shimla in June, can be fulfilled. [97]

Sentence 96 can be presented as:

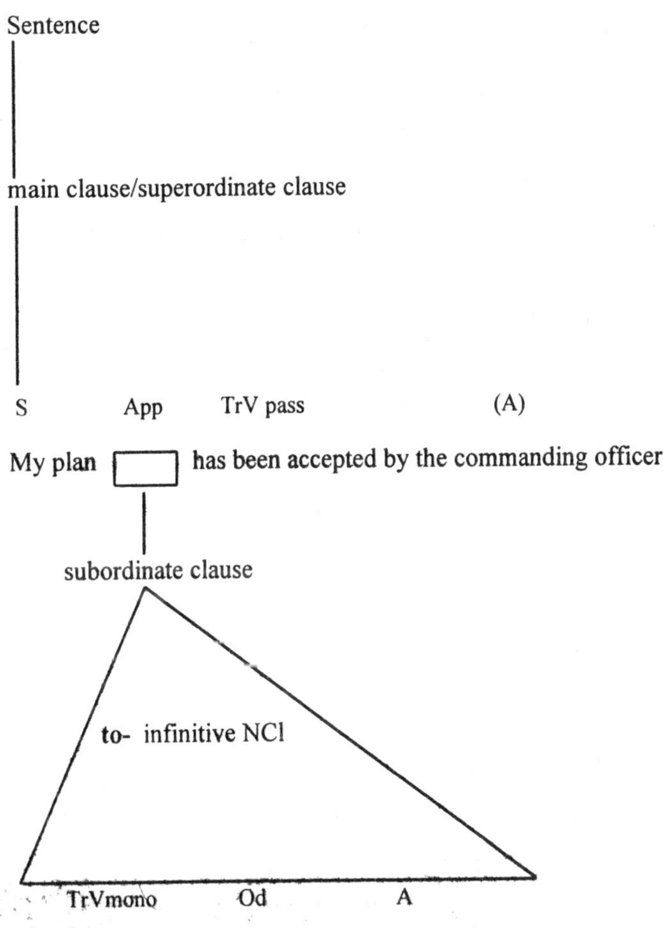

Adjectival complement:

I am keen **to do this project.** [98]

Vikram is very eager **to meet you.** [99]

Sentence 98 is derived from two simple sentences:

S	LV		Cs	
I	am	keen	for something	[a]
		Adj	postmodifier	

I do this project. [b]

Sentence **b** is inserted in sentence **a** at the position of the postmodifier, so that we get **c**.

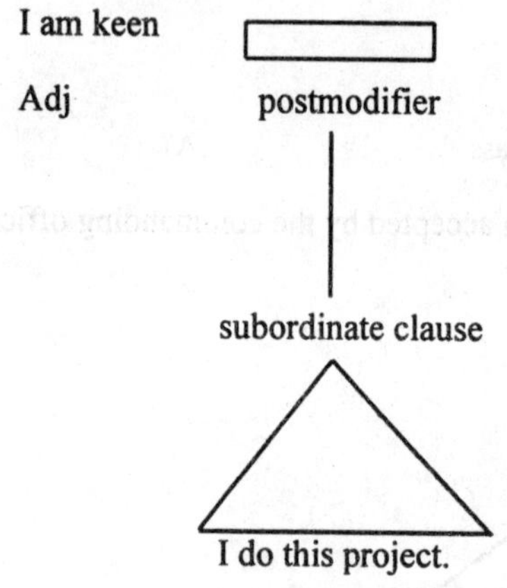

Using **for-to** as subordinating conjunction, we get:

I am keen **for me to do this project.** [d]

As the subject of the main clause and the subject of the subordinate clause are common referents, **for-me** in the subordinate clause can be dropped and we get sentence 98.

Extraposed subject:

It is easy **to solve this problem.** [100]

It is important **for you to go there.** [101]

As in the case of the other extraposed clauses, the **to-** infinitive clause is derived from the subject position. For example, 100 can be derived from 100a and 101 from 101a.

To solve this problem is easy. [100a]

For you to go there is important. [101a]

Exercise 15

***Combine these pairs of sentences in such* a *way that sentence* b *is used as a* to- *infinitive clause in place of* it/something/this *in sentence* a:**

1. a. She likes something.
   b. Her friends visit her.
2. a. The director instructed all the officers something.
   b. The officers are punctual.
3. a. It is my dream.
   b. I visit London.
4. a. She seems something.
   b. She is temperamental.
5. a. I told her something.
   b. She met me at the station.
6. a. She persuaded me something.
   b. I took up the job.
7. a. She is very keen on something.
   b. She meets you.
8. a. He is sure of this.
   b. He will pass the examination.
9. a. It is extremely disgraceful.
   b. An army withdraws like that.
10. a. The best remedy is this.
    b. One sleeps for two hours.

Exercise 16

Analyse these sentences into the main clause/superordinate clause and the subordinate clause, and label the elements of each clause:

1. To do one's best is the right thing.
2. Manohar instructed the constable to control the traffic.
3. I would like to see him tomorrow.
4. My plan is to visit my grandma during the summer vacation.
5. Our proposal, to start a new department, has been accepted.
6. It is fun to watch this film.
7. She was very happy to meet you.
8. For a country to survive such an economic disaster in the twentieth century is a great achievement.
9. He forced Nirmal to go by bus.
10. Your plan to visit your grandma during the summer vacation, is absolutely great.

7.5.1.6 -ing clauses

In traditional grammar **-ing** clauses have been treated as gerunds but we shall treat them as non-finite clauses for a better understanding of their structure. These clauses can function as subject, direct object, subject complement, appositive, adjectival complement (though limited) and prepositional complement.

Subject:

Walking on sand can be great fun. [102]

Kapil's surpassing Hadley's record was a milestone for Indian cricket. [103]

Sentence 102 can be analysed as follows:

This sentence is derived from two simple sentences:

S

It can be great fun. [a]

One walks on sand. [b]

Sentence b is inserted in sentence **a** in the subject position as shown in **c.**

S

can be great fun [c]

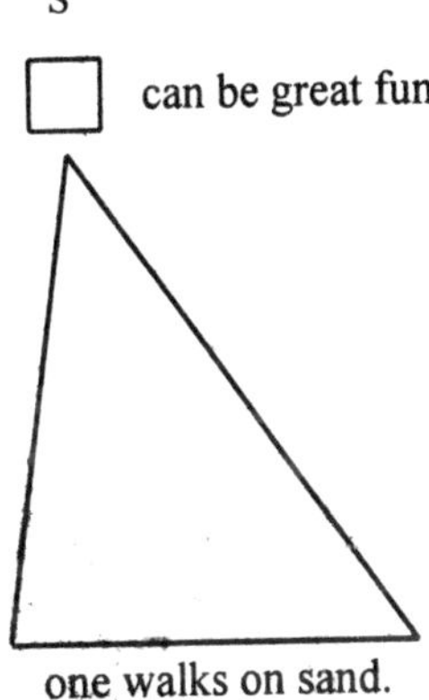

one walks on sand.

As in the case of **to-** infinitive clauses, where **for-to** as conjunction is used, in the case of **-ing** clauses, the conjunction NP's (genitive case), **V + ing** is used in the above sentence. **NP's** is used for the subject and **V + ing** for the verb of the subordinate clause. Thus we get:

One's walking on sand can be great fun. [d]

However, if the subject has an indefinite person reference **it** may be dropped and we get sentence [102].

Therefore, 102 can be presented as follows:

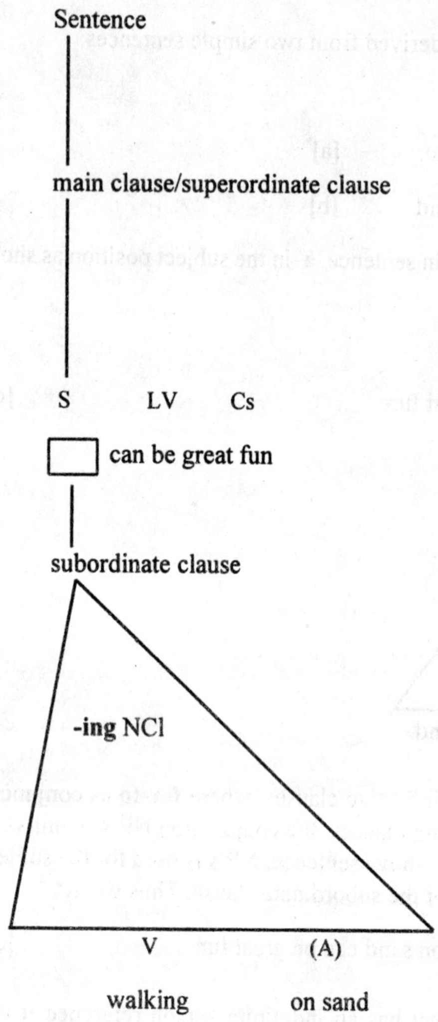

Similarly, 103 can be presented as:

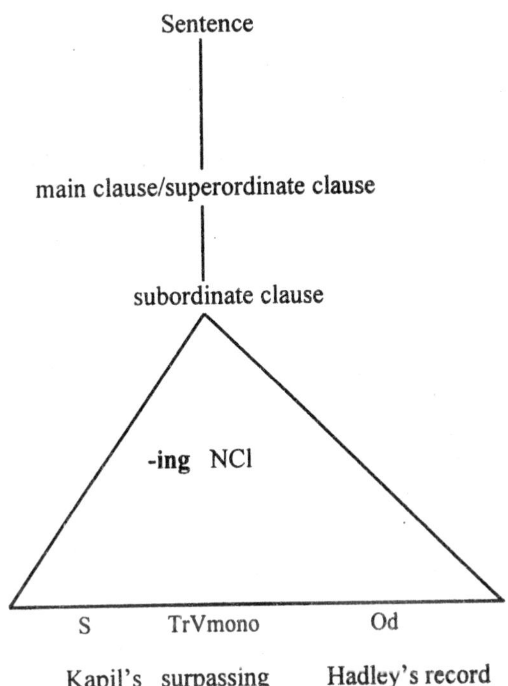

Direct object:

Meena enjoys **playing hockey.** [104]

Manisha can't bear **Mohan drinking all evening.** [105]

She can't bear **him drinking all evening.** [106]

Sentence 104 can be analysed on the basis of the rules mentioned for the subject position. The subject of the subordinate clause in sentence 104 has been dropped because it has a common referent in the subject of the main clause i.e. *she*. Sentences 105 and 106 need some explanation. They can be analysed as follows:

Sentence 105/106 is made of the following two simple sentences:

Manisha can't bear it. [a]

He drinks all evening. [b]

Sentence **b** is inserted in sentence **a** in the position of the direct object.

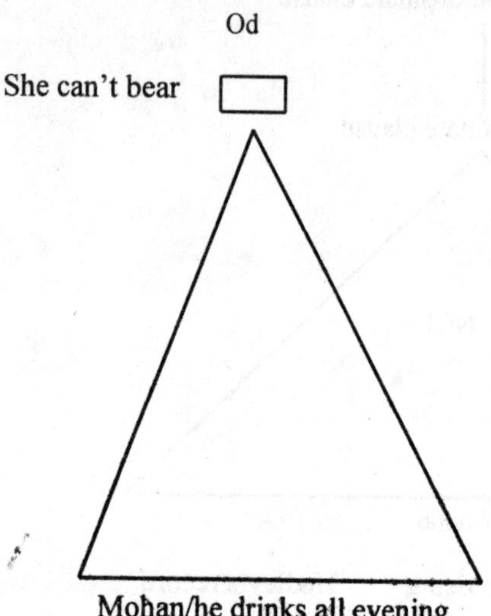

The conjunction (NP's V + **ing**) used for the subject position does not work here, though in 104 we use NP's - V + **ing** only. For inserting sentence **b** into **a** in the sentences above, the conjunction NP -**ing** is used. In the case of nouns the common case is used and in the case of pronouns the objective case is used. It is possible to use NP's -V + **ing** for 106, so that we have:

She can't bear **his drinking all evening.** [107]

NP + V + **ing** may be used in the informal style and NP's - V + **ing** in the formal style. Therefore, sentence 106/107 can be presented as:

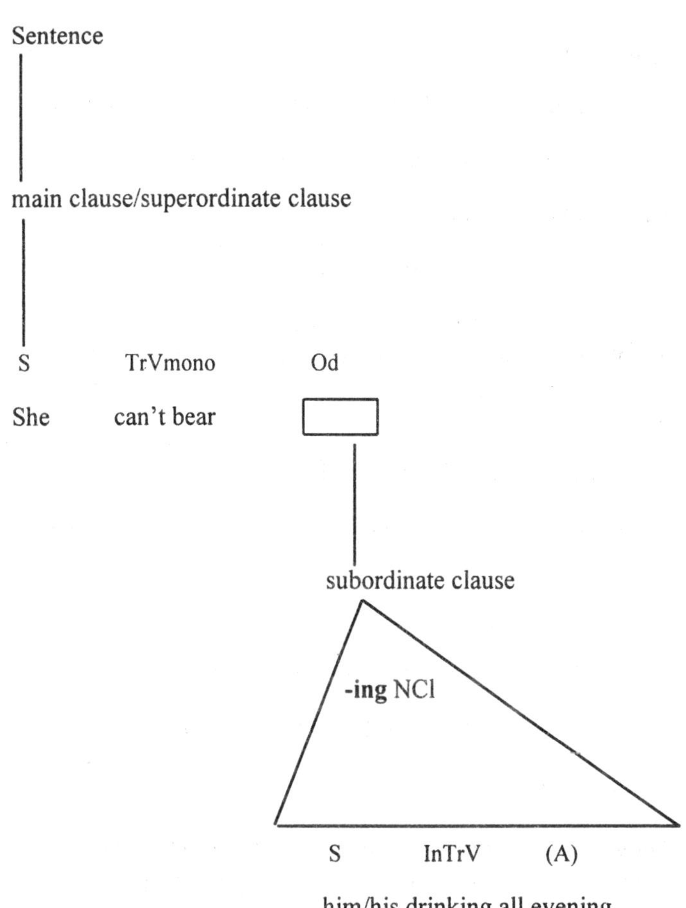

Subject complement:

His pastime is **watching TV.** [108]

The best moment was **our staging *Macbeth* in the open-air theatre.** [109]

Appositive:

His proposal, **reducing the annual deficit,** seems good. [110]

Her hobby, **reading novels,** keeps her busy. [111]

Adjectival complement:

They are busy **drafting letters.** [112]

There is restricted use of the **-ing** nominal clauses as adjectival complements, because most of the adjectives require prepositions to be followed by an **-ing** nominal clause. Even sentence 112 can be rewritten as:

They are busy in **drafting letters.** [113]

and in such a case the **-ing** clause becomes the complement of a preposition.

Preposition complement:

I am keen on **joining the swimming club.** [114]

She is not capable of **taking up any responsibility.** [115]

Exercise 17

***Combine these pairs of sentences in such a way that sentence* b *is used as an* - ing *nominal clause in place of* it/something/this *in sentence* a:**

1. a. I don't like it. b. He sings in the classroom.
2. a. It used to be a cricketer's delight. b. The cricketer watched Gavaskar on the field.
3. a. The best event was this. b. Niraj played for our team.
4. a. Her job is this. b. She prepares the annual balance sheet.
5. a. Dilip regrets it. b. He talked to you rudely.

6. a. It is a serious matter. b. Ravi fell in the playfield.
7. a. Rita is responsible for this. b. She declares the results.
8. a. It is injurious to health. b. One smokes.
9. a. Sameer loves it. b. He visits hill stations.
10. a. Her ambition was this. b. Her son reached the top.

Exercise 18

Analyse these sentences into the main clause/superordinate clause and the subordinate clause, and label the elements of each clause:

1. Your playing loud music disturbs us at night.
2. Her job is ringing the bell in school.
3. She enjoyed listening to classical music.
4. Rekha is not capable of doing anything.
5. She is busy cooking lunch.
6. I don't like people driving their cars fast.
7. Playing games can develop a child's mind.
8. He is hopeless at preparing bills.
9. They appreciated my working on Sundays.
10. Sending your son to hostel was a mistake.

Exercise 19

Analyse these sentences into the main clause/superordinate clause and the subordinate clause, and label the elements of each clause:

1. The assumption is that the war will end.
2. Ajay assumed that you would join our team.
3. I want to sleep for an hour.
4. Her ambition, to become an army officer, requires our support.
5. She is keen on joining the armed forces.

8

Complex Sentences - II

8.1 Relative/adjectival clauses:

As discussed in chapter 3.3.2.2, a relative clause functions as a postnomional modifier.

The girl < who is standing near the counter > is a television actress. [1]

The table < which we bought yesterday > is made of teak wood. [2]

A relative clause is introduced by a relative pronoun - **who, whom, which, that** or **whose,** or by a relative adverb - **where, when or why.**

8.1.1 The use of *who* and *whom*

a. **Who** and **whom** are always used in relative clauses referring to human beings. **Who** is the subject of the relative clause.

The gentleman **who came in the morning** has left a note for you. [3]

Sentence 3 consists of two simple sentences:

The gentleman has left a note for you. [a]

He came in the morning. [b]

The gentleman in sentence **a** and *he* in sentence **b** refer to the same person. Sentence **b** is inserted in sentence **a** so that sentence **b** modifies the *gentleman*.

The gentleman < he came in the morning > has left a note for you. [c]

He which is the subject of **b** and refers to the gentleman is replaced by the relative pronoun *who,* so that we get,

> The gentleman < who came in the morning > has left
> a note for you. [d]

> I met the coach who trained you. [4]

This sentence can be presented as:

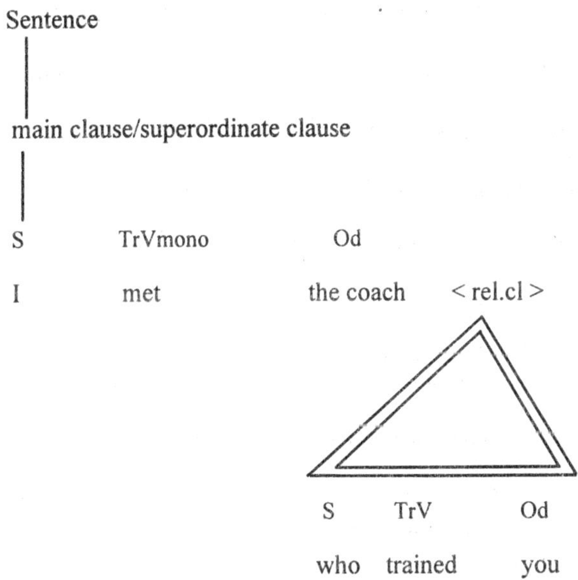

(Note: We have used two labels for *the coach* in sentence 4. One is the functional label Cs and the second is the formal label NP, because the relative clause modifies the NP. Secondly, we have used the < > for the relative clause rather than the ▭ that we used for nominal clauses. The reason for using < > relative clauses is that whereas the nominal clause is used in place of an element of the main clause, the relative clause does not replace an element of the main clause. The double lines for the triangle are also used to indicate this difference.)

b. **Whom/who: Whom** may be used as the object of the relative clause. However, nowadays **who** can also be used as the object of the relative clause. The difference between the use of **whom** and **who** as the object of the relative clause is that **whom** is used in a formal context and **who** is used in an informal context.

The girl < whom you selected > has drafted this letter. [5a]

The girl < who you selected > has drafted this letter. [5b]

In an informal context, it is possible to drop **whom/who.**

The girl < you selected > has drafted this letter. [5c]

Sentence 5a and 5b can be derived from two simple sentences:

The girl has drafted this letter. [a]

You selected her. [b]

Sentence **b** is inserted in sentence **a** so that sentence **b** modifies *the girl* in sentence **b.**

The girl < you selected > has drafted this letter. [c]

The girl of sentence **a** and *her* which is the direct object of sentence **b** are common referents. Therefore, *her* is replaced by **whom/who.**

The girl < you selected whom > has drafted this letter.

As a general rule the relative pronoun should be placed next to the noun it modifies. Therefore we get:

The girl whom you selected has drafted this letter.

Sentences 5a and 5b may be presented as:

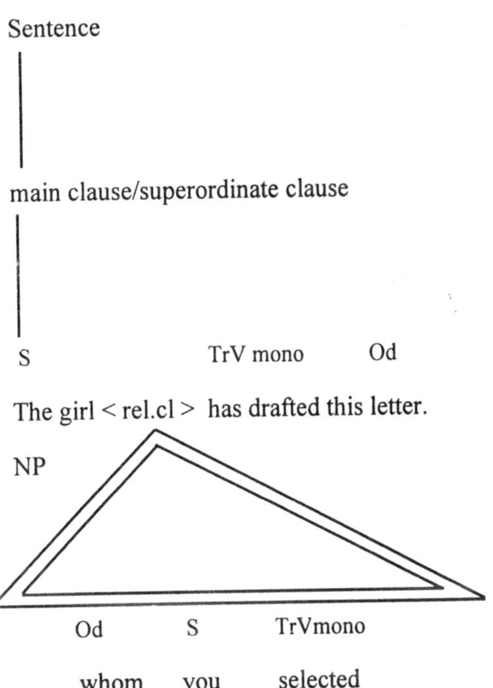

c. **Whom** is also used as the object of a preposition in a relative clause.

> The lady < with whom you travelled to Delhi > has sent you a card. [6a]
>
> She is the girl < for whom I bought these books >. [7a]

It is possible to separate the preposition from the relative pronoun and use the preposition towards the end of the relative clause. In such constructions, it is possible to use **who** or **whom.** However, some native speakers of English do not find this acceptable.

The lady < who you travelled with to Delhi > has sent you a card [6b]

She is the girl < who I bought these books for >.

Sentence 6a can be presented as follows:

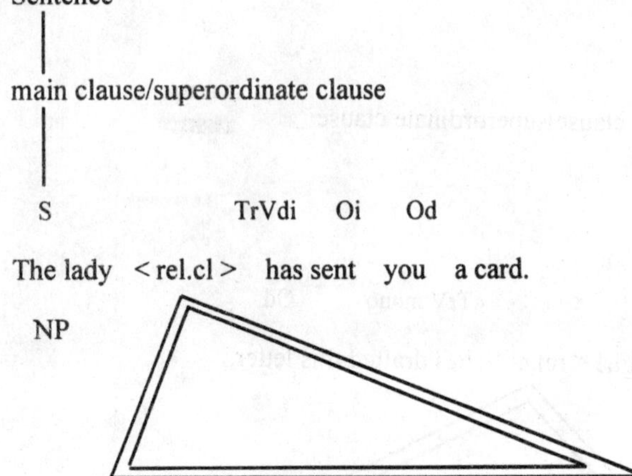

(A) S InTrV (A)

with whom you travelled to Delhi

prep object of prep

8.1.2 Which is used as a relative pronoun for non-human nouns like *dog, cow, table, chair, book* etc.

It can be used as the subject, object or object of preposition.

The scooter < which is lying under the shed > has been painted recently. [8]

I have bought the book < which you had recommended >. [9]

The house < in which I was born > was constructed in the nineteenth century. [10]

Sentence 8 can be split into two simple sentences:

The scooter has been painted recently. [a]

It is lying under the shed. [b]

Sentence **b** is inserted in sentence **a** so that we get:

The scooter < it is lying under the shed > has been painted recently. [c]

Notice that *it* (which refers to *the scooter* in sentence **a** is the subject of **b. It** is replaced by *which,* so that we get:

The scooter < which is lying under the shed > has been painted recently. [d]

Notice that *which* is the subject of the relative clause.

Sentence 9 can be presented as follows:

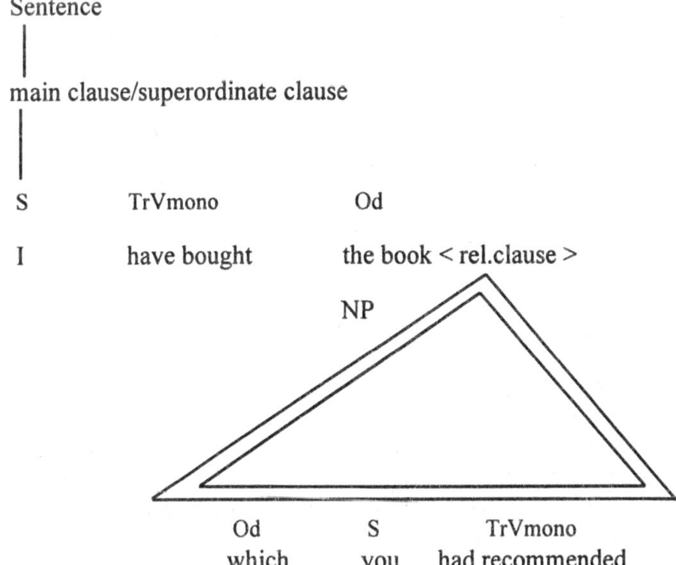

8.1.3 That can be used instead of **who, whom,** or **which.** This means that **that** can be used to refer to either human or non-human nouns and it can be used as the subject, the object or the object of a preposition in a relative clause.

I know the girl {who / that} was sitting next to you in the plane. [11]
[**who/that** is the subject]

The girl {whom / that} we have selected wants to meet you. [12]
[**whom/that** is the object]

The dog {which / that} ran after you was very ferocious. [13]
[**which/that** is the subject]

This is the pen {which / that} I found on the floor. [14]
[**which/that** is the object]

There is no general rule which can account for the use of **that** in all the contexts. In some cases **that** is interchangeable with **who/whom/which.** In other cases, there may be restrictions on the use of **that.** The following details may help in understanding the use of **that, who, whom** or **which.**

a. When the noun head modified by the relative clause is human and the relative pronoun is the subject of the relative clause, **who** is favoured to **that,** though there is nothing odd in the use of **that.**

   The girl **who** won the gold medal ... [14a]

   The girl **that** won the gold medal ... [14b]

b. When the noun head modified by the relative clause is human and the relative pronoun is the object of the relative clause, **that** may be preferred to **whom.** However, **that** and **whom** may occur with equal frequency.

The cricket players **that** we met ... [14c]

The cricket players we met ... [14d]

The cricket players **whom** we met ... [14e]

c. **Whom/which** are obligatory after prepositions, although **that** is possible if the preposition is not used before the relative pronoun but is used at the end of the sentence.

The girl **to** whom you were speaking is my cousin. [14f]

The girl **that** you were speaking to is my cousin. [14g]

The girl you were speaking to is my cousin. [14h]

d. **That** as subject and **that/ø** as object of the relative clause are preferred to **who(m)/which** after non-personal *all*, *anything* and *everything*.

All **that** glitters is not gold. [14i]

Everything (**that**) he mentioned was true. [14j]

Anything (**that**) you give me is acceptable. [14k]

e. **That/ø** relative pronoun, if it is not a subject, is used after a noun which has a superlative as a pronominal modifier.

He is the best teacher (**that**) I have ever known. [14l]

This serial is the most expensive TV programme (**that**) we've ever made. [14m]

f. When the noun head of the relative clause is non-human and is only preceded by **the, that** may be preferred to **which.**

I'll show you the house **that** your grandfather built. [14n]

g. **Who/which** is generally preferred to **that** if the relative clause is separated from the noun head by one or more phrases.

I like the girl sitting by the door whom you were teaching English a few moments ago. [14o]

I have bought a book on Shakespeare which was written two centuries ago. [14p]

8.1.4 Whose is a relative pronoun that is used to indicate possession. This is always used before a noun because it does not replace the noun head but the possessive form of the noun or pronoun in a relative clause.

The lady < whose house you bought > is on the phone. [15]

Sentence 15 can be split into two simple sentences:

The lady is on the phone. [a]

You bought her house. [b]

Notice that *her* of *her house* in sentence **b** has a common referent to the lady in sentence **a**. Sentence **b** is inserted in sentence **a** to get:

The lady < you bought her house > is on the phone. [c]

Her is replaced by *whose* to get:

The lady < you bought whose house > is on the phone.

As the relative pronoun should be placed next to the noun head it refers to, and as *whose* cannot be separated from the noun head *house,* the object, *whose house* is placed next to *the lady.*

The lady < whose house you bought > is on the phone. [15]

Whose can be used to refer to people, countries, animals, things etc.

The table < whose leg was broken > has been sold. [16a]

It is also possible to use 16b instead of 16a.

The table < the leg of which was broken > has been sold. [16b]

Some people prefer 16b to 16a because they prefer the use of **whose** only for human nouns. However, sentence 16 b is rather cumbersome.

India, < whose economic growth has improved during the last fifty years >, is one of the leading industrialised countries. [17]

Exercise 1

***Combine the following pairs of sentences so that sentence* b *of each pair is changed into the relative clause of sentence* a:**

1. a. The doctor is available in the evening.
   b. My father usually consults him.
2. a. The story has appeared in *The Times of India.*
   b. I was talking to him about this story.
3. a. The boy is my neighbour.
   b. He has stood first in school.
4. a. The newspaper has been started recently.
   b. He works for it.
5. a. The man left for Australia.
   b. She was working with him.
6. a. I am waiting for the girl.
   b. She joined our class yesterday.
7. a. The mechanic has come to see you.
   b. You met him at the garage yesterday.

8. a. The lady has migrated to the USA.
   b. You constructed her house last month.
9. a. The chair is made of pine.
   b. It is lying in the corner.
10. a. The girl is the daughter of an ambassador.
    b. I talked to her yesterday.

Exercise 2

Analyse the following sentences into the main clause/superordinate clause and the subordinate clause and label the elements of each clause:

1. The director who made this film has been selected for the National Award.
2. I met the man to whom you sold your house last year.
3. The bungalow in which he lives is government accommodation.
4. This is the girl who has been looking for you.
5. That is the lawyer you wanted to consult.
6. I met a girl whose mother is your colleague.
7. We live in an area which is threatened by floods every year.
8. The bank for which he works has been opened recently.
9. An officer whom your father knew has been of great help.
10. She is the girl who coaches our team.

8.1.5 The use of *when*, *where* and *why* as relative adverbials

When can be used in a relative clause when the clause is preceded by a noun referring to time, or a period of time like *year, day, week* etc.

> The decade < when the economic boom took place > was a period of great prosperity. [18a]

> The decade < during which the economic boom took place > was a period of great prosperity. [18b]

Sentences 18a and 18b can be derived from two simple sentences:

The decade was a period of great prosperity. [a]

The economic boom took place during that decade. [b]

Inserting sentence **b** in sentence **a** we get:

The decade < the economic boom took place during that decade > was a period of great prosperity. [c]

Using the earlier rules of the replacement of the non-human noun we get:

The decade < the economic boom took place during which > was a period of great prosperity. [d]

The decade < during which the economic boom took place > was a period of great prosperity. [e]

The decade < when the economic boom took place > was a period of great prosperity. [f]

Therefore, sentences 18a and 18b can be presented as follows:

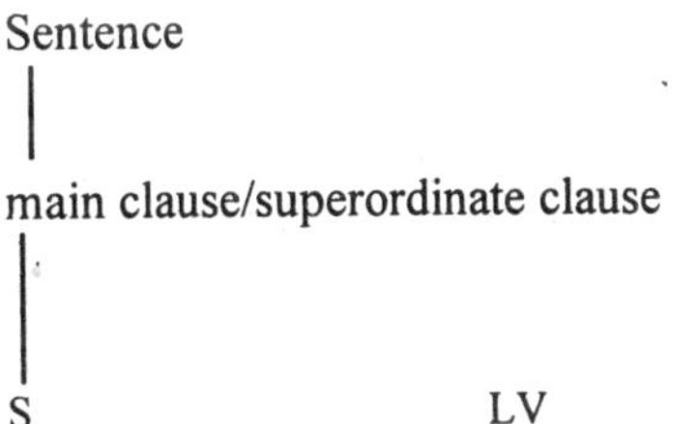

The decade < rel.cl. > was a period of great prosperity.

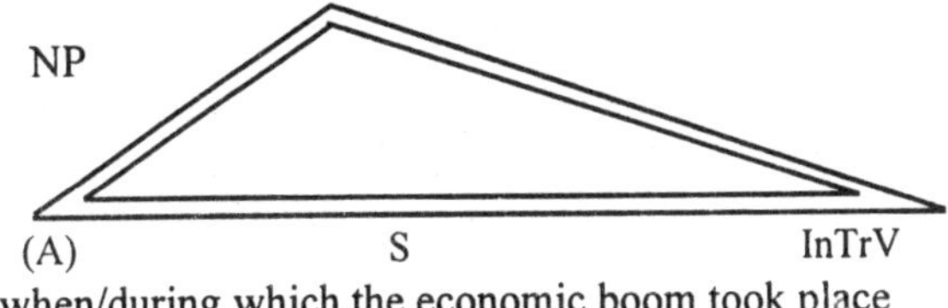

when/during which the economic boom took place

Where is preceded by a noun referring to a place.

This is the house < where I was born >. [19a]

This is the house < in which I was born >. [19b]

The office < where my father works > is at the corner. [20]

Why is used after the noun, *reason.*

That is the reason < why he didn't attend the meeting >. [21]

Exercise 3

Analyse the following sentences into the main clause/superordinate clause and the subordinate clause. Label the elements of each clause:

1. The bank where I work deals in foreign exchange also.
2. The year when we gained independence was also a year of great turmoil.
3. This is the reason why we have a strong workforce.
4. This is the time when we can start our new business.
5. This is the shop where you can get good suits.

8.1.6 Restrictive and non-restrictive clauses

Sentences 1 - 21 discussed above are examples of restrictive relative clauses. A restrictive or defining clause is used to identify a noun.

The man < who is drinking coffee > is an army officer. [22]

The films < that Doordarshan telecasts > are good entertainment. [23]

The relative clause *who is drinking* coffee identifies or restricts the noun head *the man* in sentence 22. The relative clauses in sentences 22 and 23 answer the questions *which man* and *which films* respectively.

A non-restrictive or non-defining relative clause, on the other hand, is used to give extra information about the noun head. It is not used to identify the noun which is identified either from the context or because it is a proper noun:

Dr Singh, < who is sitting in the library > wants to see you. [24]

Notice that *Dr Singh* is a proper noun and does not need a relative clause to identify it. It would be quite all right to say:

Dr Singh wants to see you. [25]

Who is sitting in the library gives us extra information about Dr Singh.

My sister < who lives in Delhi > is a pilot. [26]

I met Sharda < who had also come for the dinner >. [27]

Usually commas are used before and after non-restrictive clauses.

8.2 Appositive clauses

As discussed in chapter 7, section 7.5.1.1, an appositive clause is a nominal clause. The appositive clause resembles a relative clause as it is introduced by **that.**

The message that the Prime Minister was arriving
by car reached us in the morning. [28]

The appositive clause differs from the relative clause in four ways:

1. Whereas the **that** of the appositive clause is the subordinating conjunction it is a relative pronoun in the relative clause.

2. The **that** of a relative clause, being a relative pronoun, replaces a noun. However, the **that** of an appositive clause, being a subordinate conjunction, is added to the clause.

3. The relative clause can modify many nouns but the appositive clause can only modify a limited number of general abstract nouns like *answer, message, story, news, reply, fact* etc.

4. When the linking verb be is placed between the noun and appositive clause we get a grammatical sentence. However, when the linking verb be is placed between the noun and its relative clause, we do not get a grammatical sentence.

   The news item << that Farida had been selected for the National Award >> was covered in the evening news. [29a]

   The news story < that you told me > was covered in the evening bulletin. [29b]

   The report << that the thief has been caught >> is true. [30a]

   The report < that you have given me > is true. [30b]

   Sentence 29a can be analysed as two simple sentences:

   The news item was covered in the evening news. [a]

   Farida had been selected for the National Award. [b]

   Sentence **b** can be inserted in **a** to get:

   The news item < Farida had been selected for the National Award > was covered in the evening news. [c]

   The subordinating conjunction **that** is placed before the appositive clause.

   The news item << that Farida had been selected for the National Award >> was covered in the evening news. [d]

   Sentence 29b can be analysed as two simple sentences:

   The news story was covered in the evening news. [a]

   You told me the news story. [b]

Sentence **b** is inserted in **a** to get:

The news story < you told me the news story > was covered in the evening news. [c]

The news story of **a** and **b** have the same referent. Therefore, *the news story* of **b** can be replaced by the relative pronoun **that** so that we get:

The news story < you told me that > was covered in the evening news. [d]

The relative pronoun **that** should be placed next to the noun it refers to:

The news story < that you told me > was covered in the evening news. [e]

that you told me is the relative clause.

By a simple test, we can distinguish between the appositive clause and the relative clause by using the linking verb **be.**

Sentence 30a, *The report is that the thief has been caught*, is a grammatical sentence, therefore it is an appositive clause.

Sentence 30b, * *The report is that you have given me*, is an ungrammatical sentence and is therefore a relative clause.

8.3 Adverbial clauses

We will first discuss the forms of adverbial clauses. Adverbial clauses can be both finite and non-finite.

Finite adverbial clauses are introduced by a subordinating conjunction.

When I reached his house, he was writing a letter. [31]

I gave him money **because he was stranded.** [32]

Non-finite adverbial clauses are of the following types:

a. **-ing participle clauses:**

I saw her **while entering the room.**
(*while I was entering the room*) [33]

On reaching the airport, she rang up her brother.
(*when she reached the airport*) [34]

b. **-ed participle clauses:**

When defeated, the enemy laid down their arms. [35]
(*when they were defeated*)

Although found on the hillls, this wood can be grown in the plains too. [36]
(*although it is found in the hills*)

c. **to- infinitive clauses:**

She ran fast **to catch the train.**
(*so that she could catch the train*) [37]

To open the door, press this button.
(*in order to open the door*) [38]

d. **verbless clauses:**

When in difficulty, take a deep breath. [39]
(*when you are in difficulty*)

While on vacation, I completed the book. [40]
(*while I was on vacation*)

Position of adverbial clauses: The usual position of an adverbial clause is right after the main clause.

I reached the station **before the train left.** [41]

An adverbial clause can also be placed before the main clause as in,

> **When she reached the office,** she didn't find anyone there. [42]

Sometimes an adverbial clause can be used in the middle of the main clause. However, this is quite rare.

> My uncle, **when he was young,** was a bank officer. [43]

There are a few adverbial clauses that can only be used before the main clause and there are a few others that can be used only after the main clause.

8.3.1 Adverbial clauses of time

Adverbial clauses of time are used to refer to a period of time or to another event. The subordinating conjunctions that are usually used to introduce an adverbial clause of time are: **when, before, after, since, while, once, as, until.**

> I met Renu **after I had finished my work.** [44]
>
> I have not seen him **since I left Bahrain.** [45]
>
> **When I first saw him,** I thought he was a lawyer. [46]
>
> He joined **after having his dinner.** [47]
>
> **On passing your MBA,** you'll immediately be appointed manager. [48]
>
> **Once published,** your novel will be reviewed. [49]
>
> **While in Delhi,** I visited all the leading educationists. [50]

Notice that sentences 44 - 46 have finite adverbial clauses, sentences 47 and 48 have non-finite **-ing** adverbial clauses, sentence 50 has a verbless adverbial clause.

Sentence 44 can be represented as:

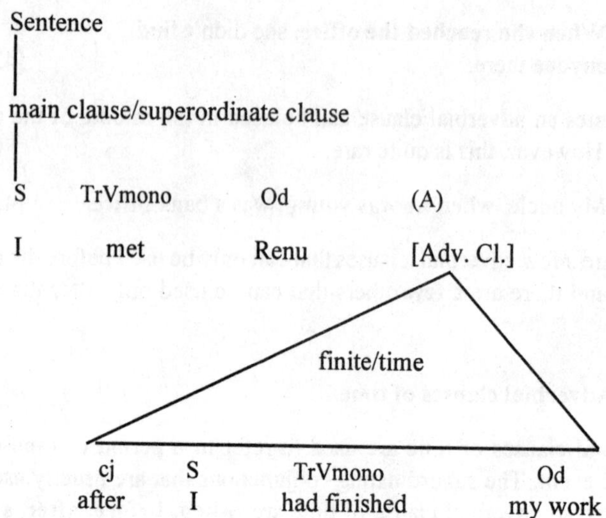

Sentence 50 can be represented as:

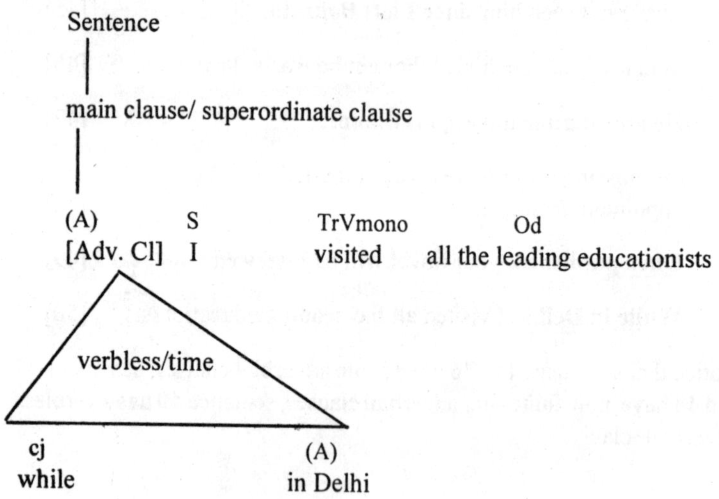

8.3.2 Adverbial clauses of place

Adverbial clauses of place may be introduced by the subordinating conjunctions **where** and **wherever.**

Where there was a temple, we found an absolutely new building. [51]

Water coolers were placed, **wherever possible.** [52]

8.3.3 Adverbial clauses of reason

Adverbial clauses of reason are used to indicate the reason for the action in the main clause. The subordinating conjunctions generally used for clauses of reason are, **because, as, since.**

I could not meet you **because you were very busy.** [53]

As he was the airport manager, he had to listen to the passenger's complaint. [54]

Since Rajesh is the captain, he should introduce the team to the chief guest. [55]

Notice that an adverbial clause of reason can be used either at the beginning or at the end of the main clause. However, when an adverbial clause of reason is used at the beginning of the main clause, the conjunction used is either **as** or **since.**

Knowing my temper, I kept quiet. [56]
(*as I knew my temper*)

Having completed the bridge, I asked for the payment of the money. [57]
(*as I had completed the bridge*)

Neglected by her parents, she stayed with her friend. [58]
(*as she was neglected by her parents*)

Disguised at her behaviour, I terminated
her services. [59]
(*as I was disgusted with her behaviour*)

Sentences 56 and 57 are non-finite **-ing** adverbial clauses of reason, 58 is a non-finite **-ed** adverbial clause of reason and 59 is a verbless adverbial clause of reason.

Sentence 56 can be represented as follows:

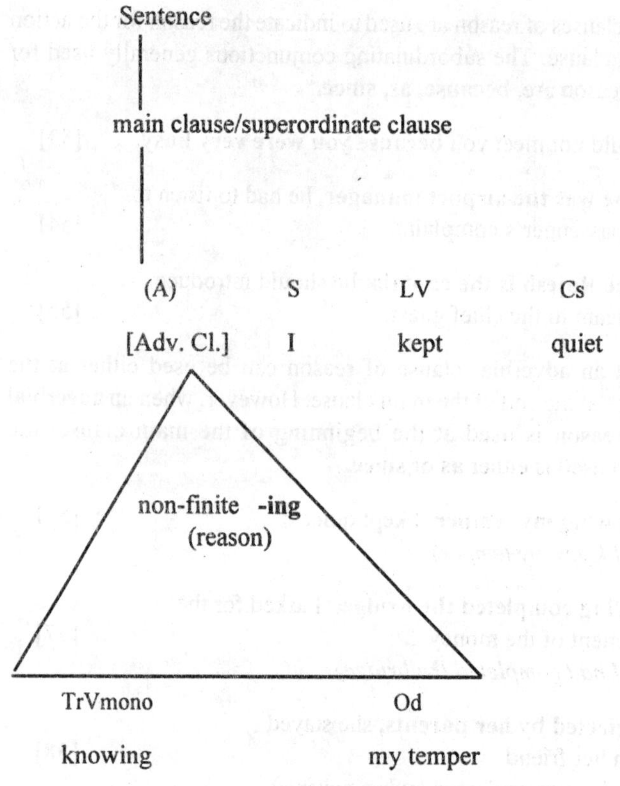

8.3.4 Adverbial clauses of condition

The common subordinating conjunction to introduce an adverbial clause of condition is **if**. The other subordinating conjunction is **unless,** which introduces a negative condition. Some other subordinating conjunctions are **as long as, in case, provided (that)** etc.

A conditional clause is used to indicate that the situation in the main clause is dependent on the fulfilment of the condition in the conditional clause.

a. **Open condition:** A conditional clause may contain an open condition. An open condition is a condition which is a real condition and can be fulfilled.

If I go to college, I'll speak to the Principal. [60]

If Sonia takes up this job, she will be paid well. [61]

If you heat water under pressure, it changes into steam. [62]

You can become a good swimmer, if you swim everyday. [63]

Notice that in 60 and 61 the conditional clauses are in the simple present tense and the main clauses have **will/shall + the first form of the verb.** Such constructions are used to talk about situations which may exist in the future.

However, in 62 and 63 both the conditional clause and the main clause are in the simple present tense. Such conditions are used to talk about situations which we know to exist or are true.

b. **Hypothetical condition:** A conditional clause may contain a hypothetical condition, which cannot be fulfilled. Such clauses are used about situations which we know do not exist.

If he behaved well, I would help him. [64]

If she worked hard, she'd pass. [65]

Notice that in 64 the conditional clause, *if he behaved well,* has a hypothetical condition that means *that there is no possibility of his behaving well* and 65 can be paraphrased as *there is no posssibility of her working hard* and, *therefore, she will not pass.* Notice that the simple past tense is used in the conditional and a modal auxiliary in the past tense in the main clause.

c. **Unfulfilled condition in the past:** The conditional clause contains a condition, which was not fulfilled in the past.

If he had written to me, I would have arranged a taxi for him. [66]

If we had taken our raincoats, we would not have got wet. [67]

Notice that the conditional clauses in 66 and 67 are in the past perfect tense (**had** + the past participle form of the verb) and the main clauses have the structure **would** + **have** + the past participle form of the verb.

It is possible to drop **if** in 66 and 67 and use **had** before the subject.

Had he written to me, I would have arranged a taxi for him. [68]

Had we taken our raincoats, we would not have got wet. [69]

Unless introduces a negative meaning:

Unless you work hard, you cannot pass. [70]

Unless I meet him, I cannot decide on this matter. [71]

Conditional clauses with other conjunctions can also be used:

In case he meets you, you may inform him of our decision. [72]

I shall help him **provided he writes to me.** [73]

If and **unless** may be used with non-finite and verbless conditional clauses.

If hit hard, this ball won't bounce. [74]

Unless told, you may not leave this gate. [75]

Exercise 4

Combine each of the following pairs of sentences so that sentence* b *of each pair is changed into an adverbial clause and is used in place of the underlined word/phrase in italics. Use an appropriate subordinating conjunction before the adverbial clause.

1. a. She lived in Delhi *then.*

   b. I last met her.

2. a. I saw her *then.*

   b. She was crossing the road.

3. a. Please inform me *then.*

   b. You reach Raipur.

4. a. Lata started clearing up the mess *then.*

   b. The guests had left.

5. a. They will go home *then.*

   b. They have taken the examination.

6. a. Wait for me until *then.*

   b. I return.

7. a. Neena went to Dehradun *for this reason.*

   b. Her father was ill.

8. a. *For this reason,* I stopped eating at the mess.

   b. The food is too spicy.

9. a. *Then,* she looked very tired.

   b. I met her.

10. a. I rang her up *for this reason.*

    b. I had to give her a message.

Exercise 5

Analyse the following sentences into the main clause/superordinate clause and the subordinate clause, and label the elements of each clause:

1. I went to office today because the registrar had called me.
2. She rang us as soon as she reached Satara.
3. While on vacation, I saw both the films.
4. While I was driving home, I saw Sunita near Odeon.
5. Once opened, the can should be kept in the fridge.
6. They landed where the plane had crashed.
7. As she knew me well, she visited me at home.
8. He felt nervous on entering the room.
9. Having completed the course, we went on a picnic.
10. When she was young, she was quite plump.

8.3.5 Adverbial clauses of concession

There are two main subordinating conjunctions - **although** and **though** which can introduce an adverbial clause of concession.

> **Although there was a shortage of sugar in the country,** the Government was able to control the sugar prices. [76]
>
> The film was very interesting **though the director was a teenager.** [77]
>
> **Though tired,** she went with me to the airport. [78]

Though living beyond his means, he could always manage his finances. [79]

Notice that 76 and 77 are finite and 78 and 79 are non-finite.

There are a few other subordinators like **whatever, when, while,** which can be used with adverbial clauses of concession.

While I don't want to interfere, I request you to change the topic. [80]

Whatever you may say, he is the best cricket player. [81]

8.3.6 Adverbial clauses of manner

Adverbial clauses of manner are used to talk about someone's behaviour or the way something is done. Subordinating conjunctions that are usually used with clauses of manner are **as, as if,** and **as though.**

She behaves **as if she were the boss.** [82]

His face looked **as if it had been painted.** [83]

She looked **as if she had not slept for days.** [84]

In formal English we use **were** instead of **was** in clauses of manner beginning with **as if** or **as though.**

8.3.7 Adverbial clauses of contrast

Whereas and **while** introduce adverbial clauses of contrast.

While his elder brother is an officer, his younger brother is a teacher. [85]

Our country has progressed economically, **whereas many other developing countries are facing problems of financial mismanagement.** [86]

8.3.8 Adverbial clauses of purpose

Adverbial clauses of purpose are used to indicate the purpose of an action. The most common conjunctions used to indicate clauses of purpose are **to, in order to, so that** and **in order that. To** and **in order to** are followed by non-finite clauses are more frequent. **So that** and **in order that** are followed by finite clauses.

My father gave me a piece of land **to build a house.** [87]

I worked hard **in order to pass the examination.** [88]

He took the car with him **so that his son would not drive it.** [89]

Sentence 87 can be represented as:

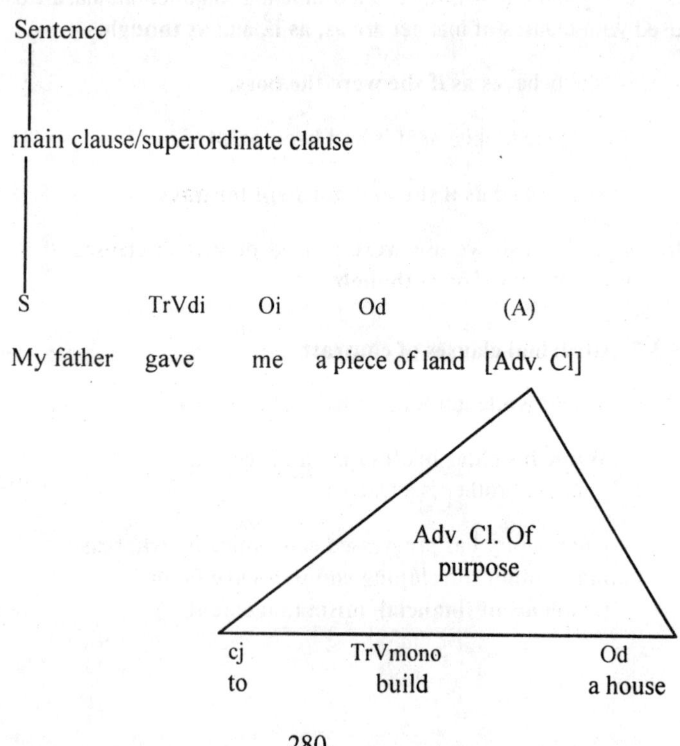

Notice that we often use **can, could, will, would,** or **needn't.**

8.4 Analysis of complex sentences

In chapter 7 and in the earlier sections of this chapter, we dealt with complex sentences with two clauses, a main clause/superordinate clause and a subordinate clause, for the sake of convenience. The following labels have been used for the analysis of sentences:

1. Function labels such as S (subject), V (verbal), O (object), C (complement) and A (adverbial) for the main elements of a clause.

2. N Cl, R Cl, App Cl and Adv Cl for nominal clauses, relative clauses, appositive clauses and adverbial clauses respectively.

3. A single line triangle to represent nominal clauses and adverbial clauses.

4. A double line triangle to represent an indirect subordinate clause, e.g., a relative clause or an appositive clause. A relative clause or an appositive clause does not take the position of a sentence element (S, O etc) but modifies an element in the sentence.

5. cj, p, NP to represent a conjunction in a subordinate clause, a preposition and a noun phrase respectively.

6. ⊔ to link the interrupted elements in a verbal phrase and + to indicate coordination and a semicolon (;) or a comma (,) to indicate 'unlinked coordination' (Leech *et al:* 1982).

Let us analyse a sentence using tree diagrams:

> This proposal has been formulated at a time when the entire matter of pensionary benefits to Central Government employees is under active review by the Fifth Central Pay Commission which was appointed in July . [90]

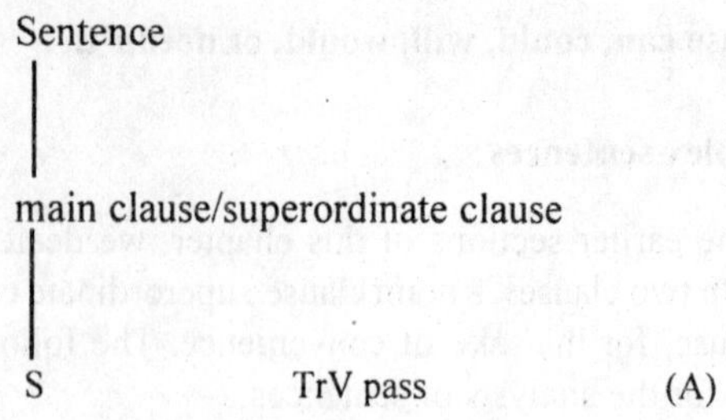

This proposal has been formulated at a time < rel.cl >

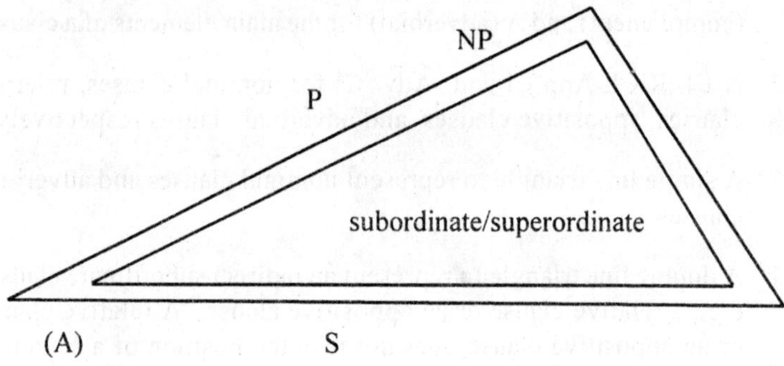

when the entire matter of pensionary benefits to Central Govt. employees

V (A) (A)

is under active review by the Central Pay Commission < rel.cl >

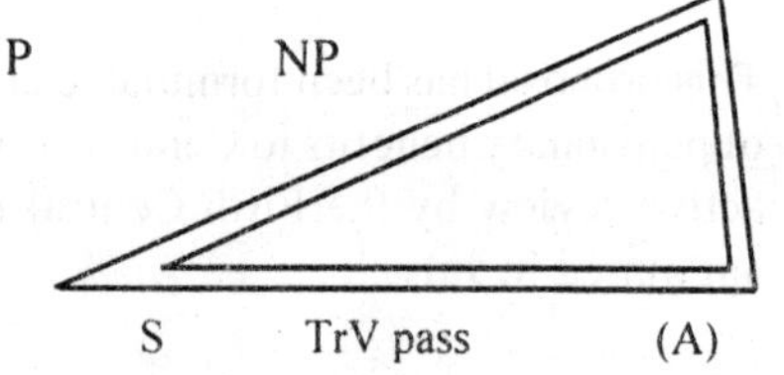

which was appointed in July

Following Leech *et al* (1983), we can leave out the actual words used and can represent the above sentence as:

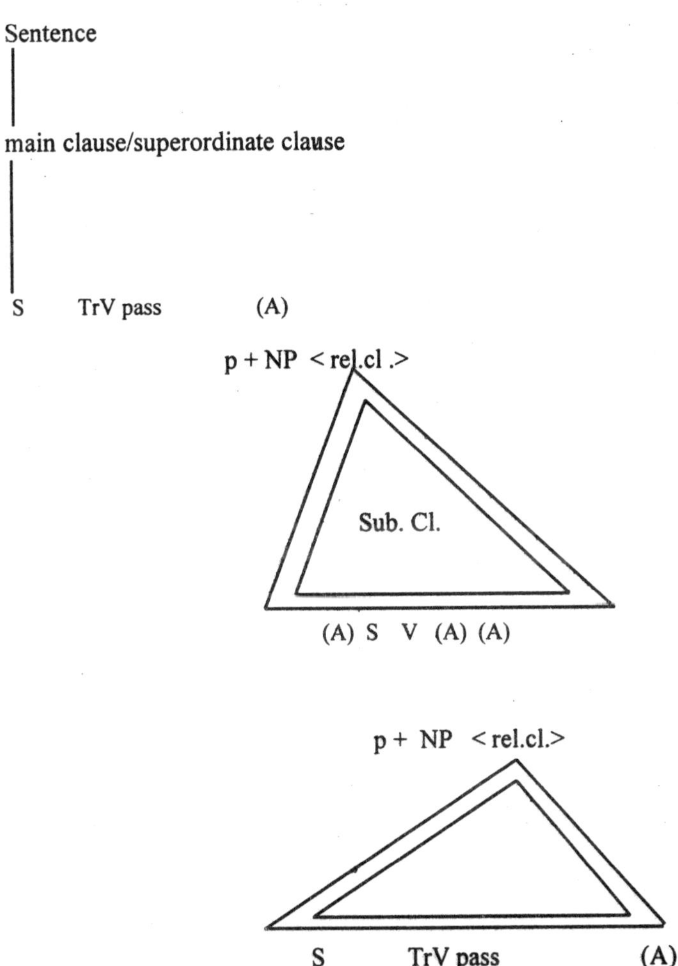

David Basnett says that if the State Earnings Related Pension Scheme were abolished, those in occupational pension schemes would pay considerably increased National Insurance Contributions for considerably reduced benefits. [91]

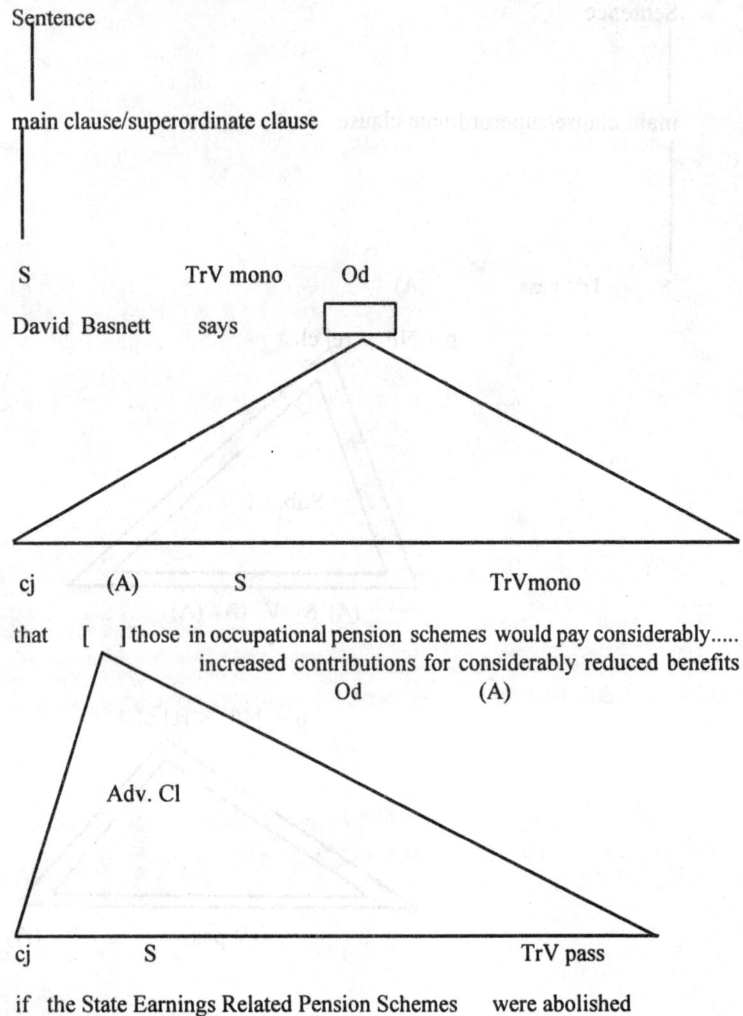

We can represent the same information as:

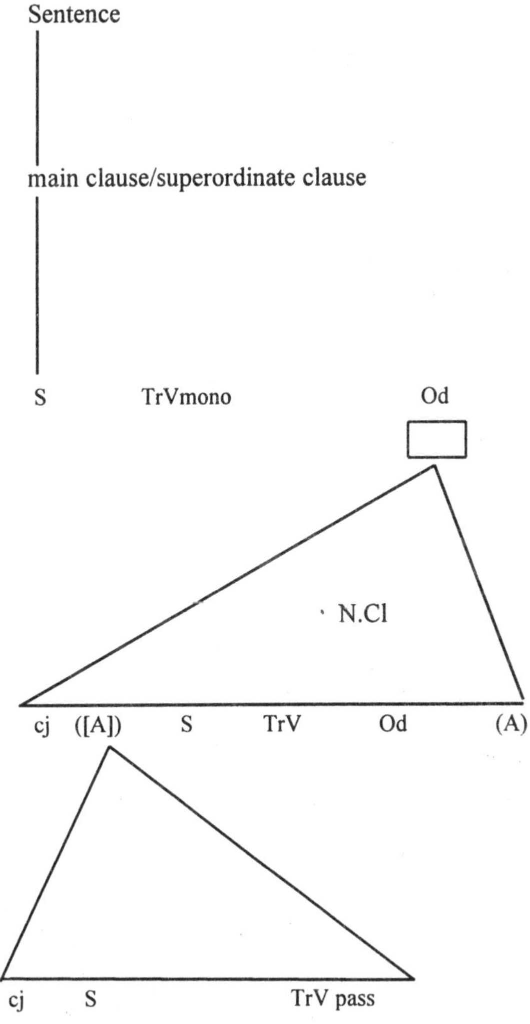

The tall doctor whom you met at the party last night told me that he slipped over the bar while talking to the Governor. [92]

The basic structure analaysis of sentence 92 is:

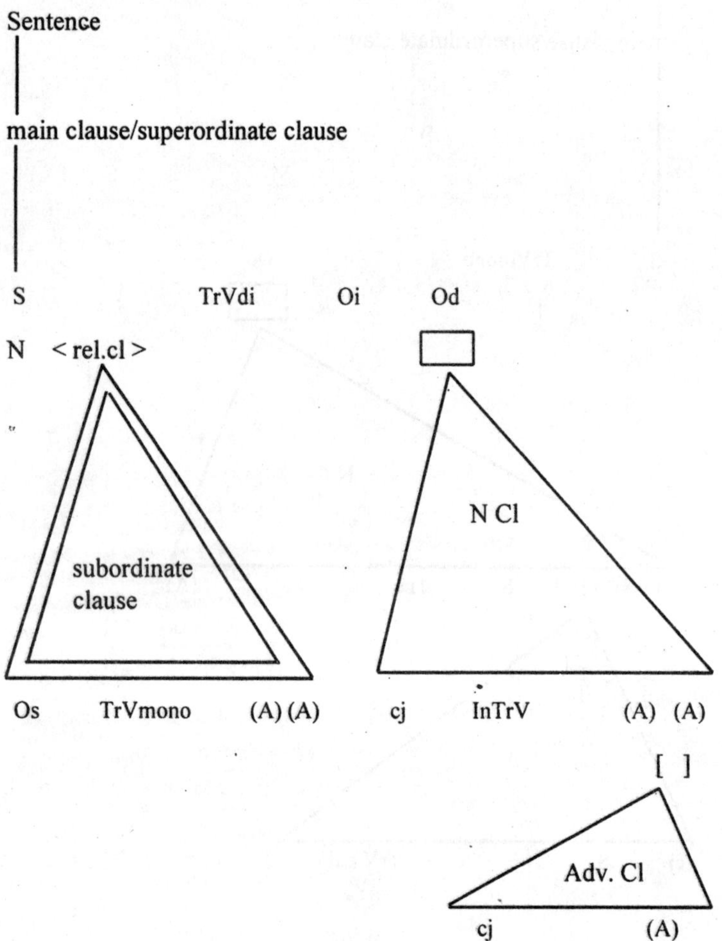

When the old lady came to our house, my father informed her that her son had been awarded the Vir Chakra. [93]

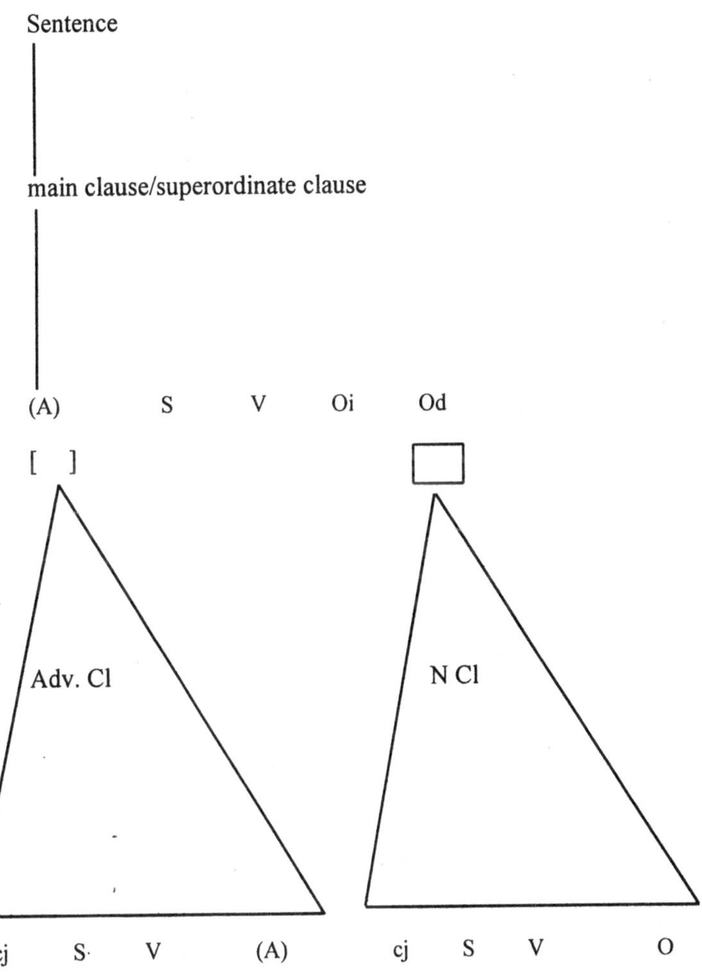

It is a pity that Reema met him at a time when he had lost his business. [94]

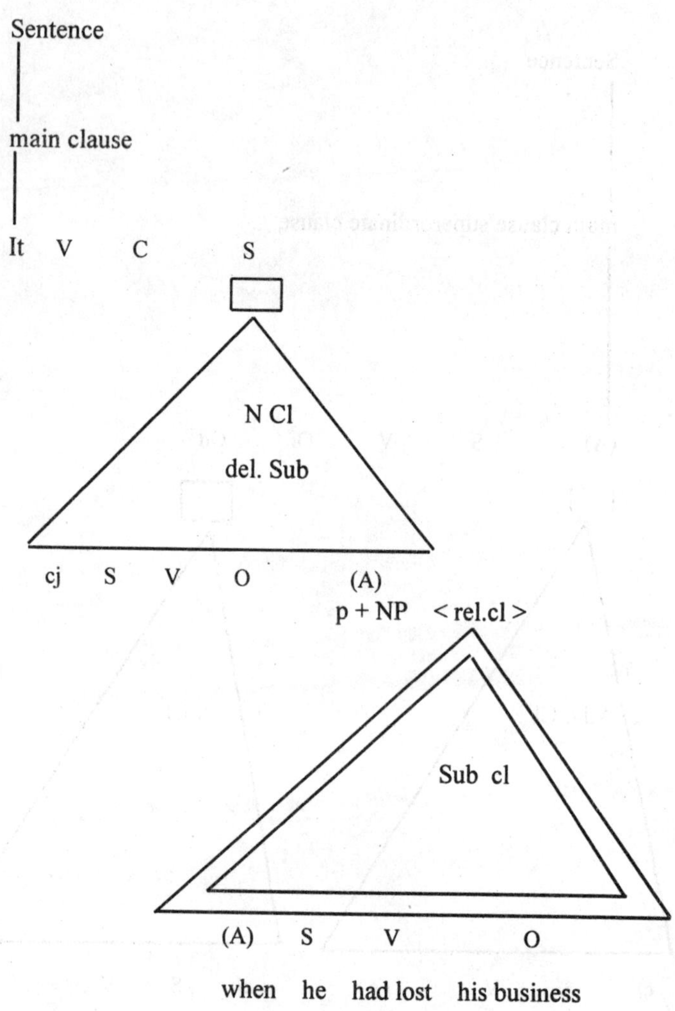

I have never asked him to work in the library because this can only be done by the director. [95]

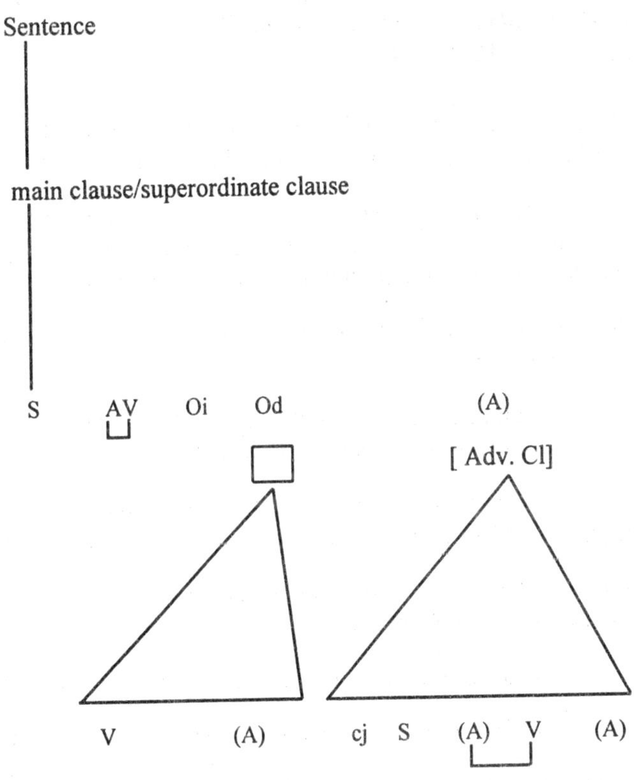

Notice the use of ⌴ to connect have asked and can be done

Exercise 6

Analyse the following sentences into main, superordinate and subordinate clauses. Identify each clause as NCl, Rel.Cl., App.Cl., or Adv. Cl. For each Adv.Cl state its type, i.e., whether it is an adverbial clause of time, place, reason etc. Describe the structure of each clause in terms of cj, S, V, O, C, A:

1. When she came to my office, I told her that she could meet the Manager after she had completed all the formalities.
2. Politicians who seek to change the present government's economic policies will lack credibility abroad unless they prove that they are genuine in their concern for the economy.
3. He is a person who will never return books to the library unless threatened with a fine.
4. The fact that he did not attend the meeting doesn't mean that he does not want to remain on the Board.
5. The girl whose mother gave you a present at the party last night would like to meet you after you have finished the lecture.
6. Entering the room, he noticed that his secretary had rearranged the furniture in his absence.
7. I enjoy reading a novel at night when everyone is fast asleep.
8. I want to tell you that your playing music disturbs us at night.
9. We were not sure what she would do when we told her that her son was missing from school.
10. After I returned home last night, I ate everything that was lying on the table.

Exercise 7

Explain the differences between each of the following pairs of sentences:

1. a. I know where she has left the keys.

   b. I know the place where she has left the keys.

2. a. His brother who is a university professor is getting married next month.

   b. His brother, who is a university professor, is getting married next month.

3. a. The story that he was arrested has appeared in all newspapers.

   b. The story that you told me last night has appeared in all newspapers.

4. a. The man who is standing in the corridor is a lawyer.

   b. The man who you met in the corridor is a lawyer.

5. a. He would like to meet the Chief Minister.

   b. He went there to meet the Chief minister.

6. a. It is good that Nina has passed the examination.

   b. I am sure that Nina will pass the examination.

7. a. I want to be an astronaut.

   b. I want her to be an astronaut.

8. a. I asked him to complete the paper.

   b. I wanted him to complete the paper.

9. a. While I was crossing the road I saw Vimal standing with her son.

   b. While Ram is aggressive, his brother is docile.

10. a. If I become the Prime Minister, I'll appoint you the Finance secretary.

    b. If I became the Prime Minister, I'd appoint you the Finance secretary.

9

Coordination

9.1 Introduction

Coordination is grammatical process by which two or more words or phrases of the same rank are conjoined:

> **Kumar is a college lecturer and his wife is a computer professional.** (*two clauses coordinated*) [1]
>
> The **old man and the young woman** were playing chess in the room. (*two NPs coordinated*) [2]
>
> He **ran** and **hit** the ball. (*two verbs coordinated*) [3]

9.2 Compound sentences and coordinate clauses

A compound sentence comprises two or more coordinated clauses. Coordinated clauses are linked by coordinating conjunctions. Typical coordinating conjunctions are **and, or** and **but.**

> Arpit plays hockey and his brother plays tennis. [4]
>
> The Principal was angry but he didn't say anything. [5]

Sentence 4 can be presented as follows:

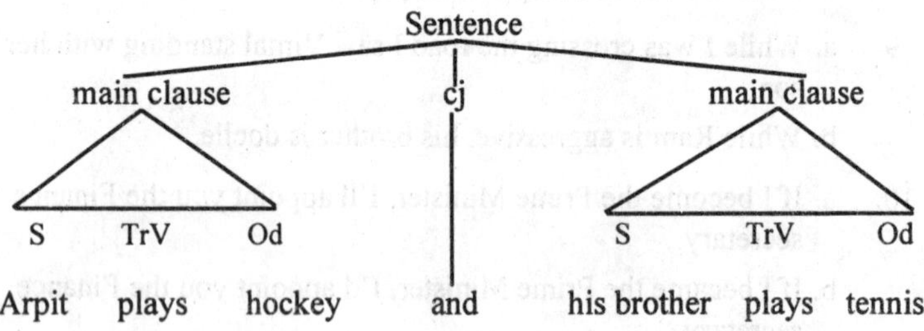

It is also possible that the main clause(s) of a compound sentence has/ have one or more subordinate clauses:

> Mukesh told me that Rita was coming by air but his father told me that she was coming by road. [6]
>
> I felt that she had grown tall but my wife told me that she was wearing high heels. [7]

Sentence 6 can be presented as follows:

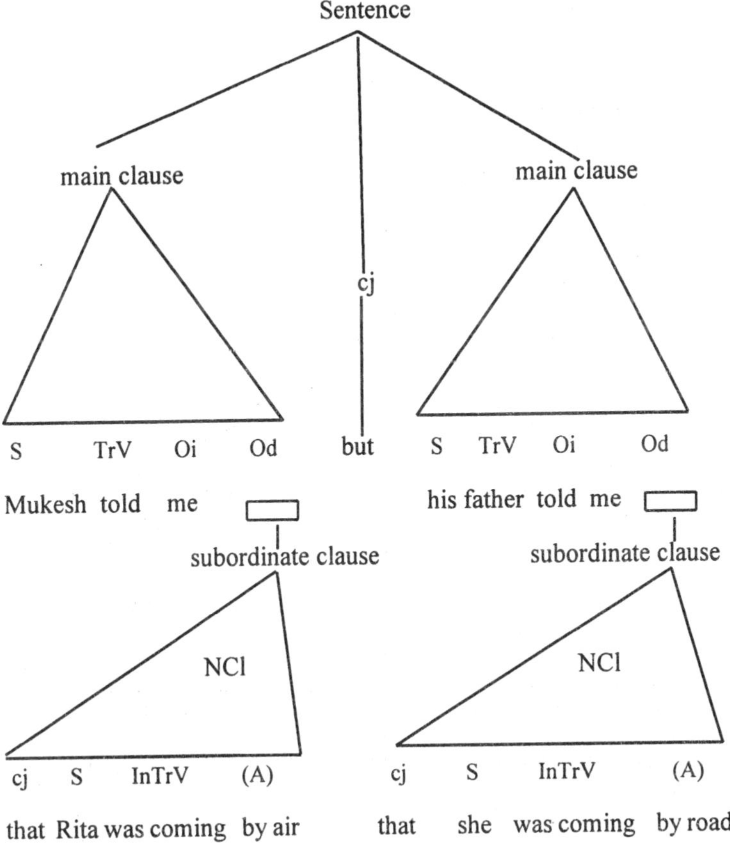

Sometimes, the subordinate clauses of a complex sentence can also be coordinated:

> I heard that Mira is going to Oxford **and**
> that her husband is going to Cambridge. [8]

> He went by car to drop Mini at her school **and**
> to see off Rekha at the station. [9]

Sentence 8 can be presented as follows:

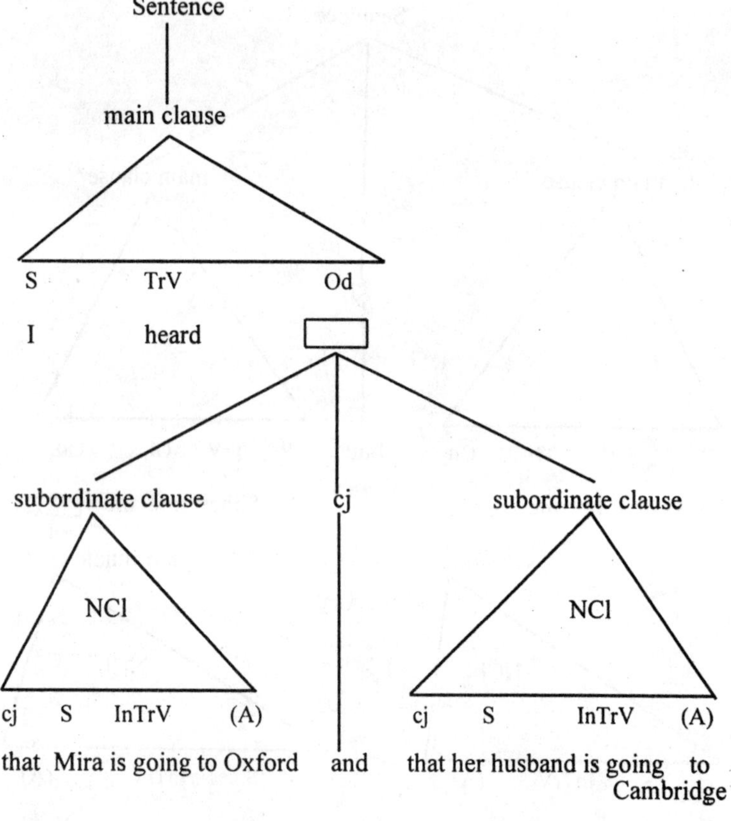

Sentence 9 can be presented as follows:

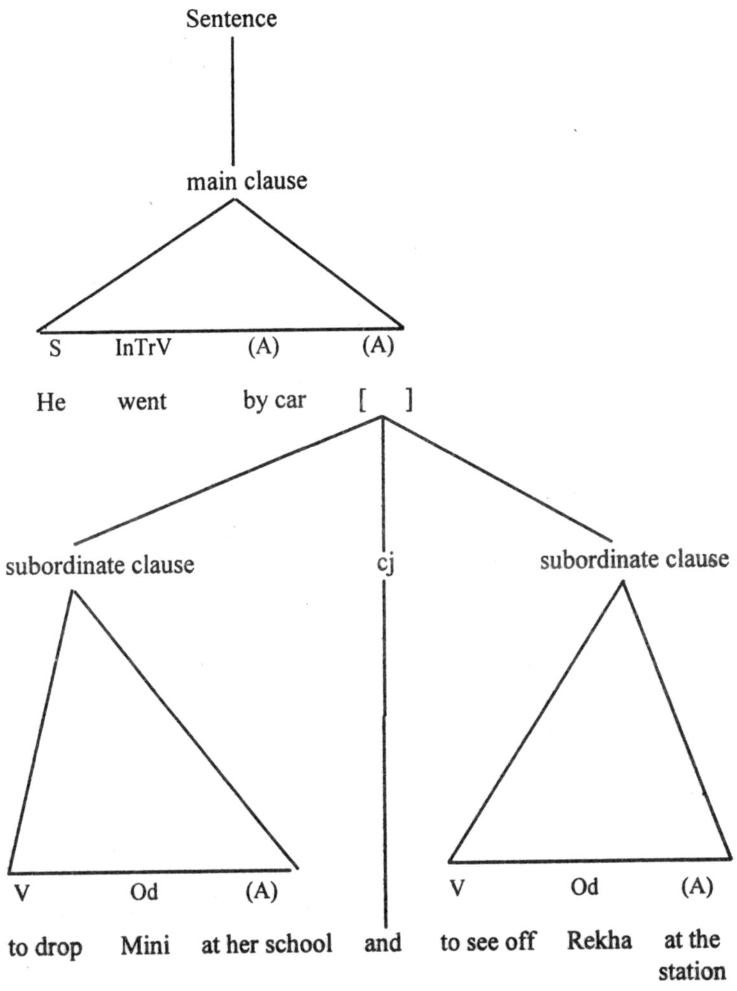

Exercise 1

Analyse these sentences into the main clause, coordinate clause and subordinate clause, if any:

1. We ate potatoes and they ate beans.
2. The District Magistrate told the Minister that he would visit the village and that his wife would go around to visit the school.
3. She was unhappy or she was upset.
4. That the earth is round and that it revolves around the sun are obvious facts.
5. She told Neena that she was going to Mumbai but she told Ravi that she was going to Goa.
6. I went to the railway station and she went to the airport.
7. I don't know whether he did it or whether his wife did it.
8. She has asked me to meet him today and he has asked Meena to meet her tomorrow.
9. He tried hard but he couldn't succeed.
10. What I wear in the morning and what I wear in the evening depend on the weather.

9.3 Ellipsis in coordinated clauses

Often words or phrases are omitted in successive coordinated clause(s) because their structure and meaning can be recovered from the first clause.

a. **Ellipsis of subject:** Identical subjects of coordinated clauses are ellipted.

Meera opened the fridge and (*Meera*) put the milk in it. [10]

He chained the dog and (*he*) tied it to the door. [11]

b. **Ellipsis of subject and auxiliaries:** If the subjects and auxiliaries are identical, they may be ellipted in the successive clause.

Rita has opened the room, and (*Rita has*) cleaned it. [12]

Farida must have reached Delhi and (*Farida must have*) met Indira. [13]

c. **Ellipsis of auxiliary only:** The subjects of coordinated clauses may be different but the auxiliaries may be identical. In such a case, the auxiliaries may be ellipted.

Sudha may be playing in the field, and Arvind (*may be*) swimming in the pool. [14]

d. **Ellipsis of the verbal group:**

She works with Air India, and her husband (*works*) with the Indian Airlines. [15]

My father was presented a certificate of merit and my mother (*was presented*) a gold medal. [16]

e. **Ellipsis of the verbal group and complement of the subject:**

She was Miss Universe in 1992, and her sister (*was Miss Universe*) in 1994. [17]

Haldar is a lecturer at Oxford and Bimal (*is a lecturer*) at Cambridge. [18]

f. **Ellipsis of the auxiliary/verbal group and direct object:**

Mohan opens the library at 9 o' clock and Rakesh (*opens the library*) at 10 o' clock. [19]

Rita will play tennis in the evening and Shailaja may (*play tennis*) in the morning. [20]

g. **Ellipsis of the direct object:**

Mohan opens (*the library*) and Rakesh closes the library. [21]

h. **Ellipsis of the whole predication:**

Iqbal will construct the house and Amrit might (*construct the house*) too. [22]

i. **Ellipsis of elements of the noun phrase:**

One player was hit and another (*player was*) injured during the game. [23]

I wanted boiled mutton but he gave me fried (*mutton*). [24]

Exercise 2

State which elements in these sentences are ellipted. Rewrite these sentences giving the full forms of the ellipted elements within brackets for your analysis:

1. She was ironing clothes and singing away.
2. Rajesh goes to office by car and Vanita to the bank on scooter.
3. My brother is travelling by bus and my sister-in-law by train.
4. Quader should be in his apartment and Kajol in the library.
5. She wrote a novel and published it herself.
6. Krishna must have received the letter and informed Mohinder.
7. A boy was injured and another killed during the expedition.
8. She was the President of the Students' Union last year and her brother this year.
9. Sunit must be sleeping and Punit playing in the room.
10. I met Mohan and spoke to him for an hour.

9.4 Meaning related to coordinating conjunctions

a. **Related facts:** Two related facts can be conjoined by **and.**

He works in a school and **his wife in a college.** [25]

She has finished her BA (Hons.) **and now plans to join MA.** [26]

b. **Consequence or result:** The second coordinated clause can be the consequence or result of the first clause.

I gave him fifty thousand rupees **and** he bought a second hand car with it. [27]

The clerk did not accept his application, **and** (therefore), **he reported the matter to the office.** [28]

c. **Sequence:** The second coordinated clause can be the chronological sequence of the first.

I was born in Shimla **and studied in Chandigarh.** [29]

India gained independence in 1947, **and became a Republic in 1950.** [30]

d. **Contrast:** In introducing a contrasting fact, one usually uses **but**, though **and** is also possible.

Shakila is single **but lives in a big house.** [31]

Joshi is a good teacher **but he is a poor scholar.** [32]

Rajesh is an introvert **and his brother is an extrovert.** [33]

e. **Alternative: Or** can introduce an alternative.

He is in his room **or is in the library.** [34]

You may go to the club **or watch a movie** in the evening. [35]

Exercise 3

Identify the meanings of coordinated conjunctions in these sentences:

1. Brazil has Pele and Argentina has Maradona as the soccer superstar.
2. Germany went to war in 1939 and attacked a number of European countries.
3. Norway scored a goal in the first half and Belgium in the second.
4. Meenakshi is good at planning but is bad at executing rules.
5. We may appoint a new Principal or may ask Mrs Kapoor to look after the school for a year.
6. She came to college yesterday and attended all the classes.
7. She may go to Mumbai by train or by bus.
8. Monish has gone to Florida and Iqbal is going to Washington.
9. We won the cricket trophy and the Principal declared the following day a holiday.
10. He suffers from a heart ailment but attends his office regularly.

9.5 Coordination of the constituents of the sentence

a. **Coordination of noun phrases:** Two or more noun phrases may be coordinated and such coordinated noun phrases may function as subject, object, complement, etc.

Harish and Mona have finished their work. (subject) [36]

They served us **chicken and potatoes.** (object) [37]

Aparna is a **good teacher and a fine scholar.** (complement) [38]

b. **Coordination of adjectives:** Two or more objectives functioning at the subject complement position can be coordinated.

Varun is **friendly and helpful.** [39]

The Steamer Point Hotel is **inexpensive but the best** in the city. [40]

Two or more adjectives functioning as prenominal modifiers can also be coordinated.

She met a **friendly and helpful lady** on the train. [41]

He is a **bright and intelligent** boy. [42]

She has a **red and blue** umbrella. [43]

c. **Coordination of verbs**

i. Coordination of the main verbs

He has **constructed and furnished** his house. [44]

They **ate and talked** in the bedroom. [45]

ii. Coordination of the auxiliaries is not very frequent.

He **can and should** play cricket. [46]

iii. Coordination of the verb phrases

We **started in the morning and drove till the afternoon.** [47]

Manoj **can drive but cannot service** your car. [48]

d. **Coordination of adverbs/adverbials**

He spoke **quickly but softly.** [49]

She will speak to you **today or tomorrow.** [50]

I will ring you up **in the morning or in the afternoon.** [51]

Renu is going to **Hyderabad and to Mumbai** next month. [52]

She lectured **softly but with great force.** [53]

Exercise 4

Identify and underline the coordinated constituents in these sentences. Also mention the form of the coordinated items:

1. She swept and polished the floor.
2. The red and white scooter is very striking.
3. Surinder and Rita got married on Tuesday.
4. They will play in Lucknow or in Amritsar.
5. That house is very small but expensive.
6. She is singing and dancing in the hall.
7. He may buy a fridge or a TV next month.
8. Mira is thin but healthy.
9. They played and ate in the stadium.
10. They slept in the morning and played in the evening.

10

Focus

10.1 Simple sentences and focus

In chapter 1, we discussed the concept of the simple sentences and all the examples of simple sentences were declarative sentences. We also discussed that the basic sentence patterns in English are of the following types:

1. S + InTrV + (Adv)
2. S + LV + Cs
3. S + TrVmono + Od + (Adv)
4. S + TrVdi + Oi + Od + (Adv)
5. S + TrVcomp + Od + Co + (Adv)
6. S + TrVcomp + Od + Adv

Thus the discussion of the simple sentence was based on the structure of declarative sentences. A declarative sentence begins with the subject and is followed by the verb. If there is an intransitive verb, the sentence may be complete or may be followed by an adverbial. A linking verb is followed by a complement and a transitive verb is followed by an object. Such sentences are neutral or unmarked as the focus is on the last constituent of the sentence. However, in real life communication, we need to focus on a constituent other than the last constituent of the sentence. In such an event, the sentence is a **marked sentence.**

I like ice cream (S TrVmono Od, *unmarked*) [1]

Ice cream, I like (Od S TrVmono, *marked with focus on the Od*) [1a]

Leander Paes is a great player.
(S LV Cs, *unmarked*) [2]

A great player, Leander Paes is.
(Cs S LV *marked with focus on the Cs*) [2a]

They call her Cleopatra.
(S TrVcomp Od Co, *unmarked*) [3]

Cleopatra they call her.
(Co S TrVcomp Od, *marked with focus on Co*) [3a]

I met him last night.
(S TrVmono Od Adv, *unmarked*) [4]

Last night I met him.
(Adv S TrVmono, Od *marked with focus on Adv*) [4a]

In some cases when an adverb with a negative meaning (*never, hardly, little, seldom,* etc.) is **fronted** there is a subject auxiliary inversion also.

He never visited my house. (S Adv TrVmono Od) [5]

Never did he visit my house. (Adv S TrVmono Od) [5a]

All the a sentences above have a special meaning and are used in restricted contexts and are thus less frequent than unmarked sentences.

Exercise 1

Write the structure of each one of these sentences and identify which element has been fronted:

1. Rita her name is.
2. Little did he know that his manager was a crook.
3. *Gone with the Wind* I have seen five times.
4. Into the river, the burning plane fell.
5. This paper I wrote fifteen years ago.

6. Suddenly we saw a tiger in front of our car.
7. A good grade you call it.
8. Your case the judge has decided.
9. An IAS officer he has become.
10. Fifteen years ago I wrote this paper.

10.2 Cleft sentences

Another grammatical device to focus or highlight an element of a sentence is the cleft sentence device. A simple sentence is changed into a cleft sentence as:

It + be + the element to be focussed + clause.

Thus a simple sentence is changed into a cleft sentence with two clauses: for example, sentence 6 below can have several cleft sentences, depending upon the element which we want to focus.

Pavan had ice cream at the party last night. [6]

It was Pavan who had ice cream at the party last night.
(S as focus) [6a]

It was ice cream that Pavan had at the party last night.
(Od as focus) [6b]

It was at the party that Pavan had ice cream last night.
(A of place) [6c]

It was last night that Pavan had ice cream at the party.
(A of time) [6d]

Sometimes Co as focus can be used in a cleft sentence.

It was captain that they appointed him. [7]

Whereas in a relative clause, the noun can be followed by **who, whom, that, which, and whose,** in a cleft sentence the noun is frequently followed by **that** and in some cases by **who.**

10.3 Pseudo-cleft sentences

A pseudo cleft sentence, like a cleft sentence, has two clauses and is used to focus an element of a sentence.

He needs some rest. [8]

What he needs is some rest. [8a]

The cleft sentence with **what** is used either as the subject or complement of the verb **be,** the most frequent position being the subject position.

What we require is more money. (S of **be**) [9]

More money is **what we require.** (C of **be**) [10]

Usually, a pseudo-cleft sentence focusses the complement or the verb element of a sentence.

What he is, is an enigma. (focus on C) [11]

What he did was (to) jump over the wall. (focus on V) [12]

When the focus is on the predicate/the verb element, the verb of the **wh-** clause is **do** and the verb of the other clause is either the **to-** infinitive or the bare infinitive.

Exercise 2

Write the unmarked or unfocussed sentence for each one of the following focussed sentences. Also mention which constituent in each one of these sentences has been focussed.

1. It is the press that is responsible for this story.
2. It is this cow that he purchased at the fair.
3. This room is what we need.
4. It is Rita who is knocking at the door.
5. It was cheese that we had for dinner.

6. What he wrote was a good script.
7. It was last month that I paid the electricity bill.
8. It was in school that I met her.
9. What she bought was very expensive.
10. What she requires is some sleep.

10.4 Extraposition

We discussed the concept of extraposition in chapter 7 in detail. Extraposition involves the postponement of the clausal subject (finite or non-finite) to the end of the sentence and the subject position is replaced by it which is the anticipatory or unreal subject. The rule is as follows:

Subject + predicate → It + predicate + subject
(extraposed delayed subject)

That the earth is round is a fact. [13]

It is a fact that **the earth is round.**

How you treat him does not matter. [14]

It does not matter **how you treat him.**

To fail in the examination is unpardonable. [15]

It is unpardonable **to fail in the examination.**

Though we treat the delayed subject as an element for focus, it is the sentence with the delayed subject which is more frequent.

10.5 Existential sentences with introductory 'there'

Existential sentences begin with an introductory **there** and in this way resemble cleft sentences. For example, it would be unusual to use 16; one would rather use 16a.

A pen is on the table. [16]

There is a pen on the table. [16a]

Notice that the subject is postponed and its position is taken by *there*. However, the rule for this delay of the actual subject is that the subject is an indefinite subject like, **someone, anyone,** or beginning with **a/an** and the verb has a form of **be** either as the main verb or as auxiliary. Introductory *there* can be used with any of the sentence patterns.

The rule can be presented as

Indefinite subject + be - (V) + predicate

→ There + be (V) + indefinite subject + predicate

S LV C

Someone is sick. [17]

→ There is someone sick.

A cow is grazing outside. [18]

→ There is a cow grazing outside.

Someone is knocking at the door. [19]

→ There is someone knocking at the door.

S TrV Od (A)

A man is opening your house. [20]

→ There is a man opening your house.

A girl is watering the trees in your garden. [21]

→ There is a girl watering the trees in your garden.

S TrV Di Oi Od

Someone is buying her a book. [22]

→ There is someone buying her a book.

S TrVcomp Od Co

A man is dyeing his shirt red. [23]

→ There is a man dyeing his shirt red.

11

Prepositions and Phrasal Verbs

11.1 Prepositions

11.1.1 Introduction

A preposition is a word which is usually followed by a noun or a noun phrase which is the object of the preposition.

I met him **at the bank.** [1]

The girl in **the blue dress** is a flight engineer. [2]

A preposition along with the noun/noun phrase forms a **prepositional phrase.** Prepositional phrases have syntactic functions:

a. Postnominal modifier in a noun phrase: As discussed in section 3.3.2.1, a prepositional phrase is the most frequent postnominal modifier in English.

   The book **on Hardy** is lying on my table. [3]

   We visited the garden **beside the river.** [4]

b. Adverbial: As mentioned in section 4.4.3, prepositional phrases are most frequently used to modify a verb.

   We played cricket **in the afternoon.** [5]

   She slept **during the recess.** [6]

c. Complementation: A prepositional phrase can also function as the complement of an adjective.

   I was mad **at him.** [7]

   She is very fond **of me.** [8]

Two of the syntactic functions of the prepositional phrase mentioned above are subject to ambiguity. Sometimes it is difficult to make out whether a prepositional phrase modifies the noun head or the verb head.

He waved at the girl **with a smile.** [9]

We saw the play **on the terrace.** [10]

Exercise 1

Identify the prepositional phrases and mention their syntactic functions in the following sentences:

1. This bag is full of coins.
2. The Principal waited for the results in his room.
3. The girl in the blue dress is his sister.
4. The boy with the red tie caught the ball in time.
5. She was angry with me.
6. We played games in the evening with our neighbours.
7. The dog with a black collar is very ferocious.
8. She is terribly afraid of her father.
9. The flowers in the basket were bought yesterday at the flower show.
10. They went into the building.

11.1.2 Prepositions and adverbs

Some of the words treated as prepositions can also function as adverbs:

He looked **up** the stairs. (*preposition*) [11]

He looked **up.** (*adverb*) [12]

All of us waited **below** the bridge. (*preposition*) [13]

All of us waited **below.** (*adverb*) [14]

11.1.3 Simple and compound prepositions

Most of the prepositions which are commonly used in English are simple one-word prepositions:

above	*across*	*among*	*at*	*before*
behind	*between*	*by*	*during*	*for*
from	*on*	*to*	*till*	

Compound prepositions can be two-word or three-word sequences.

Some of the two-word compound prepositions are:

as far	*due to*	*away from*	*contrary to*
ahead of	*instead of*	*but for*	*because of*
according to	*prior to*	*next to*	*inside of*

Three-word compound prepositions usually have the structure:

preposition 1 + noun + preposition 2

on account of	*in accordance with*	*by means of*
in aid of	*by way of*	*in front of*
in case of	*on top of*	*in lieu of*

11.1.4 Meanings of prepositions

11.1.4.1 Prepositions of place:

Prepositions of position: *in*, *at* and *on*

Study the following figures and expressions:

in:

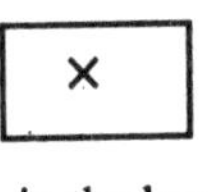

in the box

in the glass

in the house

There is a biscuit **in the box.** [15]

There is some milk **in the glass/cup.** [16]

She is singing **in the house/in the garden.** [17]

She always carries books **in her bag/in her car.** [18]

at:

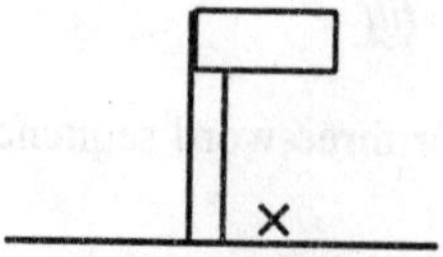

at the bus stop/station

at the window/door

She met me **at the bus stop/at the station.** [19]

There is a lady standing **at the door/at the window.** [20]

on:

on the window

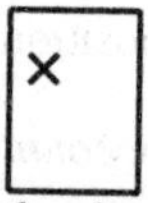

on the door

The books are lying **on the table.** [21]

There is a butterfly **on the window.** [22]

You haven't written anything **on the paper.** [23]

a. We also use **in** for a continent, a state, a town, a city or a village.

He was born **in Germany.** [24]

Madhu is **in Sri Lanka** at present. [25]

Rakesh lives **in Coimbatore.** [26]

There are many good houses **in the village.** [27]

b. We use **in** for a road, a street, a room and any other enclosed space big enough to be all around a person.

Meena lives **in Victoria street.** [28]

She is sitting **in her office.** [29]

It was dark **in the cinema hall.** [30]

Manish was sleeping **in the garden.** [31]

c. We use **at** to describe a position.

Khalil was waiting for me **at the railway station.** [32]

She was standing **at the door.** [33]

d. We use **at** for a house or an address.

He lives **at 32, Lower Circular Road.** [34]

We were **at home** in the evening. [35]

e. **On** has the meaning of on the surface.

We pasted the notice **on the board.** [36]

They were practising **on the field.** [37]

There is a TV set **on the shelf.** [38]

f. One can use **in** or **at** with school/college and with other buildings. **In** is used when one treats school/college as a building or a three-dimensional structure. **At** is used when the function of the building is referred to.

Shailaja is **in school/at school.** [39]

I was **at Krishna's house** last night. [40]

The rooms **in Krishna's house** are very spacious. [41]

Exercise 2

1. The minister is attending an international conference .... Russia.
2. I'll meet you .... the airport.
3. I met her .... the bus stand.
4. The cows are grazing .... the field.
5. Dilip was waiting for me .... the hall.
6. She has a scar .... her forehead.
7. The insurance office is .... 19, Gandhi Marg.
8. Lucknow is situated .... the river Gomti.
9. They held the meeting .... the open ground.
10. That picture hanging .... the wall is hundred years old.

Movement towards: *to*, *into*, *onto*

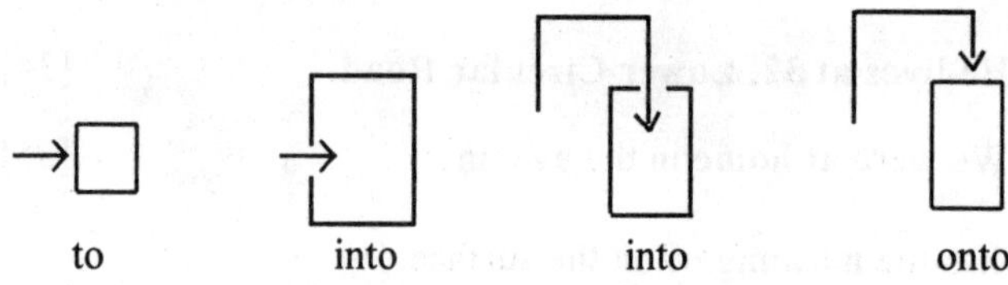

To indicates movement towards a building, place, country, etc.

They went **to the market** in the evening. [42]

I go **to work** in the morning. [43]

She drove **to the airport** with her friend. [44]

I have been **to Nepal** twice. [45]

He always walks **to college.** [46]

Into indicates movement into a room, building, rivers etc.

She ran **into the room.** [47]

He dived **into the river.** [48]

Onto indicates movement on to the top of a building/vehicle etc.

We got **onto the bus.** [49]

Sanjeev climbed **onto the roof.** [50]

Prepositions of position: *above, below, over, by, beside* and *behind*

These prepositions can best be explained with the help of a figure:

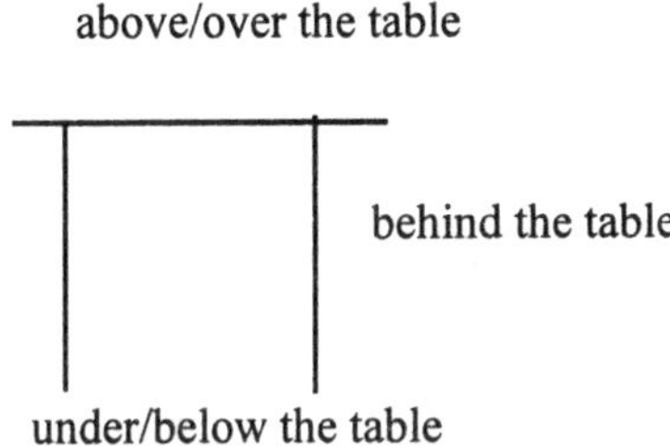

The bird is flying **over the tree.** [51]

The cat was sleeping **under the table.** [52]

Mira stood **beside the car.** [53]

Over and **above, under** and **below** are sometimes a matter of confusion.

Over and **above** are sometimes used interchangeably but **over** means vertically **above** and thus indicates *nearness*.

He had a cut **over his lip.** [54]

We hung our clothes **over the fireplace.** [55]

Above on the other hand, means *higher than.*

They live in a flat **above ours.** [56]

Whereas sentences 54 and 55 only indicate that the *cut* was vertically *above his lip* and the *clothes* were vertically *above the fireplace*, sentence 56 indicates *that they live in a flat which is at a place higher than our flat*. Similarly, *under* means vertically below and thus indicates *nearness*.

He had a **cut under his lip.** [57]

Our cat always sleeps **under my bed.** [58]

Below means lower than:

We saw small houses **below us from the plane.** [59]

The preposition **behind** has the meaning of *at the back of something* and by or **beside** has the meaning of *by the side of*.

He left the car **behind the garage.** [60]

She stood **behind the door.** [61]

He left the car **beside the garage.** [62]

She stood **beside the door.** [63]

Exercise 3

Fill in the blanks with appropriate prepositions:

in into onto above over under below behind by beside

1. I 'm not feeling well. I'm going .... bed.
2. I saw an aeroplane flying .... our houses.
3. She has a mole .... her eye.
4. A bird flew .... the room through the window.
5. She has been sleeping .... the room for the last two hours.
6. Our college is situated .... the temple.
7. Your letter is lying .... the books.
8. I've been .... Canada.
9. We could see the river .... us from the bridge.
10. She climbed .... the running train.

Prepositions of space: *between, among, around* and *round*

Between relates to the position of a person/ thing to two other persons/ things. However, it can also be used if we have a definite number in mind.

Flora is standing **between Sheikh and Smita.** [64]

Flora is standing **between Sheikh, Smita and Terry.** [65]

Madhya Pradesh lies **between U. P., Rajasthan, Bihar, Gujarat, Maharashtra, Orissa and Andhra Pradesh.** [66]

Among relates to the position of a person/thing to more than two persons/ things, when we do not have any definite number in mind.

Flora was standing **among her friends.** [67]

Our flat is the biggest **among all the flats in the building.** [68]

Around and **round** refer to a circular motion or position around another object.

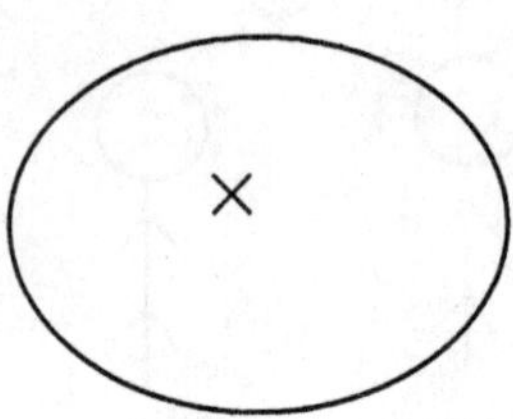

The children were running **around** the building. [69]

The earth revolves **round** the sun. [70]

Around can also mean *in the area of*, or *in various positions.*

All of us were hanging **around the courtroom.** [71]

There are many gardens **around the lake.** [72]

Prepositions of passage: *across* and *through*

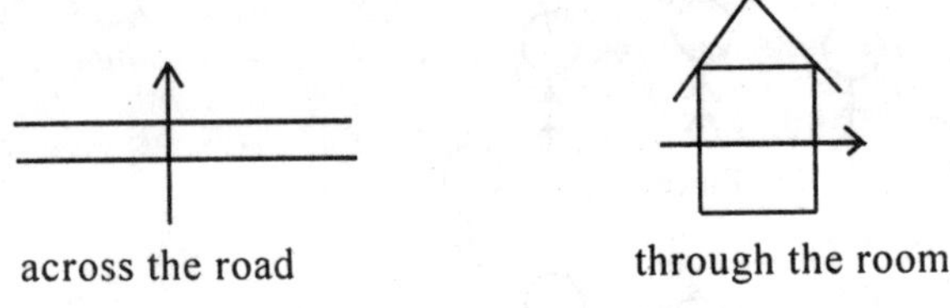

He drove the car **across the road.** [73]

The bullet went **through the room.** [74]

Prepositions of movement: *up, down, along, across.*

along the road

up the hill

down the hill

She ran **up the hill.** [75]

We came **down the hill.** [76]

Monica ran **along the road.** [77]

Monica ran **across the road.** [78]

11.1.4.2 Prepositions of time

Prepositions of time position: *at*, *on* and *in are* used with

a. an exact point of time like *at 5o'clock, at 9.30, at midnight.*

b. with meal times like *at lunch, at dinner* and

c. with festivals like *at Xmas, at Dussehra*, etc.

We'll have ameeting **at five o'clock.** (exact time) [79]

We shall discuss it **at breakfast.** (at meal time) [80]

They're going to have a party **at Diwali.** (a festival) [81]

On is used with a more general point of time like *days of the week, dates* and *parts of the day.*

He gave us a test **on Wednesday.** [82]

His birthday falls **on 18 May.** [83]

I visited her **on Friday evening**. [84]

In is used with *months, years, seasons, centuries* and *parts of the day.*

The elections will be held **in February.** [85]

India got Independence **in 1947.** [86]

We have a long vacation **in summer.** [87]

Many countries became industrialised **in the twentieth century.** [88]

There is a thick mist **in the morning.** [89]

Exercise 4

***Fill in the blanks with* at, on *or* in:**

1. The examination will begin .... ten o'clock.
2. All of us meet .... lunch everyday.
3. Our academic session begins .... August and ends .... April.
4. Many scientific instruments were invented .... the nineteenth century.
5. Jawaharlal Nehru was born .... 1889.
6. Her mother is a doctor .... this hospital but she is .... leave at the moment.
7. This shop was established .... 1982.
8. The old students of our school are meeting .... Christmas.
9. We posted the letter to you .... Tuesday.
10. The evening show begins .... 6.30 .... the evening.

Prepositions of duration: *for, during, over, through, throughout*

a. **for** is used to express a period of time:

for two years *for five hours* *for ten weeks*

We played football **for two hours.** [90]

They lived in Behrampur **for five years.** [91]

She will be in London **for a week.** [92]

b. **during** is used with known periods of time such as:

during winter *during the vacation*

It was very cold **during the winter** last year. [93]

Prices had gone up **during the Second World War.** [94]

We went to Ooty **during the vacation.** [95]

She fell asleep **during the film.** [96]

over, through and **throughout** have a meaning of *all through.* **Over** is followed by nouns/noun phrases denoting shorter periods of time like *holidays* and *through* or *throughout* is used with longer periods of time. *Over Sunday, over the weekend, throughout the middle ages, through the last month*

However, recently **over** has also been used with longer periods: *over the last four years*

We played cricket **over the weekend.** [97]

Agriculture was the main source of income for the majority of the people **throughout the middle ages.** [98]

from, from ...to, until, upto, between and *after*

a. **from:** is used to indicate the time when something starts.

People will be allowed in **from eight** in the morning. [99]

They travelled by train **over Sunday.** [100]

There is a great demand for autorickshaws **from six** in the evening. [101]

b. **from ... to/until/upto** is used to express duration.

We waited for you at the theatre **from six until/ upto eight** in the evening. [102]

It rained heavily from **Monday to Thursday** last week. [103]

c. **between ... and** is used to express a period of time by indicating the starting and end point but may not refer to the entire time.

You can see me **between 9 and 11 in the morning.** [104]

I'll ring you up **between breakfast** and lunchtime. [105]

Notice that whereas **from ... to/until/upto** express the complete duration, **between ... and** indicates sometime/anytime between the two points mentioned.

by, until/till

a. **by** is used to express *not later than.*

We'll reach your house **by 5 o'clock.**
(at 5 or earlier) [106]

She always gets up **by six in the morning.** [107]

b. **until/till** is used to indicate that a situation continues for some time and then stops.

We worked in the library **until eight o'clock.** [108]

All of us danced **until four in the morning.** [109]

until/till can also be used to indicate that something did not/ will not happen before a particular time.

The library was not opened **till 11 o'clock.** [110]

The guests will not arrive **until five in the evening.** [111]

after/before

Open this envelope **after 10. 0'clock**. [112]

Don't open this envelope **before 10.0'clock.** [113]

Lunch will be served **after the meeting.** [114]

A short meeting will be held **before lunch.** [115]

Exercise 5

Fill in the blanks with appropriate prepositions:

1. We waited .... the bus stop .... half an hour but couldn't get a bus.
2. A few students were talking .... his lecture.
3. The tickets are sold .... ten in the morning.
4. She has to pay the fees .... Monday.
5. They've been in this business .... the last three generations.

6. We met all our friends .... our stay in Dubai.
7. I'll not leave office .... six o'clock.
8. He worked hard the whole week and then took leave .... two days.
9. It is very hot .... summer .... Hyderabad.
10. I attended a computer course .... the summer vacation.

11.1.4.3 Prepositions of means: by is used for means of transport and communication.

a. We use **by** and a noun without the article **the** to indicate means of transport.

by bus, by train, by car, by air

We travelled from Delhi to Amritsar **by train.** [116]

They went to Lucknow **by car.** [117]

I'm going to Udaipur **by air.** [118]

b. We may also use **by** and a noun for means of communication.

I received the interview call **by fax.** [119]

You could inform him **by phone.** [120]

11.1.4.4 Prepositions of instrument and agentive: with and by

a. **with + noun phrase** is used to express the sense of instrument. **With** is usually followed by an inanimate noun.

with a key *with a stone* *with a stick*

She opened the door **with a key.** [121]

Marina broke the window **with a stone.** [122]

He pulled down the rag **with a stick.** [123]

b. **by + noun** is used to indicate the agentive role of a noun in the passive sentence. The agent is inanimate noun.

My mother received a letter today. (*active*) [124a]

A letter was received **by my mother today.**(*passive*) [124b]

This picture was painted **by Rohit.** [125]

c. Occasionally, **by + an inanimate noun** may be used for instrumental function.

The wall was damaged **by the storm.** [126]

The wall was damaged **by the branch of a tree.** [127a]

The wall was damaged **with the branch of a tree.** [127b]

Sentences 126 and 127a do not include a human agent. Sentence 127b indicates that *the wall was damaged by a human being with the branch of a tree.*

11.1.4.5 Prepositions of manner/resemblance: *like* and *as*

a. Manner/comparison can be expressed by **like:**

He danced **like a man possessed.** [128]

She worked **like a demon.** [129]

b. **as** expresses the sense of a role.

He delivered the lecture **as a Professor.** [130]

She speaks **as a lawyer.** [131]

11.1.4.6 Some other prepositions - I: *with, for, against*

a. **with** can express the meaning of *in the company of* or *together with* with animate noun phrases.

Ritika went to Shimla **with her father.** [132]

She always goes out in the evening **with her father.** [133]

b. **for** and **with** can be used to express solidarity and **against** is used to express opposition.

All of us spoke **for him.** [134]

We are **with you** on this issue. [135]

He spoke **against the motion.** [136]

Exercise 6

Fill in the blanks with appropriate prepositions:

1. I received this message .... telegram.
2. She behaves .... a great political leader.
3. I watched the film .... my friends.
4. They operated the lift .... a single pulley during the power breakdown.
5. She was .... this plan from the beginning and therefore she didn't vote .... it.
6. He goes to school .... bus.
7. I went to Mauritius .... my family.
8. The building was damaged .... lightning.
9. The leader of the opposition spoke .... the budget.
10. He received the question papers .... speed post.

11.1.4.7 Some other prepositions - II:

a. **Of** as a postnominal modifier similar to the genitive function.

the leg of a table *the barrel of a gun*

b. **With reference to** is used in business/official letters.

With reference to your application dated July 23 1998, I'm pleased to inform you that .... [137]

c. **In spite of** is used to express the meaning of concession.

> **In spite of** heavy rain, Ms Chandran came to the Centre. [138]

Exercise 7

Identify the meaning of each one of the prepositions in the following sentences:

1. They travelled to Anantapur by car.
2. A meeting of the faculty will be held at three o'clock on 22 March.
3. Monish and Pervez are playing beside the building.
4. We watched several films over the weekend.
5. We are going to renovate our house during the winter vacation.
6. Gurdaspur is a prosperous town in Punjab.
7. Your father is waiting for you in the bank.
8. I saw her while she was getting into her car.
9. She has fixed the fan right over your desk.
10. The letter was sent to him by registered post.

11.2 Phrasal verbs

A phrasal verb in English is a combination of two or three words and has a single meaning. A phrasal verb of two words may consist of a verb + an adverb + a preposition. Both the adverb or the preposition when used after a verb in a phrasal verb is called a **particle.** Thus one can say that a phrasal verb consists of a **verb + a particle** and the particle can be an adverb or a preposition.

> My car **broke down** on the main road. (*verb + adverb*) [139]
>
> We **worked out** the solution to this problem. (*verb+adverb*) [140]
>
> He **got over** his failure in the examination after a few days. (*verb + preposition*) [141]

There are a number of phrasal verbs comprising three words: **a verb + an adverb + a preposition:**

I **look forward to** meeting her. [142]

He **has gone back** on his word. [143]

Notice that an adverb or a preposition in a phrasal verb is an integral part of the phrasal verb and both the verb and the adverb, or the verb and the preposition or the verb and the adverb and the preposition contribute to the total meaning of the phrasal verb.

11.2.1 Two-word phrasal verbs

Two-word phrasal verbs can be of four types:

a. intransitive verb + adverb

b. transitive verb + adverb

c. intransitive verb + preposition

d. transitive verb + preposition

11.2.1.1 Intransitive verb + adverb: A phrasal verb (intransitive verb + adverb particle) can be intransitive, i.e., it does not require an object after it but one can use an adverbial as an optional element.

My car **broke down on the road.** [144]

Some common phrasal verbs of this type are given below with their meanings and examples:

break down: fail to work, to stop working (*used for machinery, vehicles*)

I have given my refrigerator for repair as it **broke down** last week. [145]

catch on: understand (*used with people*)

I couldn't **catch on** to her lecture. [146]

chip in: many people putting money together

All the boys in our class **chipped in** to raise the Drougt Relief Fund. [147]

come down: to fall, to lower (*of prices, rates, temperature etc.*)

The finance minister announced that the interest rates would **come down.** [148]

die down: become quieter

The commotion in the hostel **died down** after two hours. [149]

fall apart: break into pieces because of being old or badly made.

The table **fell apart** because it was made of cracked wood. [150]

fall through: fail to be completed (*used with plans, agreements, meetings, contracts etc.*)

His plan **fell through** due to lack of support from his colleagues. [151]

go on: continue

They **went on** with the work until midnight. [152]

hold on: wait (*used for people, for polite commands/requests or in indirect speech, commonly used in telephone conversation.*)

Could you **hold on** for a while?
I'll finish my speech in a second. [153]

pass away: die (*of people*)

I'm sorry to know that Monica's father **passed away.** [154]

set in: to begin and continue

The winter has **set in** early this year. [155]

set out: start a journey

What time did they **set out** this morning? [156]

take off: start or leave the airport

The plane **took off at 6p.m.** [157]

turn up: arrive

She **turned up** late for the meeting. [158]

Exercise 8

Rewrite the following sentences choosing a suitable phrasal verb in the right grammatical form for the underlined words in each sentence:

break down	drag on	fall apart
break out	drop in	fall off
catch on	drop out	fall out
come down	doze off	fall through
stay up	turn up	get along
pass away	go on	set in
hold on	settle down	make off
stand out		

1. Autumn had already begun.
2. I don't have a friendly relationship with Vijaya.
3. They did not arrive at the conference venue.
4. They disagreed with each other on a petty matter.
5. He left the course after two months at the university.
6. Their scheme ended without success after it was found that they were lying.
7. I remained awake last night because I had to finish my project.
8. Wait a minute; I'll see if Rakhee is around.

9. The General could be noticed among all the senior officers.
10. Her mother made a will before she died.
11. On seeing the police inspector, the thief escaped in a hurry.
12. John is sitting comfortably near the fireplace.
13. The meeting could not take place as many members objected to many items on the agenda.
14. We had to spend the night in a hotel because our bus stopped working on the way.
15. This statue may break into pieces as it has not been set properly.
16. She fell asleep during the concert.
17. He continued delivering his lecture even after the bell had rung.
18. The student enrollment has decreased this year.
19. This case has gone on slowly for ten years now.
20. The second world war started suddenly in 1939.
21. I visited her without prior announcement and surprised her.
22. Our teacher has taught us grammar for six months but we have failed to understand it.

11.2.1.2 Transitive verb + adverb: This type of phrasal verb requires an object as an obligatory element.

You can **put on** the light. [159]

She **called up** John. [160]

The object of a phrasal verb of this type can be used either before or after the adverb. Notice that in 159 and 160, the objects, *the light* and *John* have been used after the adverb particles **on** and **up.** However, it is possible to use the objects before the adverb particles in the above sentences.

You can switch the light on. [161]

She called John up. [162]

If the object is a pronoun, then it has to be used before the adverb.

You can **fill it up.** [163]

She **called him up.** [164]

Some more phrasal verbs with their meanings and examples:

carry out: complete or fulfil a promise, task, duty, job etc.

The major **carried out** the Government's orders. [165]

draw up: prepare the plan for something

She **has drawn up** a plan for starting a new paper for the course. [166]

fill in: complete details in a form etc.

You can **fill in** this form for hotel booking. [167]

give up: stop doing or having something

Vidyadhar **has given up** the idea of going to Spain. [168]

hush up: hide information from public knowledge

The principal has **hushed up** the matter. [169]

look up: find out a piece of information from a source of reference

She **looked up** his telephone number in the directory. [170]

mess up: spoil something

He **messed up** the maths paper. [171]

phase out: stop using something gradually

The Indian Air Force is **phasing out** the old aircraft. [17

put off: delay or postpone something

The deputy Commissioner has **put off** the meeting of the citizen's Council to next week. [173]

rule out: reject an idea or action

The minister **ruled out** higher wages to public sector workers at a meeting on Wednesday. [174]

see off: go with someone to the railway station, bus stop, or airport to say goodbye to him/her.

I went to the station to **see** my brother **off.** [175]

sort out: organise things like books, luggage etc. in categories, find solutions to problems

She is **sorting out** the old books in the library. [176]

try out: test something

The new car was **tried out** on the road last month. [177]

Exercise 9

Rewrite the following sentences choosing the correct phrasal verb to be used in place of the underlined words in each sentence making any other changes that may be necessary:

bring about	fill up	make out	set aside
bring up	find out	mess up	set up
call off	fix up	pack off	set out
call up	give up	phase out	sort out
carry out	hand over	pull down	step up
cook up	hush up	put off	take down
cross out	knock down	rule out	try out
draw up	let down	see off	win over
fill in	look up	set aside	wipe out

1. The municipal corporation destroyed the old building to raise a new one.
2. Indian Oil corporation has increased oil production in recent weeks.
3. She was disappointed with her children.
4. Ranjit dressed himself in his school blazer in the afternoon as the Principal was going to visit his class.
5. The company has postponed its annual board meeting because the chairman is ill.
6. He deleted the amount and wrote down a new figure on the cheque.
7. I was able to understand that she had not attended the meeting.
8. She was hit and killed by a speeding truck.
9. I sent him to a hostel.
10. We have been able to make them support us.
11. The war has completely destroyed the countryside.
12. I've arranged a meeting with the managing Director.
13. They have prepared a plan to start a new construction company.
14. Mukesh invented a false story about his book.
15. I couldn't understand the last part of his speech.
16. Rakesh's mother educated and reared Rakesh with great love and care.
17. We gave our cabin baggage to the flight attendant on entering the plane.
18. I've saved a lakh for my son's college education.
19. She may complete this form for admission to the B.C.A course.
20. The Director has hidden the case regarding the kickbacks.
21. He can write whatever is dictated very fast.
22. We have tested this book in different countries.

23. You need to <u>organise</u> your luggage at the railway station.
24. All of us went to the railway station to <u>say goodbye</u> to our English teacher.
25. The university may <u>cancel</u> the examinations.
26. He <u>completed</u> his work to the satisfaction of his employer.
27. Please <u>fill</u> this glass with coke and ice cream.
28. They have <u>built</u> a monument in memory of the late Prime Minister.
29. You must <u>find out</u> the meaning of a word that you don't know in a dictionary.
30. Manish is planning to <u>stop</u> smoking.
31. I am going to <u>telephone</u> her in the morning.
32. His marriage <u>caused</u> a great change to his personality.
33. The national airlines is going to <u>stop using</u> small aircraft.
34. The foreign minister has <u>rejected</u> any talks with the extremists.
35. He has <u>spoiled</u> the whole plan.

11.2.1.3 Intransitive verb + preposition: There are some phrasal verbs which have an intransitive verb followed by a preposition. The preposition is followed by a noun phrase. The preposition and the noun phrase form a prepositional phrase.

I don't **approve of** his conduct. [178]

Notice that in 178 **approve of** is the phrasal verb and *his conduct* is the noun phrase used as the object of the preposition **of** and *of his conduct* is the prepositional phrase. This means that *his conduct* is not the direct object of the phrasal verb **approve of.**

Some of the important phrasal verbs of the type intransitive verb + preposition are given below with their meanings and examples:

account for: a. explain how something happened
b. explain how money was spent

He will have to **account for** his silly behaviour. [179]

She was asked to **account for** the missing amount. [180]

bank on: rely on somebody/something

We were **banking on** your support in the board election. [181]

break into: enter a house illegally by breaking a lock, a door or a window

The thieves **broke into** the house in the early hours on Monday. [182]

call on: visit someone (a short visit)

We **called on** the vice-chancellor yesterday. [183]

count on: depend on someone for help

She can **count on** her family for support. [184]

dispose of: get rid of

He has **disposed of** his old car. [185]

fall for: be attracted to someone.

She **fell for** the little child as soon as she entered the orphanage. [186]

get over: recover from an unpleasant experience or problem

It took years for her to **get over** the death of her son. [187]

laugh at: make fun of or mock at someone

She **laughed at** his stupidity. [188]

look after: take care of someone or something

She **looked after** our business when we were abroad. [189]

look into: to investigate or examine facts

The chief minister himself **looked into** the case as it concerned the security of the state. [190]

part with: to give away something valuable

She **parted with** her piece of land for the sake of her children. [191]

reckon with: take into account, consider

I had not **reckoned with** the fact that he had no experience at all. [192]

run into: to face, experience, meet by chance

He has **run into** financial difficulties in his business. [193]

take after: have the qualities of someone in the family

He **takes after** his father. [194]

Exercise 10

Fill in the blanks with suitable phrasal verbs:

1. Meenakshi is .... an agency.
2. This book .... the effects of drugs on health.
3. This area .... the jurisdiction of the municipal corporation.
4. I .... the existence of God.
5. Try as he might he could not .... to his father as all the telephone lines had snapped in the storm.

11.2.1.4 Transitive verb + preposition: Phrasal verbs of this type are followed by two noun phrases. The first noun phrase is used after the transitive verb and is, therefore, the object of the verb. The second noun phrase is used after the preposition and is the object of the preposition.

Germany **drew** many European countries into war in 1939. [195]

Notice that in 195, the phrasal verb used is **drew into.** There is an object, *many European countries* used after the main verb **drew** and there is a second object *war* used after the preposition **into.**

Some important phrasal verbs of this type are given below with their meanings and examples:

assure of: give certainty or promise of one's willingness, support etc.

Rakesh has **assured me** of financial assistance for starting the factory. [196]

build into: to make something a permanent part of something else

The **cupboard was built into the wall.** [197]

build on: use something as a base

Our economy **has been built on our potential for agricultural growth.** [198]

engage in: to make busy or occupy people in some activity

Our teacher **engaged us in a lively discussion on the nuclear policy.** [199]

hold against: blame someone for his failure, mistake etc.

He **holds an unnecessary grudge against me.** [200]

lay before: present an idea, argument etc. before a person or a group

The plan **was laid before the group.** [201]

leave to: assign responsibility to someone

My father **has left the construction of the house to me.** [202]

put through: connect the telephone call to another person

I'll **put you through to the Dean**. [203]

read into: find something which does not exist

He unwarrantedly **reads bluff into everything you write.** [204]

thrust upon: force something upon someone

This work **has been thrust upon me.** [205]

11.2.2 Three-word phrasal verbs

Three-word phrasal verbs comprise verb + adverb + preposition: *boil down to, catch up with, get away with* etc.

He **can get away with** anything because he is the minister's son. [206]

Notice that **anything** is the object of the preposition **with.**

Such phrasal verbs are mostly restricted to informal spoken discourse. Most of the three-word phrasal verbs are intransitive, though there are a few transitive phrasal verbs in this category.

11.2.2.1 Intransitive verb + adverb + preposition: Some of the important verbs of this type are:

come up with: think of a plan

She may **come up with** a good selection. [207]

come down with: affected by

Rohit has **come down with** measles. [208]

come in for: be the target of

Builders have **come in for** a lot of criticism by the common people. [209]

cry out for: need something very much

University teachers are **crying out for** better employment benefits. [210]

fall back on: rely on something after other alternatives have failed

She has **fallen back on** her brother's support. [211]

grow out of: develop from something smaller to something bigger

He has **grown out of** his youthful pranks. [212]

look up to: respect someone

He **looked up to** his elder brother as his moral mentor. [213]

walk away with: win a prize etc. very easily

He **walked away with** the first prize in the contest. [214]

11.2.2.2 Transitive verb + adverb + preposition: There are a few three-word transitive phrasal verbs.

put down to: ascribed to

We **put our development down to industrialisation.** [215]

Notice that our development is the object of the verb put and industrialisation is the object of the preposition to.

let in for: feel one has got involved in something difficult

I didn't realise what I had let myself in for. [216]

play off against: set one person off against another to get an advantage.

She played her sister off against her brother. [217]

12

Word Formation

12.1 Root, base and affix

In order to understand the different processes of word formation in English, it is important to understand the concepts of **root, base** and **affix.** The root is that part of the word which carries the main or the principal meaning of the word. An affix is added to the root of a word. In the word *unhappy, happy* is the root because it carries the principal meaning and **un-** is the affix because it is added to the root *happy*. Some other examples are:

a. affix + root

il- + legible (illegible)
re- + play (replay)
dis- + honest (dishonest)
un- + able (unable)
anti- + tank (antitank)

b. root + affix

boy + -s (boys)
free + -dom (freedom)
walk + -ing (walking)
rain + -y (rainy)
teach + - er (teacher)

c. affix + root + affix

pre- + history + -ic (prehistoric)
anti- + nation + -al (antinational)
in- + able + -ity (inability)
hyper- + act + -ive (hyperactive)
under- + cook + -ed (undercooked)

The root can, usually, be used independently as a word, but an affix requires a root or a base to which it can be attached. The base is that part of a word, which may be a root or a root + an affix and to which we can attach affixes. For example, we can analyse the words *hyperactive* and *undercooked* as follows:

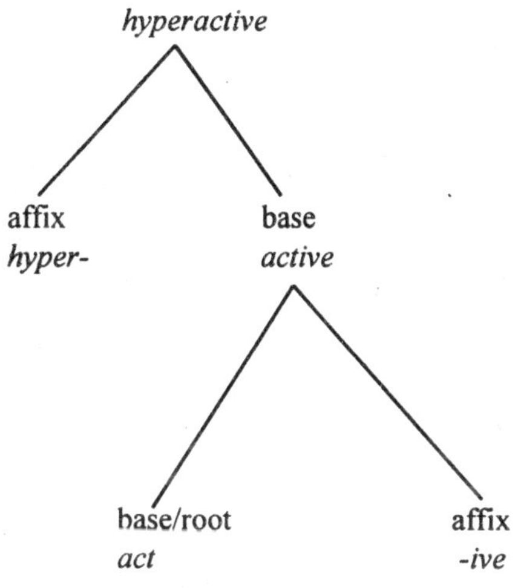

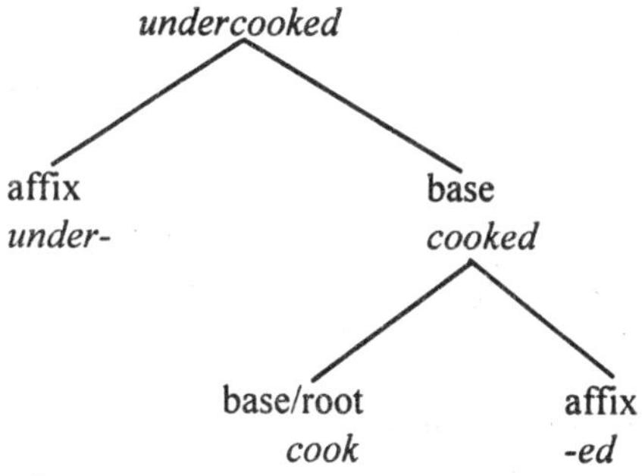

As the above analysis indicates, a root is also the base but a base may not necessarily be the root. A base can be a root or a root + affix (-es) to which other affix (es) can be attached.

Exercise 1

Identify the root and affix(es) in the following words:

multinational	funds	preschool
teaching	humanity	underground
idolise	machinery	responsibility

Exercise 2

Analyse the folowing words into base, root and affix (es). One example has been done for you:

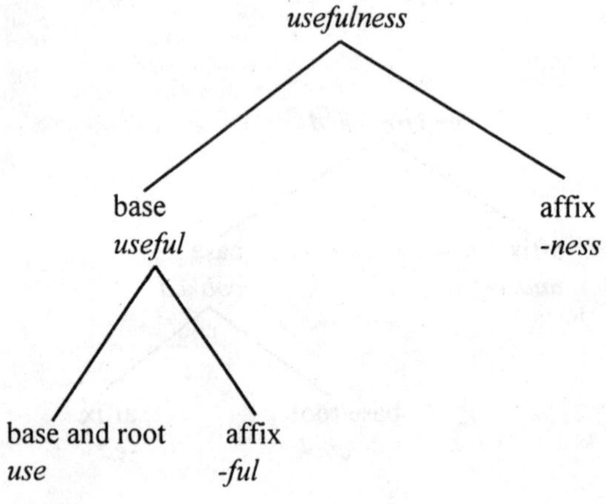

denationalisation pre-professional uncomfortable
functional post-modernism disagree
bimonthly interdisciplinary immoral

12.1.1 Affixes

Affixes are of three types: **prefixes, infixes** and **suffixes.** Prefixes are those affixes which occur before roots or bases. For example:

ante-room **irr**egular **sub**way **un**able **post**war

There are no infixes in English.

Suffixes are those affixes whish occur after roots or bases:

truth**ful** nation**al** abil**ity** book**s** talk**ing**

Suffixes can be further divided into **inflectional** and **derivational** suffixes. Inflectional suffixes are those which do not change the part of speech of the word to which it is attached. For example, the noun phrase suffix, **-s** or **-es** is an inflectional suffix because it is attached to a singular noun to form a plural noun.

pen - pen**s** dog - dog**s**

Similarly, the present participle suffix **-ing** is also an inflectional suffix, as it does not change the part of the speech of a verb to which it is attached.

run - runn**ing** watch - watch**ing**

There are eight inflectional suffixes in English:

1. noun plural -s or -es *doors, boxes*
2. noun possessive 's or -s' *girls', John's*
3. present third person -s or -es *walks, fries*
4. present participle -ing *walking, frying*

5.	past tense	-d or -ed	*forced, talked*
6.	past participle	-d or -ed	*forced, talked*
7.	comparative	-er	*higher, greater*
8.	superlative	-est	*highest, greatest*

All other suffixes are derivational suffixes. Derivational suffixes, usually, though not always, change the part of speech of the root or base to which it is attached:

adjective	noun	verb	noun	adjective	verb
happy	*happiness*	*sing*	*singer*	*quick*	*quicken*
true	*truth*	*break*	*breakage*	*simple*	*simplify*
able	*ability*	*act*	*action*	*sad*	*sadden*

Differences between English inflectional and derivational suffixes:

1. Inflectional suffixes are limited in number. Derivational suffixes, on the other hand are greater in number though they too can be listed.

2. An inflectional suffix is combined to a large number of roots but a derivational suffix is combined to a limited number of roots. For example, we can add -s or -es to a large number of singular nouns to form plural nouns:

   book - books   car - cars   dish - dishes

   However, in order to change an adjective into a noun we use different derivational suffixes with different words.

adjective	noun	derivational suffix used
true	truth	-th
free	freedom	-dom
able	ability	-ity

3. As mentioned earlier, an inflectional suffix does not change the part of speech, whereas a derivational suffix usually changes the part of speech of the root or base to which it is added.

4. An inflectional suffix closes off a word whereas a derivational suffix doesn't. This implies that it is possible to add another suffix, either derivational or inflectional, after a derivational suffix. For example,

nation national nation**alise** national**ised**

However, once **-s** is added to *nation* and we get *nations*, the word is closed off and no other suffix can be added.

Exercise 3

In the following pairs of words the word in the second column is formed by adding a derivational suffix. Indicate the part of speech of each word under both the columns.

play	playful ....
free	freedom ....
modern	modernise ....
harm	harmless ....
quick	quickly ....
hospital	hospitalise ....
conspire	conspiracy ....
inform	informant ....
ideal	idealism ....
care	careful ....
day	daily ....
arrange........................	arrangement ....

Exercise 4

Write down the word in column B according to the part of speech indicated in brackets of the corresponding word in Column A:

A		B	
response	(noun)	....	(adj)
final	(adj)	....	(v)
attest	(v)	....	(n)
drive	(v)	....	(n)
mouth	(n)	....	(adj)
wide	(adj)	....	(n)
fame	(n)	....	(adj)
happy	(adj)	....	(adv)
code	(n)	....	(v)
legal	(adj)	....	(v)

12.2 Simple, complex and compound words

12.2.1 Simple words

Simple words comprise either the root or the root + an inflectional suffix:

boy - boys   walk - walking - walked
strong - stronger - strongest

12.2.2 Complex words

Complex words comprise the root and one or more prefixes and/or one or more derivational suffixes:

national   nationalise   nationalisation   denationalisation

Prefixes usually denote some meaning to the root or base to which they are attached.

1. Negative prefixes:

un-	unhappy	uncomfortable
dis-	disagree	dishonest
in-	incapable	injustice
il-	illegible	illegal
im-	impossible	impatient
ir-	irregular	irrelevant

2. Prefixes denoting place:

inter-	(between)	international	interdepartmental
intra-	(within)	intranational	intradepartmental
mid-	(in the middle of)	midday	midway
sub-	(below)	subway	subterranean
fore-	(front)	forearm	forehead

3. Prefixes denoting degree or size:

mini-	(little)	minibus	miniauditorium
arch-	(supreme)	archduke	archbishop
super-	(more than)	supernatural	supermarket

4. Some other important prefixes:

mis-	(wrongly)	misjudge	misguide
un-	(opposite action)	undo	unpack
pre-	(before)	pre-university	pre-primary
post-	(after)	post-graduation	post-war

pro-	(in favour of)	pro-Indian	pro-democracy
anti-	(against)	anti-social	anti-war
under-	(too little)	undernourished	underpaid
dis-	(reverse)	displace	dislodge
ex-	(former)	ex-director	expupil
re-	(again)	replay	re-enter
bi-	(two)	bilingual	bicycle
multi-	(many)	multicultuaral	multinational

Derivational suffixes

1. Suffixes of concrete nouns

   -er/-or: teacher, actor　　-ee: trainee, employee

   -ist: feminist, columnist　　-ant/-ent: assistant, attendant

2. Suffixes of abstract nouns

   -tion, -ion: action, examination　　-ness: kindness, greatness

   -ment: agreement, contentment　　-dom: kingdom, freedom

   -ity: mentality, stupidity　　-ing: clothing, drawing

   -ship: hardship, scholarship

3. Verb derivational suffixes

   -ise/-ise: privatise, nationalise　　-en: widen, broaden

   -ify: qualify, purify

4. Adjective derivational suffixes

   -able: capable, acceptable　　-ic: dramatic, artistic

   -ful: beautiful, careful　　-less: meaningless, hopeless

-ous: dangerous, voluminous   -y: healthy, funny

-ive: active, expensive   -al: musical, original

Exercise 5

a. ***Change the following words into concrete nouns:***

own	drive	edit	build	train
produce	tour	novel	pay	add

b. ***Change the following words into abstract nouns:***

invite	discuss	pay	develop
martyr	garden	arrange	responsible
feel	refuse		

c. ***Change the following words into verbs:***

beauty	class	modern	popular	deep

d. ***Change the following words into adjectives:***

power	harm	effect	health	thirst
greed	nation	culture	fame	courage

12.2.3 Compound words

A compound word is formed with more than one root but functions as a single word. Usually, though not always, a compound word in English comprises two roots only.

greenroom   blackbird   footlight

It is sometimes possible to have a compound word in which a derivational suffix is attached to either of the roots.

walking stick   washing machine

We must distinguish between a compound word which is a single word and a phrase comprising two different words. One way could be to look at the overall meaning of the compound. For example, *greenroom* as a compound word is not a *room* which is *green* but is a *room where stage actors get ready*. However, a *blue room*, as a noun phrase is a *room which is blue in colour*. Similarly, *blackbird* as a compound word is the name of a bird but a *black bird* as a phrase is *a bird which is black in colour*.

The second way to distinguish a noun phrase and a compound word is to contrast their stress patterns. A noun phrase has the primary stress on the second element whereas a compound word has the primary stress on the first element.

Noun phrase	**Compound word**
black ˈbird	ˈblackbird
small ˈroom	ˈgreenroom

Compound nouns: There are different types of compound nouns:

1. *noun + noun*

   earthquake handbag teacup letterbox handshake

2. *adjective + noun*

   blackboard heavyweight darkroom greenhouse

3. *present participle as verbal noun + noun*

   dining room frying pan swimming pool
   drawing room printing ink

4. *verb + noun*

   drawbridge grindstone pickpocket
   killjoy scarecrow

5. *pronoun + noun*

he-goat she-goat he-man

Compound adjectives:

1. *noun + adjective*

homesick taxfree foolproof

colourblind watertight

2. *adjective + adjective*

reddish-brown dark blue Anglo-French

Indo-American deaf-mute socioeconomic

3. *noun + present participle functioning as adjective*

lifegiving Hindi-speaking heart-breaking

4. *noun + past participle functioning as adjective*

handmade typewritten

frostbitten citybred

5. *adjective + present participle functioning as adjective*

goodlooking far-reaching well-meaning

6. *adjective + past participle functioning as adjective*

widespread loudmouthed

drycleaned freshbaked

Compound verbs:

underestimate overreact overact overdo

Exercise 6

Identify the following words as simple, complex or compound words:

homeless	talking	breakage	wider
flowers	brotherhood	steamengine	fireproof
incapable	highsounding	dissatisfied	stardom
Sino-Pak	honest	living room	window pane
coffee time	minicab	rebuild	usefulness

Exercise 7

Analyse the following compound words into the two base forms and then identify each one of them:

heartbeat	pushbutton	franking machine
chairman	seasick	rockhard
brick-red	recordbreaking	long-awaited

12.3 Other processes of word formation

12.3.1 Clipping

Clipping is the process of shortening a word by cutting the beginning, the end or sometimes even the middle of a word. Such a form is called a clipped word.

ad	from *advertisement*	(*the beginning of the word is retained but the end is clipped off*)
phone	from *telephone*	(*the end of the word is retained but the beginning is clipped off*)
flu	from *influenza*	(*the middle of the word is retained but the beginning and the end are clipped off*)

Some other examples are:

lab	*laboratory*	*plane*	*aeroplane*
prof	*professor*	*gas*	*gasoline*
fridge	*refrigerator*		

Exercise 8

Write down the words from which the following have been derived:

photo	memo ....
fax	demo ....
rail	exam ....
intercom	mike ....

12.3.2 Acronymy

Acronymy is the process by which a word is formed using the initial letters of a succession of words. In some acronyms, each letter is pronounced separately.

IAS	Indian Administrative Service
NDA	National Defence Academy
VIP	Very Important Person

Some acronyms on the other hand, are pronounced and sometimes spelled as single words:

SAARC (South Asian Association for Regional Cooperation)

NATO (North Atlantic Treaty Organisation)

RADAR (Radio Detecting and Ranging)

Exercise 9

Expand these acronyms:

UNDP	PC	laser	PS	CBI
Aids	WHO	TV	scuba	PCS

12.3.3 Blending

Blending is a process of word formation which combines parts of two words. Usually the first part of one word is combined with the last part of another word to form a blend:

> **brunch** is formed from two words *breakfast* and *lunch* by blending **br-** of breakfast and **-unch** of lunch.

The blend carries the meanings of both the original words from which it has been derived.

Some other blends are:

transistor: transfer + resistor

paratroops: parachute + troops

camcorder: camera + recorder

Exercise 10

Write down the words from which these have been formed:

smog	newscast ....
telecast	travelogue ....
moped	interpol ....
motel	telex ....
heliport	handycam ....

12.3.4 Back-formation

This is the reverse of the common method of forming a related word by adding a derivational suffix. In back-formation, historically, a noun comes to exist with a derivational suffix like **-er/ -or/ -ar/** or **-ing** and later the suffix is dropped to form the verb. For example, nouns like *editor, beggar* and *television* existed in the English language before the words *edit, beg* and *televise.*

Some other words formed through back-formation are:

swindle *babysit* *brainwash*

sleepwalk *sightsee* *lipread*

12.3.5 Reduplication

Reduplicatives may be treated as compound words, in which two or more elements are closely related in form:

zig-zag *hocus-pocus* *teeny-weeny*

As illustrated above, in some case the medial vowels differ and in some cases the initial consonants differ. Other examples of reduplication are:

walkie-talkie *ding-dong* *hanky-panky* *wishy-washy*

flip-flop *ping-pong* *tip-top*

12.3.6 Antonomasia

This is a process of word formation when a word is derived from a proper name. For example, the word sandwich is derived from the Earl of Sandwich. Similarly hamburger is derived from Hamburg in Germany.

Other examples are:

sideburns *boycott* *denim* *cashmere* *caesarean*

Key to Exercises

(Note: For exercises in brackets possible answers are given)

Chapter 1

Exercise 1

	Subject	Predicate
1.	Her younger brother	is a famous doctor
2.	The finance minister	has given us tax concessions
3.	Meera	runs very fast
4.	The food	smells good
5.	All the old employees	are unhappy
6.	Her teachers	consider her intelligent
7.	Varun	is sitting in the corner
8.	The Board's decision	has made us happy
9.	The university	has framed a new rule
10.	The old students	have gone out for dinner

Exercise 2

1. while their parents are away 2. with a pen 3. whenever they see a dog 4. there 5. when they are on leave 6. fast 7. in the room 8. loudly 9. to her office, in the afternoon 10. continuously

Exercise 3

	LV	Cs: NP/Adj		LV	Cs: NP/adj
1.	were	busy: adj	6.	is	tasty: adj
2.	were	the winners: NP	7.	No LV	
3.	No LV		8.	is	industrious: adj
4.	is	a fool: NP	9.	is	a doctor: NP
5.	may be	right: adj	10.	was	a great leader

(Exercise 4)

1. His book was very exhaustive/on the shelf. 2. Delhi is the capital of India/ in the north. 3. Mukesh was the captain of the cricket team/ in his room. 4. The

meeting will be quite interesting/in the evening. 5. The cricket team has been very popular/in the hotel. 6. The car is very old/ under the tree. 7. The players were our friends/in the dressing room. 8. Her grandfather is a doctor/ upstairs. 9. Professor Kapoor is the Head of the Department/in the laboratory. 10. The policeman was very helpful/in the jeep.

Exercise 5

	NP_1	V	NP_2
1.	Rajesh	is	a doctor.
	S	LV	Cs
	NP_1	V	Prep Phr
2.	The students	played	in the ground
	S	InTrV	Adv
	NP_1	V	NP_2
3.	My brother	has become	a professor.
	S	LV	Cs

	NP_1	V		NP_1	V	Adj.
4.	The comedian	laughed.	5.	His sister	is	tall.
	S	InTrV		S	LV	Cs
	NP_1	V	Prep Phr	NP_1	V	Adj.
6.	The cat	slept	under the table. 7.	I	feel	fine.
	S	LV	Cs	S	InTrV	Adv.
	NP_1	V	Adj.	NP_1	V	A
8.	Mary	seemed	sad. 9.	Vinod	talks	softly.
	S	LV	Cs	S	InTrV	Adv.

	NP_1	V	NP_2
10.	Kalpana	must have been	the thief.
	S	LV	Cs

(Exercise 6)

1. was 2. anxious 3. Vidya 4. continuously for three hours 5. an army officer 6. will sing at the function 7. awful 8. are 9. accurately 10. tired

Exercise 7

TrV: 1, 3, 6, 7, 10; InTrV: 5, 8; LV: 2, 4, 9

Exercise 8

	NP_1	V	NP_2	Prep Phr
1.	John	has been	a university professor	for five years.
	S	LV	Cs	Adv.

	NP_1	V	NP_2	Prep Phr
2.	She	boarded	the train	with her baggage.
	S	TrV/mono	Od	Adv.

	NP_1	V	NP_2	Prep Phr
3.	The servant	polished	the car	on Friday.
	S	TrVmono	Od	Adv.

	NP_1	V	A
4.	The driver	turned	sharply.
	S	InTrV	Adv

	NP_1	V	NP_2	Prep Phr
5.	The vice-chancellor	delivered	the speech	in the hall.
	S	TrVmono	Od	Adv.

	NP_1	V	NP_2	Prep Phr
6.	The leader of the opposition	criticised	the Government	at the press conference.
	S	TrV mono	Od	Adv.

	NP_1	V	Adj	Prep Phr
7.	Rita	looked	unhappy	at the party.
	S	LV	Cs	Adv.

	NP_1	V	NP_2	Prep Phr
8.	The policeman	carried	his rifle	on his shoulder.
	S	TrV mono	Od	Adv.

	NP_1	V	NP_2	Prep Phr
9.	I	bought	this book	in Delhi.
	S	Trvmono	Od	Adv.

	NP_1	V	NP_2	A
10.	She	followed	him	everywhere.
	S	TrV mono	Od	Adv.

(*Exercise 9*)

1. has built 2. seems 3. her house, in June 4. likes, biscuits 5. the Principal of this school 6. enjoyed 7. trees 8. played, in the afternoon 9. ran, fast 10. to the left

(Exercise 10)

1. us, a story 2. her, a letter 3. Hyder, his wages 4. her teacher a question 5. him, leave

Exercise 11

1. Radha sent a box of biscuits for her brother. 2. My mother bought a bicycle for me. 3. Mr Kapoor wrote a letter to me. 4. He found a house for her. 5. Sham paid the money to me.

Exercise 12

1. through Rita 2. on Monday 3. in the last semester 4. through an estate agent 5. yesterday

(Exercise 13)

1. taught us English grammar
2. gave us a good rebate on the TV set
3. offered me his scooter
4. bought his friend a good pen
5. sent his son a gift
6. has sent us his brief
7. has granted us leave
8. lent his officers the jeep to fetch their families
9. served us tea
10. paid his driver a bonus for his good work

Exercise 14

	NP_1	V	NP_2	NP_3	Prep. Phr	S
1.	His mother	gave(TrVdi)	Peter(Oi)	an apple(Od)	in the morning(Adv)	
2.	The sun	rises (InTrv)			in the east(Adv)	
3.	Uma	will become (LV)	a pilot(Cs)		next year(Adv)	
4.	We	watch (Trvdi)	television (Od)		every evening (Adv)	
5.	The company	offered (TrVdi)	her (Oi)	a high salary (Od)		
6.	The minister	considers (TrV comp)	his secretary (Od)	very patient.(Adj. Phr.Co		
7.	Neeta	called (TrVcomp)	Roshan(Od)	a fool (Co)		
8.	She	sleeps (InTrV)			till (Adv)eight in the morning(Adv) A)	
9.	Our gardener	has planted (TrVmono)	cauliflower(Od)		recently(Adv)	
10.	The General Manager	asked	him	difficult questions	during the interview(Adv).	
11.	Meena	looked (LV)	(Adj) cheerful(Cs)		at the party(Adv)	
12.	The child	was crying(InTrV).				
13.	Our finance minister	is(LV)	(Adj) far-sighted.(Cs)			
14.	The Doordarshan	has started(TrV mono)	five satellite channels (Od)			
15.	The Principal	declared (TrVcomp)	Monday(Od)	a holiday (Co)		

Exercise 16

1a.	S InTrv Adv	b.	S TrVmono Od
2a.	S LV Cs	b.	S TrVmono Od
3a.	S TrVdi Oi Od	b.	S TrVcomp Od Co
4a.	S TrVmono Od Adv	b.	S InTrV Adv
5a.	S MV NP	b.	S TrVmono Od
6a.	S TrVcomp Od	b.	S TrVdi Oi Od
7a.	S InTrV Adv	b.	S TrVmono Od
8a.	S TrVmono Od Adv	b.	S TrVdi Oi Od Adv
9a.	S TrV comp Od Co	b.	S TrVmono Od Adv
10a.	S Trv mono Od Co	b.	S LV Cs

Exercise 17

	Agentive	Affected		Agentive	Affected
1.	Rita	letter	4.	The dog	the cat
2.	My younger sister	the book	5.	My mother	a book
3.	Standard IV students	the play			

Exercise 18

	Agentive	Instrument	Affected	Attributive	Beneficiary
1.	a thief		My father's car		
2.	My mother	a stick	the ball		
3.	Seema	a knife	the potatoes		
4.	That girl			my friend	
5.	They		him	President	
6.	That building			very impressive	
7.	Rajesh		a bicycle		his son
8.			the milk	sour	
9.	They		her	the captain of the hockey team	
10.	They		a house		her

Exercise 19

1. Her sister has been a dancer for several years.
   S affected LV Cs attributive Adv Temporal
2. It is humid in Mumbai during the rains.
   S LV Cs attributive Adv locative Adv temporal

3. She | is boiling | milk | in the kitchen.
   S Agentive | TrVmono | Od affected | Adv locative
4. The milk | is boiling.
   S affected | InTrV
5. Monish | is | my cousin.
   S Affected | LV | Attributive
6. The Principal | made | him | the monitor | of the class.
   S Agentive | TrVcomp | Od | affected | Co attributive
7. My uncle | remained | silent.
   S affected | LV | Cs attributive
8. The opposition | supported | the new bill.
   S Agentive | TrVmono | Od affected
9. The dog | was hit | by a train
   S affected | TrVmono | Adv instrument
10. She | was presented | a watch | on the occasion.
    S | TrVdi | Od affected | Adv locative

Exercise 20

1. interrogative, complaining
2. declarative, statement
3. declarative, apologising
4. exclamatory, praising
5. interrogative, requesting
6. declarative, reprimanding
7. declarative, permission
8. declarative, statement
9. declarative, inviting
10. declarative, advising

Exercise 21

1. have	2. has/have	3. is	4. has/have	5. has
6. work	7. have	8. seems	9. is/are	10. is

Chapter 2

Exercise 1

1. These fans need repair. 2. These chains are made of stainless steel. 3. Cats dislike dogs. 4. I bought books yesterday. 5. TV sets are sold at a lower price these days. 6. Children below five years are not allowed inside the planetarium. 7. The Bajaj company has manufactured good scooters. 8. Computers have become essential for most organisations. 9. I own cows. 10. Monkeys can be dangerous.

Exercise 2

1. son 2. neighbours 3. books 4. sunflower 5. chairs
6. man 7. girl 8. potatoes 9. mice 10. children

Exercise 3

1. a loaf of bread 2. a pot 3. a glass of milk 4. a piece of paper 5. a pen 6. a piece of cake 7. an apple 8. a tree 9. a dog 10. a cup of tea

Exercise 4

1, 6, 9	2, 4, 7	3, 8	5, 10
generic	non-generic specific definite cataphoric reference	non-generic non-specific	non-generic specific indefinite

Exercise 5

1, 3, 5, 7, 9, 10, 12, 13, 14, 17: a 2, 4, 6, 8, 11, 15, 16, 18: an

Exercise 6

1. a, ø, ø 2. a, a 3. an ø 4. a, ø, ø, ø 5. ø, ø, ø
6. a, a 7. ø, ø 8. ø, ø 9. ø, ø, ø 10. ø, ø, ø

Exercise 7

1. ø, generic 2. ø, generic 3. ø, proper noun 4. an, indefinite noun 5. a, generic 6. ø, meal 7. a, modified by adjective 8. ø, function not building 9. a, singular, countable noun 10. a, mode of transport

Exercise 8

1. ø 2. the 3. the 4. the, the 5. the, ø 6. the 7. ø, the 8. the, the 9, 10 the

Exercise 9

1. the, the, a, a, the, the, the 2. an, a, the 3. the, the, the, the 4. ø, the, an 5. a, a 6. a 7. a, a, the 8. the 9. the, the, a, the 10. ø, a

Exercise 10

1. ø bed 2. The Times of India (before names of newspapers) 3. ø Oil(generic) 4. the evening (times of the day) 5. the dog (situational reference) 6. the best player (superlative) 7. the shirts (cataphoric reference) 8. a dog (sing.

uncountable noun used for thr first time) 9. the Chopras (surnames of couples or families) the Governor (situational reference) 10. a film (sing. noun used for the first time), the Mayfair theatre (theatre), the film (anaphoric reference)

Chapter 3

Exercise 1

1. boy, captain	2. car	3. house	4. brother	5. son
6. dog	7. girl	8. book	9. novel, romance	10. teacher

Exercise 2

	Pre-D	D	PD	PD	NH
1.	both	his			<friends>
2.	three times	her			<salary>
3.	her		first	three	<books>
4.	twice	a			<day>
5.			little		<water>
6.			a few		<men>
7.	half the				<amount>
8.		the	last	six	<months>
9.		Arun's	twentieth		<birthday>
10.		Ayesha's	last		<wish>

(Exercisc 3)

1. new	2. old	3. good	4. long	5. ferocious
6. palatial	7. latest	8. political	9. colour	10. wooden

Exerscise 4

1. rather heavy 2. very tall 3. very long 4. a fairly old 5. very heavy 6. extremely high 7. very old 8. fairly sensible 9. very faithful 10. rather fierce

Exercise 5

1. morning 2. steel 3. copper 4. village 5. insurance 6. film 7. chemistry 8. iron 9. tennis 10. finance

Exercise 6

1. her extremely old village house	2. my new college friend
3. that rather tall football player	4. the latest Doordarshan channel

5. that fairly young army captain
6. his formal grammar notebok
7. that red metal box
8. his compact English dictionary
9. a very bright young man
10. this absolutely pure mineral water

Exercise 7

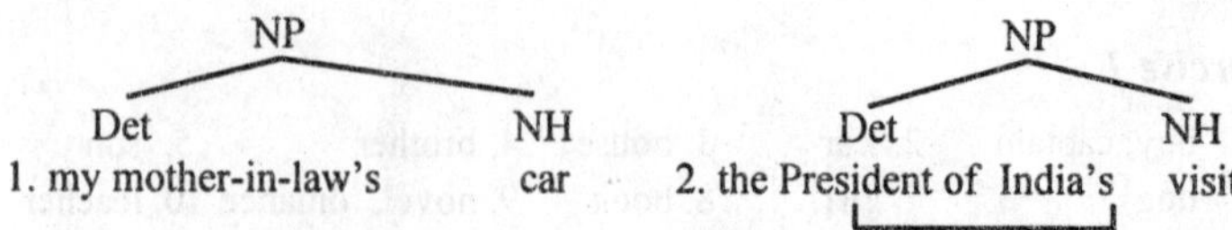

3. The Professor of linguistics' room 4. The F.M of India's speech

5. Edward VIII's reign

Exercise 8

1. with four headlights 2. in a black suit 3. from London to York
4. of English 5. of his house

(Exercise 9)

1. There is a dog barking at the cat outside. 2. She was sitting in the boat sailing slowly. 3. Namita pointed at the plane flying in the air. 4. She wants to meet the teacher writing on the blackboard. 5. He saw a crow eating bread on the tree.

(Exercise 10)

1. Passive: A machine has recently been made by our engineers.
   NP: a machine made by our engineers
   Sentence: A machine made by our engineers will be displayed at the exhibition.
2. Passive: A film was shown by them on TV this week.
   NP: a film shown on TV this week
   Sentence: The film shown on TV this week has been nominated for the national award.
3. Passive: A letter was written by Manoj.
   NP: a letter written by Manoj
   Sentence: We have received a letter received by Manoj.
4. Passive: A problem has been mentioned above by them.
   NP: a problem mentioned above
   Sentence: I can solve the problem mentioned above.

5. Passive: The Discovery of India was written by Pandit Jawaharlal Nehru.
   NP: The Discovery of India written by Pandit Jawaharlal Nehru.
   Sentence: I recently read the Discovery of India writen by Pandit Jawaharlal Nehru.

Exercise 11

1. The place to stay is the Institute hostel. 2. We need students to study this problem. 3. He is the right man to take a deision. 4. I need something to eat. 5. That is the most suitable time to practise.

Exercise 12

1. I saw a girl swimming in the pool. 2. That man standing under the tree wants to meet you. 3. The problem mentioned above is quite difficult. 4. Your willingness to attend the meeting has been appreciated. 5. She asked me to bring the book lying on the table. 6. The scooter parked near the gate is for sale. 7. You have no reason to refuse it. 8. The boy running in the field is my cousin. 9. The candidates to be interviewed by us have arrived. 10. Everyone liked the dress designed by your mother.

Exercise 13

1. the (D) tall (adj) <boy> (NH) standing near the door (present participle clause) 2. both (Pre-D) his (D) younger (adj) <brothers> (NH) who studied with me (rel cl) 3. Her (D) most expensive (adj phrase) <pen> (NH) that she bought at an auction (rel.cl) 4. a (D) few (PD) back <issues> (NH) of our college magazine (prep phr) 5. the (D) seventh (PD) UGC (N) <Refresher course> (NH) for teachers of English (prep phr) 6. all (Pre-D) those (D) tall (adj) hockey (N) <players> (NH) running with their sticks (pres part cl) 7. his (D) small (adj) white (adj) (NH) which he bought last year (rel.cl.) 8. both (PreD) his (D) elder (adj) <sisters> (NH) sitting near the door (past part cl.) 9. the (D) long (adj) garden(N) <fence> (NH) of my house (prep phr) that was built two years ago (rel.cl)

Chapter4

Exercise 1

	General Analysis	Specific Analysis
1.	T + (be + -ing) + MV	past + be + -ing + *sing*
2.	T + (have + -en) +MV	pres + have + -en + *finish*
3.	T + MV	pres + *go*

4.	T + (be + -ing) + MV	pres + be + -ing + *play*
5.	T + (M) + (have + -en) + MV	pres + must + have + en + *reach*
6.	T + (M) + (have + -en) + do	past + may + have + -en + *do*
7.	T + (have + -en) + (be + _ ing) + MV	pres + have + -en + be + -ing + *sleep*
8.	T + (be + - ing) + MV	past + be + -ing + *talk*

(Exercise 2)

1. She could have examined her on Wednesday. 2. Rita works in a bank. 3. He was running fast in the ground. 4. She might have met Rohit at the party. 5.They have been practising for the Republic Day since October. 6. They could have been playing in the lawn. 7. Diana sang well at the concert. 8. Star TV will telecast a new soap opera next week. 9. He was driving fast around the city. 10.We shall go to Delhi next week.

Exercise 3

	General Analysis	Specific Analysis
1.	T + (be + -en) + MV	past + be + -en + *examine*
2.	T + (be + -ing) + (be + -en) + MV	pres + be + -ing + be + - en + *consider*
3.	T + (have + -en) + (be + -en) + MV	pres + have + -en + be + -en + *visit*
4.	T + (M) + (be + -en) + MV	pres + will + be + -en + *deliver*
5.	T + (M) + (have + -en) + (be + -en) + MV	past + may + have + -en + be + -en + *do*

Exercise 4

	Finite	Non-finite		Finite	Non-finite
1.	has been sleping		2.	know	has left
3.	saw	coming	4.	wants	to see
5.	can be	to work	6.	has finished	
7.	got up	to catch	8.	went	having completed
9.	asked	could attend	10.	noticed, was	

Exercise 5

1. normally F 2. always F 3. softly M 4. fully De 5. rarely F 6. firmly M 7. generally D beautifully M 8. deeply De 9. regularly F 10. inside P

11. always F carefully M 12. rarely F carelessly M 13. seldom F 14. Often F, coldly M 15. strongly De 16. upstairs P 17. always D here P 18. indefinitely D 19. peacefully M 20. awkwardly M sideways P

Exercise 6

1.	this evening (NP)	2.	the whole night (NP)	3.	carefully (A)
4.	a great deal NP	5.	rarely (A)	6.	a little while (NP)
7.	next time (NP)	8.	upstairs (A)	9.	a little while (NP)
10.	vividly (A)	11.	this way (NP)	12.	the next day (NP)
13.	occasionally (A)	14.	easily (A)	15.	soon (A)

Exercise 7

1. in the library: place 2. for four days: duration 3. by train: means 4. in the morning: time 5. in the meantime: duration 6. because of the holiday: reason 7. towards me: direction 8. in the conference room: place during the lunch break: duration on 28th July: time 9. during the film: duration 10, to the Rashtrapati Bhavan: place in the horse carriage: means

Exercise 8

1. behind the fences: amb 2. in college: adv 3. with a hammer: adv, in two minutes adv 4. with the stick: amb 5. behind that fence: adj 6. between the pages: amb 7. in the red shirt: adj, into the pool: adv 8. in the auditorium: adv, for two hours: adv 9. with three legs: amb 10. in the blue suit: adj

Exercise 9

1. walking around the room: MV 2. written by my father: MN 3. was in pieces: MV 4. frowning at Ravi: MV 5. laughing at Jivan: MN 6. played at the party: MN 7. smiling gently MV 8. sitting at the table: MN 9. shaken by the event: MV 10. standing near the school: MN

Exercise 10

1. last night (NP), sitting on the chair: -ing cl; 2. firmly: A with the other country's propaganda: prep phr. 3. if you need any help: adv cl 4. at Clark Avadh: prep phr; this evening : NP 5. a little while: NP 6. when he lived in Lucknow: ad. cl 7. always: A with gusto: prep. phr. 8. wounded by the bullet: -ed cl. 9. because he had migrated to the U. S. A: adv.cl 10. never: A 11. gently 12. since she came back from England: adv.cl. 13. waving at all of us: -ing cl. 14. occasionally: A, these days: NP 15. always A, to office: prep phr, by car: prep phr 16. unless you pay back the money: adv. cl. 17. there: A , encircled by admirers: -ed cl. 18. in the hall: prep phr, 19. upstairs: A 20. on Monday: prep phr

Chapter 5

Exercise1

1. extremely: intensifier; happy: adj; to hear this: to- infinitive; adj. comp
2. a little: intensifier; hesitant: adj.; to say this: to- infinitive, adj. comp
3. very: intensifier; eager: adj.; to meeet you: to- infinitive; adj.comp
4. devoted: adj.; to her son: to- infinitive, adj comp
5. doubtful: adj.; of passing the examination: prep phr. adj comp
6. afraid: adj.; that his sister might not return: that- cl. adj comp
7. certain: adj.; that he'll attend the meeting: that- cl: adj comp
8. surprised: adj.; that I knew the story: that- cl. adj comp
9. willing: adj.; to accompany you: to- infinitive, adj comp
10. fraught: adj.; with danger: prep phr. adj comp

Exercise 2

1. There is a weekly train from Lucknow to Kanyakumari. (attr) 2. I'm afraid it can't be done. (pred) 3. That tall girl wants to speak to you. (attr) 4. It was a wonderful show. (attr) 5. I'm not answerable to you. (pred) 6. She's unwilling to take up this job. (pred) 7. He has been made the GOC-in -C of the eastern command. (attr) 8. There used to be an occasional get-to-gether of the residents of our building last year. (attr) 9. I am glad to know it. (pred) 10. She was delighted to meet us. (pred) 11. He is fond of good food. (pred) 12. She is incapable of doing it. (pred) 13. He was very thin as a baby. (pred) 14. The Times of India is a daily newspaper. (attr) 15. You are liable to pay the tax. (pred) 16. I was very tired in the evening. (pred) 17. My elder brother is a colonel in the army. (attr) 18. She is always very anxious. (pred) 19. Rekha was very pleased with me. (pred) 20. There is a wide road behind that building. (attr)

Exercise 3

		Quality	Colour	Classifier	
1.	a	little	white	metallic	box
2.	the	calm		western	wind
3.	the	new		political	party
4.	a	heavy		commercial	vehicle
5.	a	beautiful	blue	dress	
6.	the	new		agricultural	equipment
7.	a	delicious	red	Kashmiri	apple
8.	the	famous		Victorian	building
9.	the	weak		military	regime
10.	the	successful		national	party

Exercise 4

1. She is waiting for you downstairs. 2. We had to wait long at the airport. 3. She always arranges the table neatly. 4. They went southward in search of the missing dog. 5. She would do it happily. 6. They arrived at the station at 10 and I gave them your letter then. 7. This toy runs clockwise. 8. The plane is landing shortly. 9. She looked at him suspiciously because he had a revolver in his hand. 10. I get up very early in the morning.

Exercise 5

1. however (c) 2. luckily (d) 3. personally speaking (d) 4. at the party (a) ; on Tuesday (a) ; in college (a); on Wednesday (adj); however (c); to college (a) as she fell ill after the party (a) 5. while he was travelling by the Rajdhani to Mumbai (a); fortunately (d) in the same coach (a) therefore (c), immediately (a) 6. When I reached her place (a); already (a); for office (a) 7. surprisingly (d); late (a); in the market (a) 8. greatly (a); incidentally (a) 9. therefore (c); again (a) 10. happily (a); actually (d)

Exercise 6

1. always (verb) there (verb) 2. rather (adj) 3. below (NP) 4. just (verb) 5. aloud (verb) 6. right (prep phr) 7. quite (NP) 8. simply (adj) 9. economically (adj) 10. pretty (adv) 11. up (verb) there (verb) 12. rarely (verb) carelessly (verb) 13.highly (adj) during the train journey (verb) 14. close (prep phr) 15. almost (pre-D) 16. always (verb); very (adverb), softly (verb) 17. upstairs (NP) 18. fairly (adj) 19. pretty (adv) well (verb) 20. nearly (pre-D)

Exercise 7

1. under the tree (place, position), while we were chatting here (time, duration) 2. temporarily (time, duration) 3. as if he were the boss (manner) 4. from our point of view (point of view) 5. kindly (courtesy) 6. on Monday (definite time) 7. recently (indefinite time) 8. completely (intensity, amplifier) 9. generally (restrictive focussing), office (place, position), at 9.30 a.m. (definite time)

Chapter 6

Exercise 1

1. habitual action 2. future 3. natural phenomenon 4. thoughts/feelings of the present moment 5. historic simple present with reference to the work of a writer 6. habitual action 7. future 8. habitual action 9. commentary 10. demonstrations

Exercise 2

1. seems, is wearing 2. am listening, hope, can hear 3. owns 4. has 5. is waiting, want 6. belongs 7. needs, is working 8. think, is waiting 9. tastes, is eating 10. remember

Exercise 3

1, 3, 5, 6: happening in progress at the present time 2, 8: future with reference to a definite time 4, 7: temporary situation 9, 10: repeated action referring to the habitual

Exercise 4

1. recent past 2. resultative 3. action in progress from the past to the present 4. indefinite past 5. continuative 6. hot news 7. result of recent past events seen now 8. completion 9. continuative 10. indefinite past

Exercise 5

1a and b: no difference 2a: the action is complete b: the action is in progress 3a and b: no difference 4a and b: no difference 5a: the action is complete b: the action is in progress

Exercise 6

1, 4, 9: past event 2, 7: polite attitude 3,5, 10: unreality/hypothetical 6, 8: reported speech

Exercise 7

(2 & 9: no difference) 1a.probably I am not ill now. b. I am ill at the moment 3a. Kiran Kumar got the award in the past and its effect is not felt now. b. Its effect is felt now. 4a.The Mayor is dead and hence the use of the past. b. The school exists and therefore can be used at the subject position in the present perfect tense. 5a. In the past. b. In the recent past and the effect is still visible. 6a. In the past: hence the use of the simple past tense. b. His theory influences scientists even today: hence, present perfect tense. 7a. His sister is not alive. b.His sister is alive. 8a. Came and has probably left. b. He came and is still there. 10a. Probably in the past. b.Probably it is running in a theatre in the city.

Exercise 8

1, 7, 8, 10: past perfect: past in the past 2. simple past: indicates what happened second 3. past perfect: rules of reported speech 4. past perfect: unfulfilled condition 5. past progressive: action started early in the morning and probably continued till much later 6. past perfect progressive: action happened over a period of time 9: past progressive: action in progress in the past.

Exercise 9

1: a fixed event as a result of a 'natural law 2, 4: result of a pre-planned arrangement 3, 7: prediction 5, 6: to express an official plan 8: something probably going to happen soon 9: foreseeing what is going to happen 10: reference to a definite plan

Exercise 10

(Note: Each sentence in these items have been numbered a,b, c ... for convenience)
1. a. simple past: past event b. past perfect: past in the past c. simple past: a past event d. past progressive: happening at the time of action of 'a' e. past perfect: past in the past f,g,h. simple past: past event i. past perfect: reported speech
2. a, b, f. present perfect: recent past; c: present perfect progressive: action in progress from the past to the present d: simple present: at the present moment e: future action to happen soon. 3. a, b and c.simple present: demonstration
4.a. present progressive: future reference for a definite plan. b.shall+main verb: opinion c. will + be + present participle: action in the future, a result of a pre-planned arrangement d. simple present: fixed plan e. will + main verb; shall + main verb: prediction f. will + main verb: opinion g. will + main verb: prediction
5.a. past progressive: action in progress in the past b. simple past: past event; past progressive: action in progress in the past c. past progressive and simple past: action in progress in the past and past event d. past progressive: action in progress in the past e. simple past: past event; past perfect: past in the past
6. a, b. present perfect: recent past c, d, g, h. simple present: thought/attitude at the present momentf. present perfect progressive: action in progress from the past to the present g and h. simple present: attitude thought at the present moment i. will + main verb: opinion 7. a, b, c, d and e. simple present: commentary
8. a. be + to + main verb: to express plan for the future; b. simple past: past event c and d. will + main verb: prediction 9. a, b. present perfect: indefinite past
10. a.simple past: past event; past progressive: action in progress in the pastb.simple past: past event; past perfect progressive: action over a period of time upto a past time c. simple past: past event d. simple past: past event; past progressive: action over a period of time to a past time

Exercise 11

1. We will not play football this evening. 2. John cannot carry heavy loads. 3. They may not visit us tomorrow. 4. She could not finish her work in time. 5. You should not write to him. 6. You must not sit here. 7. They should not visit the hostel. 8. Renu will not attend class on Monday. 9. Vijay may not take your car. 10. She cannot attend my lecture today.

Exercise 12

1. Will Prof. Kumar take our class tomorrow? 2. Could I meet you at the bus stand? 3. Will he go now? 4. Can I eat this piece of bread? 5. May we leave the room now? 6. Can you see me in the evening? 7. May I borrow your car? 8. Will you open the window? 9. Shall we watch this film? 10. Ought we to wait for some time?

Exercise 13

1. Jane can fly a plane 2. Can I drive this car? 3. Rehman could attend... 4. She can walk... 5. Could I borrow... 6.They could operate ... 7. Could we take... 7. May we attend ... 9. He may participate... 10. You can borrow ...

Exercise 14

1. I could/might win ... 2. The best pilots can make ... 3. Mira may be ... 4. John may visit ... 5. The state can be placed ... 6. Kailash may be ... 7. The enemy may be ... 8. Our team could/ may win ... 9. The house may still be vacant. 10. Rita may pass ...

Exercise 15

1. Would you have ... 2. Will you switch on ... 3. Shall we have ... 4. Can I drink ... 5. Could you lend ... 6. Could I meet ... 7. May I borrow ... 8. You should visit ... 9. Would you drop ..... 10. We could walk down ......

Exercise 16

1. You must see ... 2. Enakshi ought to ... 3. She must use ... 4. We should respect ... 5. They ought to have seen ... 6. We must finish ... 7. He should have taken ... 8. Visitors should park ... 9. You ought to report ... 10. Students must wear ...

Exercise 17

1, 4, 5, 7, 10: needn't   2, 3, 6, 8, 9: mustn't

Exercise 18

1. could: tentative possibility 2. would: hypothetical, unreal situation 3. would: hypothetical, unreal situation 4. can: ability 5. may: factual possibility 6. could: tentaive possibility 7. shall: suggestionn 8. may: formal permission 9. could: past ability 10. should have: tentative possibility 11. must: strong persuasion 12. might: tentative possibility 13. may: factual possibility 14. may: formal request 15. could: tentative, polite request 16. should have: a strong suggestion 17. mustn't: obligation 18. should have: strong suggestion 19. might: tentative possibility 20. should: strong obligation

Chapter 7

Exercise 1

	Matrix clause	Subordinate clause	Conjunction
1.	The fact is	that he has never attended the meeting	that
2.	I shall help you	if you pass this examination	if
3.	He noticed	that she was wearing his dauhter's dress	that
4.	I shall see you	after I have finished my lecture	after
5.	He told me	that the Prime Minister would visit Lucknow	that
6.	I couldn't see the Principal	although I reached college at 9 a.m.	although
7.	The rumour was	that she had been dismissed	that
8.	We went out for a week as Shakti had returned early		as
9.	You may leave the class	as soon as you have finished the paper	as soon as
10.	I last met him	when he lived in London	when

Exercise 2

Passive verbs: TrVpass

1. Sentence

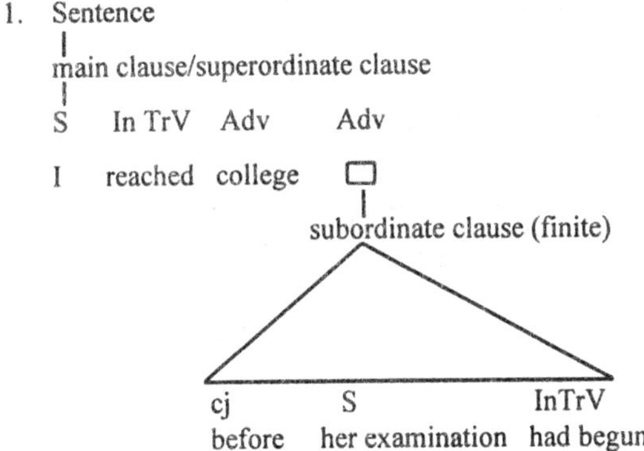

2.

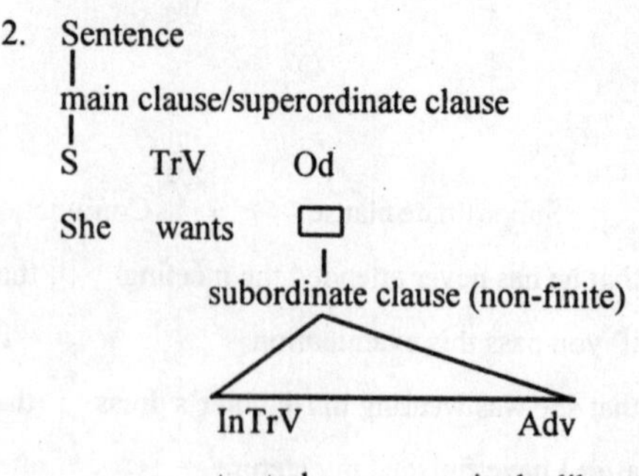

3. Sentence

main clause/ superordinate clause

subordinate clause (finite)

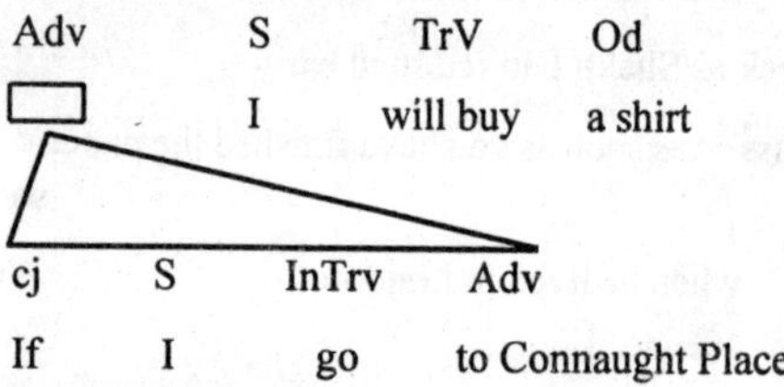

4. Sentence

main clause/superordinate clause

S TrV Od

He proved

subordinate clause (finite)

cj S LV Cs

that his results were correct

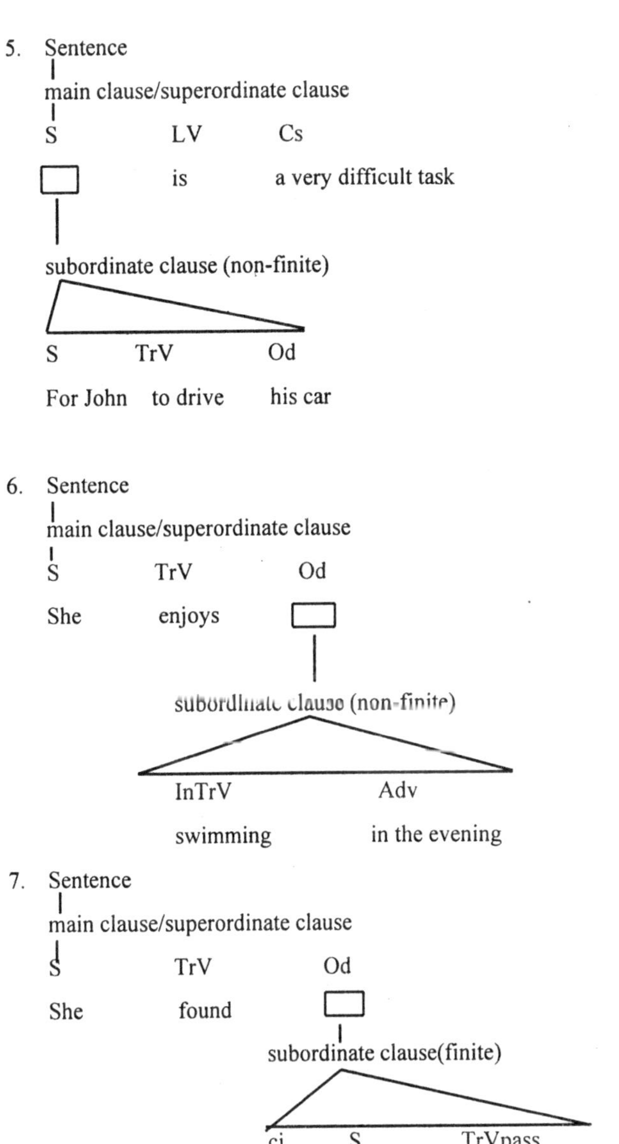
5. Sentence
main clause/superordinate clause
S
LV
Cs
is
a very difficult task
subordinate clause (non-finite)
S
TrV
Od
For John
to drive
his car
6. Sentence
main clause/superordinate clause
S
TrV
Od
She
enjoys
subordinate clause (non-finite)
InTrV
Adv
swimming
in the evening
7. Sentence
main clause/superordinate clause
S
TrV
Od
She
found
subordinate clause(finite)
cj
S
TrVpass
that
her locker
has been opened

8. 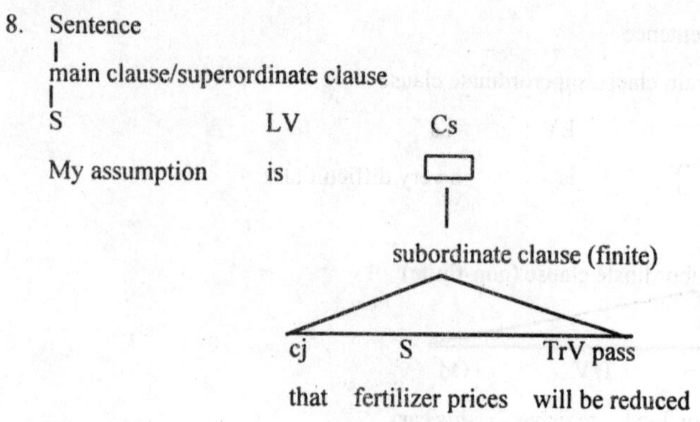
Sentence
main clause/superordinate clause
S
LV
Cs
My assumption
is
subordinate clause (finite)
cj
S
TrV pass
that
fertilizer prices
will be reduced

9. 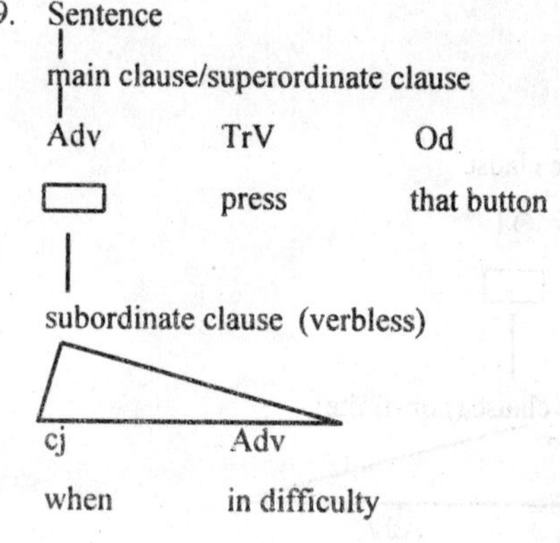
Sentence
main clause/superordinate clause
Adv
TrV
Od
press
that button
subordinate clause (verbless)
cj
Adv
when
in difficulty

10. 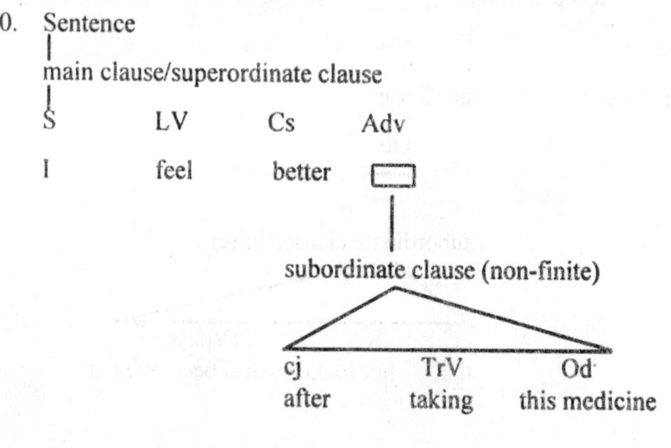
Sentence
main clause/superordinate clause
S
LV
Cs
Adv
I
feel
better
subordinate clause (non-finite)
cj
TrV
Od
after
taking
this medicine

Exercise 3

1. That India won the one-day series did not come as a surprise to anyone.
2. That Kunal has stood first in the ICSE examination has brought credit to the school.
3. That she will meet the President of the U.S.A indicates her popularity in the international community.
4. That the troops have been withdrawn has not changed our government's policy.
5. That Rajinder was promoted as Lieutenant Colonel raised the morale of the battalion.

Exercise 4

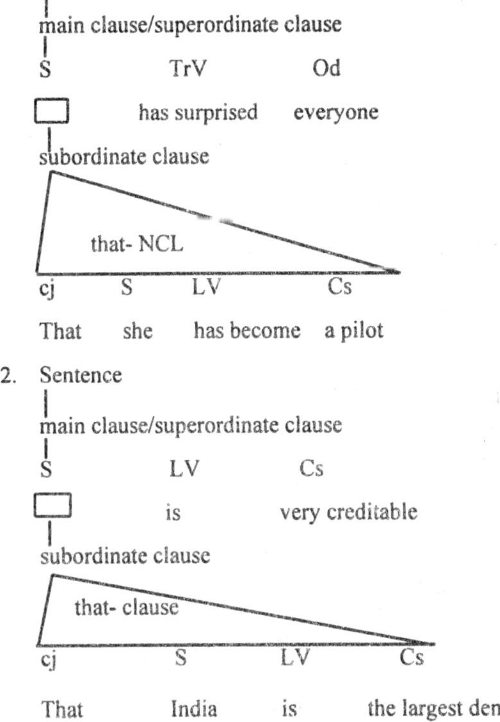

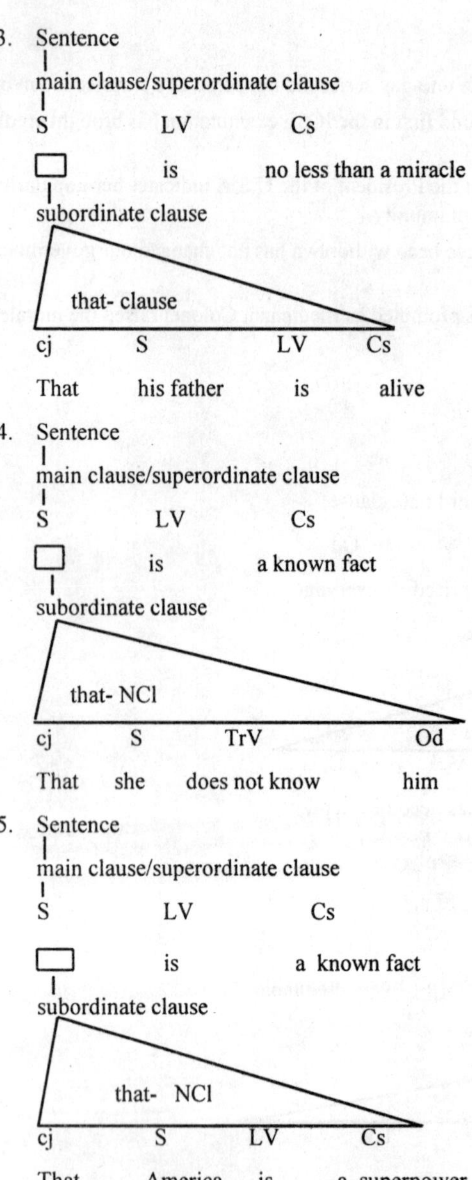
3. Sentence
main clause/superordinate clause
S LV Cs
is no less than a miracle
subordinate clause
that- clause
cj S LV Cs
That his father is alive
4. Sentence
main clause/superordinate clause
S LV Cs
is a known fact
subordinate clause
that- NCl
cj S TrV Od
That she does not know him
5. Sentence
main clause/superordinate clause
S LV Cs
is a known fact
subordinate clause
that- NCl
cj S LV Cs
That America is a superpower

Exercise 5

1. Kamlesh accepted that her sister had taken the money.
2. She told me that you were coming here on Tuesday.
3. I regret that she did not give you the discount.
4. Vikram dreamt that he had become a general.
5. We heard that you are going to the USA.

Exercise 6

1. Sentence

main clause/superordinate clause

S TrV Od

She feels

subordinate clause

that- NCl

cj S TrV Od

that we should buy a car

2. 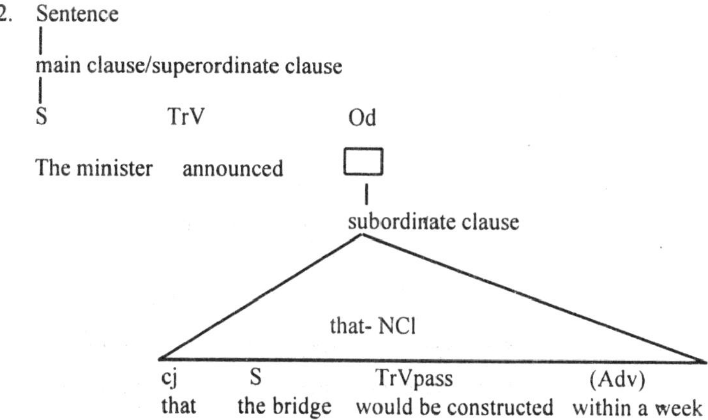

3\.

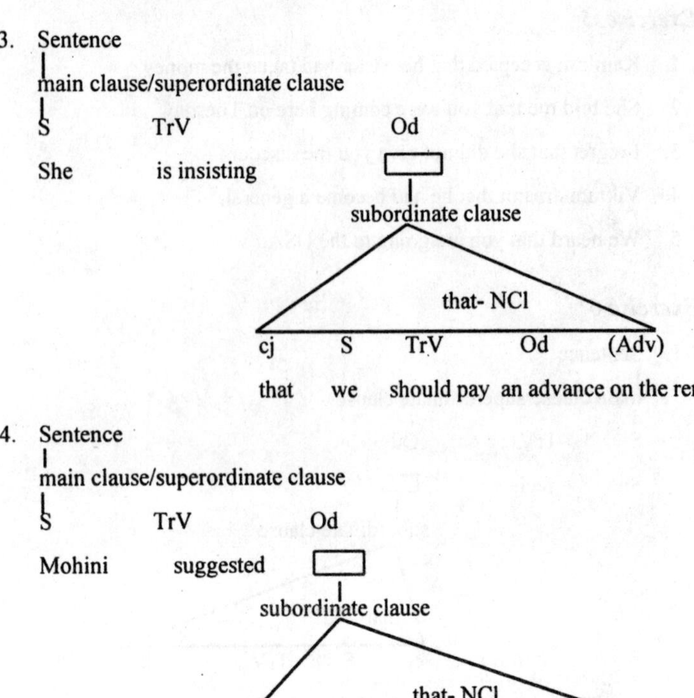
Sentence
main clause/superordinate clause
S
TrV
Od
She
is insisting
subordinate clause
that- NCl
cj
S
TrV
Od
(Adv)
that
we
should pay
an advance on the rent

4\.

Sentence
main clause/superordinate clause
S
TrV
Od
Mohini
suggested
subordinate clause
that- NCl
cj
S
InTrV
(Adv)
that
we
should go
on vacation

5\.

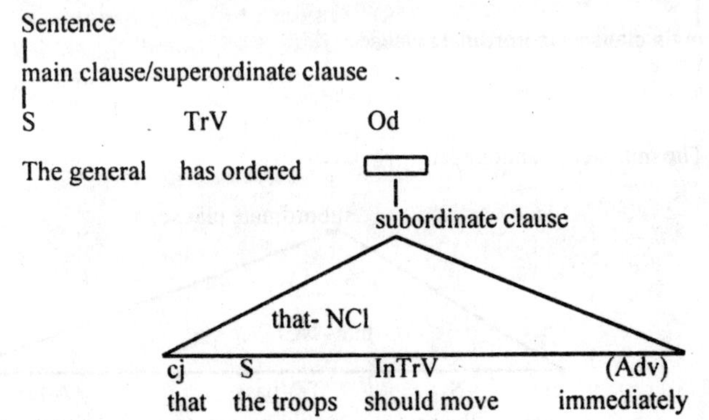
Sentence
main clause/superordinate clause
S
TrV
Od
The general
has ordered
subordinate clause
that- NCl
cj
S
InTrV
(Adv)
that
the troops
should move
immediately

Exercise 7

1. The chances are that we will win the match.
2. The suggestion was that the meeting should be held after two months.
3. The assumption is that democracy will survive.
4. The decision was that Varun would be given a scholarship.
5. My advice is that you should attend the interview tomorrow.

Exercise 8

1. Sentence

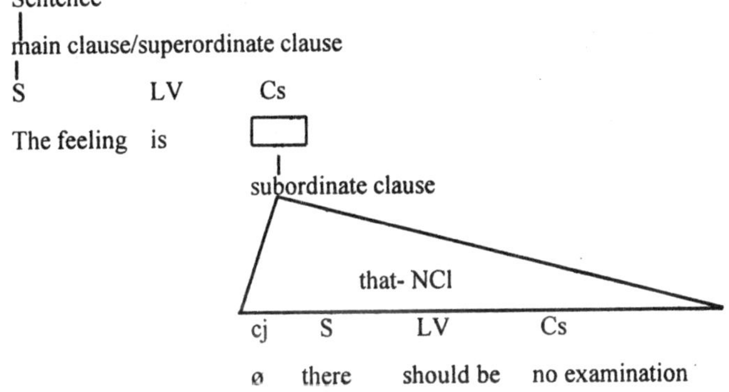

2. Sentence

main clause/superordinate clause

S LV Cs

The hope is

subordinate clause

that- NCl

cj S TrV Od

ø we shall get help

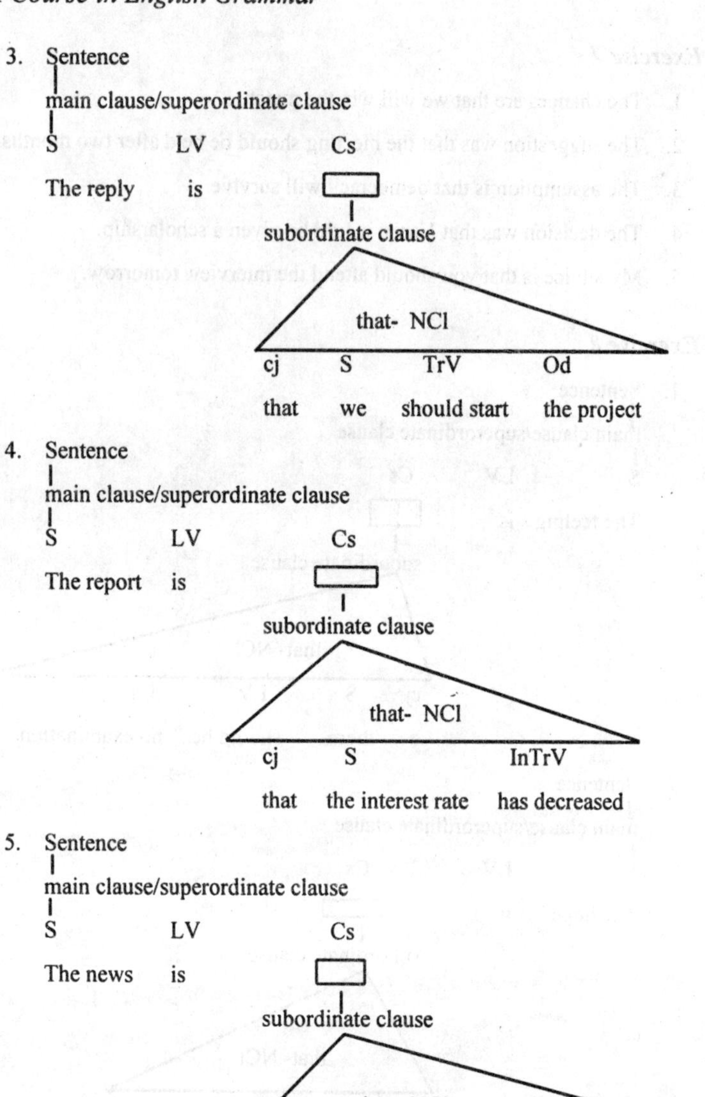
3. Sentence
main clause/superordinate clause
S
LV
Cs
The reply
is
subordinate clause
that- NCl
cj
S
TrV
Od
that
we
should start
the project
4. Sentence
main clause/superordinate clause
S
LV
Cs
The report
is
subordinate clause
that- NCl
cj
S
InTrV
that
the interest rate
has decreased
5. Sentence
main clause/superordinate clause
S
LV
Cs
The news
is
subordinate clause
that- NCl
cj
S
TrV
Od
that
India
has won
the cricket match

Exercise 9

1. Sentence

main clause/superordinate clause

S	LV	Cs	Adj. comp
Kiran	is	certain	[ ]

subordinate clause

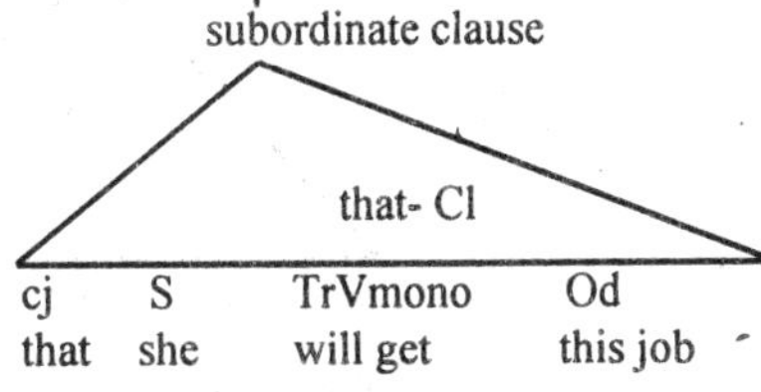

that- Cl

cj	S	TrVmono	Od
that	she	will get	this job

2. Sentence

main clause/superordinate clause

S	LV	Cs	Adj. comp
I	am	afraid	[ ]

subordinate clause

that- NCl

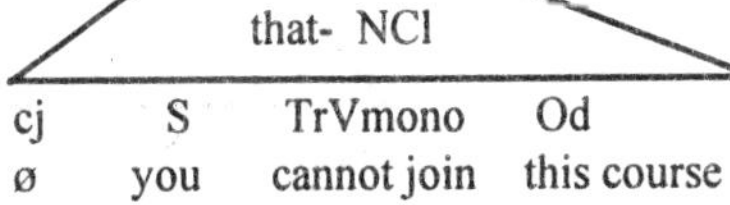

cj	S	TrVmono	Od
ø	you	cannot join	this course

3. Sentence

main clause/superordinate clause

S	LV	Cs	Adj. comp
She	is	astonished	[ ]

subordinate clause

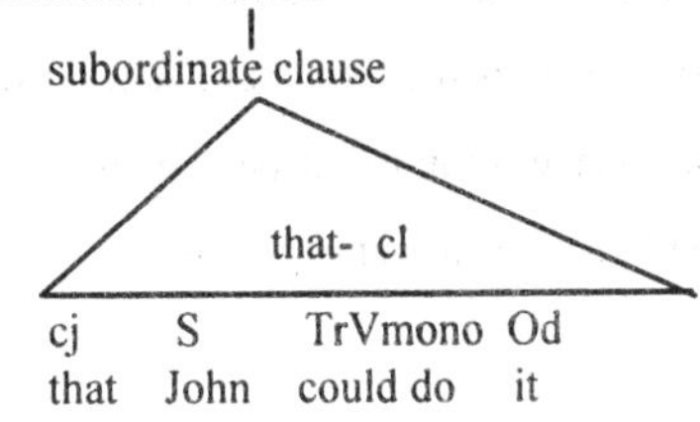

that- cl

cj	S	TrVmono	Od
that	John	could do	it

4. Sentence

main clause/superordinate clause

S LV Cs Adj.comp

I am convinced

subordinate clause

that- NCl

cj S LV Cs

that he is a great writer

5. Sentence

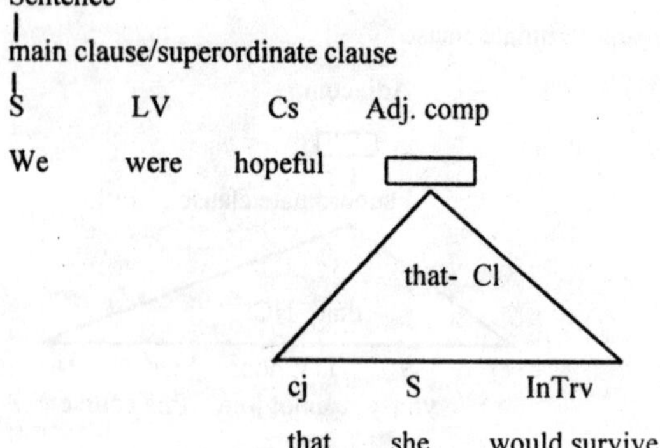

Exercise 10

1. When the Prime Minister will arrive is a secret.
2. I know why he didn't take the examination.
3. The best solution is what you have suggested.
4. How the college is run will depend on the Principal.
5. I can't tell you why she arrived late.

Exercise 11

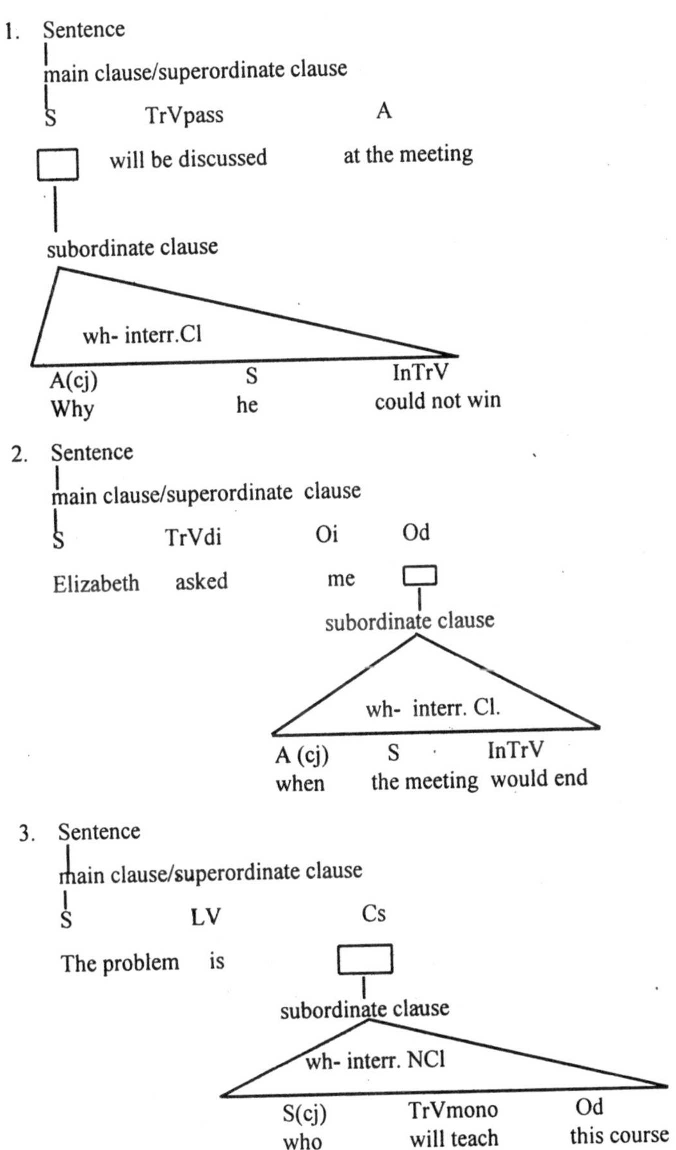
1. Sentence
main clause/superordinate clause
S
TrVpass
A
will be discussed
at the meeting
subordinate clause
wh- interr.Cl
A(cj)
Why
S
he
InTrV
could not win
2. Sentence
main clause/superordinate clause
S
TrVdi
Oi
Od
Elizabeth
asked
me
subordinate clause
wh- interr. Cl.
A (cj)
when
S
the meeting
InTrV
would end
3. Sentence
main clause/superordinate clause
S
LV
Cs
The problem
is
subordinate clause
wh- interr. NCl
S(cj)
who
TrVmono
will teach
Od
this course

4.

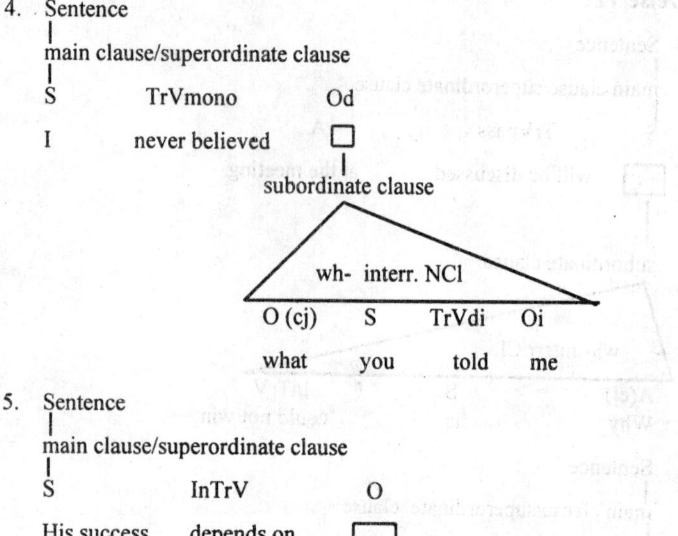
Sentence
main clause/superordinate clause
S
TrVmono
Od
I
never believed
subordinate clause
wh- interr. NCl
O (cj)
S
TrVdi
Oi
what
you
told
me

5.

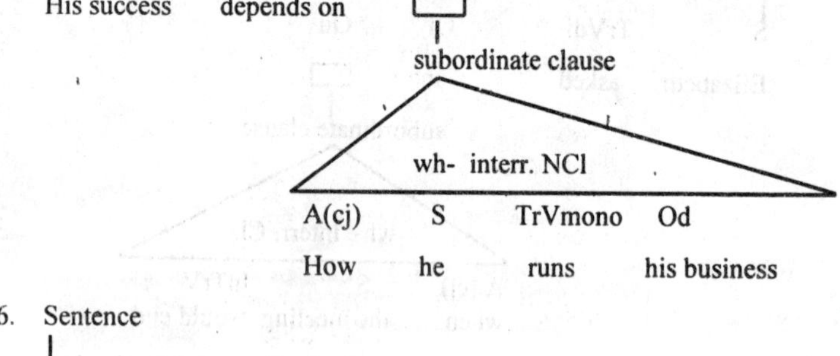
Sentence
main clause/superordinate clause
S
InTrV
O
His success
depends on
subordinate clause
wh- interr. NCl
A(cj)
S
TrVmono
Od
How
he
runs
his business

6.

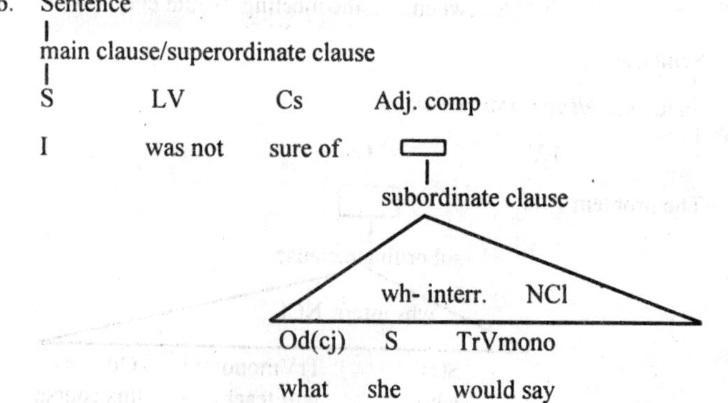
Sentence
main clause/superordinate clause
S
LV
Cs
Adj. comp
I
was not
sure of
subordinate clause
wh- interr. NCl
Od(cj)
S
TrVmono
what
she
would say

7. 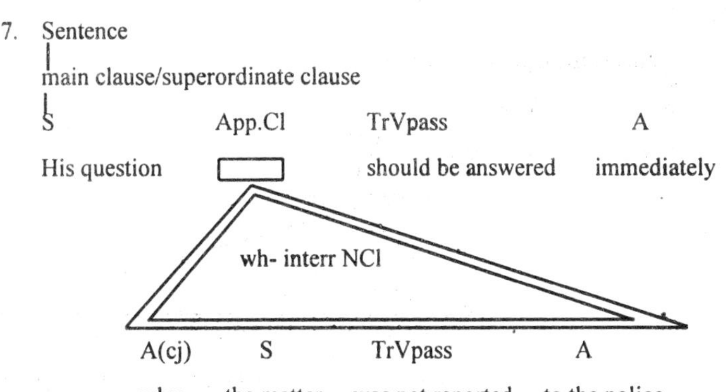
Sentence
main clause/superordinate clause
S
App.Cl
TrVpass
A
His question
should be answered
immediately
wh- interr NCl
A(cj)
S
TrVpass
A
why
the matter
was not reported
to the police

8. 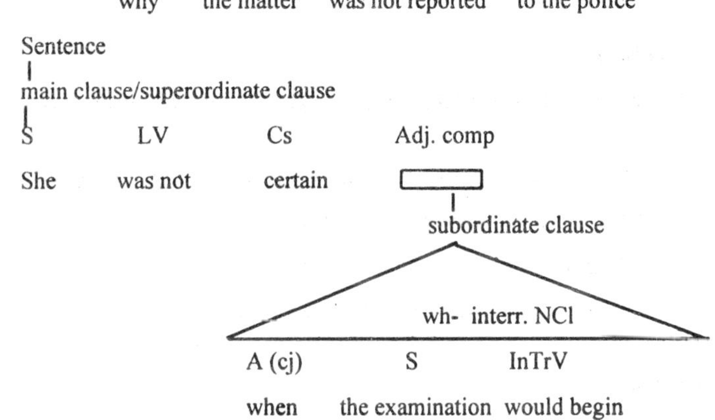
Sentence
main clause/superordinate clause
S
LV
Cs
Adj. comp
She
was not
certain
subordinate clause
wh- interr. NCl
A (cj)
S
InTrV
when
the examination
would begin

9. 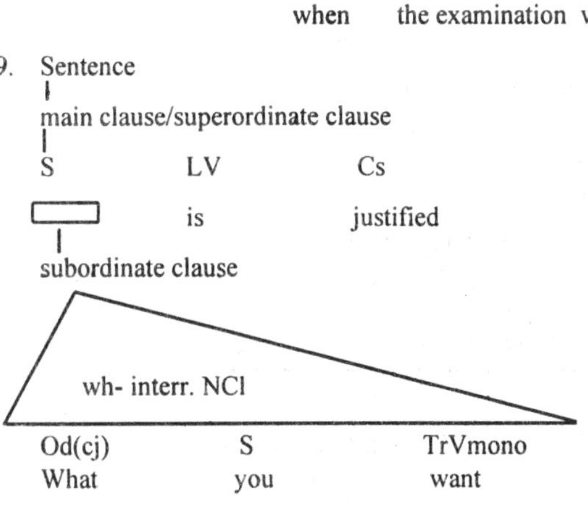
Sentence
main clause/superordinate clause
S
LV
Cs
is
justified
subordinate clause
wh- interr. NCl
Od(cj)
S
TrVmono
What
you
want

10. 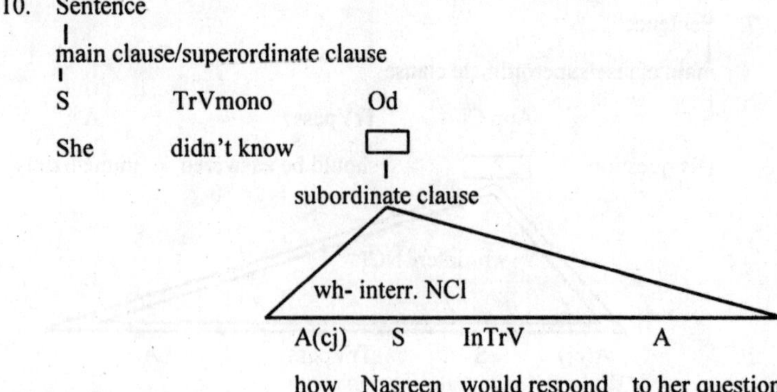

Exercise 12

1. Whether she could take part in the game depended a great deal on her recovery.
2. Our main concern is whether she will join us before lunch time.
3. Jivan asked her if she had worked earlier.
4. Whether you study or play is your decision.
5. She asked me if Meena could stay with them.

Exercise 13

1. 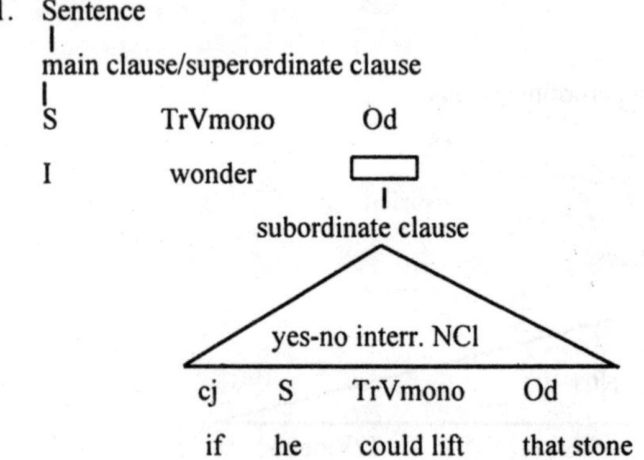

2\.

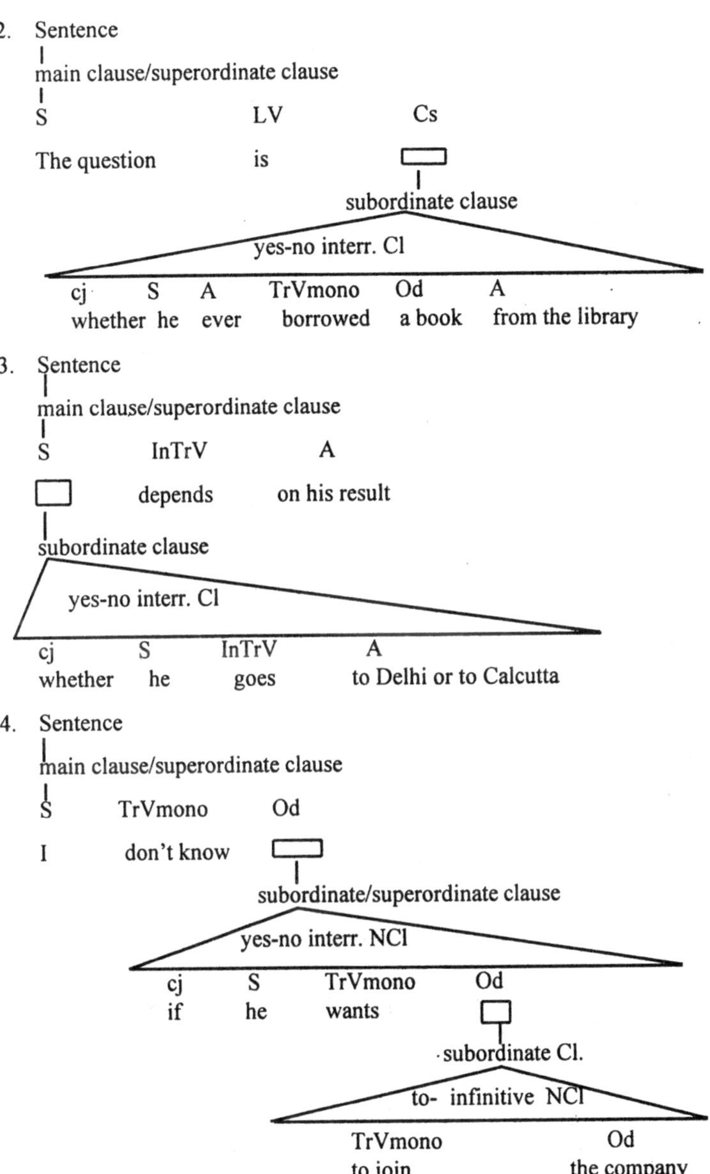
Sentence
main clause/superordinate clause
S
LV
Cs
The question
is
subordinate clause
yes-no interr. Cl
cj
S
A
TrVmono
Od
A
whether
he
ever
borrowed
a book
from the library
Sentence
main clause/superordinate clause
S
InTrV
A
depends
on his result
subordinate clause
yes-no interr. Cl
cj
S
InTrV
A
whether
he
goes
to Delhi or to Calcutta
Sentence
main clause/superordinate clause
S
TrVmono
Od
I
don't know
subordinate/superordinate clause
yes-no interr. NCl
cj
S
TrVmono
Od
if
he
wants
subordinate Cl.
to- infinitive NCl
TrVmono
Od
to join
the company

3\.

4\.

5. This sentence has been derived from:

Whether she takes part in the dance or not is immaterial.

Sentence

main clause/superordinate clause

S	LV	Cs
□	is	immaterial

subordinate clause

yes-no interr. NCl

cj	S	TrVmono	Od
if	she	takes	part in the dance or not

Using the following rule for extraposed subject:

S + LV + Cs → It + LV +Cs + extraposed subject

We get: It is immaterial whether she takes part in the dance or not.

6. Sentence

main clause/superordinate clause

S	LV	Cs	Adj. comp
I	am not	certain	□

subordinate clause

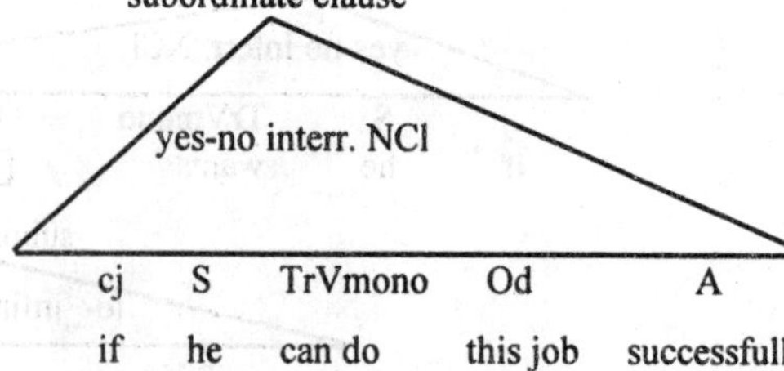

cj	S	TrVmono	Od	A
if	he	can do	this job	successfully

7.

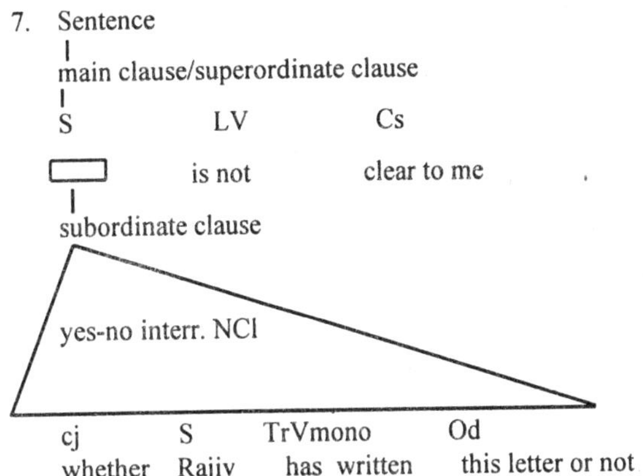

8. Same as sentence 6 analysis.

9. Same as sentence 4 analysis

10. Same as sentence 5 analysis.

Exercise 14

1.

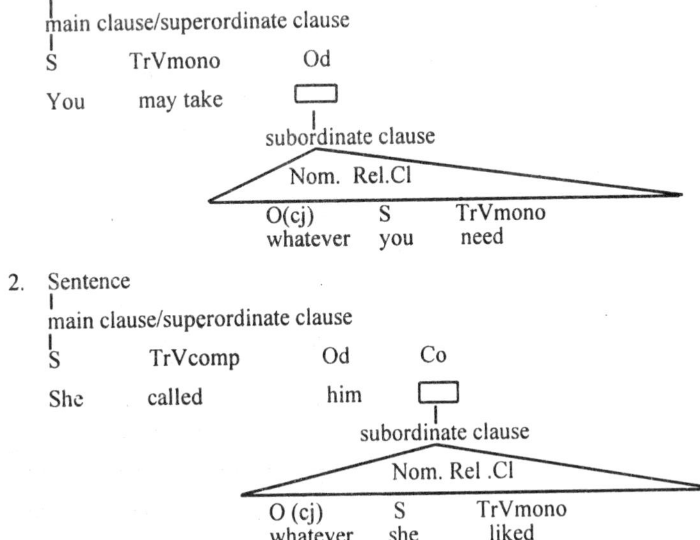

2.

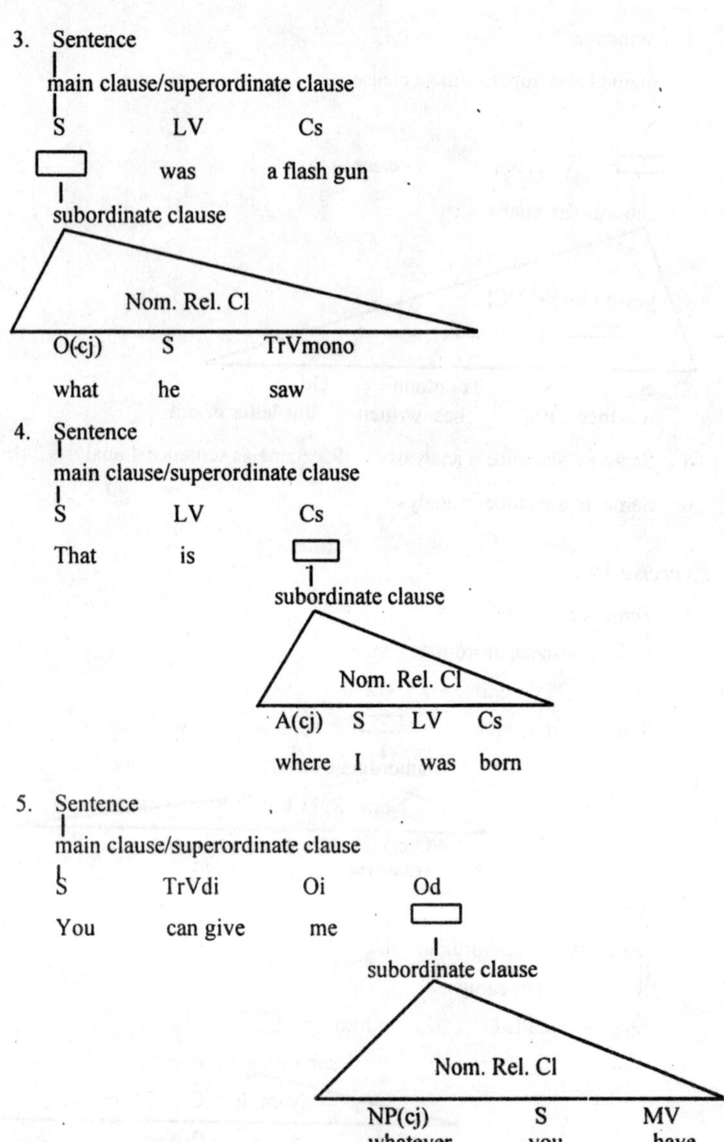

Note: *Have* is a middle verb and *whatever* is an NP and not an object (see section 1.4)

6. Sentence

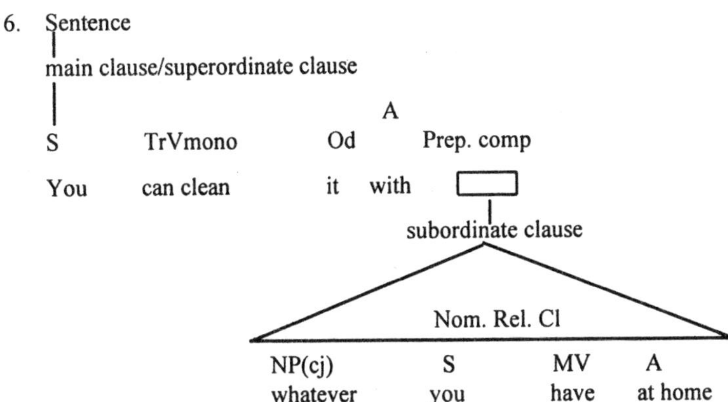

Note: *Have* is a middle verb here.

7. Sentence

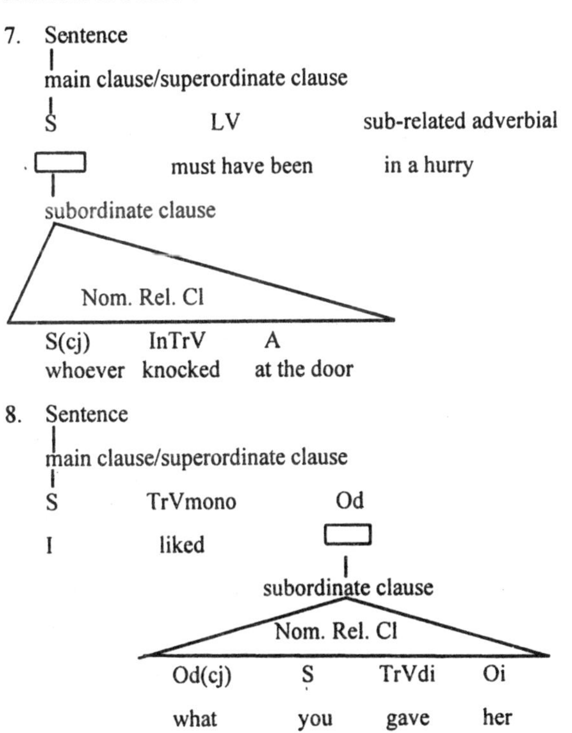

8. Sentence

main clause/superordinate clause

S TrVmono Od

I liked

subordinate clause

Nom. Rel. Cl

Od(cj) S TrVdi Oi

what you gave her

9\. Sentence

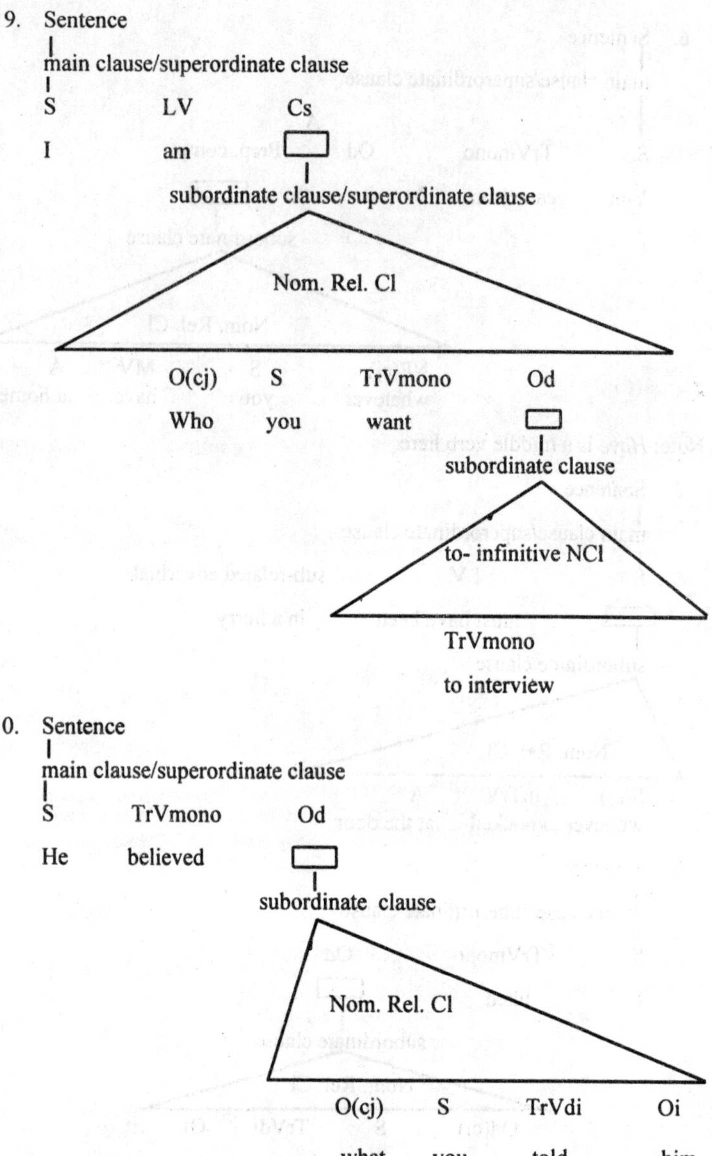

10\. Sentence

Exercise 15

1. She likes her friends visiting her.
2. The director instructed all the officers to be punctual.
3. To visit London is my dream.
4. She seems to be temperamental.
5. I told her to meet me at the station.
6. She persuaded me to take up the job.
7. She is very keen to meet you.
8. He is sure to pass the examination.
9. For an army to withdraw like that is extremely disgraceful.
   Or
   It is extremely disgraceful for an army to withdraw like that.
10. The best remedy is to sleep for two hours.

Exercise 16

1. Sentence

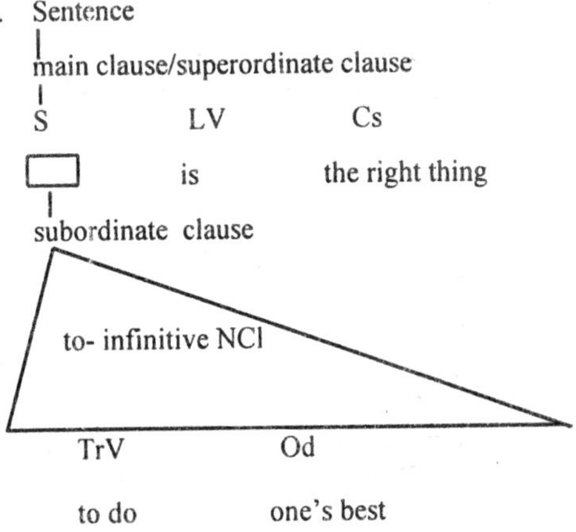

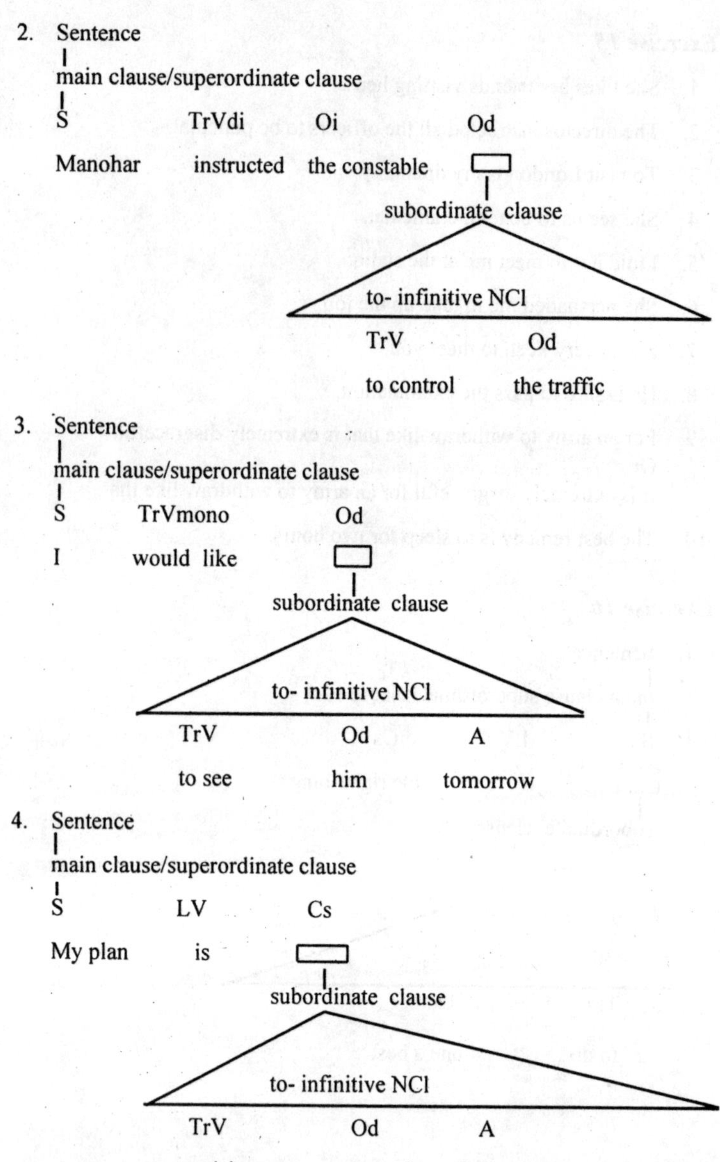
2. Sentence
main clause/superordinate clause
S
TrVdi
Oi
Od
Manohar
instructed
the constable
subordinate clause
to- infinitive NCl
TrV
Od
to control
the traffic
3. Sentence
main clause/superordinate clause
S
TrVmono
Od
I
would like
subordinate clause
to- infinitive NCl
TrV
Od
A
to see
him
tomorrow
4. Sentence
main clause/superordinate clause
S
LV
Cs
My plan
is
subordinate clause
to- infinitive NCl
TrV
Od
A
to visit
my grandma
during the summer vacation

5. 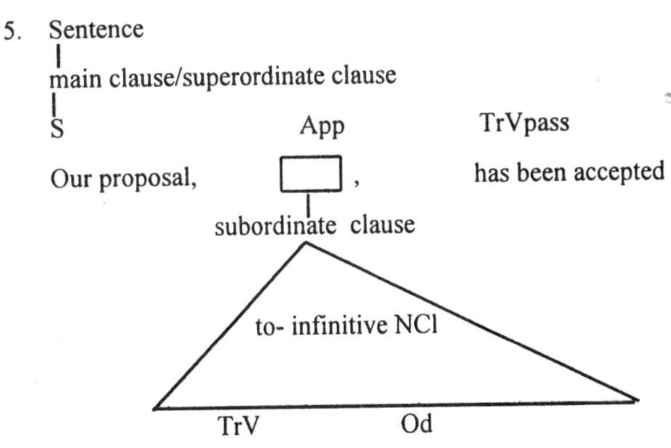

6. This sentence is derived from:

To watch this film is fun.

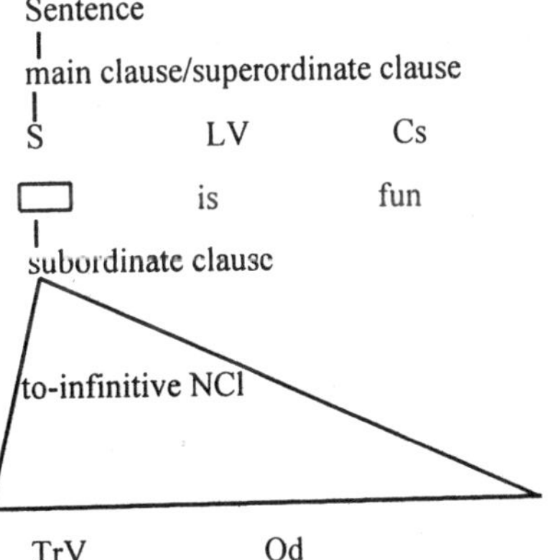

TrV Od

to watch this film

Using the following formula:

S + LV + Cs $\rightarrow$ It+LV + Cs + extraposed subject

One gets: It is fun to watch this film.

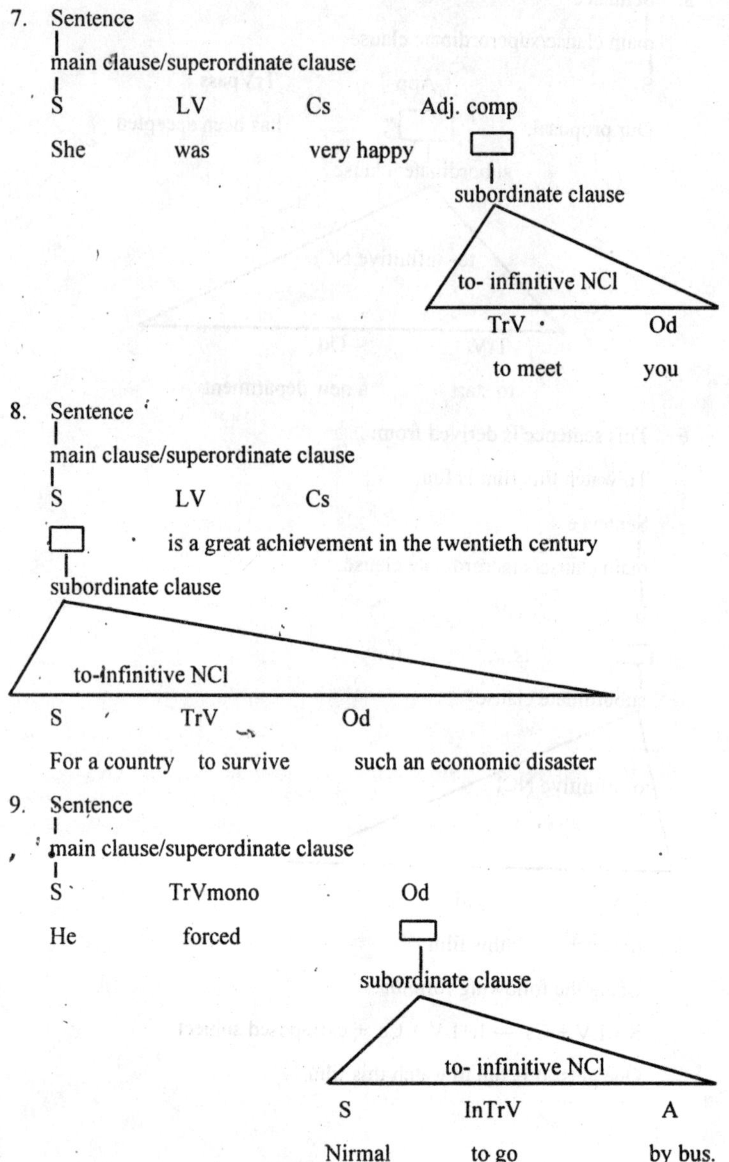
7. Sentence
main clause/superordinate clause
S
LV
Cs
Adj. comp
She
was
very happy
subordinate clause
to- infinitive NCl
TrV
Od
to meet
you
8. Sentence
main clause/superordinate clause
S
LV
Cs
is a great achievement in the twentieth century
subordinate clause
to-infinitive NCl
S
TrV
Od
For a country
to survive
such an economic disaster
9. Sentence
main clause/superordinate clause
S
TrVmono
Od
He
forced
subordinate clause
to- infinitive NCl
S
InTrV
A
Nirmal
to go
by bus.

10.

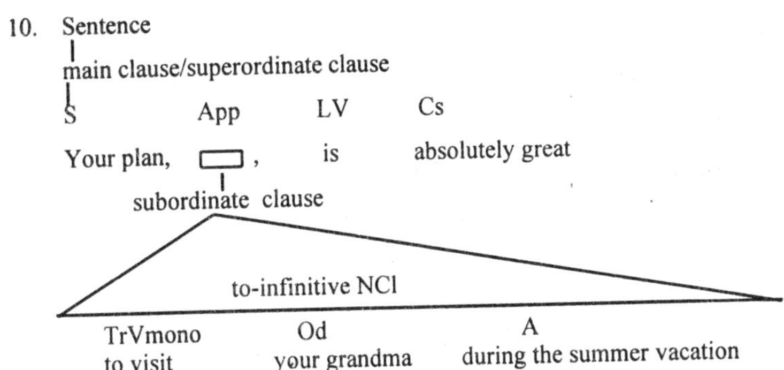

Exercise 17

1. I don't like him singing in the classroom.
2. Watching Gavaskar on the field used to be a cricketer's delight.
3. The best event was Niraj playing for our team.
4. Her job is preparing the annual balance sheet.
5. Dilip regrets talking to you rudely.
6. Ravi falling in the playfield is a serious matter.
7. Rita is responsible for declaring the results.
8. Smoking is injurious to health.
9. Sameer loves visiting hill stations.
10. Her ambition was her son reaching the top.

Exercise 18

1.

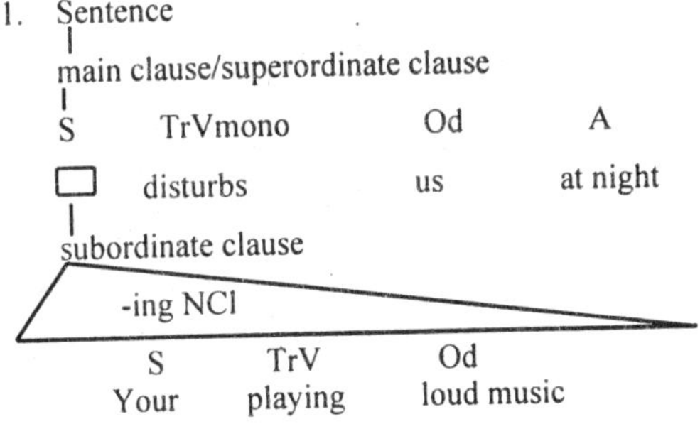

2. Sentence

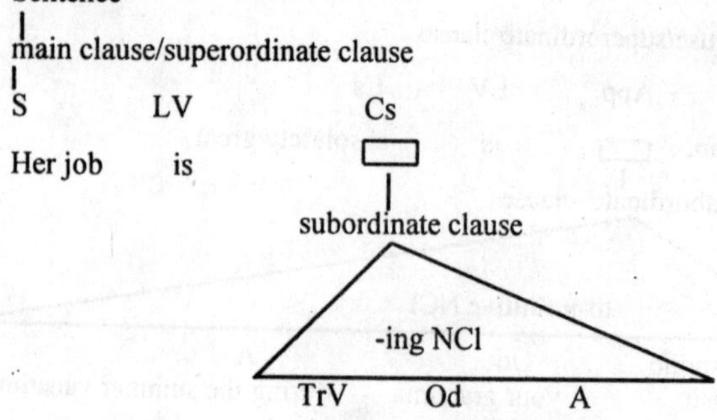

3. Sentence

main clause/superordinate clause

S TrVmono Od

She enjoyed

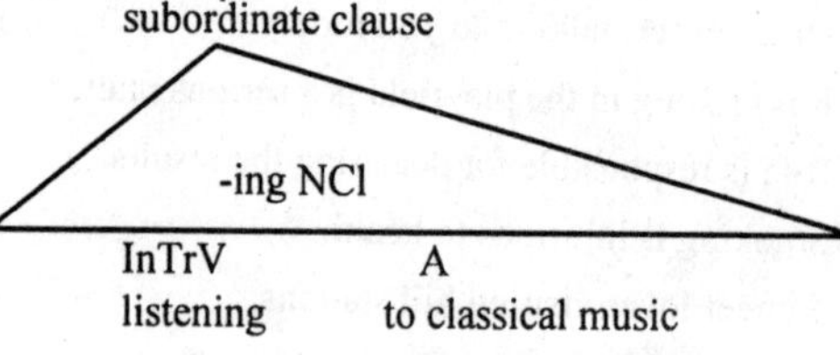

4. Sentence

main clause/superordinate clause

S LV Cs prep. comp

Rekha is not capable of

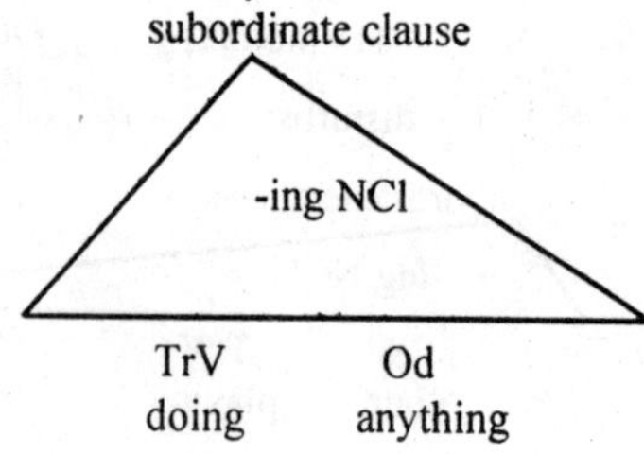

5. 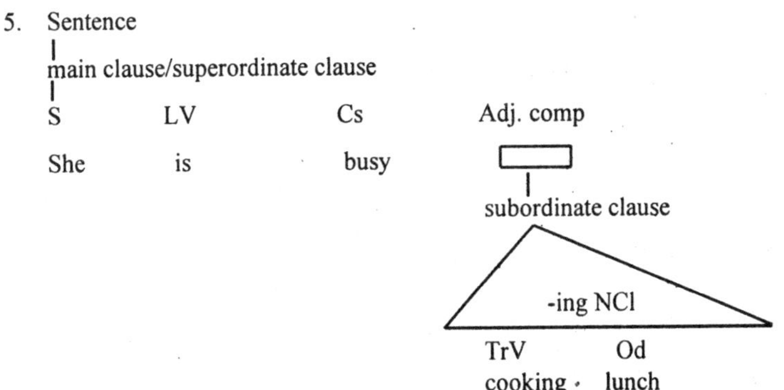

6 and 9 as for 3; 7 and 10 as for 1; 8 as for 4;

Exercise 19

1. 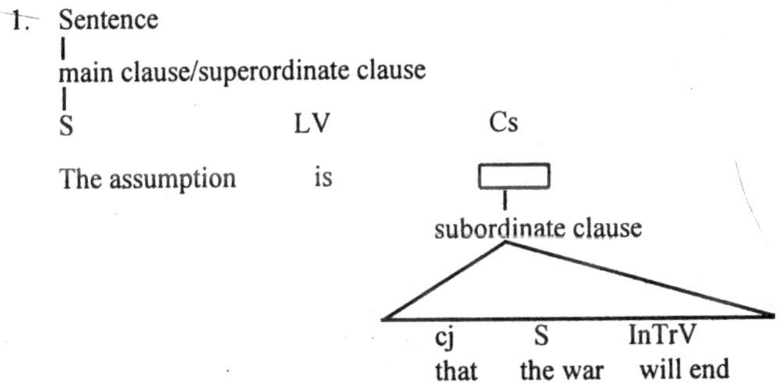

2. 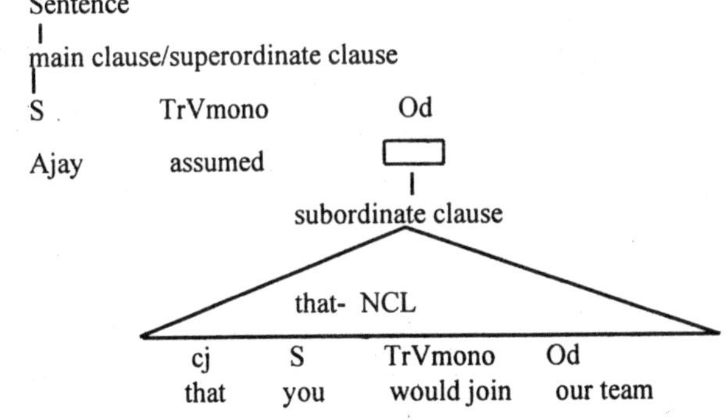

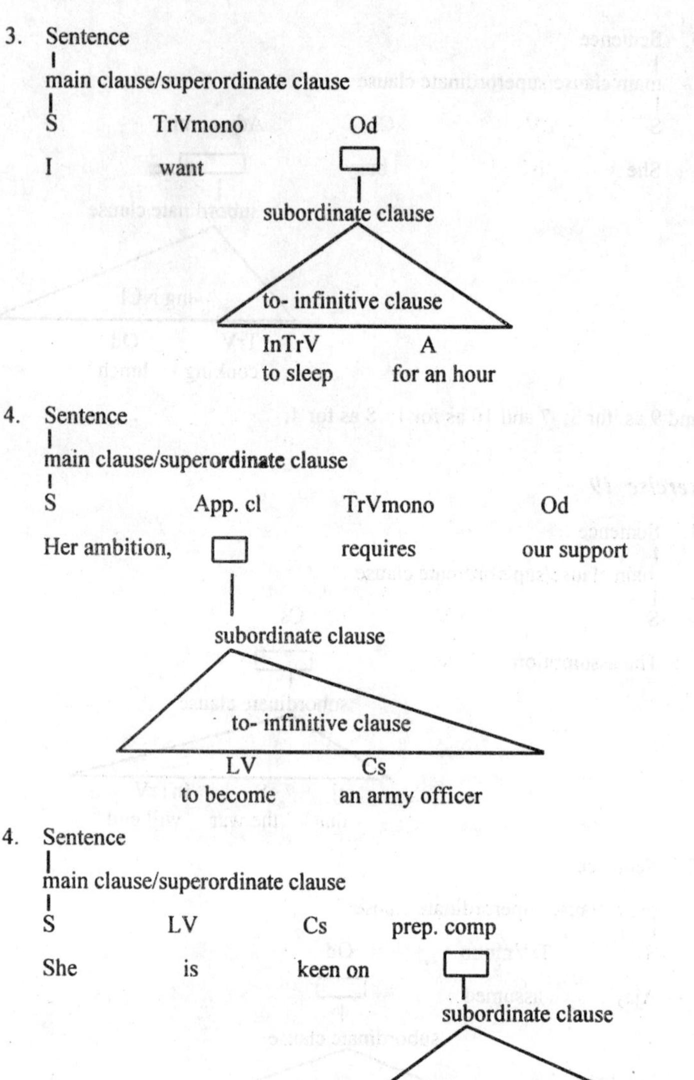
3. Sentence
main clause/superordinate clause
S
TrVmono
Od
I
want
subordinate clause
to- infinitive clause
InTrV
A
to sleep
for an hour
4. Sentence
main clause/superordinate clause
S
App. cl
TrVmono
Od
Her ambition,
requires
our support
subordinate clause
to- infinitive clause
LV
Cs
to become
an army officer
4. Sentence
main clause/superordinate clause
S
LV
Cs
prep. comp
She
is
keen on
subordinate clause
-ing NCl
TrV
Od
joining
the armed forces

Chapter 8

Exercise 1

1. The doctor whom/who my father usually consults is available in the evening.
2. The story about which I was talking has appeared in *The Times of India*.
3. The boy who has stood first in the school is my neighbour.
4. The newspaper for which he works has been started recently.
5. The man with whom she was working left for Australia.
6. I am waiting for the girl who joined our class yesterday.
7. The mechanic whom/who you met at the garage yesterday has come to see you.
8. The lady whose house you constructed last month has migrated to the USA.
9. The chair which/that is lying in the corner is made of pine.
10. The girl with whom I talked yesterday is the daughter of an ambassador.

Exercise 2

1. Sentence

main clause/superordinate clause

S InTrV Od Prep. comp

The director < rel.cl.> has been selected for the National award

S TrVmono Od

who made this film

2. Sentence

main clause/superordinate clause

S TrVmono Od

I met the man < rel.cl >

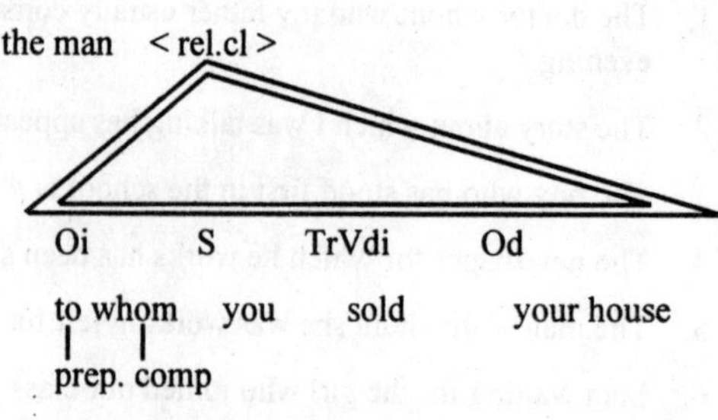

Oi S TrVdi Od

to whom you sold your house

prep. comp

3. Sentence

main clause/superordinate clause

S LV Cs

The bungalow < rel.cl. > is government accommodation

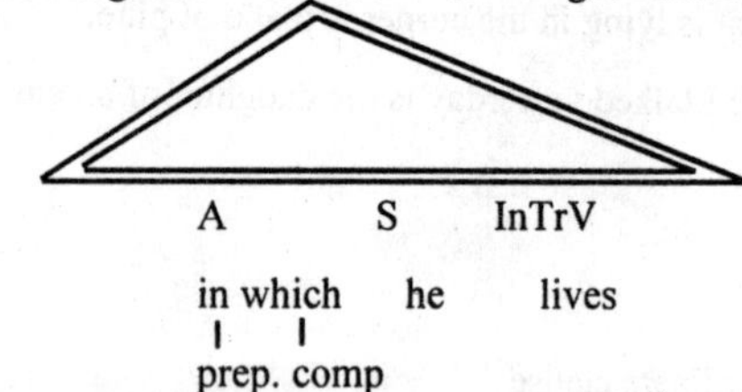

A S InTrV

in which he lives

prep. comp

4. Sentence

main clause/superordinate clause

S LV Cs

This is the girl < rel.cl. >

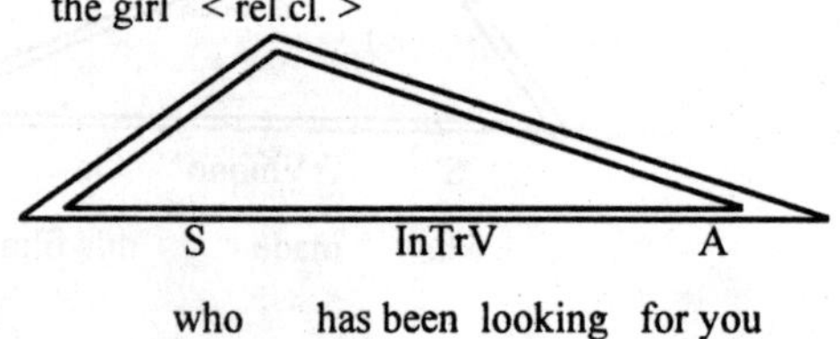

S InTrV A

who has been looking for you

5. Sentence

main clause/superordinate clause

S LV Cs

That is the lawyer < rel. cl. >

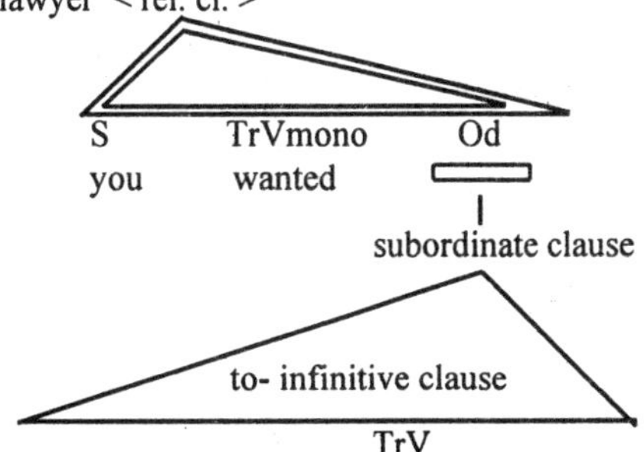

6. Sentence

main clause/superordinate clause

S TrVmono Od

I met a girl < rel.cl. >

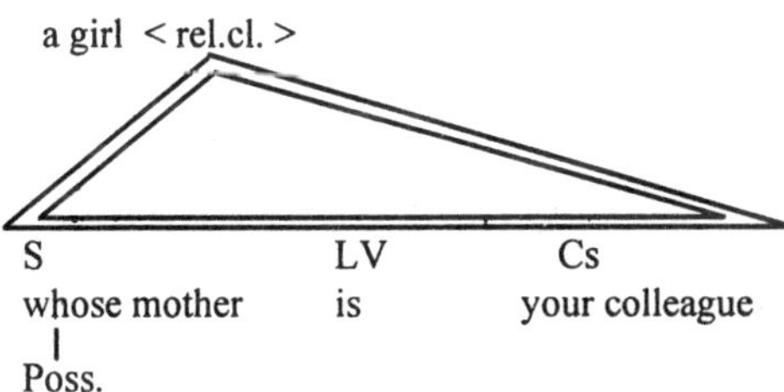

7. Sentence

main clause/superordinate clause

S InTrV A

We live in an area < rel.cl. >

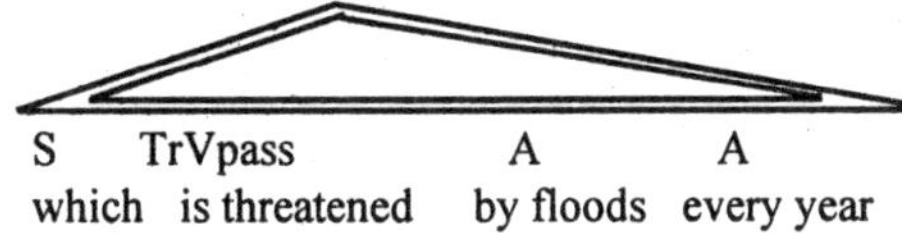

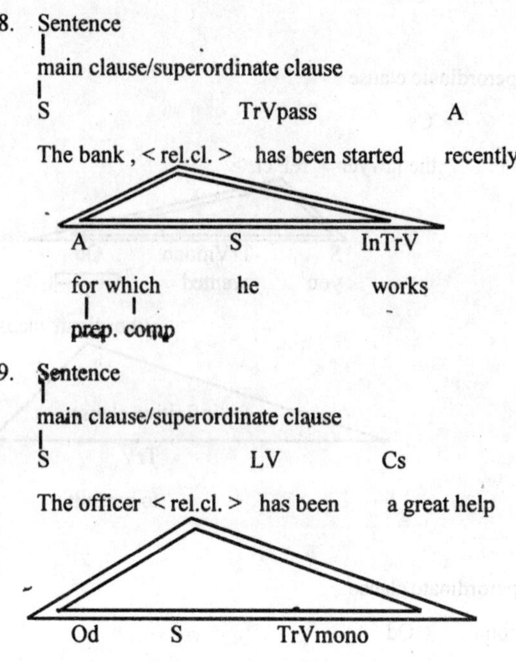

10. Same as analysis for sentence 4.

Exercise 3

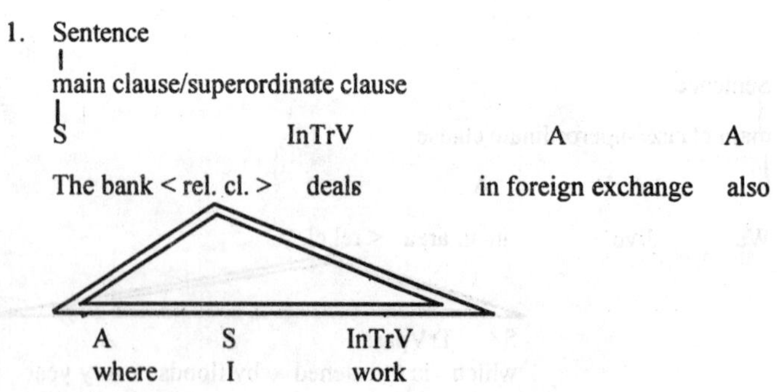

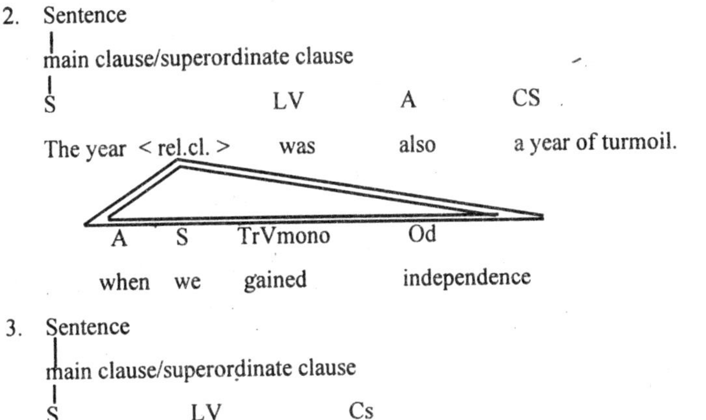

This is the reason < rel. cl. >

A S MV NP

why we have a strong work force.

Note: 'have' is a middle verb and 'a strong army' is the NP

4 and 5 same as analyses for sentence 3

Exercise 4

1. She lived in Delhi when I last met her.
2. I saw her while she was crossing the road.
3. Please inform me when you reach Raipur.
4. Lata started clearing up the mess after the guests had left.
5. They will go home after they have taken the examination.
6. Wait for me until I return.
7. Neena went to DehraDun because her father was ill.
8. As the food is too spicy I stopped eating at the mess.
9. When I met her she looked very tired.
10. I rang her up because I had to give her a message.

Exercise 5

1. Sentence

main clause/superordinate clause

S InTrV A A A

I went to office today [Adv. cl]

finite/reason

cj S TrVmono Od

because the Registrar had called me

2. 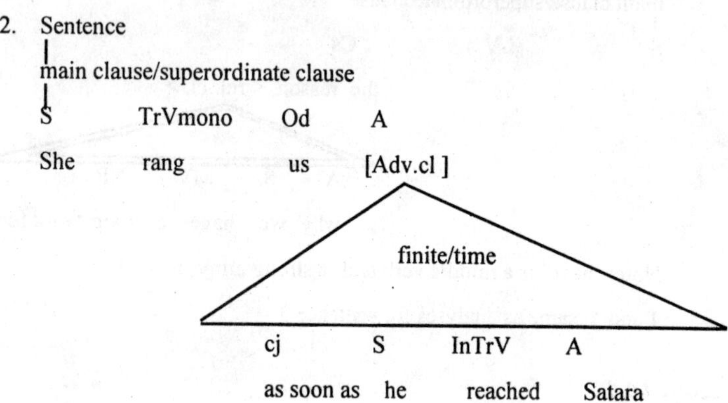

3. 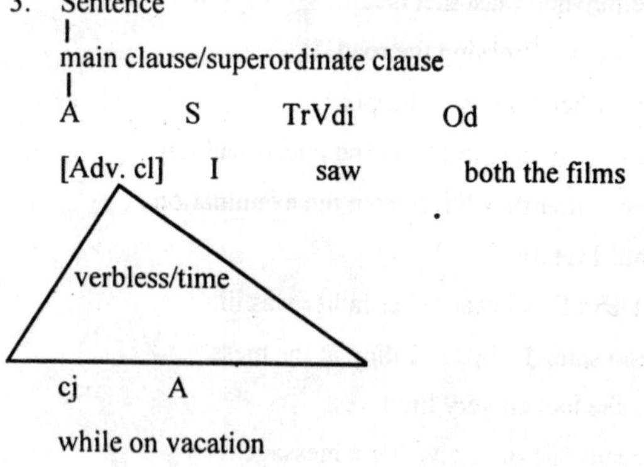

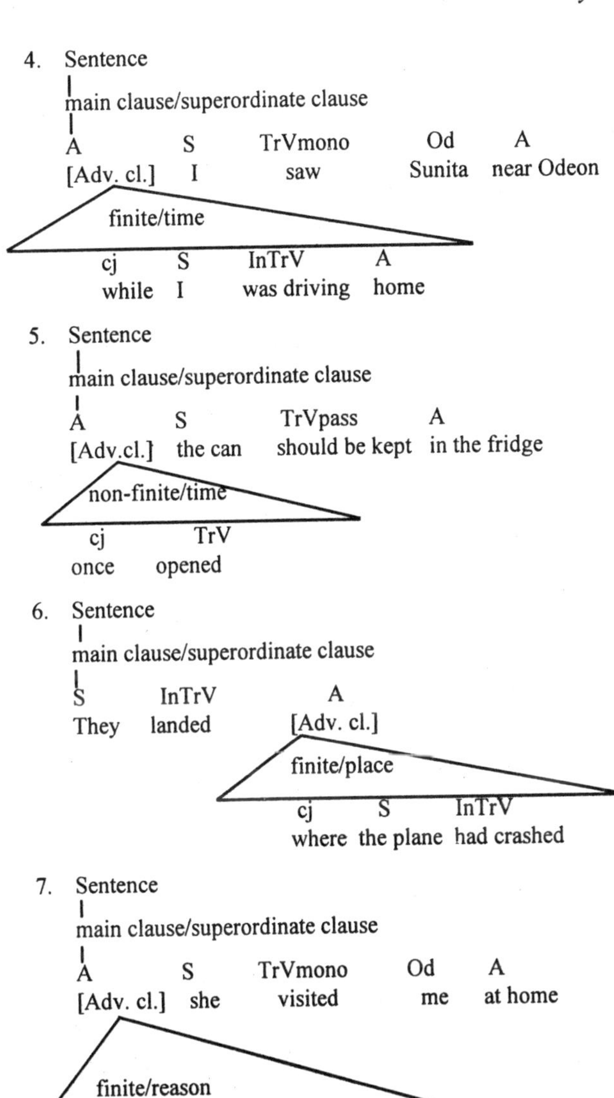
4. Sentence
main clause/superordinate clause
A S TrVmono Od A
[Adv. cl.] I saw Sunita near Odeon
finite/time
cj S InTrV A
while I was driving home
5. Sentence
main clause/superordinate clause
A S TrVpass A
[Adv.cl.] the can should be kept in the fridge
non-finite/time
cj TrV
once opened
6. Sentence
main clause/superordinate clause
S InTrV A
They landed [Adv. cl.]
finite/place
cj S InTrV
where the plane had crashed
7. Sentence
main clause/superordinate clause
A S TrVmono Od A
[Adv. cl.] she visited me at home
finite/reason
cj S TrVmono Od A
As she knew me well

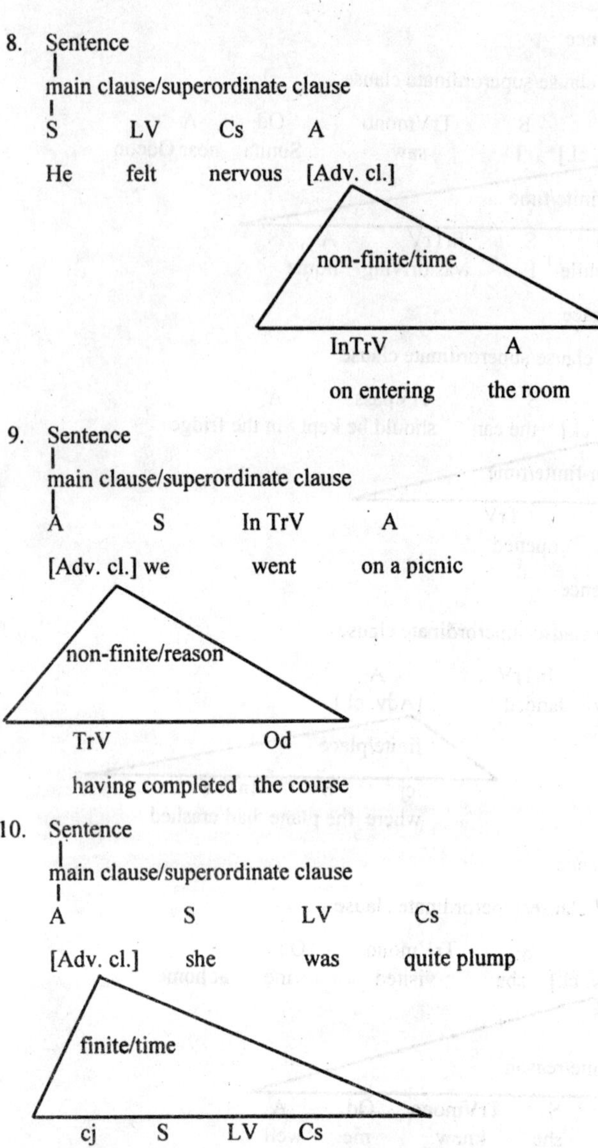
8. Sentence
main clause/superordinate clause
S LV Cs A
He felt nervous [Adv. cl.]
non-finite/time
InTrV A
on entering the room
9. Sentence
main clause/superordinate clause
A S In TrV A
[Adv. cl.] we went on a picnic
non-finite/reason
TrV Od
having completed the course
10. Sentence
main clause/superordinate clause
A S LV Cs
[Adv. cl.] she was quite plump
finite/time
cj S LV Cs
when she was young

Exercise 6

1. Sentence

main clause/superordinate clause

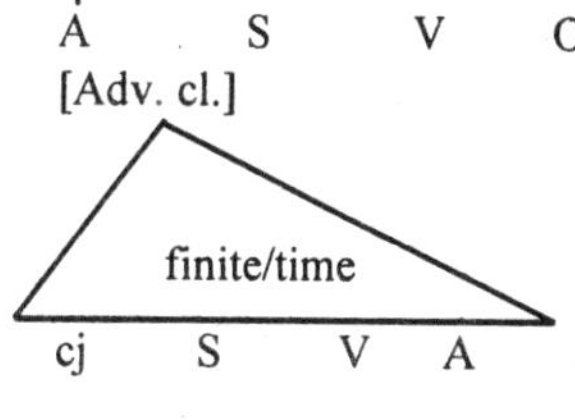

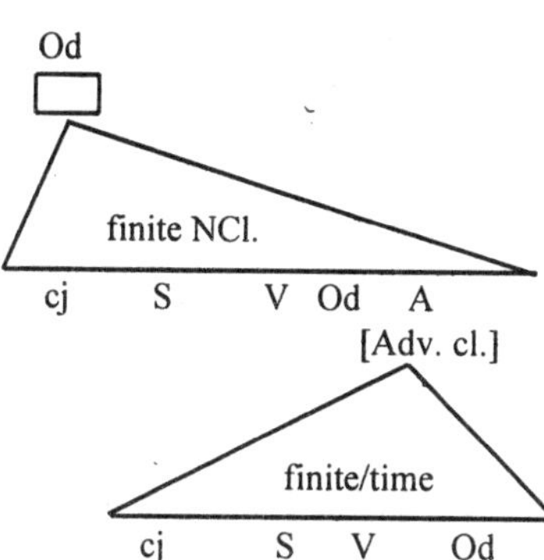

2. Sentence

main clause/superordinate clause

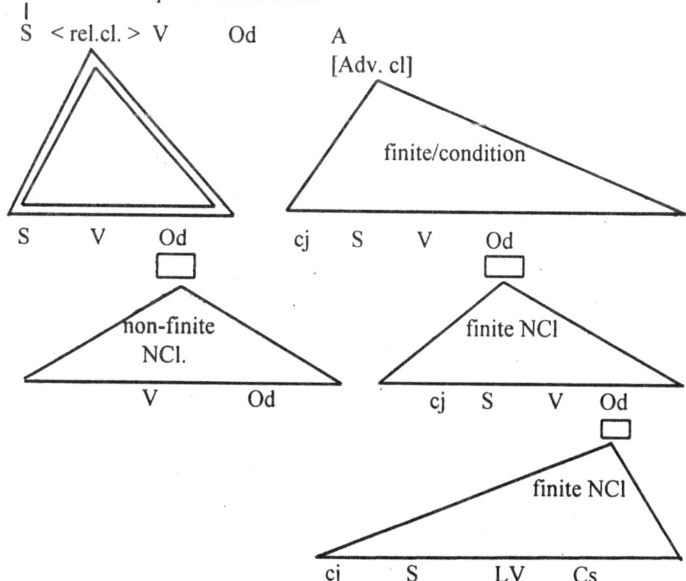

3. Sentence

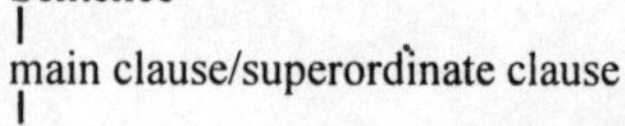

S V

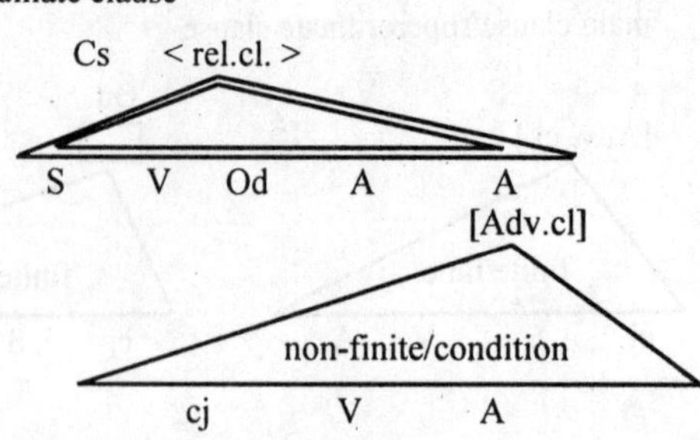

4. Sentence

main clause/superordinate clause

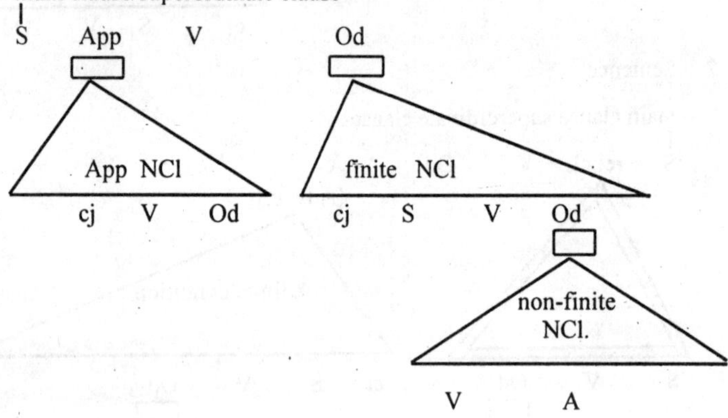

5. Sentence

main clause/superordinate clause

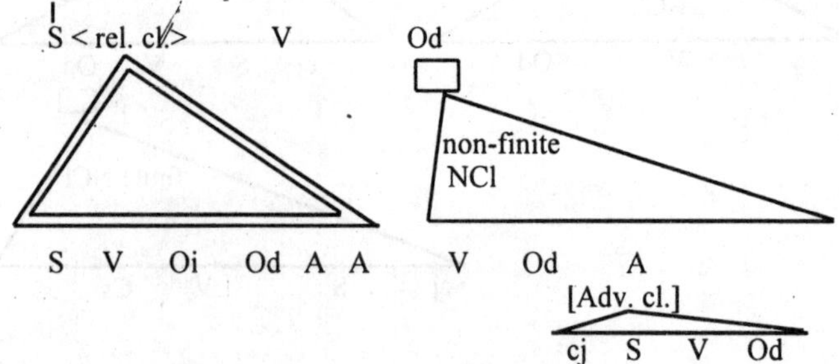

6. Sentence

main clause/superordinate clause

A S V Od

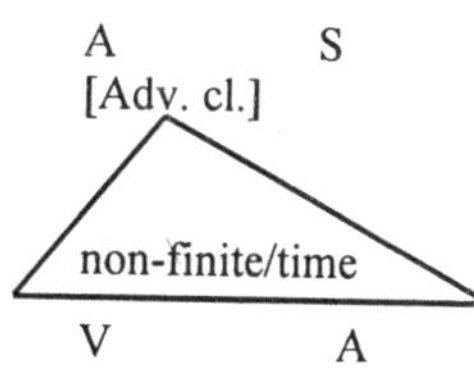

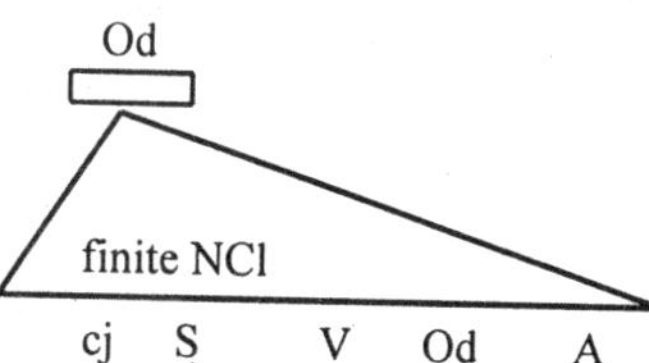

7. Sentence

main clause/superordinate clause

S V Od

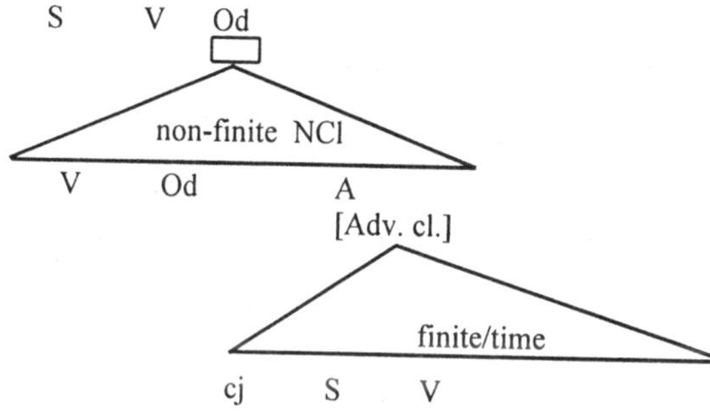

8. Sentence

main clause/superordinate clause

S V Od

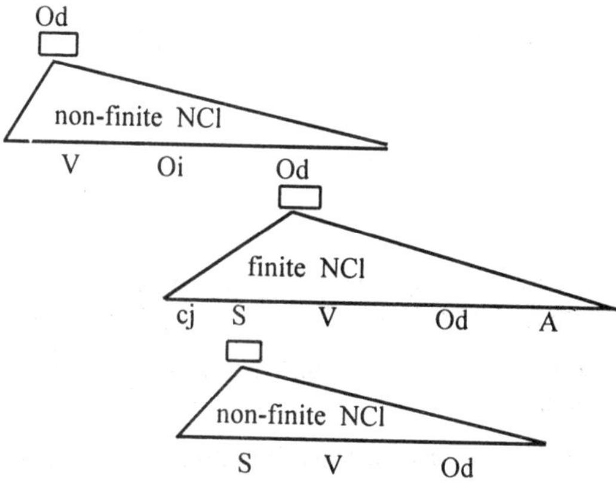

9. Sentence

main clause/superordinate clause

S V Cs Adj.comp

finite NCl

Od(cj) S V A

[Adv. cl]

finite/time

cj S V Oi Od

finite NCl

cj S V Od

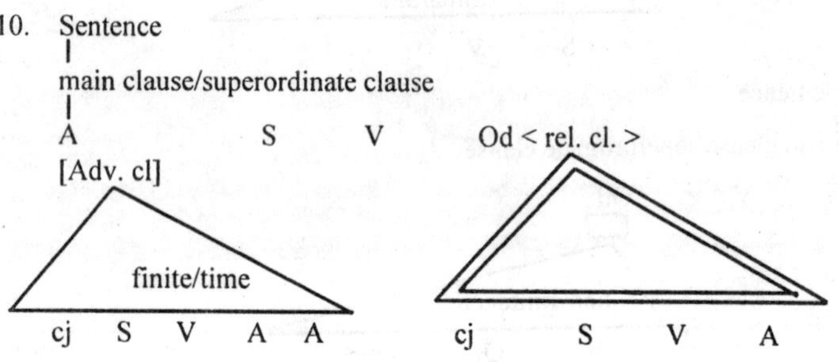

Exercise 7

1. Where she has left the keys is a wh-interrogative clause used as Od in **a** and a relative clause in **b.**

2. The relative clause is a restrictive clause in **a** and a non-restrictive clause in **b.**

3. That he was arrested is an appositive clause in **a.** That you told me is a relative clause in **b.**

4. 'Who' in the relative clause has replaced the subject in **a** and the direct object in **b.**

5. To meet the chief minister is the Od in **a** and the Adv. cl in **b.**

6. The that- NCl is a delayed subject in **a** and an adjectival complement in **b.**

7. The subject of the infinitive NCl 'to be an astronaut' is co-referential to the subject (I) of the main clause and therefore has been dropped in **a.** 'Her to be an astronaut' is a to- infinitive NCl with 'her' as subject which is not co-referential to the subject (I) of the main clause and is therefore not dropped in **b.**

8. Same as 7

9. 'While I was crossing the road' is an adverbial clause of time in **a** and 'While Johhn is aggressive' is a clause of contrast in **b.**

10. The if-clause is a clause of open condition in **a** and hypothetical condition in **b.**

Chapter 9

Exercise 1

1.

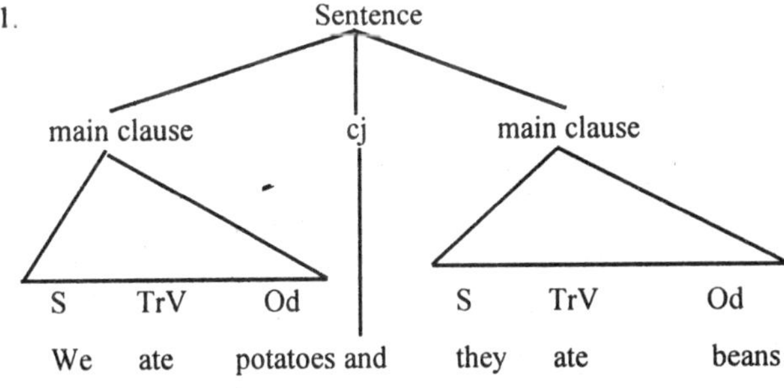

2.

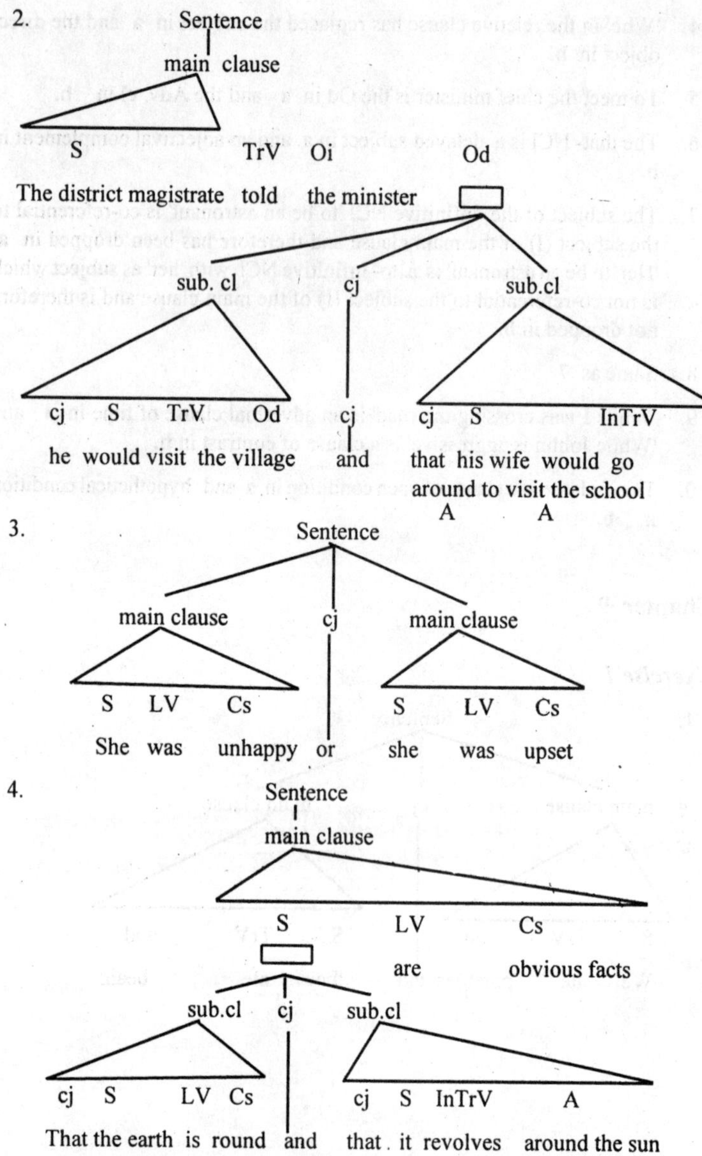
Sentence
main clause
S
TrV
Oi
Od
The district magistrate told the minister
sub. cl
cj
sub.cl
cj S TrV Od
cj
cj S InTrV
he would visit the village
and
that his wife would go
around to visit the school
A A
Sentence
main clause
cj
main clause
S LV Cs
S LV Cs
She was unhappy or she was upset
Sentence
main clause
S LV Cs
are obvious facts
sub.cl cj sub.cl
cj S LV Cs
cj S InTrV A
That the earth is round and that . it revolves around the sun

3.

4.

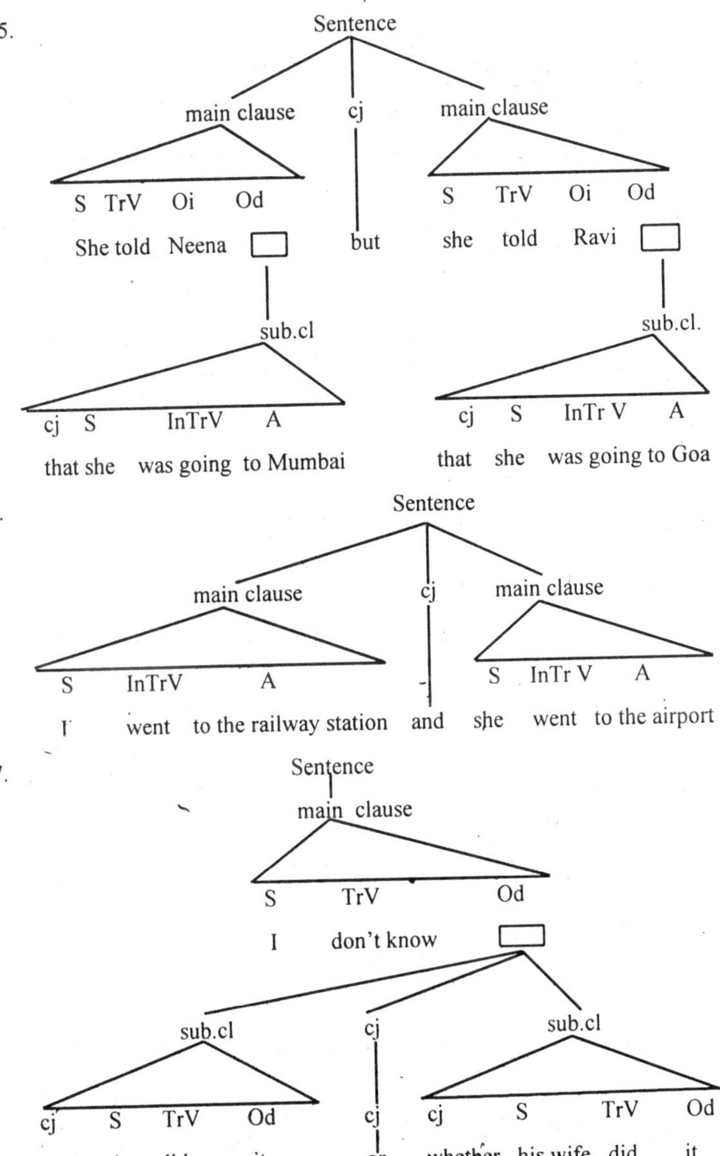
5.
Sentence
main clause
cj
main clause
S TrV Oi Od
She told Neena
but
S TrV Oi Od
she told Ravi
sub.cl
sub.cl.
cj S InTrV A
that she was going to Mumbai
cj S InTr V A
that she was going to Goa
6.
Sentence
main clause
cj
main clause
S InTrV A
I went to the railway station
and
S InTr V A
she went to the airport
7.
Sentence
main clause
S TrV Od
I don't know
sub.cl
cj
sub.cl
cj S TrV Od
whether he did it
cj
or
cj S TrV Od
whether his wife did it

8.

9.

10.

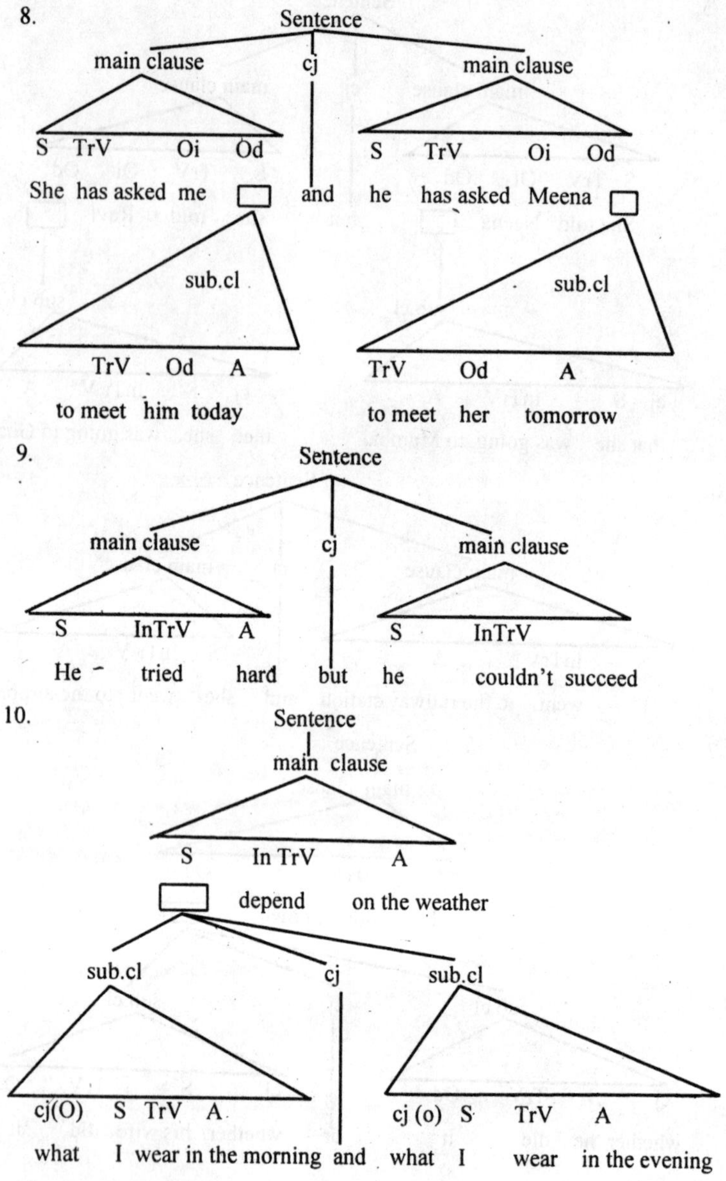
Sentence
main clause
cj
main clause
S TrV Oi Od
S TrV Oi Od
She has asked me
and
he has asked Meena
sub.cl
sub.cl
TrV Od A
TrV Od A
to meet him today
to meet her tomorrow
Sentence
main clause
cj
main clause
S InTrV A
S InTrV
He tried hard
but
he couldn't succeed
Sentence
main clause
S In TrV A
depend on the weather
sub.cl
cj
sub.cl
cj(O) S TrV A
cj (o) S TrV A
what I wear in the morning
and
what I wear in the evening

Exercise 2

1. She was ironing clothes and (she was: S + aux) singing away.
2. Rajesh goes to office by car and Vanita (goes: V) to bank by scooter.
3. My brother-in-law is travelling by air and my sister-in-law (is travelling: aux + V) by train.
4. Quader should be in his apartment and Kajol (should be: aux + V) in the library.
5. She wrote a novel and (she: S) published it herself.
6. Krishna must have received the letter and (he must have: S + aux) informed Mohinder.
7. A boy was injured and another (boy was: S + V) killed during the expedition.
8. She was the President of the Students' Union last year and her brother (was the President of the Students' Union: V + Cs) this year.
9. Sunit must be sleeping and Punit (must be: aux) playing in the room.
10. I met Mohan and (I: S) spoke to him for an hour.

Exercise 3

1 and 8: related facts 2, 6 and 9: consequence or result 3. sequence 4 and 10: contrast 5 and 7: alternative

Exercise 4

1. swept and polished: main verbs 2. red and white: adjectives as pronominal modifiers 3. Surinder and Rita: noun phrases (subject) 4. In Lucknow or in Amritsar (adverbials) 5. very small but expensive: adjectives (subject complement) 6. singing and dancing: main verbs 7. a fridge or a TV: noun phrases (object) 8. thin but healthy: adjectives (subject complement) 9. played and ate: main verbs 10. slept in the morning and palyed in the evening: verb phrases

Chapter 10

Exercise 1

1; 9: Cs S LV; Cs fronted 2; 10: A S TrV Od; A fronted 3;5: Od S Trv A; Od fronted 4. A S InTrV ; A fronted 5: Od S TrV A; Od fronted 6. A S TrV Od A fronted 7. Co S TrV Od; Co fronted 8: Od S Trv; Od fronted

Exercise 2

Focus on:

1. the press (S) 2. this cow (Od) 3. need (V) 4. Rita (S) 5. cheese (Od) 6. good script (Od) 7. last month (A) 8. in school (A) 9. what (Od) 10. some sleep (Od)

Chapter 11

Exercise 1

1. full of coins: complementation 2. for the results: adverbial, in his room: adverbial 3. in the blue dress: postnominal modifier, adverbial 4. with the red tie: postnominal modifier, in time: postnominal modifier, adverbial 5. with me: complementation 6. in the evening: adverbial, with our neighbours: adverbial 7. with a black collar: postnominal modifier 8. of her father: complementation 9. in the basket: postnominal modifier, at the flower show: adverbial 10. into the building: adverbial

Exercise 2

1, 4, 5, 9: in 2, 3, 7: at 6, 8, 10: on

Exercise 3

1, 8: to 2, 3, 4: over 5: in 6: behind/beside 7: under/behind 9: below 10: onto

Exercise 4

1, 2, 8: at 3, 4, 5, 7: in 6: in, on 9: on 10: at, in

Exercise 5

1: at, for 2: during 3: at/ before/after 4: on/by 5: for 6: during 7: before 8: for 9: during/in 10: during

Exercise 6

1, 6, 8, 10: by 2: as 3, 4, 7: with 5: against, for 9: against/for

Exercise 7

1. to: movement towards Shimla; by: mode of transport 2. at: specific time; on: specific time referring to date 3. beside: by the side of 4. over: all through

5. during: duration by: means of communication 6. in: place 7. in: place 8. in: enclosed place 9. over: vertically above 10. to: movement towards

Exercise 8

1. set in 2. get along 3. turn up 4. fell out 5. drop out of 6. fell through 7. stayed up 8. hold on 9. stood out 10. passed away 11. made off 12. settled down 13. fell through 14. broke down 15. fall apart 16. dozed off 17. went on 18. come down 19. dragged on 20. broke out 21. dropped in 22. catch on

Exercise 9

1. pulled down 2. stepped up 3. let down by 4. put on 5. put off 6. crossed out 7. make out 8. knocked down 9. packed him off 10. win over their support 11. wiped out 12. fixed up 13. drawn up 14. cooked up 15. make out 16. brought up 17. handed over 18. set aside 19. fill in 20. hushed up 21. can take down 22. tried out 23. sort out 24. see off 25. call off 26. carried out 27. fill up 28. set up 29. look up 30. give up 31. call her up 32. brought about 33. phase out 34. ruled out 35. messed up

Exercise10

1. trying for 2. deals with 3. comes under 4. believe in 5. get through

Chapter 12

Exercise 1

root: nation fund school teach human ground idol machine response

affix: multi-, -al -s pre- -ing -ity der- -ise -ry (e) -ible, -ty

Exercise 2

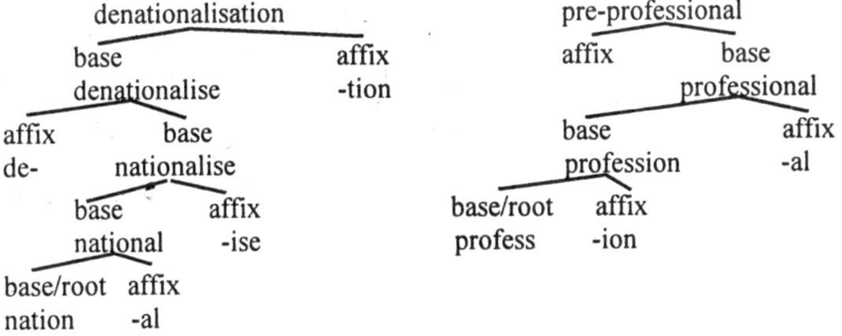

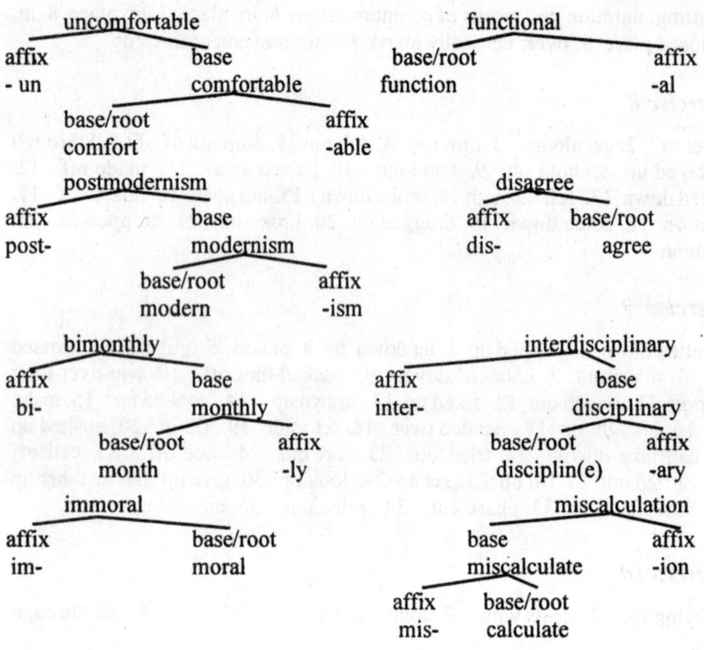

Exercise 3

1. N or V; Adj 2. Adj; N 3. Adj; V 4. N or V; Adj 5. Adj; Adv6. N; V 7. V; N 8. V; N 9. Adj; V 10. V or N; Adj 11. N; Adj 12. V; N

Exercise 4

responsible; finalise; attestation; driver; mouthful; width; famous; happily; codify/ encode; legalise

Bibliography

Curme, G. 1935. *A Grammar of the English Language.* Vol II. Parts of Speech and Accidence. Boston. D. C. Hearth and Co.

Greenbaum, S. 1996. *The Oxford English Grammar.* Oxford: Oxford University Press.

Jesperson, O. 1954. *A Modern English Grammar on Historical Principles.* London: George Allen and Unwin. (reprinted)

Leech, G. 1971. *Meaning and the English Verb.* London: Longman.

Leech, G., M. Deucher, and R. Hoogenrad, 1982. *English Grammar for Today: A New Introduction.* London: Macmillan Education Ltd.

McCawley, J. D. 1971. *Tense and time reference in English* in C. Filimore and D. Langendoen (eds.) Studies in Linguistic Semantics. New York: Holt, Rinehart and Winston.

Palmer, F.R. 1974. *The English Verb.* London: Longman.

Quirk, R., S. Greenbaum, G. Leech, and J. Svartvik, 1985. *A Comprehensive Grammar of the English Language.* London: Longman.

Van ek, J. A. and J. N. Robat. 1984. *The Student's Grammar of English.* Oxford: Basil Blackwell.

Index

acronymy 12.3.2
adjective 3.3.1.4, 5.1
  classifying 5.1.2
  colour 5.1.2
  compound 5.1.1.3
  emphasising 5.1.2
  participial 5.1.1.2
  qualitative 5.1.2
  syntactic functions of 5.1.1
  attributive 5.1.1.1
  predicative 5.1.1.1
adjective phrase 5.1
adverb 5.2
  derivational 5.2.1
  forms 5.2.1
  adjuncts 5.2.2.1
  conjuncts 5.2.3.3
  disjuncts 5.2.2.2
  grammatical functions 5.2.2
  uninflected 5.2.1
  one-word 4.4.1
  syntactic functions of 5.2.3
adverbial 1.2, 5.3
  additive 5.3.2.8
  intensity 5.3.2.7
  focussing 5.3.2.8
  noun phrase 4.4.2
  position 1.3.1, 5.3.1
  relative 8.1.5
  restrictive 5.3.2.8
  semantic functions 5.3.2
  subject-related 1.3.1
affix 12.1
agentive role 1.5
agreement, noun-verb 2.1
ambiguity 4.4.3
amplifier 5.3.2.7
antonomasia 12.3.6
appositive phrase 3.3.2.4
article 2.3
  definite 2.4.3
  indefinite 2.4.1
  zero 2.4.2
  uses of 2.4
attribute 1.5
auxiliaries 4.1, 4.2, 4.3

back-formation 12.3.4
base 12.1
basic patterns 1.3
blending 12.3.3
clause
  appositive 7.5.1.1, 8.2
  adjectival 8.1
  adverbial 4.4.4, 8.3
    non-finite,4.4.5, 8.3
    of concession 8.3.5
    condition 8.3.4
    contrast 8.3.7
    manner 8.3.6
    place 8.3.2
    purpose 8.3.8
    reason 8.3.3
    time 8.3.1
  coordinate 9.2
    ellipsis in 9.3
  matrix 7.3
  relative 8.1, 3.3.2.2
    restrictive and non-restrictive 8.1.6
  verbless 7.4.3, 8.3
subordinate 7.2
  finite 7.4.1
  functions of 7.5
  nominal 7.5.1
    adjectival 8.1
    -ing 7.5.1.6
    to- infinitive 7.5.1.5
    relative 7.5.1.4
  non-finite 7.4.2
    to- infinitive 7. 4.2.1
    wh- interrogative 7.5.1.2
    yes-no interrogative 7.5.1.3
    verbless 7.4.3
superordinate 7.2
clipping 12.3.1

Index

characterisation 1.5
complement 1.2
  adjectival 5.1
  adverbial 1.3.1
  object 1.2, 1.3.3
completion 6.1.3
concord 1.7
condition
  hypothetical 8.3.4
  open 8.3.4
  unfulfilled
conjunction
  coordinating 9.4
coordination 9.1
  of constituents 9.5

determiner 3.3.1.1
downtoner 5.3.2.7

existential sentence 10.5
extraposition 10.4

focus 10.1

genitive 2.2, 3.3.1.7
  elliptic 3.3.1.7
  group 3.3.1.7
  local 3.3.1.7
  post- 3.3.1.7
identification 1.5
illocutionary acts 1.6
intensifier 5.1
locative 1.5
marked sentence 10.1
modifier 3.3
  prenominal 3.3.1
  postnominal 3.3.2

noun
  collective 2.1
  countable,uncountable 2.1
  gender 2.1
  mass 2.1
  proper 2.1
noun phrase 3.1
  noun head 3.2
  modifiers of 3.3
    prenominal and postnominal 3.3
  parts of 3.2
  simple and complex 3.3.3
object 1.2
  direct 1.3.3
  indirect 1.3.3

participle 4.2
particle 11.2
partitive 2.1
postdeterminer 3.3.1.2
postmodification
  minor 3.3.2.5
  multiple 3.3.3
predeterminer 3.3.1.3
predicate 1.1
prefix 12.1.1
preposition 11.1
  and adverb 11.1.2
  compound 11.1.3
  of agentive and instrument 11:1.4.4
    manner 11.1.4.5
    means 11.1.4.3
    place 11.1.4.1
    time 11.1.4.2
    simple 11.1.3
prepositional phrase 4.4.3, 11.1.1
pronoun 1.2, 1.3.3

reduplication 12.3.5
reference
  anaphoric 2.3.2
  cataphoric 2.3.2
  definite and indefinite 2.3.2
  generic and non-generic 2.3.1
  situational 2.3.2
  specific and non-specific 2.3.1
relative clause 3.3.2.2
  non-finite 3.3.2.3
  infinitive 3.3.2.3
  non-restrictive
  restrictive

reported speech 6.1.7
root 12.1
semantic roles 1.5
  affected 1.5
  agentive 1.5
  attributive 1.5
  beneficiary 1.5
  characterisation 1.5
  identification 1.5
  instrument1.5
  locative 1.5
  temporal 1.5
sentence types 1.6
  complex 7.1
    analysis of 8.4
  compond 9.2
  cleft 10.2
  declarative 1.6
  exclamative 1.6
  imperative 1.6
  interrogative 1.6
  pseudo-cleft 10.3
  simple 1
speech acts 1.6
subject 1, 1.2.1
suffix 12.1.1
  derivational 12.1.1
  inflectional 12.1.1

tense 6.1
  past perfect 6.1.7
  past perfect progressive 6.1.8
  past progressive 6.1.6
  present perfect 6.1.3
  present perfect progressive 6.1.4
  present progressive 6.1.2
  simple past 6.1.5
  simple present 6.1.1
time
  future 6.1.9

verb 1.2
  action 6.1.2
  attitudinal 6.1.2
  auxiliary 4.2
  complex transitive 1.1.3
  conclusive and non-conclusive 6.1.3
  continuative 6.1.3
  ditransitive 1.3.3
  dynamic 6.1.2
  intransitive 1.2, 1.3.2, 6.1.2,
  linking 1.2, 1.3.1
  middle 1.4
  modal 6.2
    auxiliaries 6.2.1
    general characteristics of 6.2.1
    special characteristics of 6.2.1
    interpretations of 6.2.3
    ability 6.2.3.1
    necessity 6.2.3.6
    needn't and mustn't
    obligation 6.2.3.7
    permission 6.2.3.2
    possibility 6.2.3.3
    request 6.2.3.4
    suggestion 6.2.3.5
  modifiers of 4.4
  momentary 6.1.2
  monotransitive 1.3.3
  phrasal 11.2
  perception 6.1.2
  relational 6.1.2
  sensation 6.1.2
  stative 6.1.2
  transitive 1.2, 1.3.3
  verb phrase 4.1
    structure of 4.2
    finite and non-finite 4.3
voice, active and passive 1.3.3, 4.2
word
  complex 12.2.2
  simple 12.2.1